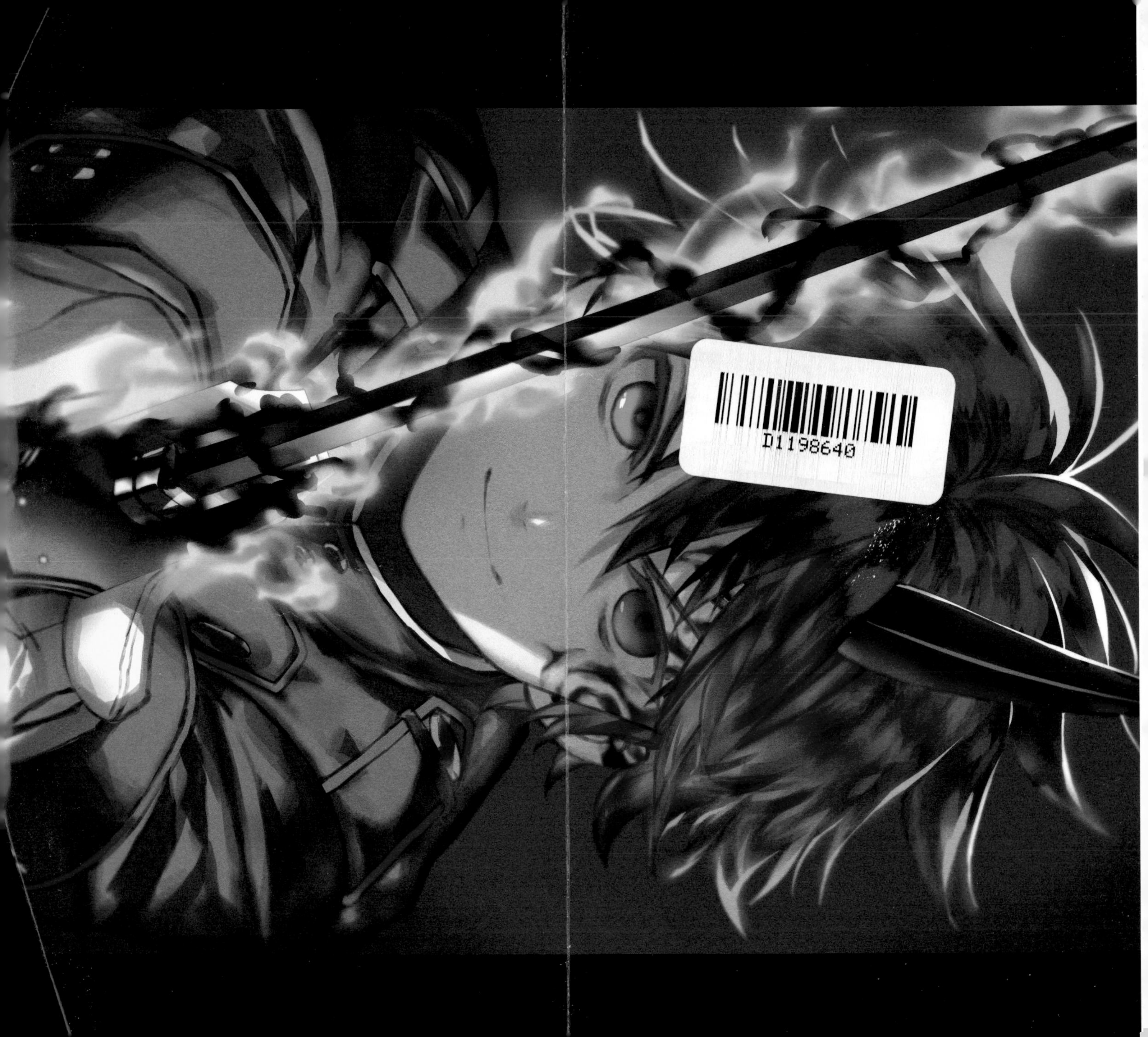

Seraph of the End

─── VAMPIRE REIGN ───

21

STORY BY **Takaya Kagami**

ART BY **Yamato Yamamoto**

STORYBOARDS BY **Daisuke Furuya**

CHARACTERS

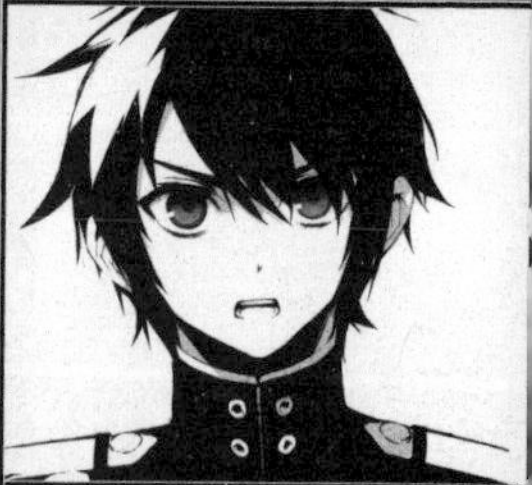

YUICHIRO HYAKUYA

A boy who escaped from the vampire capital, he has both great kindness and a great desire for revenge. Lone wolf. His Cursed Gear is Asuramaru, a katana.

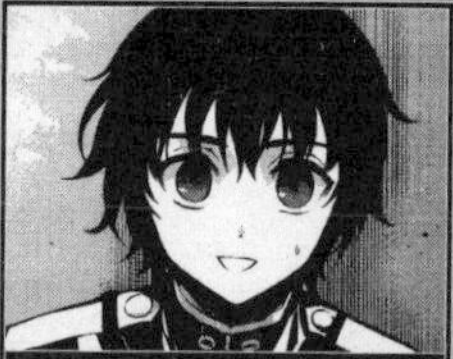

YOICHI SAOTOME

Yuichiro's friend. His sister was killed by a vampire. His Cursed Gear is Gekkouin, a bow.

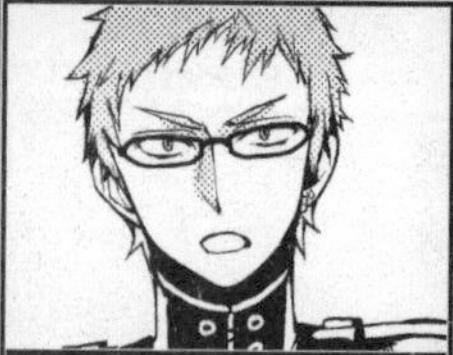

SHIHO KIMIZUKI

Yuichiro's friend. Smart but abrasive. His Cursed Gear is Kiseki-o, twin blades.

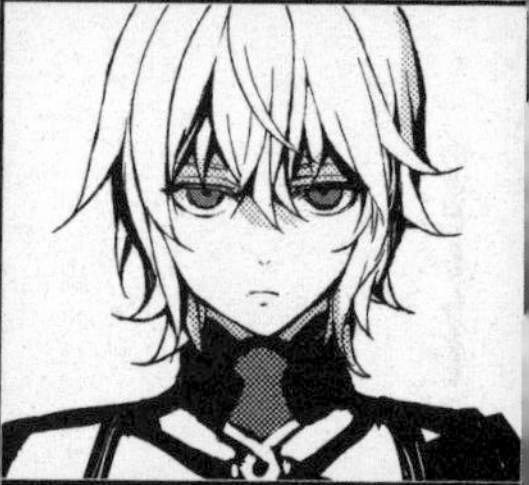

MIKAELA HYAKUYA

Yuichiro's best friend. He was supposedly killed but has come back to life as a vampire. Currently working with Shinoa Squad.

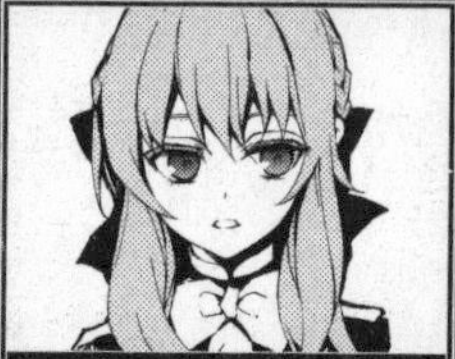

SHINOA HIRAGI

Guren's subordinate and Yuichiro's surveillance officer. Member of the illustrious Hiragi family. Her Cursed Gear is Shikama Doji, a scythe.

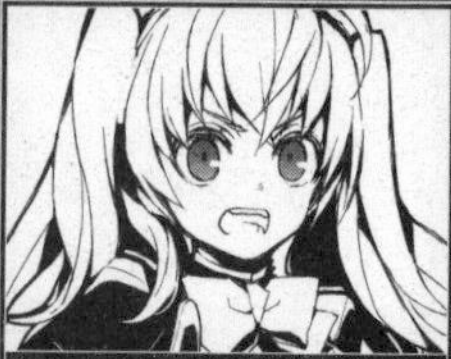

MITSUBA SANGU

An elite soldier who has been part of the Moon Demon Company since age 13. Bossy. Her Cursed Gear is Tenjiryu, a giant axe.

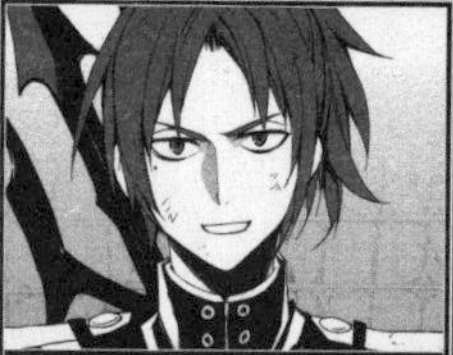

MAKOTO NARUMI

Former leader of Narumi Squad. After his entire squad died during the battle of Nagoya, he deserted the Demon Army with Shinoa Squad.

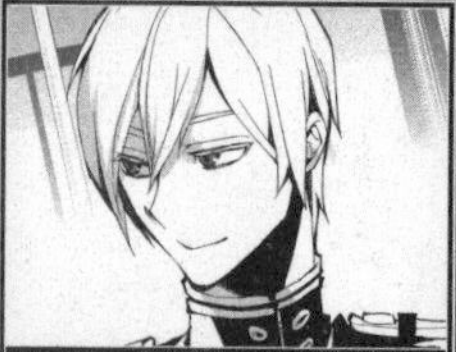

SHINYA HIRAGI

A Major General and adoptee into the Hiragi Family. He was Mahiru Hiragi's fiancé.

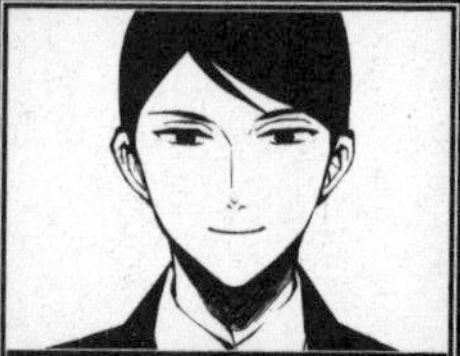

SAITO

A mysterious man somehow connected with the Hyakuya Sect. He was once a Second Progenitor vampire.

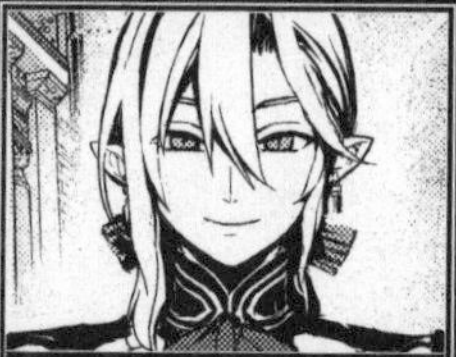

FERID BATHORY

A Seventh Progenitor vampire, he killed Mikaela.

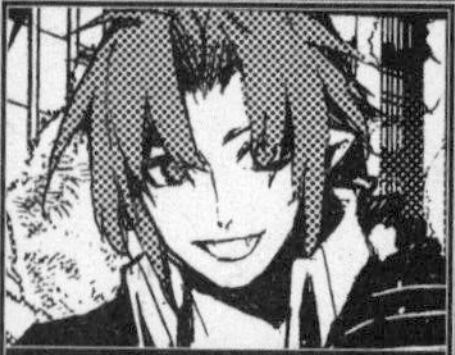

CROWLEY EUSFORD

A Thirteenth Progenitor vampire. Part of Ferid's faction.

KRUL TEPES

Third Progenitor and Queen of the Vampires. She is currently being held prisoner by Urd Geales.

MAHIRU HIRAGI

Shinoa's older sister. Most believe her dead, but she currently inhabits Guren's sword.

GUREN ICHINOSE

Lt. Colonel of the Moon Demon Company. He recruited Yuichiro into the Demon Army. During the battle in Nagoya, he began acting strangely... His Cursed Gear is Mahiru-no-yo, a katana.

SHIKAMA DOJI

The being that inhabits Shinoa's scythe. He's actually the long-missing First Progenitor of the vampires.

ASURAMARU

The demon that possesses Yuichiro's sword. A long time ago, he was a human boy named Ashera.

NOYA

The demon sealed inside Guren's sword.

STORY

A mysterious virus decimates the human population, and vampires claim dominion over the world. Yuichiro and his adopted family of orphans are kept as vampire fodder in an underground city until the day Mikaela, Yuichiro's best friend, plots an ill-fated escape for the orphans. Only Yuichiro survives and reaches the surface.

Four years later, Yuichiro enters into the Moon Demon Company, a Vampire Extermination Unit in the Japanese Imperial Demon Army, to enact his revenge. There he gains Asuramaru, a demon-possessed weapon capable of killing vampires, and a squad of trusted friends—Shinoa, Yoichi, Kimizuki and Mitsuba.

In his battles against the vampires, Yuichiro discovers that not only is Mikaela alive, but he also has been turned into a vampire. After misunderstandings and near-misses, Yuichiro and Mikaela finally rejoin each other in Nagoya.

After much chaos and confusion, the Shinoa Squad deserts the Demon Army to follow Ferid and Crowley. Navigating through both human and vampire plots, the group returns to Shibuya.

They aren't there long before Shinoa's body is taken over by Shikama Doji, a godlike being who is the First Vampire. To add to the chaos, the Hyakuya Sect, led by Saito, attacks the Demon Army's Shibuya base and takes Yuichiro hostage.

Facing their greatest threat ever, Mahiru, Guren and Noya use the Sinful Keys to seal away the First successfully. Shinoa regains consciousness, and...?

Seraph of the End
—VAMPIRE REIGN—

CONTENTS

21

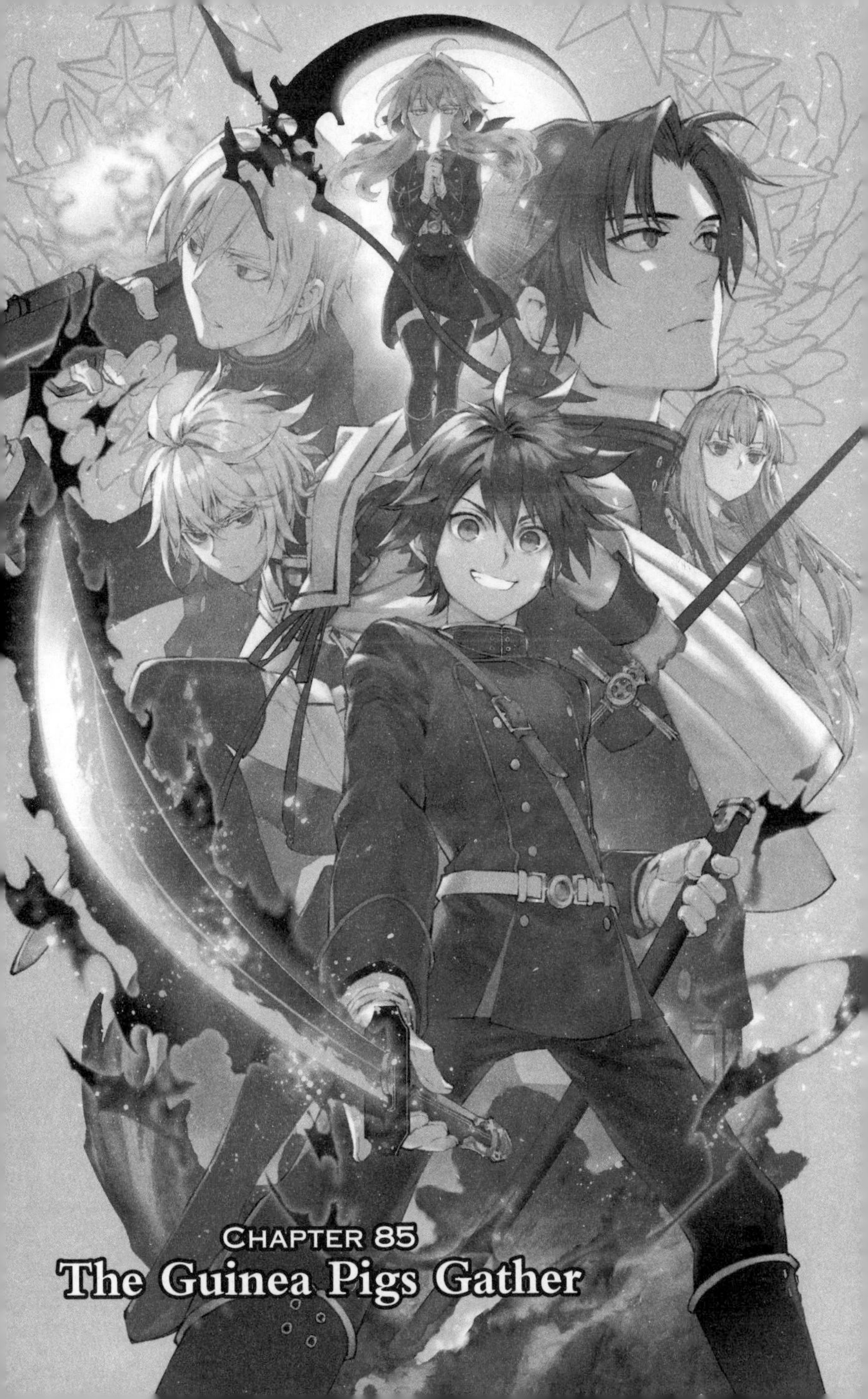
CHAPTER 85
The Guinea Pigs Gather

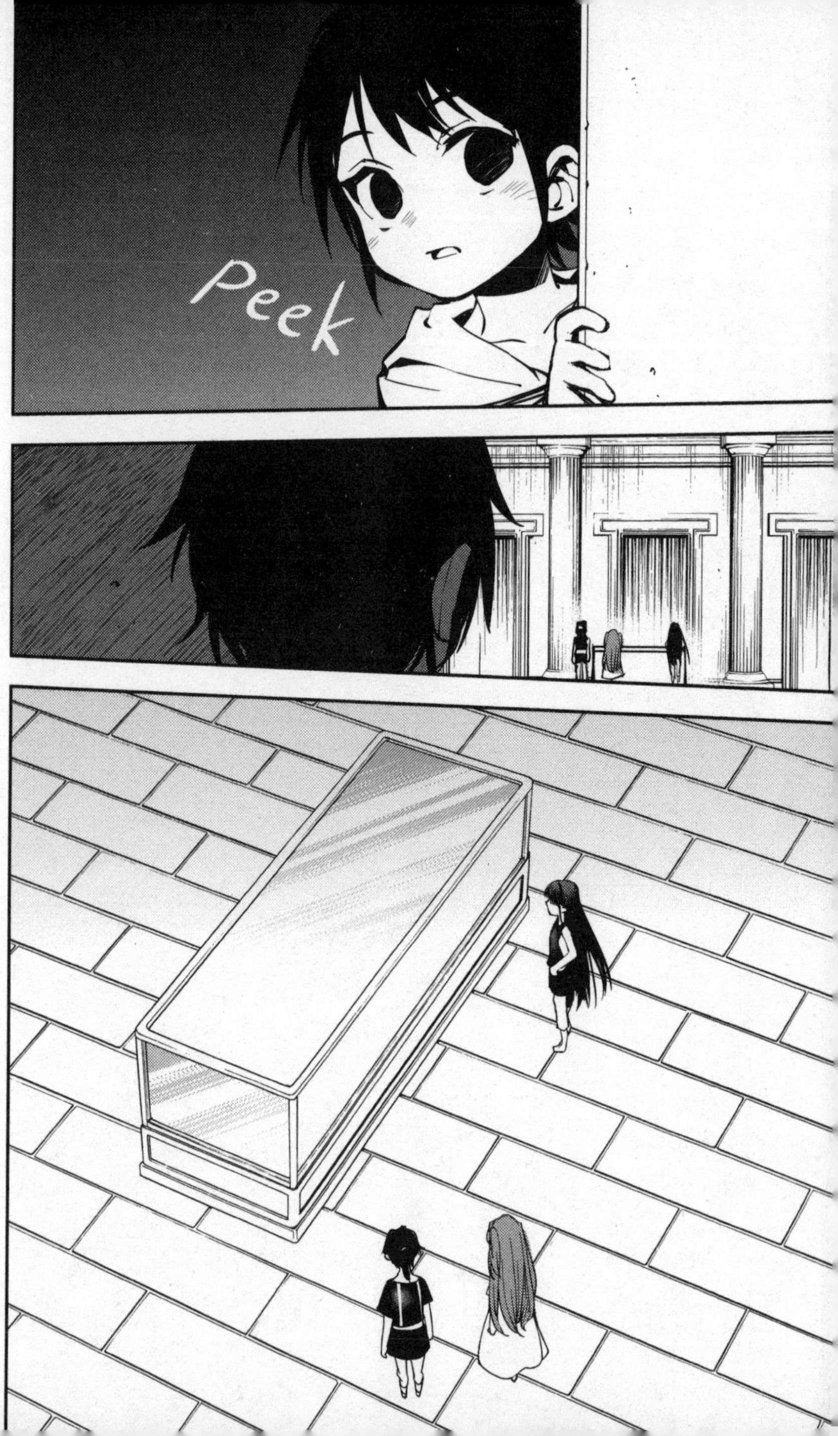
Peek

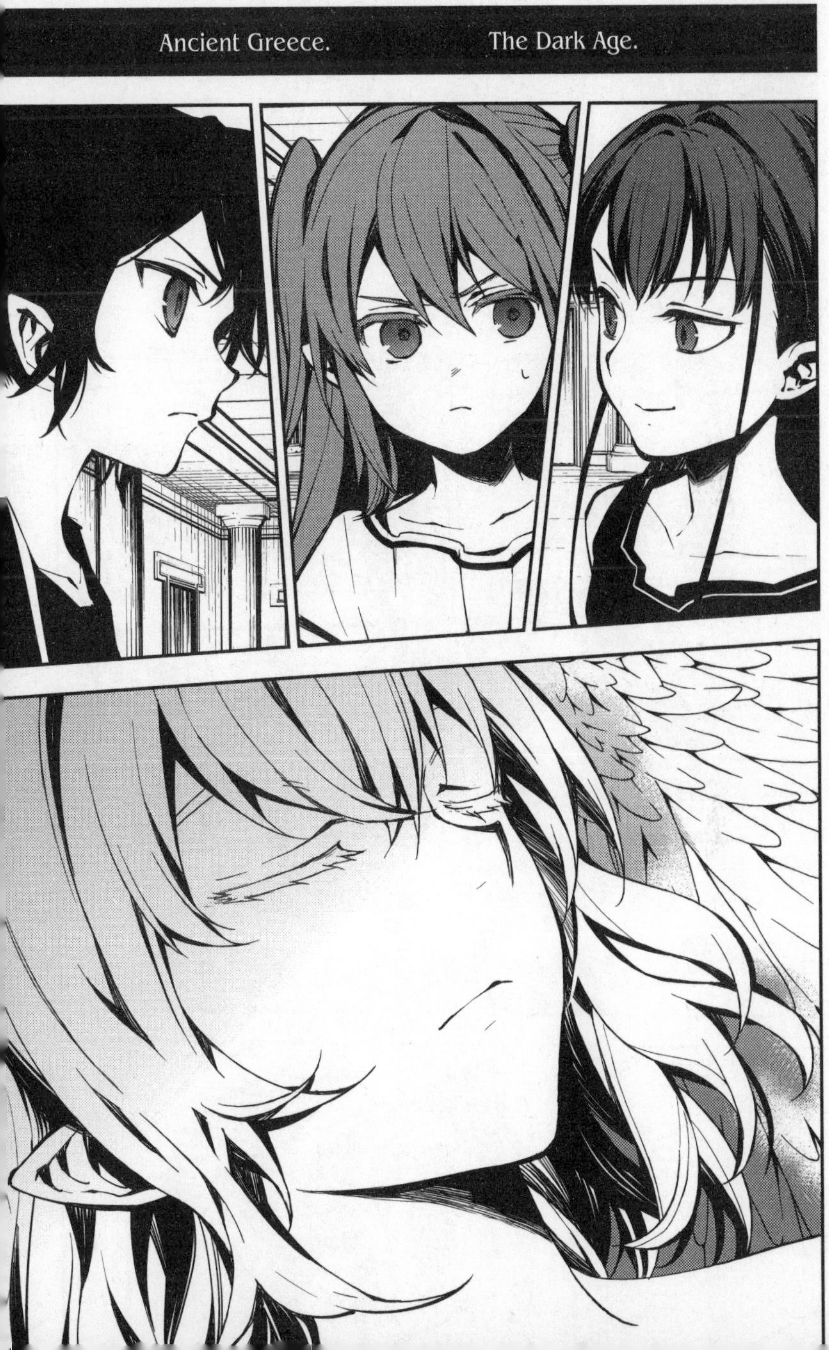
Ancient Greece.
The Dark Age.

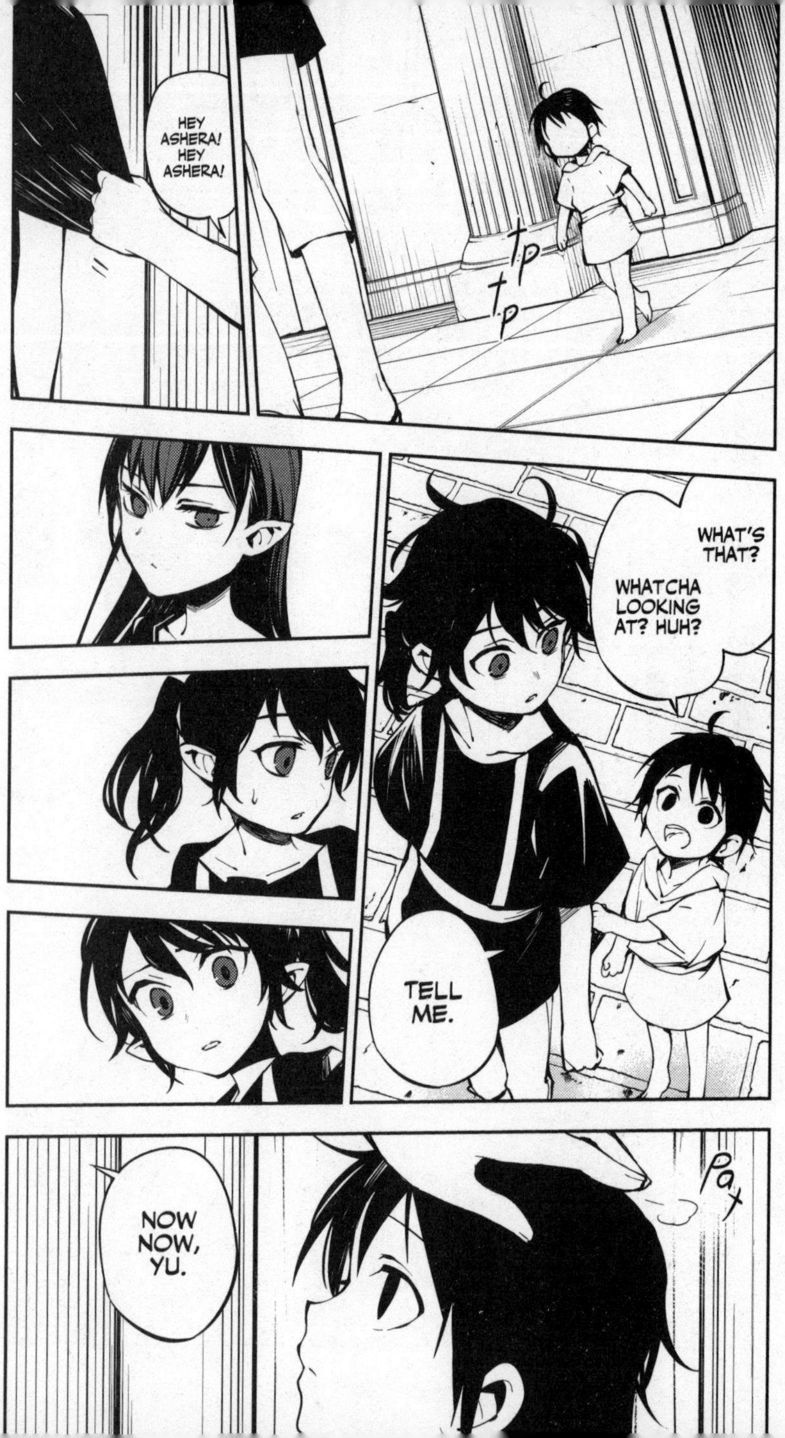
tp tp
HEY ASHERA! HEY ASHERA!
WHAT'S THAT?
WHATCHA LOOKING AT? HUH?
TELL ME.
Pat
NOW NOW, YU.

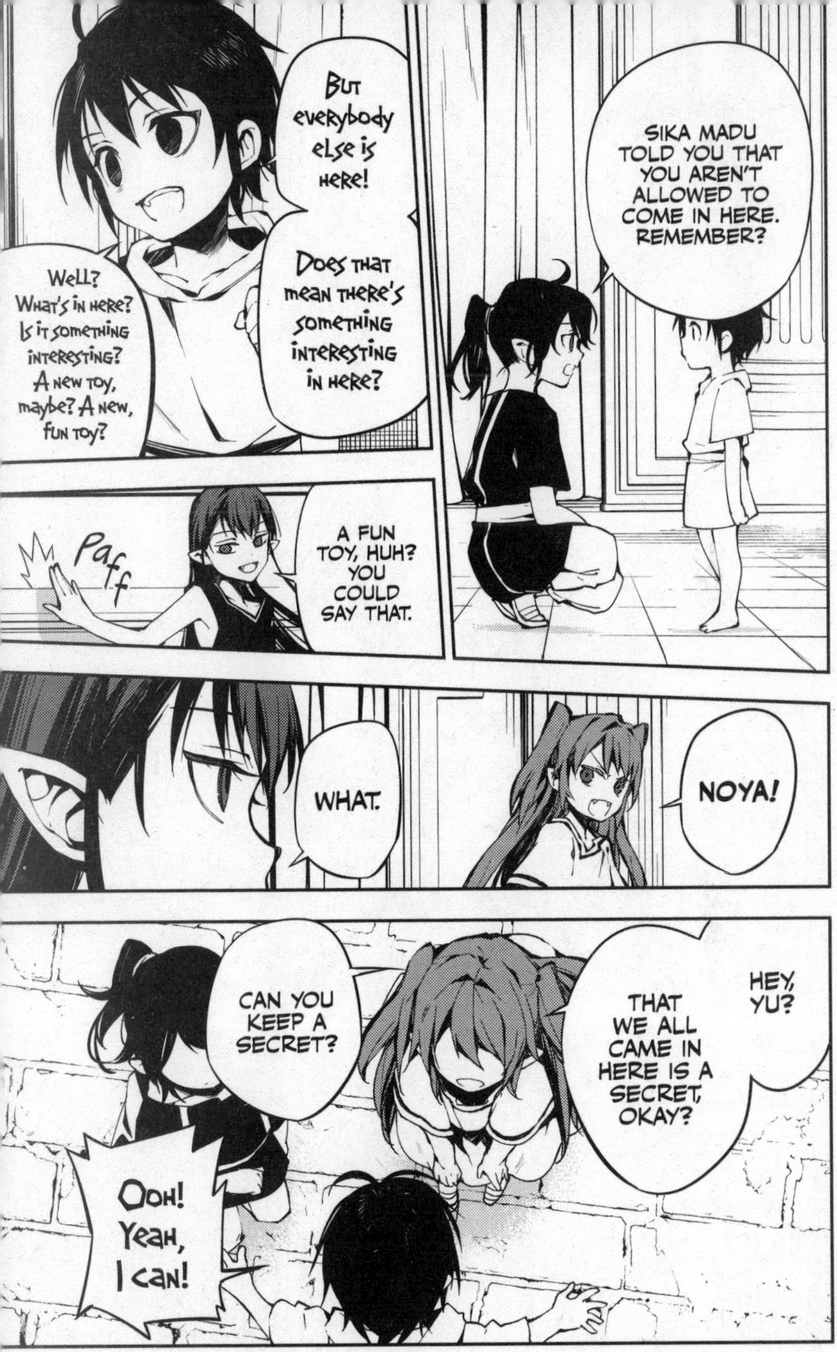

SIKA MADU TOLD YOU THAT YOU AREN'T ALLOWED TO COME IN HERE. REMEMBER?
But everybody else is here!
Does that mean there's something interesting in here?
Well? What's in here? Is it something interesting? A new toy, maybe? A new, fun toy?
A FUN TOY, HUH? YOU COULD SAY THAT.
Paff
NOYA!
WHAT.
HEY, YU?
THAT WE ALL CAME IN HERE IS A SECRET, OKAY?
CAN YOU KEEP A SECRET?
Ooh! Yeah, I can!

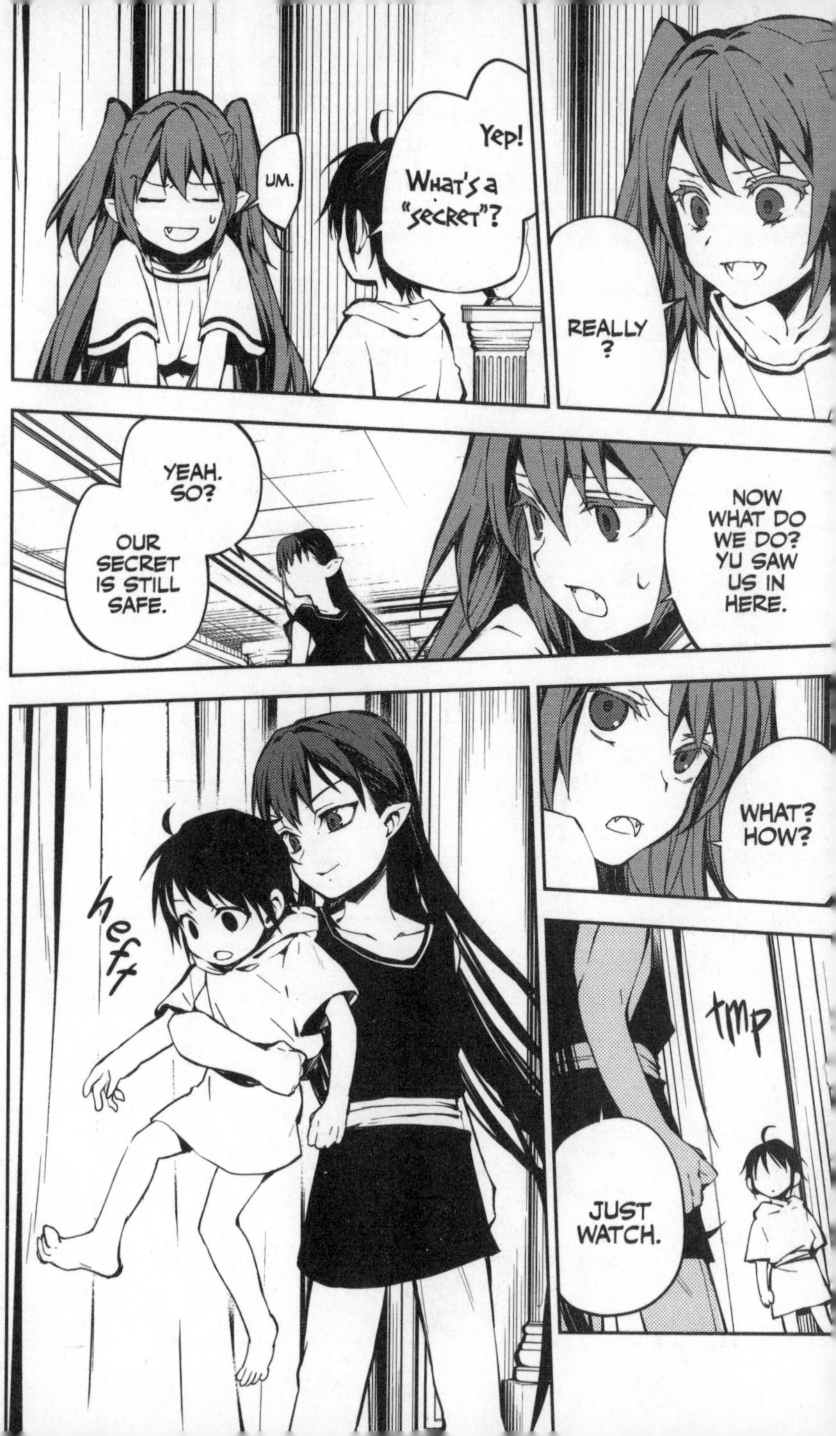
REALLY?
Yep!
What's a "secret"?
UM.
NOW WHAT DO WE DO? YU SAW US IN HERE.
YEAH. SO?
OUR SECRET IS STILL SAFE.
WHAT? HOW?
tmp
JUST WATCH.
heft

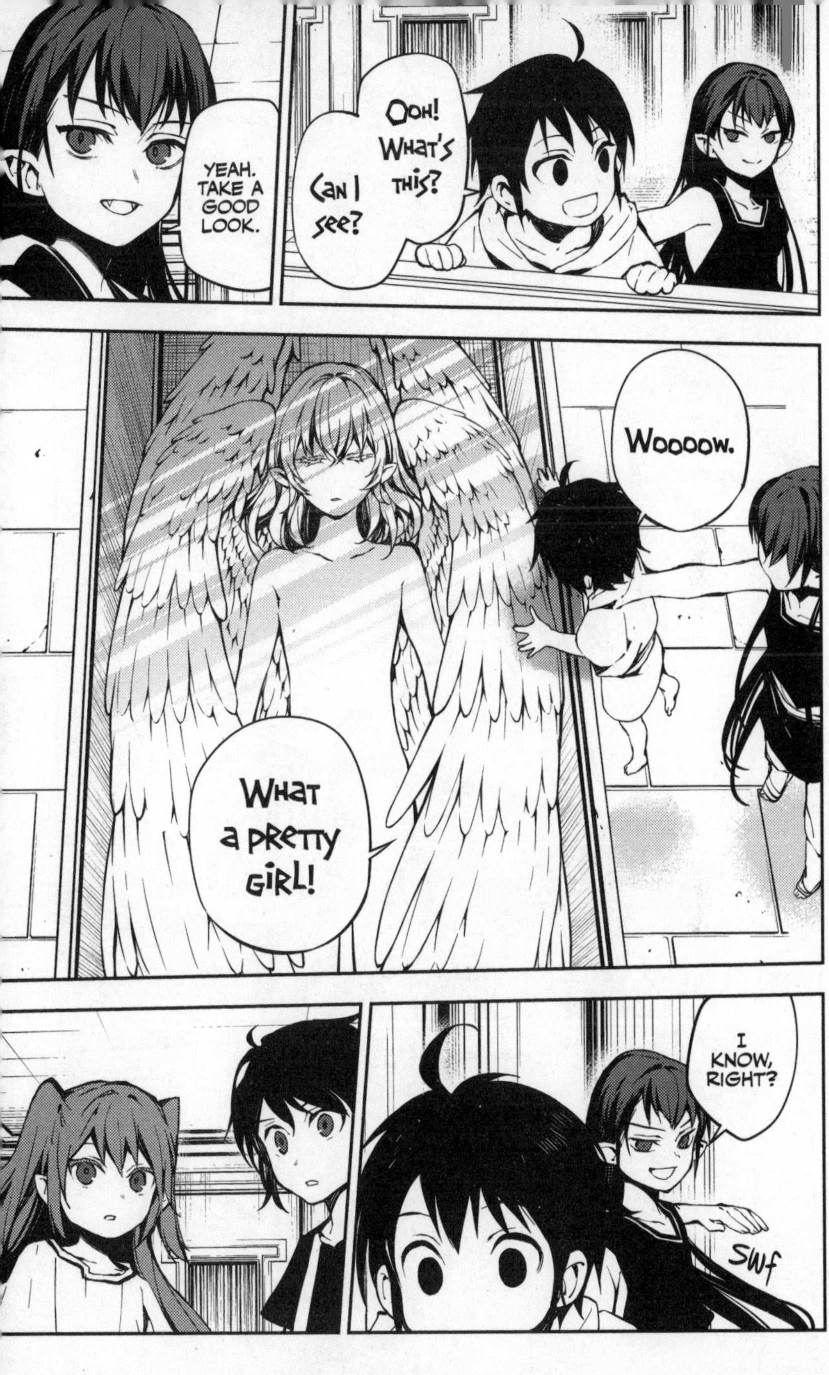
Ooh! What's this?
Can I see?
Yeah. Take a good look.
Woooow.
What a pretty girl!
I know, right?
SWf

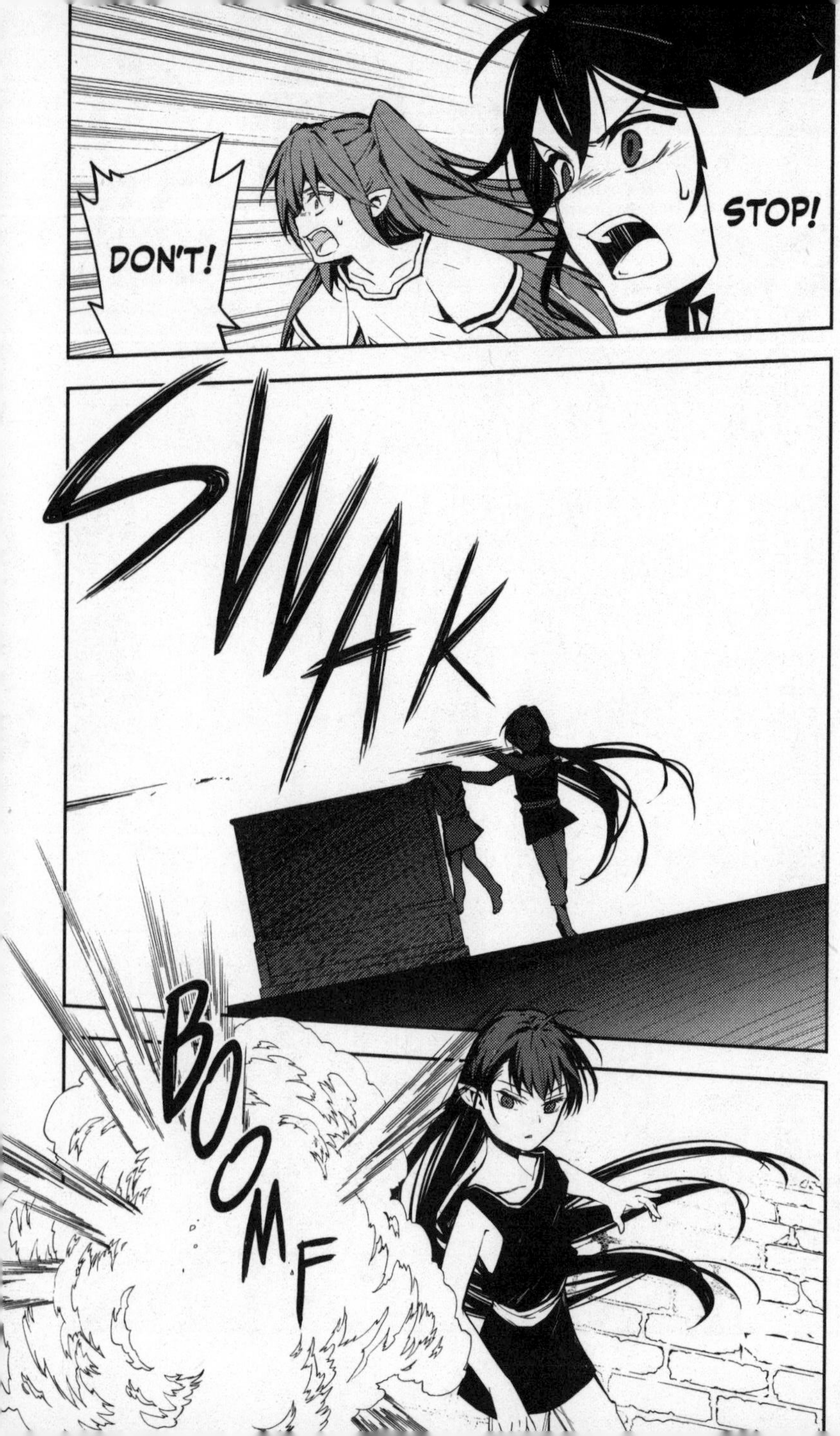
STOP!
DON'T!
SWAK
BOOMF

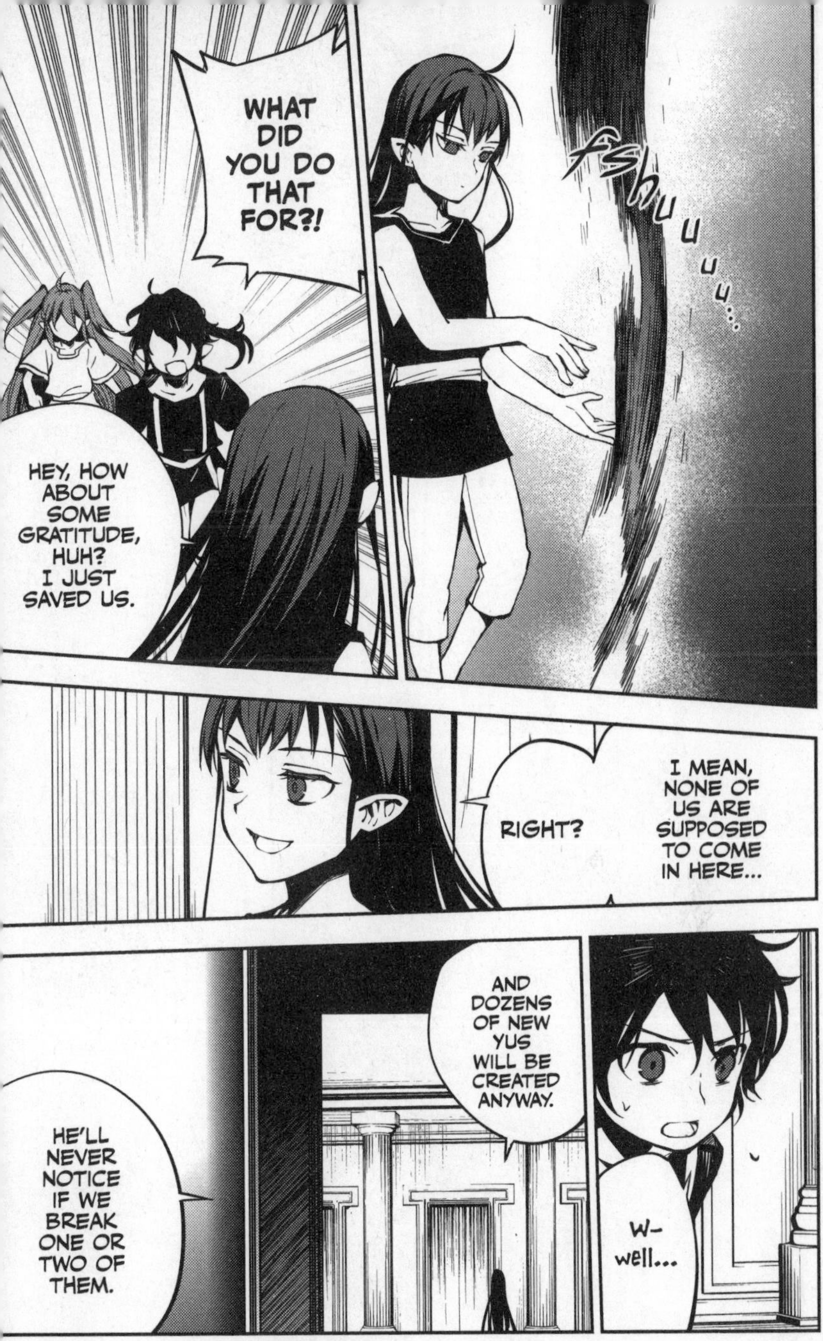
fshuuuu...
WHAT DID YOU DO THAT FOR?!
HEY, HOW ABOUT SOME GRATITUDE, HUH? I JUST SAVED US.
I MEAN, NONE OF US ARE SUPPOSED TO COME IN HERE...
RIGHT?
W-well...
AND DOZENS OF NEW YUS WILL BE CREATED ANYWAY.
HE'LL NEVER NOTICE IF WE BREAK ONE OR TWO OF THEM.

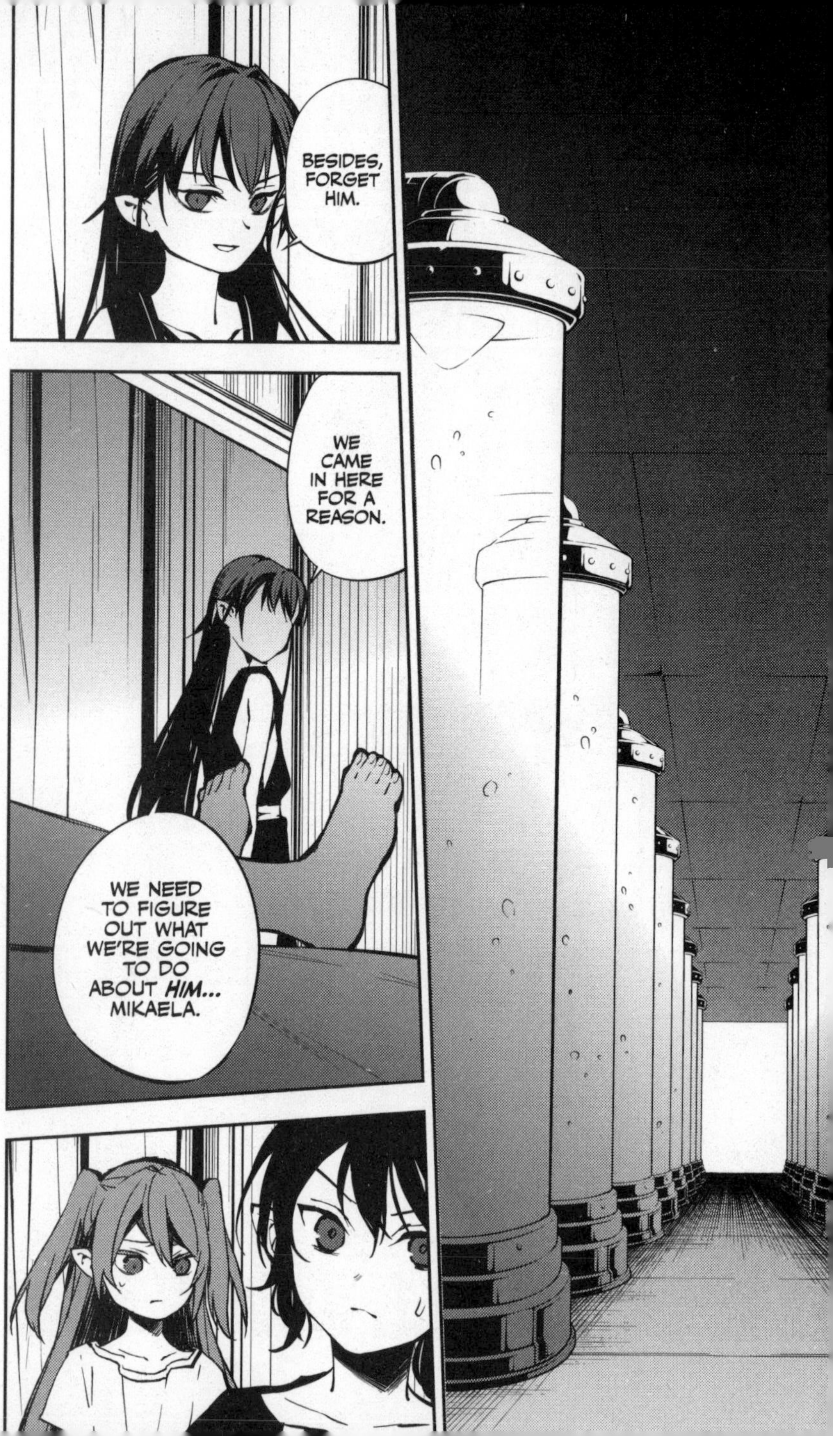
BESIDES, FORGET HIM.
WE CAME IN HERE FOR A REASON.
WE NEED TO FIGURE OUT WHAT WE'RE GOING TO DO ABOUT *HIM*... MIKAELA.

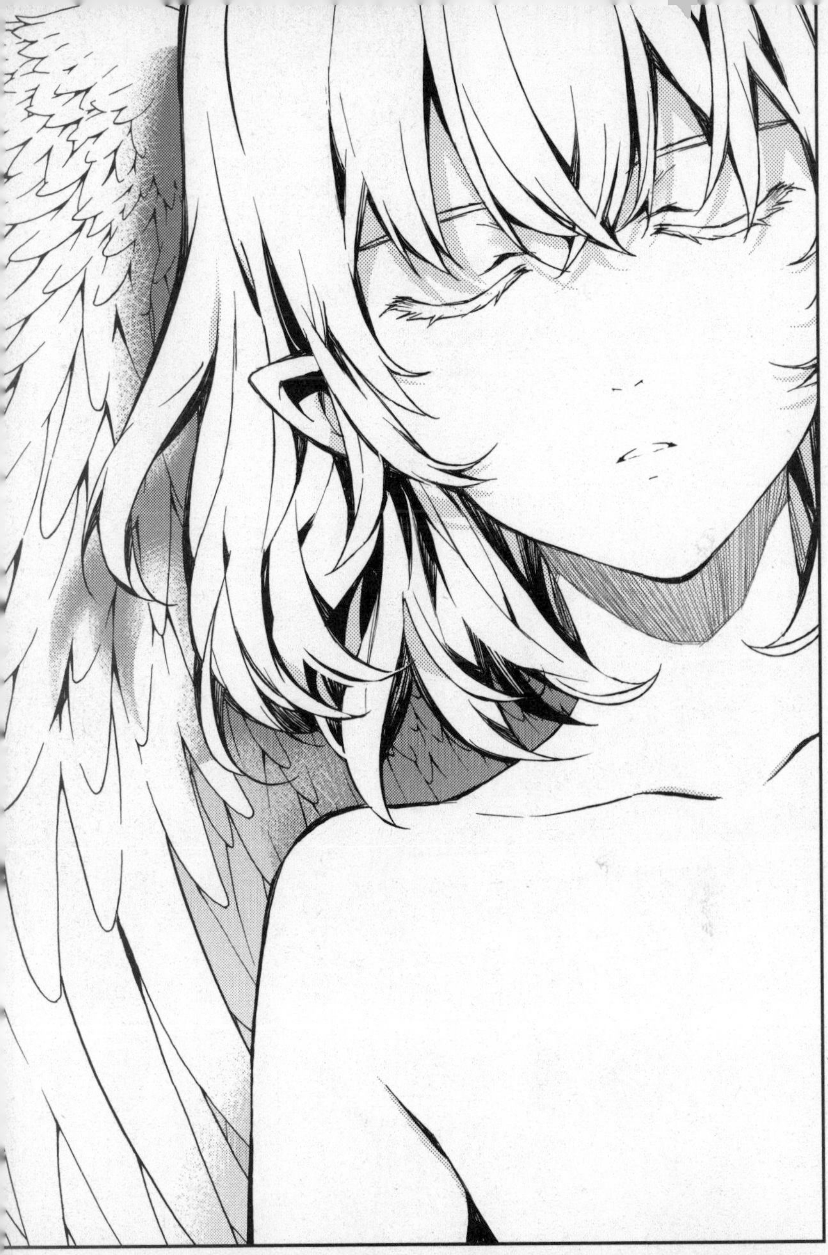

Thousands of years later, the present day.

WHAT'S THE CORRECT ANSWER?

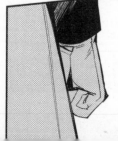

WHAT COURSE OF ACTION IS THE CORRECT ONE HERE?

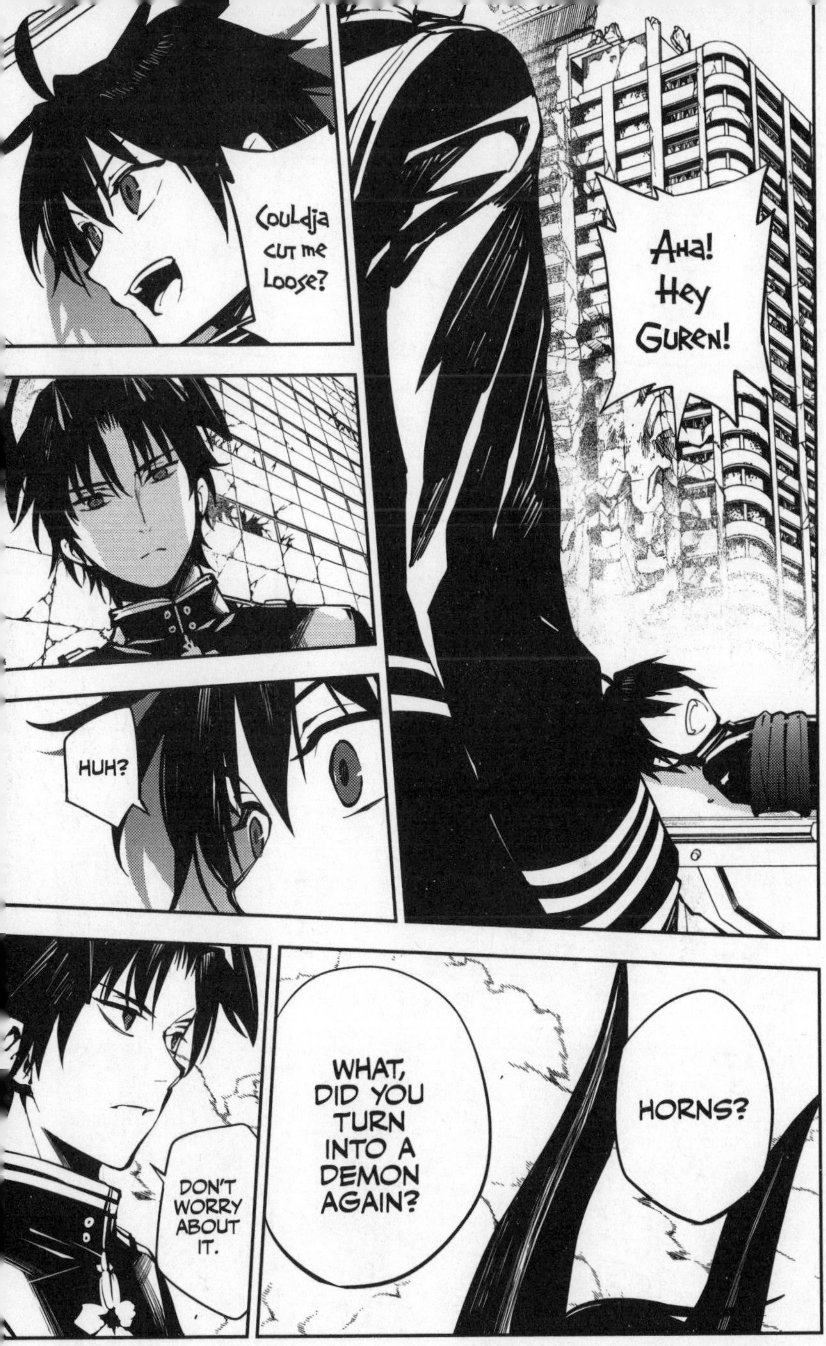
Aha! Hey Guren!
Couldja cut me loose?
HUH?
HORNS?
WHAT, DID YOU TURN INTO A DEMON AGAIN?
DON'T WORRY ABOUT IT.

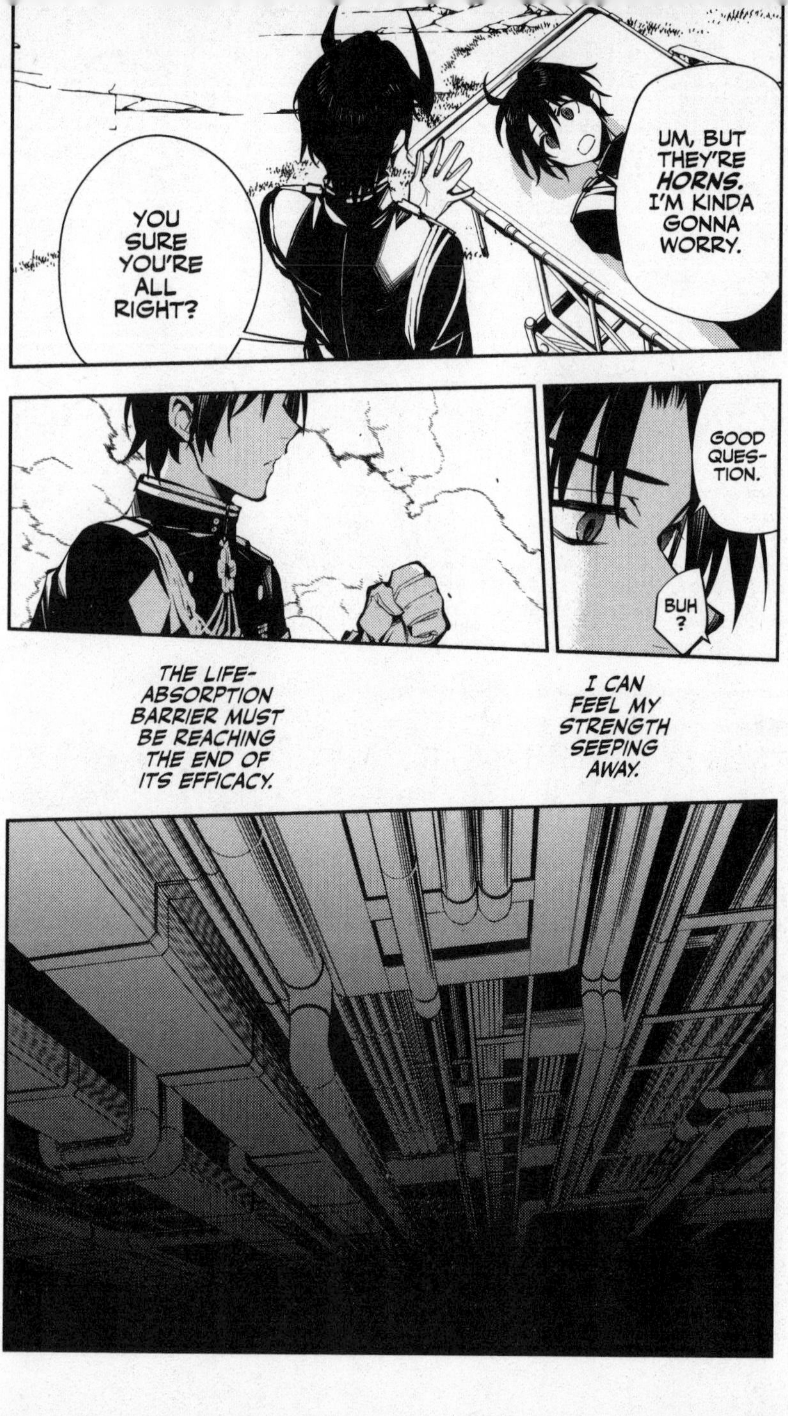
UM, BUT THEY'RE HORNS. I'M KINDA GONNA WORRY.
YOU SURE YOU'RE ALL RIGHT?
GOOD QUES-TION.
BUH?
I CAN FEEL MY STRENGTH SEEPING AWAY.
THE LIFE-ABSORPTION BARRIER MUST BE REACHING THE END OF ITS EFFICACY.

Ngh...

WHEW...

THE CHAINS ARE GONE.

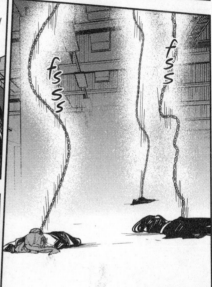

fsss

fsss

IT'S FREAKILY QUIET OUT- SIDE.

WHERE'D GUREN GET TO?

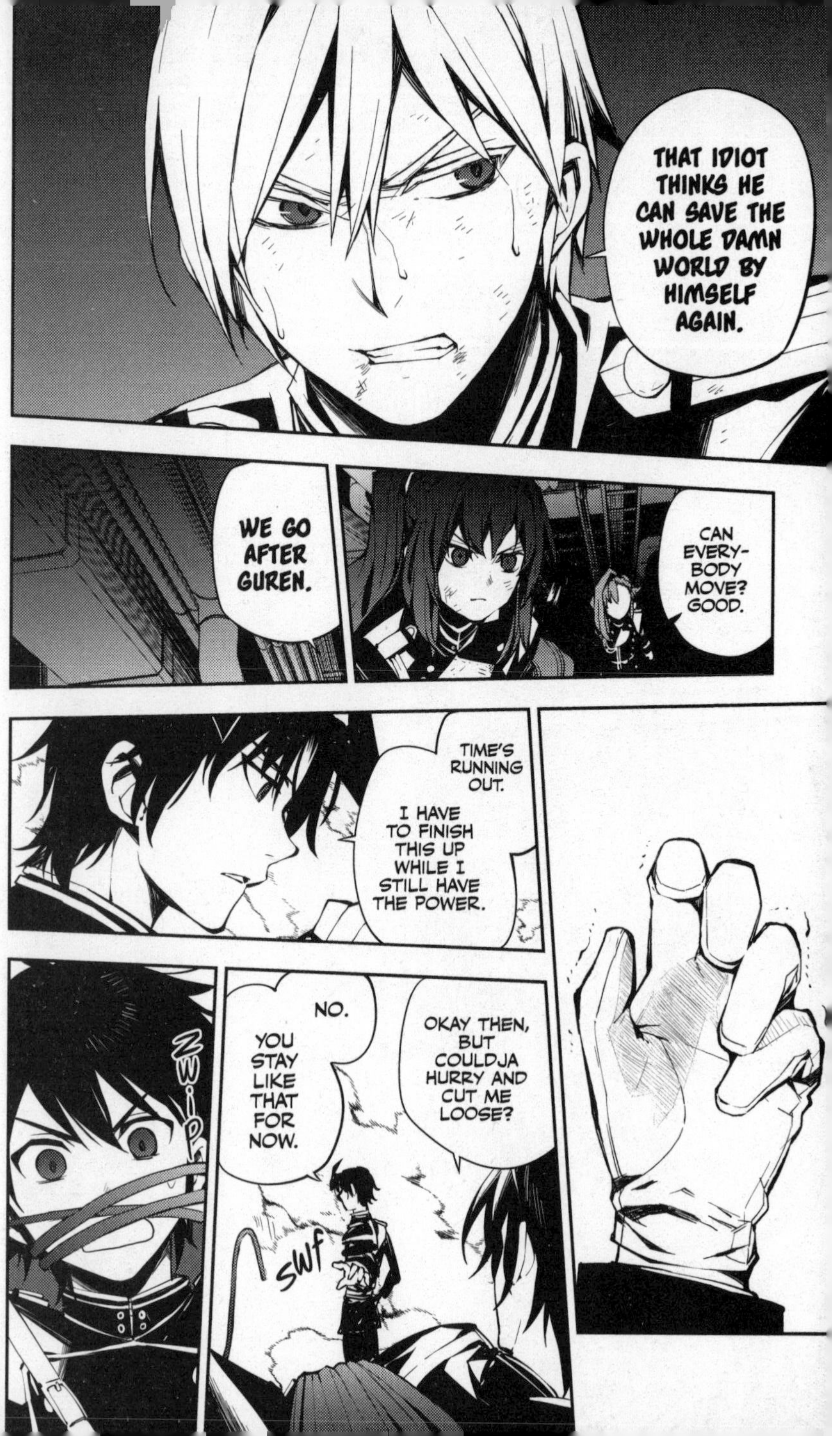
THAT IDIOT THINKS HE CAN SAVE THE WHOLE DAMN WORLD BY HIMSELF AGAIN.
CAN EVERY-BODY MOVE? GOOD.
WE GO AFTER GUREN.
TIME'S RUNNING OUT.
I HAVE TO FINISH THIS UP WHILE I STILL HAVE THE POWER.
OKAY THEN, BUT COULDJA HURRY AND CUT ME LOOSE?
NO.
YOU STAY LIKE THAT FOR NOW.
SWF
ZWIP

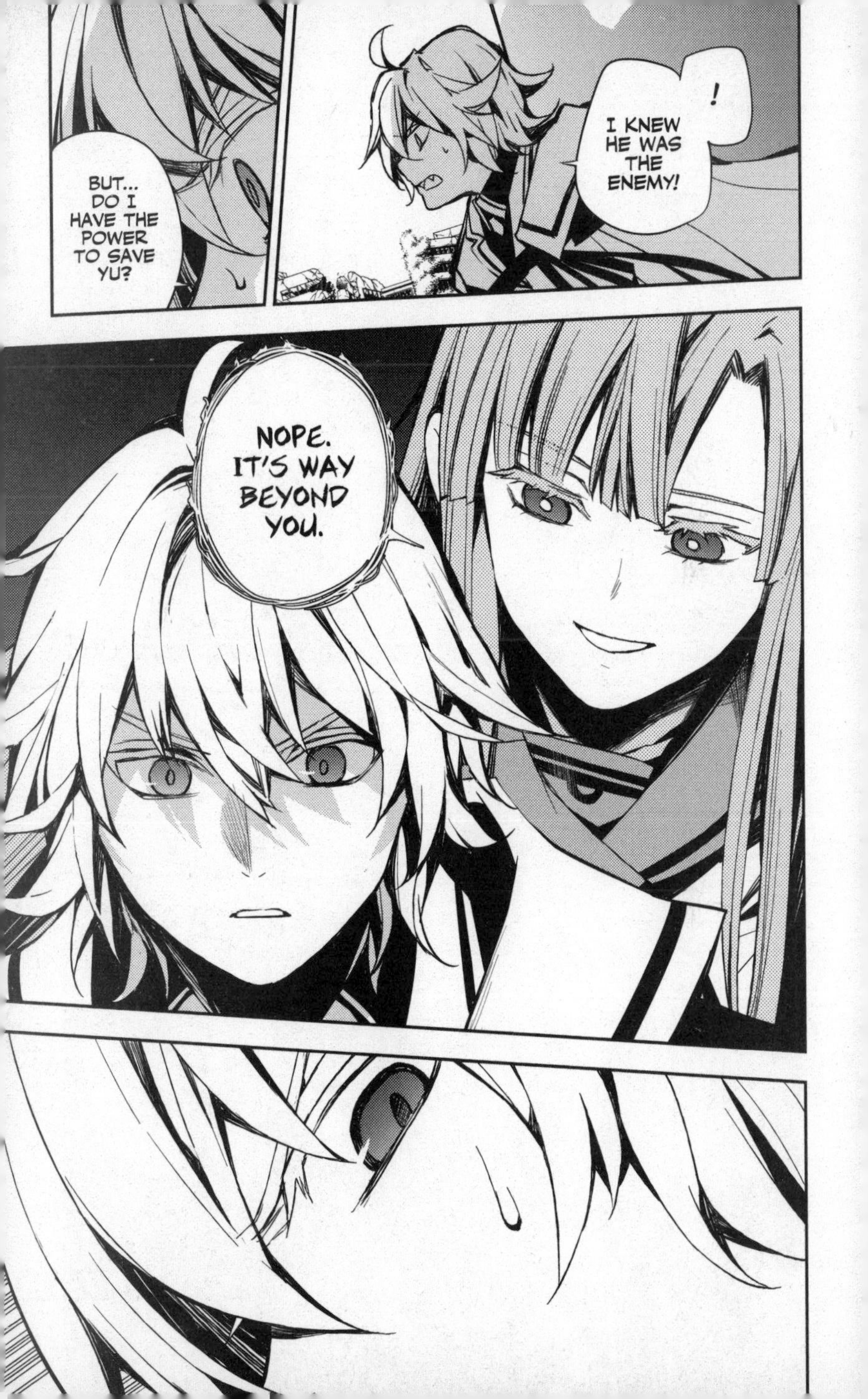
!
I KNEW HE WAS THE ENEMY!
BUT... DO I HAVE THE POWER TO SAVE YU?
NOPE. IT'S WAY BEYOND YOU.

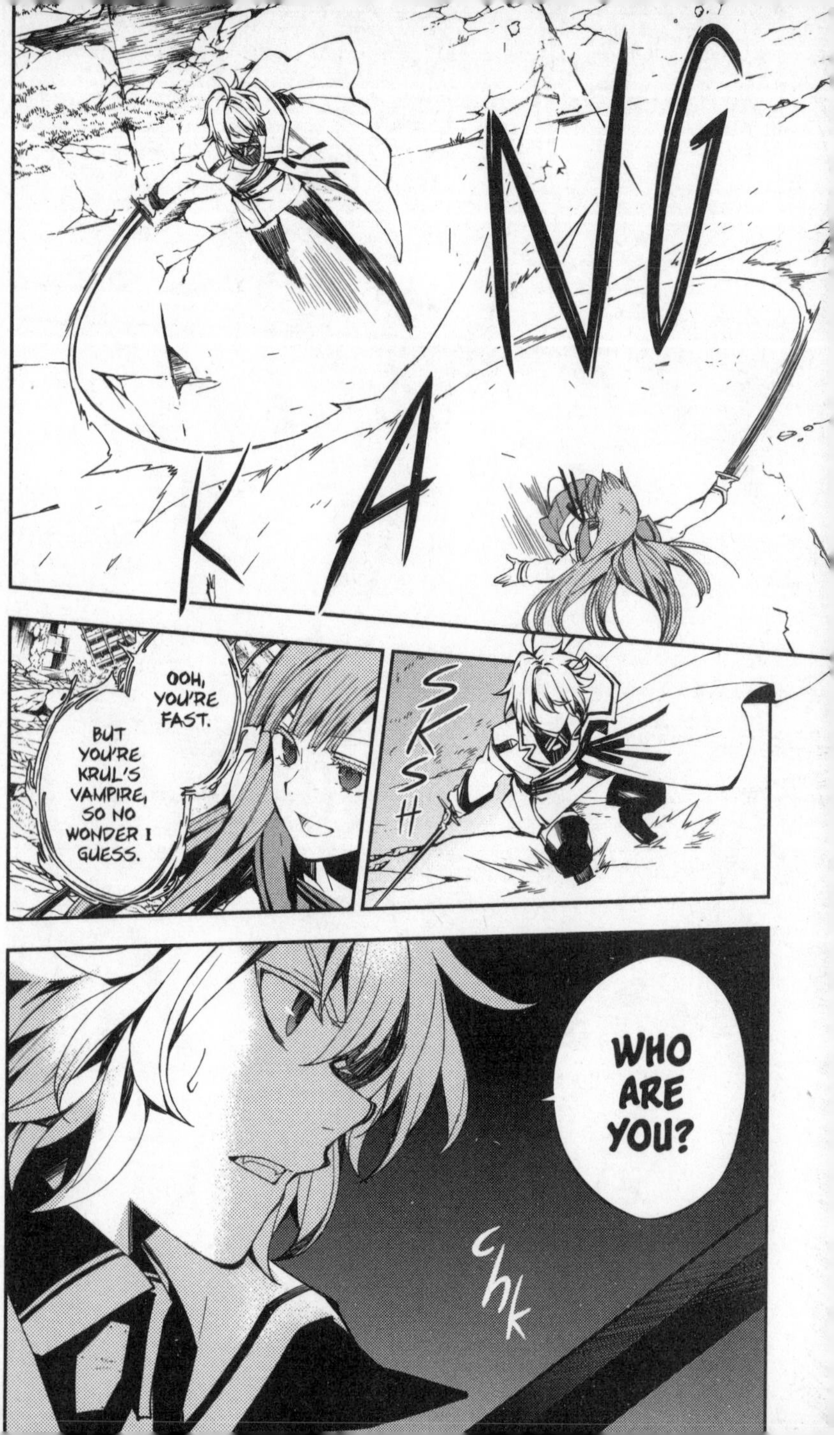
KANG
SKSH
OOH, YOU'RE FAST.
BUT YOU'RE KRUL'S VAMPIRE, SO NO WONDER I GUESS.
WHO ARE YOU?
chk

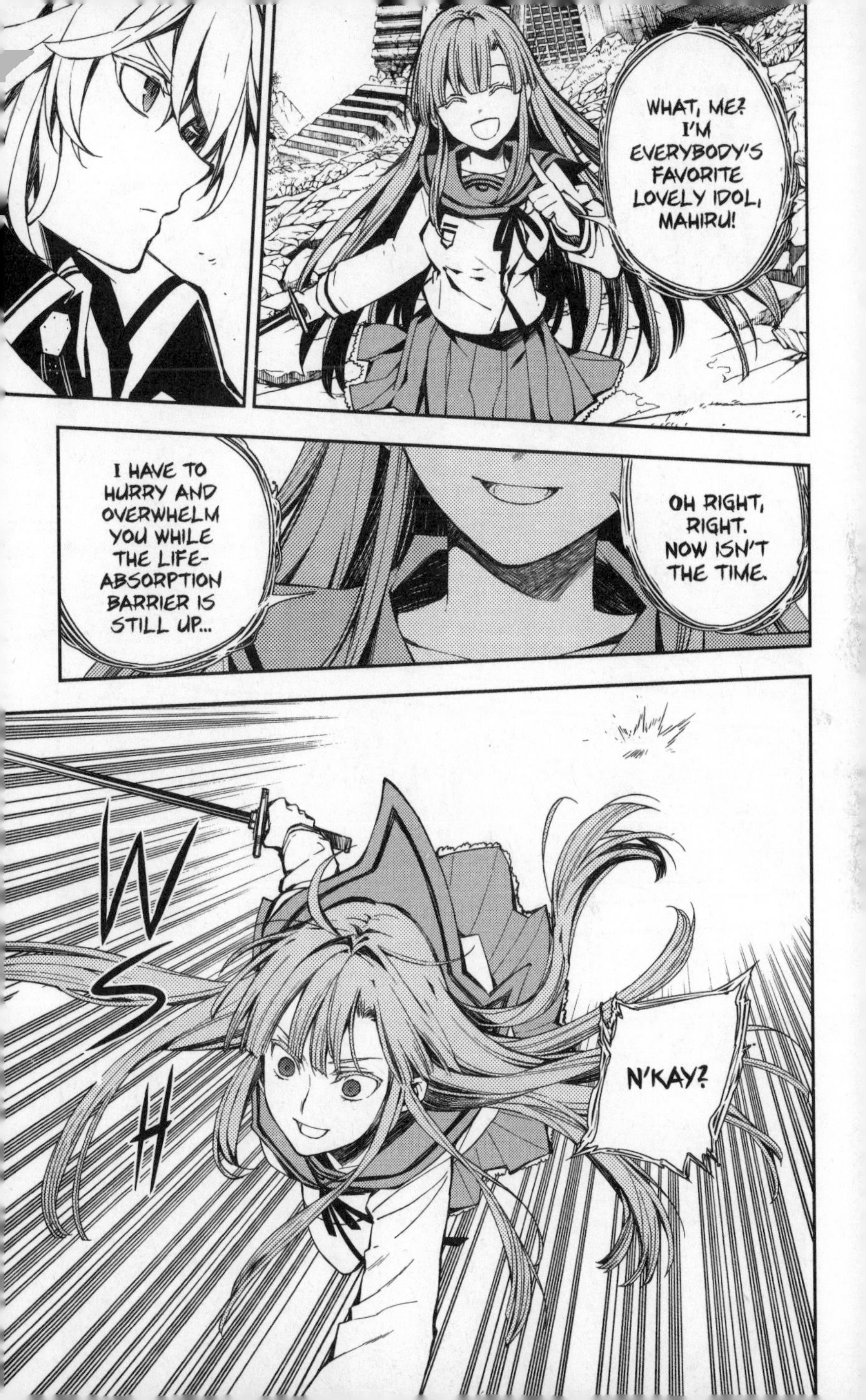
WHAT, ME? I'M EVERYBODY'S FAVORITE LOVELY IDOL, MAHIRU!
OH RIGHT, RIGHT. NOW ISN'T THE TIME.
I HAVE TO HURRY AND OVERWHELM YOU WHILE THE LIFE-ABSORPTION BARRIER IS STILL UP...
N'KAY?
WSH

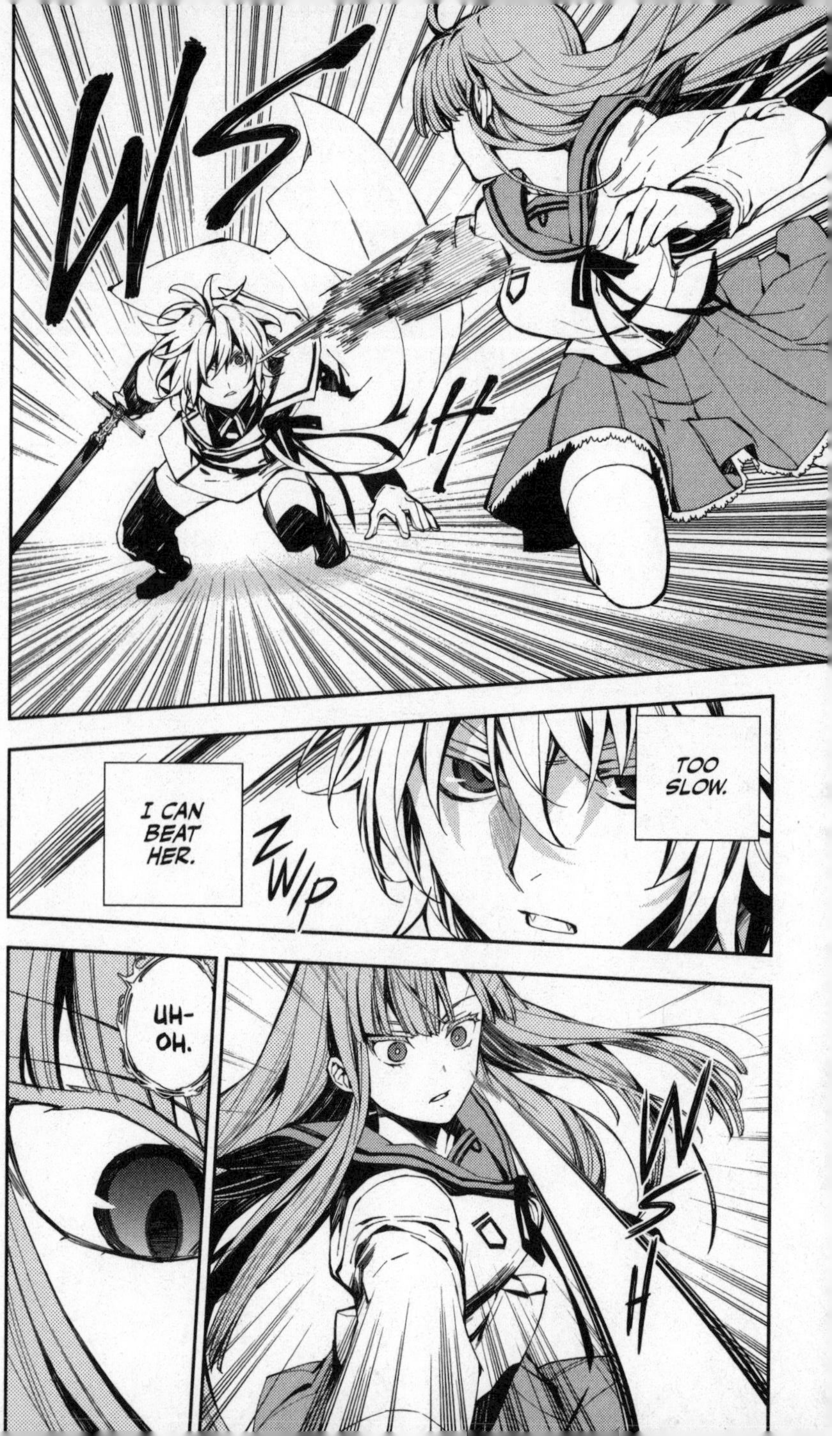
WSH
TOO SLOW.
ZWIP
I CAN BEAT HER.
WSH
UH-OH.

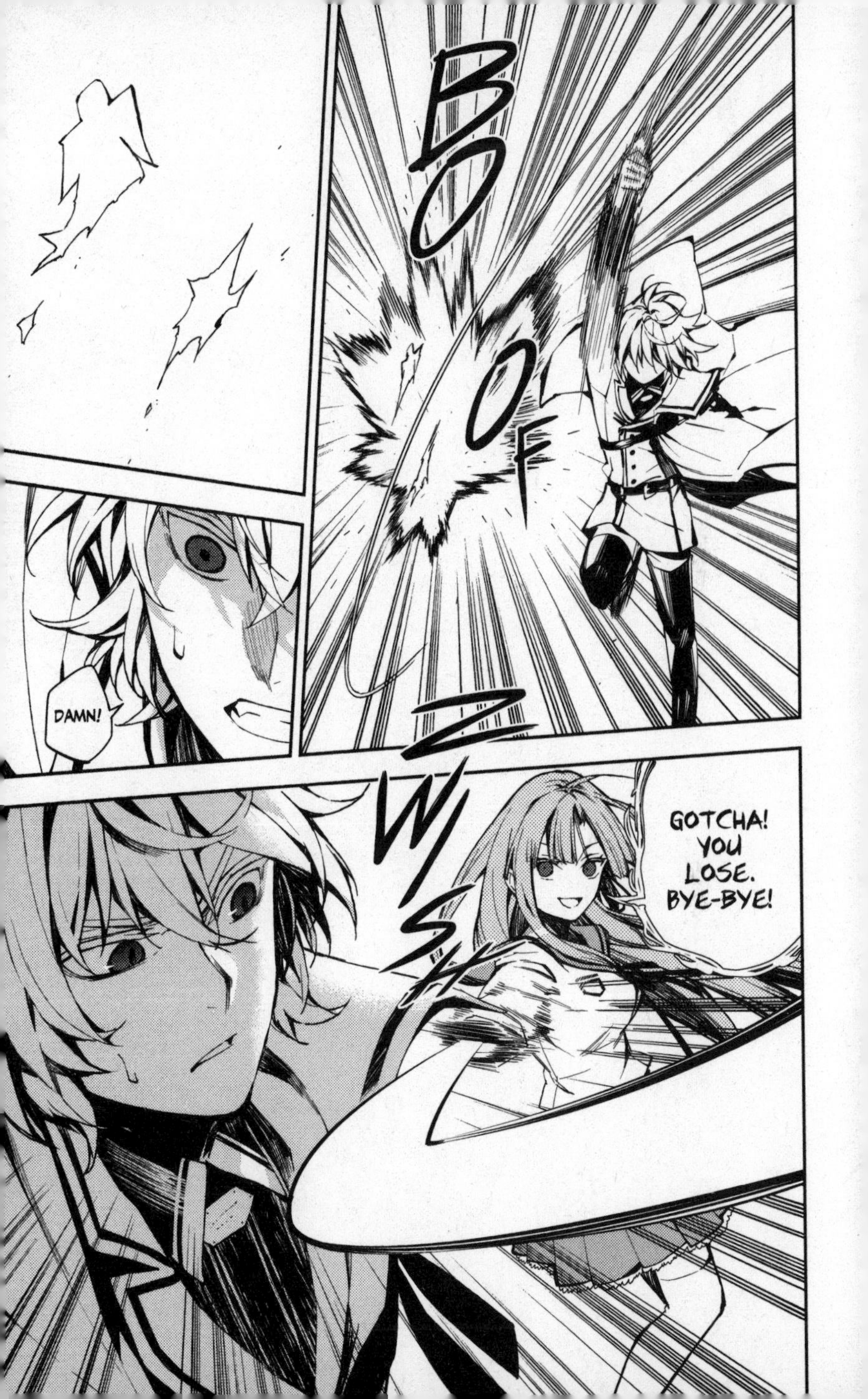
BOOF
DAMN!
GOTCHA! YOU LOSE. BYE-BYE!
ZWISH

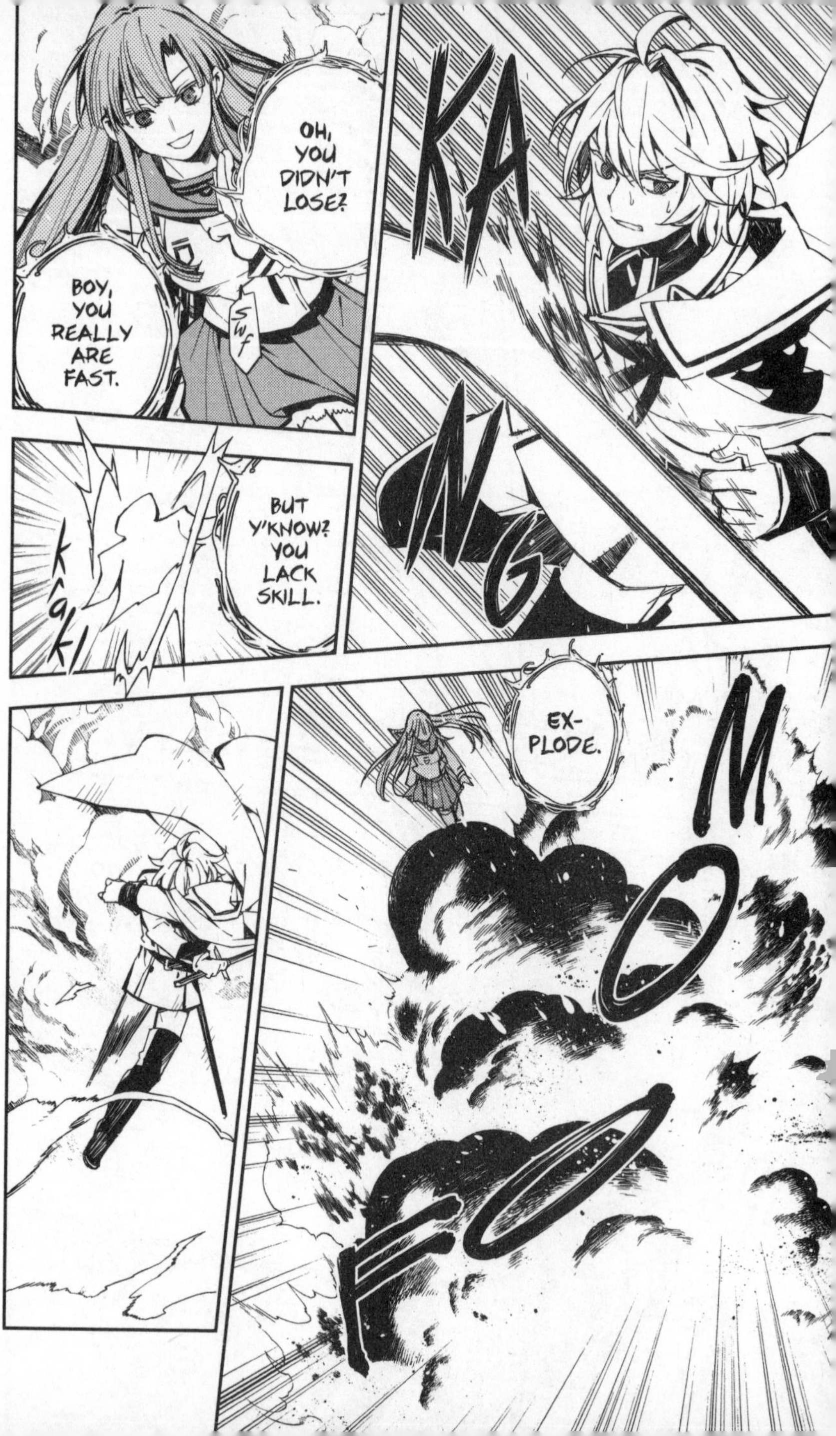
KANG
OH, YOU DIDN'T LOSE?
BOY, YOU REALLY ARE FAST.
SWF
BUT Y'KNOW? YOU LACK SKILL.
KRAKI
EX-PLODE.
FOOM

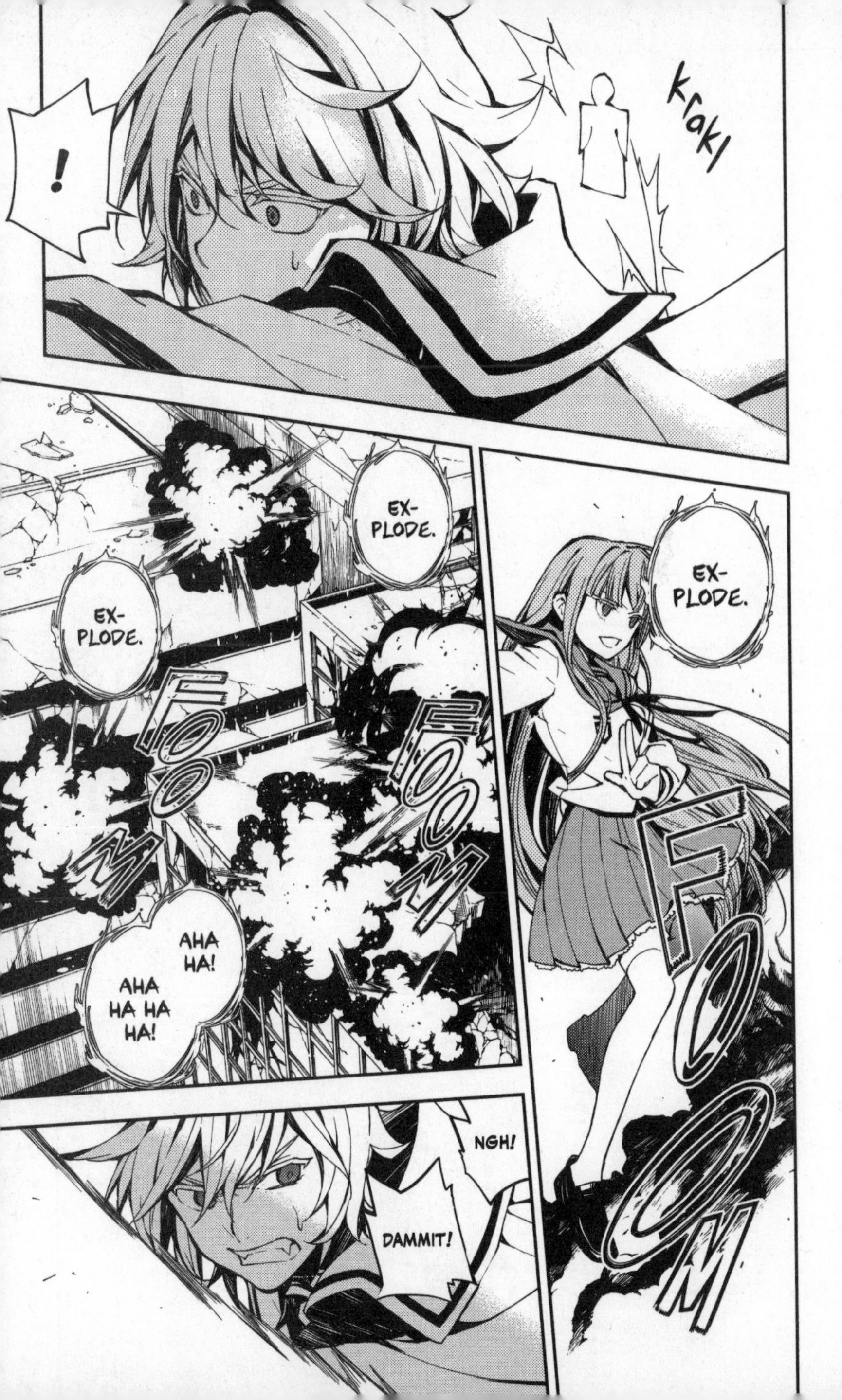
krak!
!
EX-PLODE.
FOOM
EX-PLODE.
FOOM
EX-PLODE.
FOOM
AHA HA!
AHA HA HA HA!
NGH!
DAMMIT!

FORGET HER. I HAVE TO SAVE YU.

YES, THAT'S IT.

RUN OFF AND SAVE LITTLE YU.

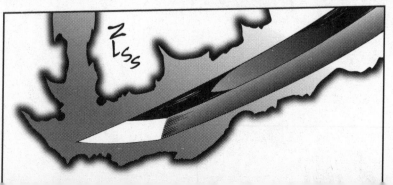

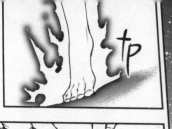

tp

NLORSH

MMMM!

THE OUTSIDE AIR TASTES SOOOO GOOD!

MNNN!

NN!

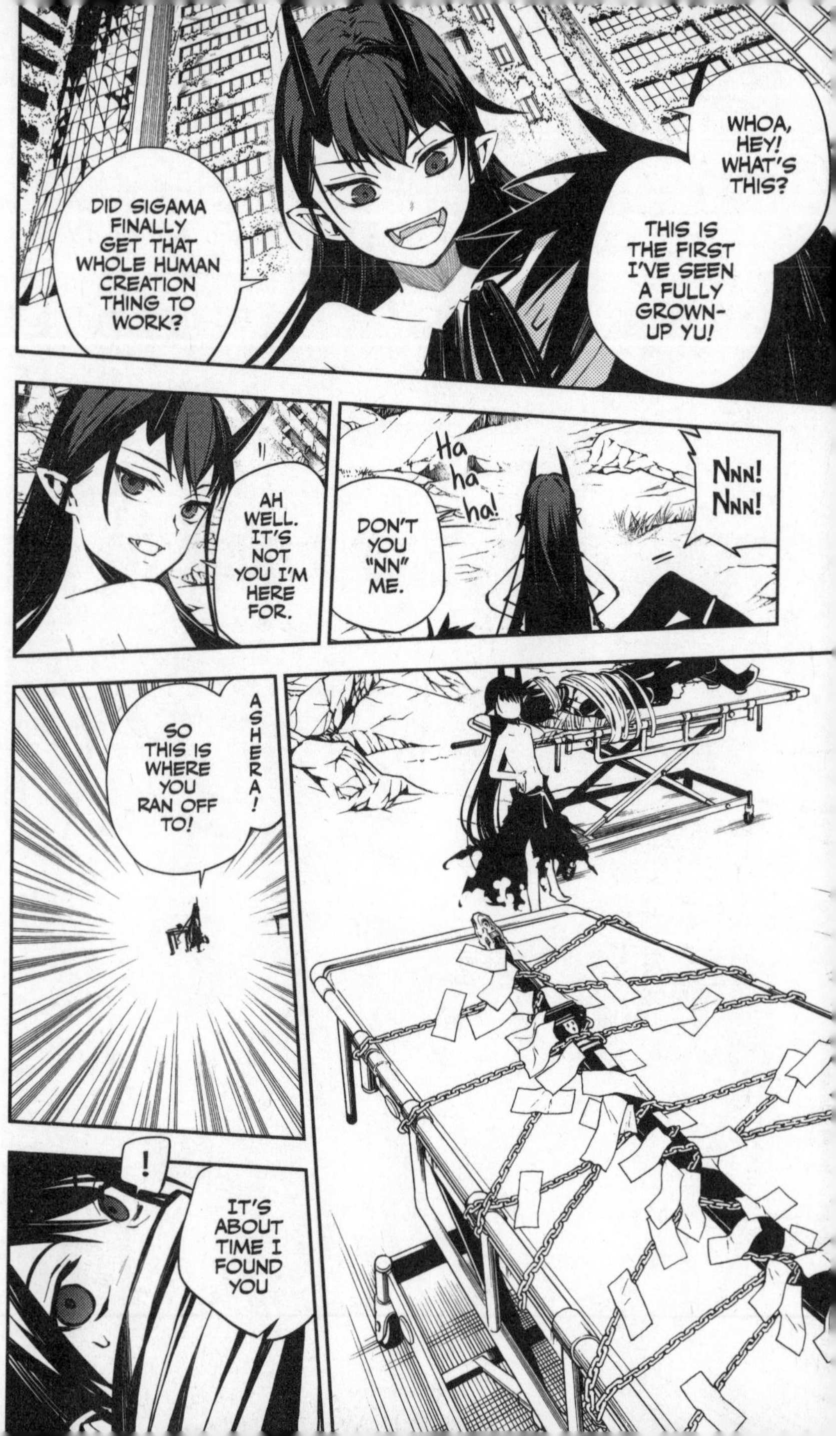
WHOA, HEY! WHAT'S THIS?
THIS IS THE FIRST I'VE SEEN A FULLY GROWN-UP YU!
DID SIGAMA FINALLY GET THAT WHOLE HUMAN CREATION THING TO WORK?
NNN! NNN!
Ha ha ha!
DON'T YOU "NN" ME.
AH WELL. IT'S NOT YOU I'M HERE FOR.
ASHERA!
SO THIS IS WHERE YOU RAN OFF TO!
!
IT'S ABOUT TIME I FOUND YOU

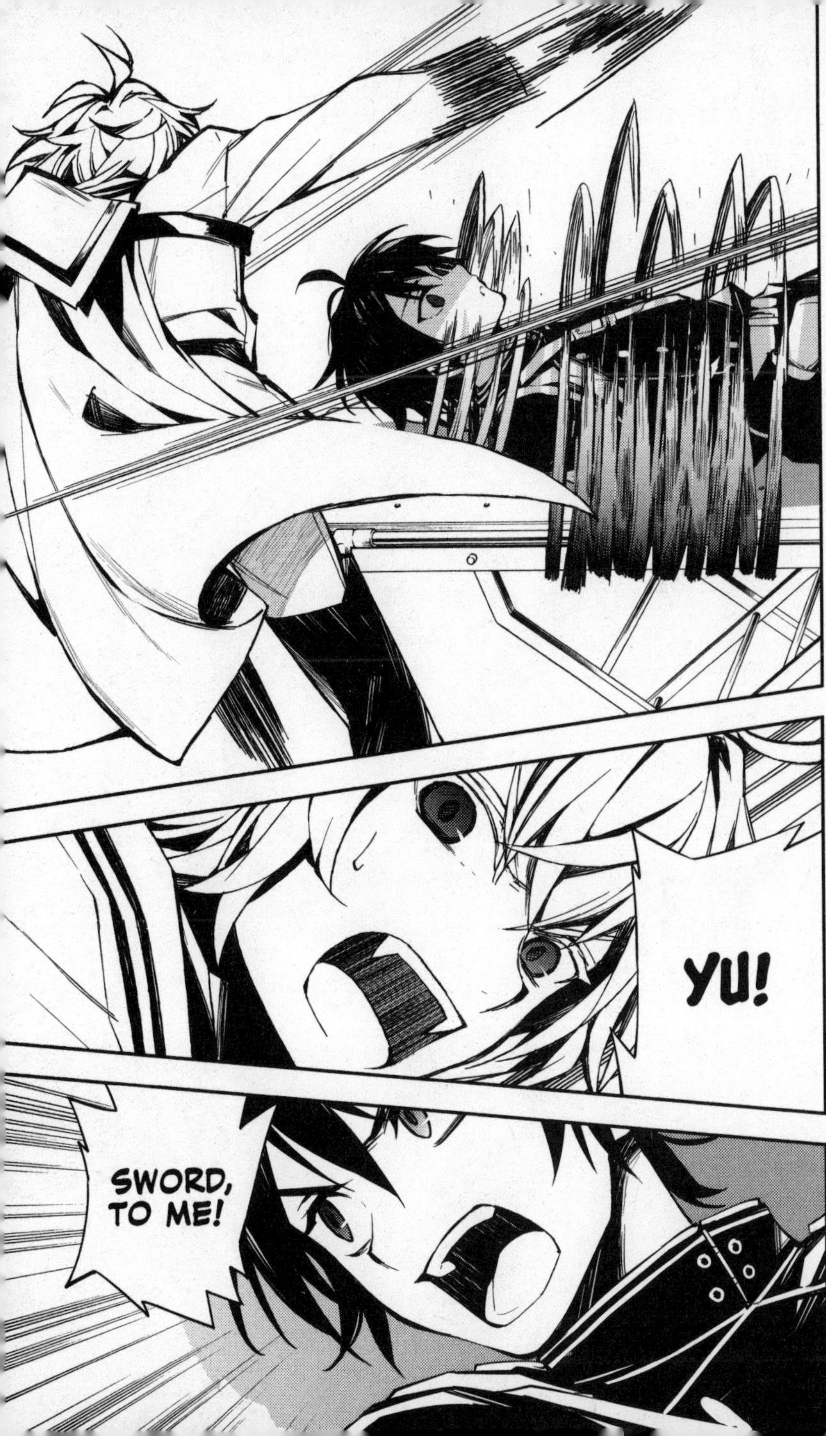
YU!
SWORD, TO ME!

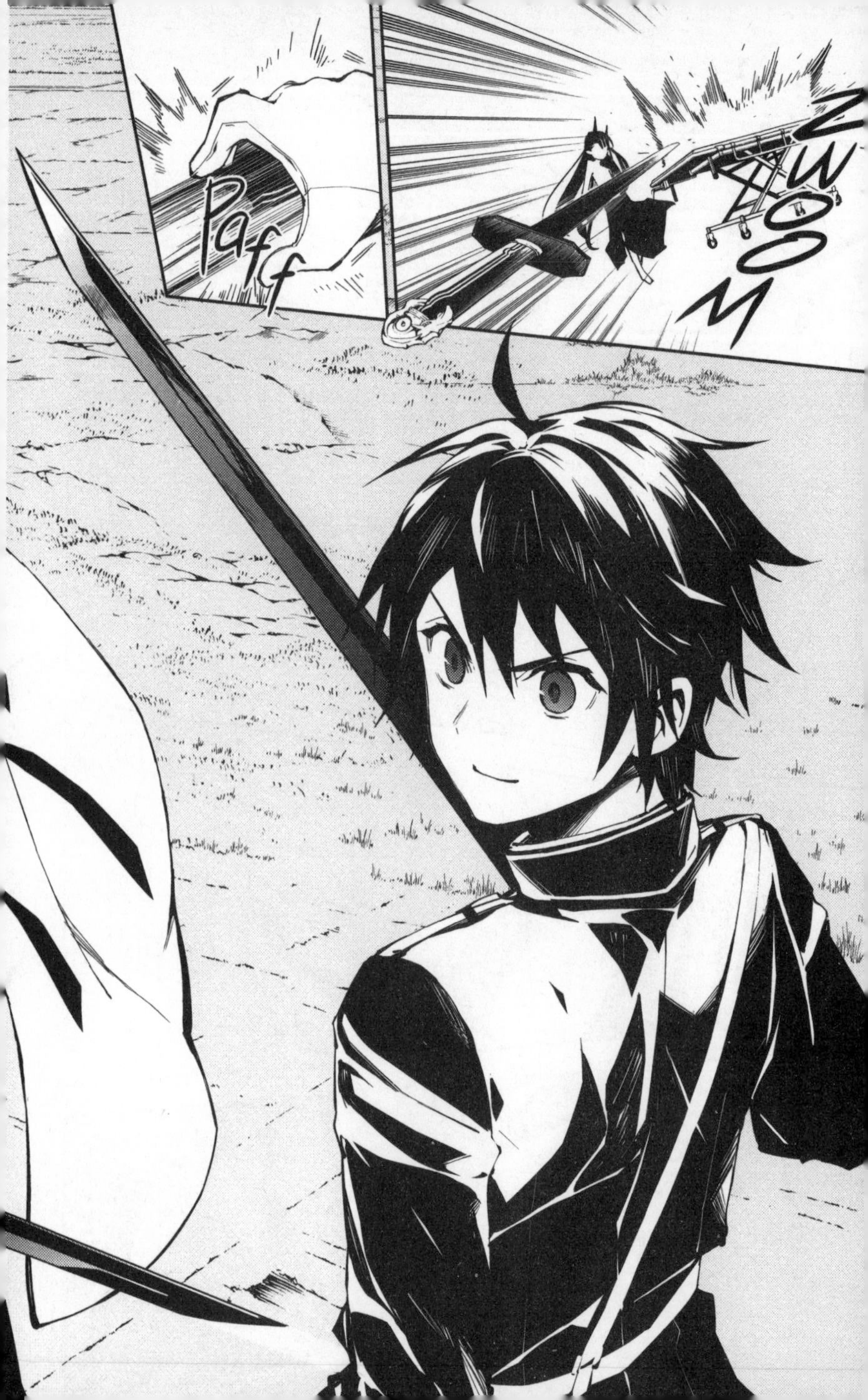
ZWOOM
Paff

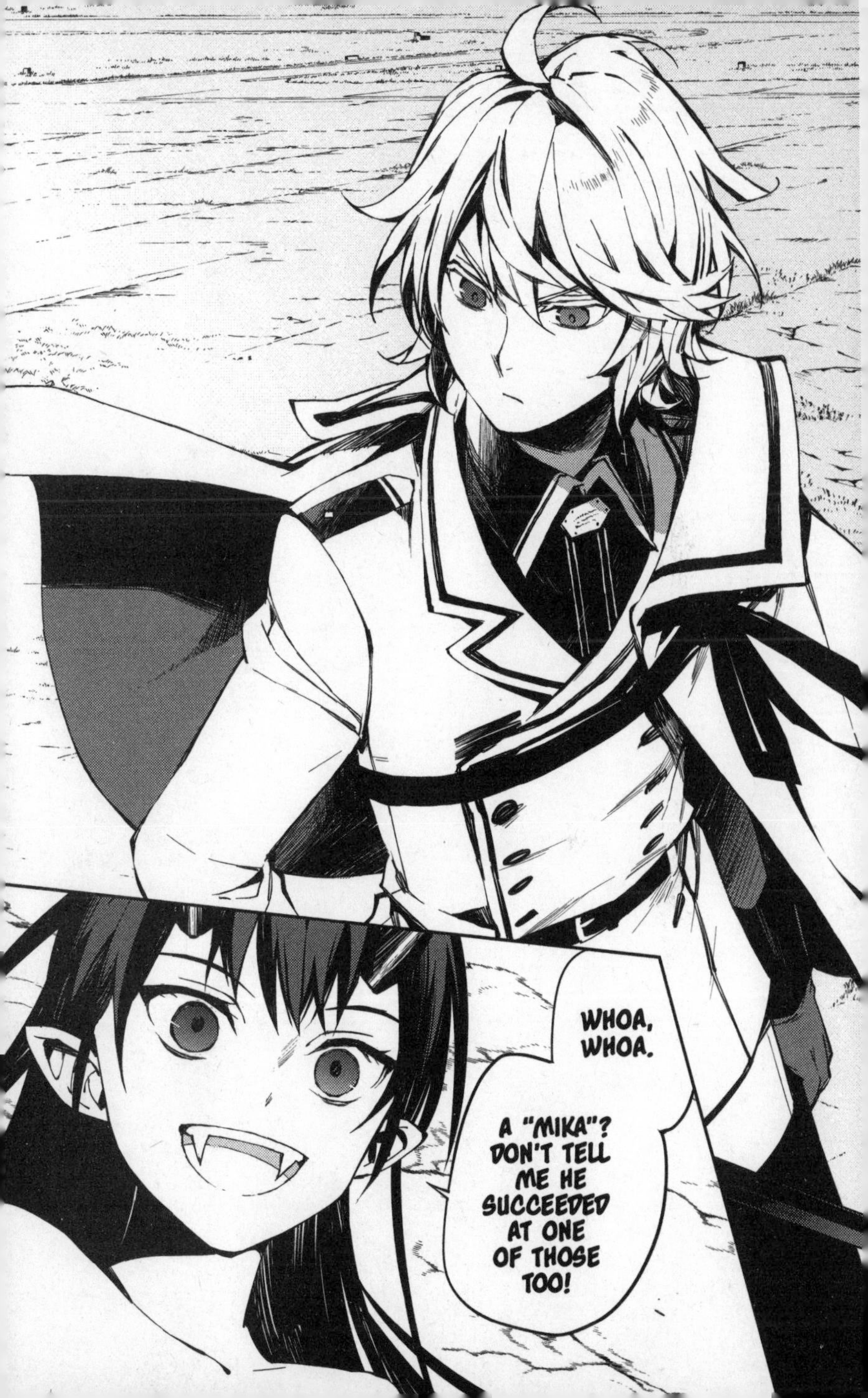
WHOA, WHOA.
A "MIKA"? DON'T TELL ME HE SUCCEEDED AT ONE OF THOSE TOO!

Seraph of the End

—VAMPIRE REIGN—

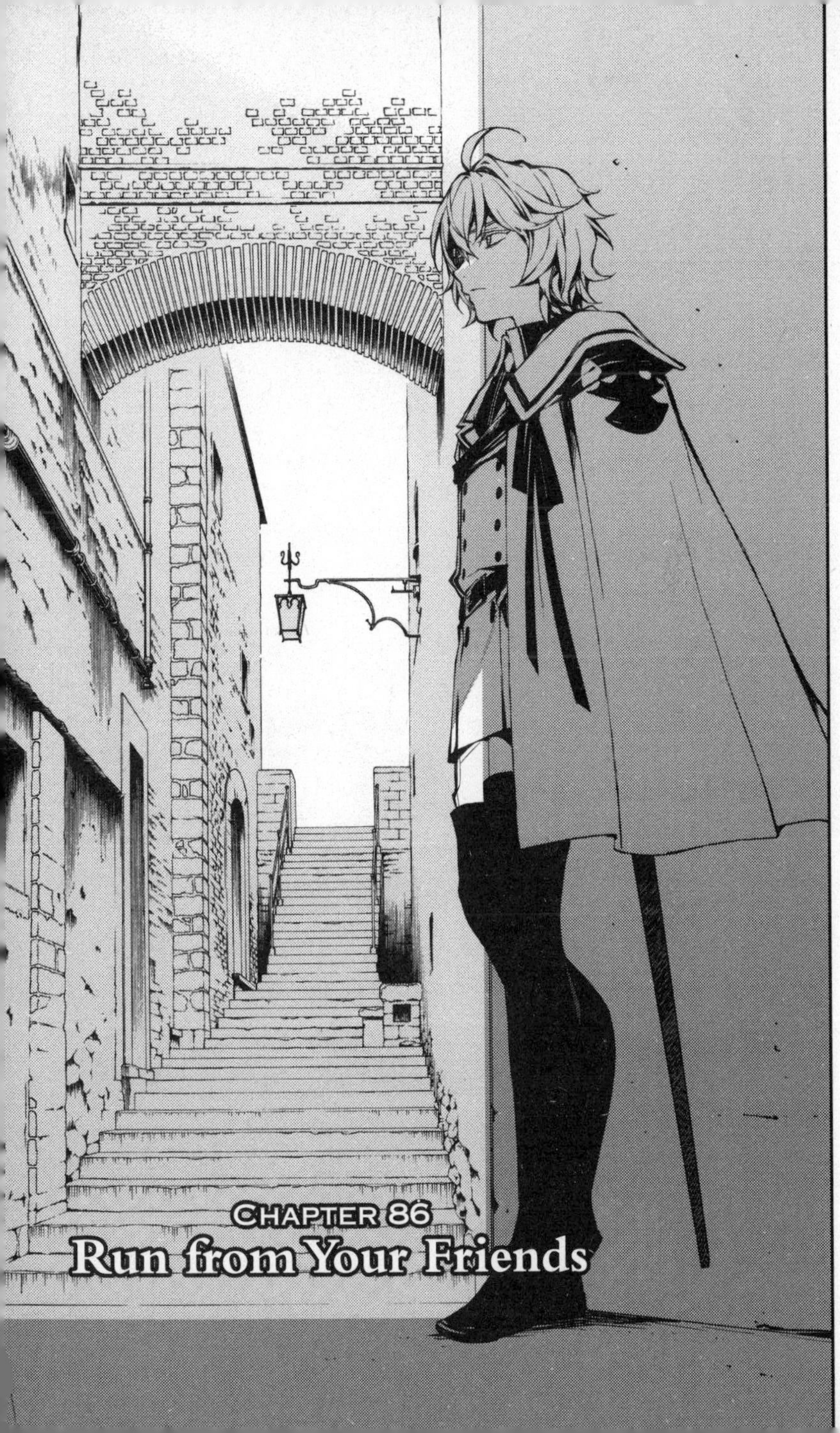
CHAPTER 86
Run from Your Friends

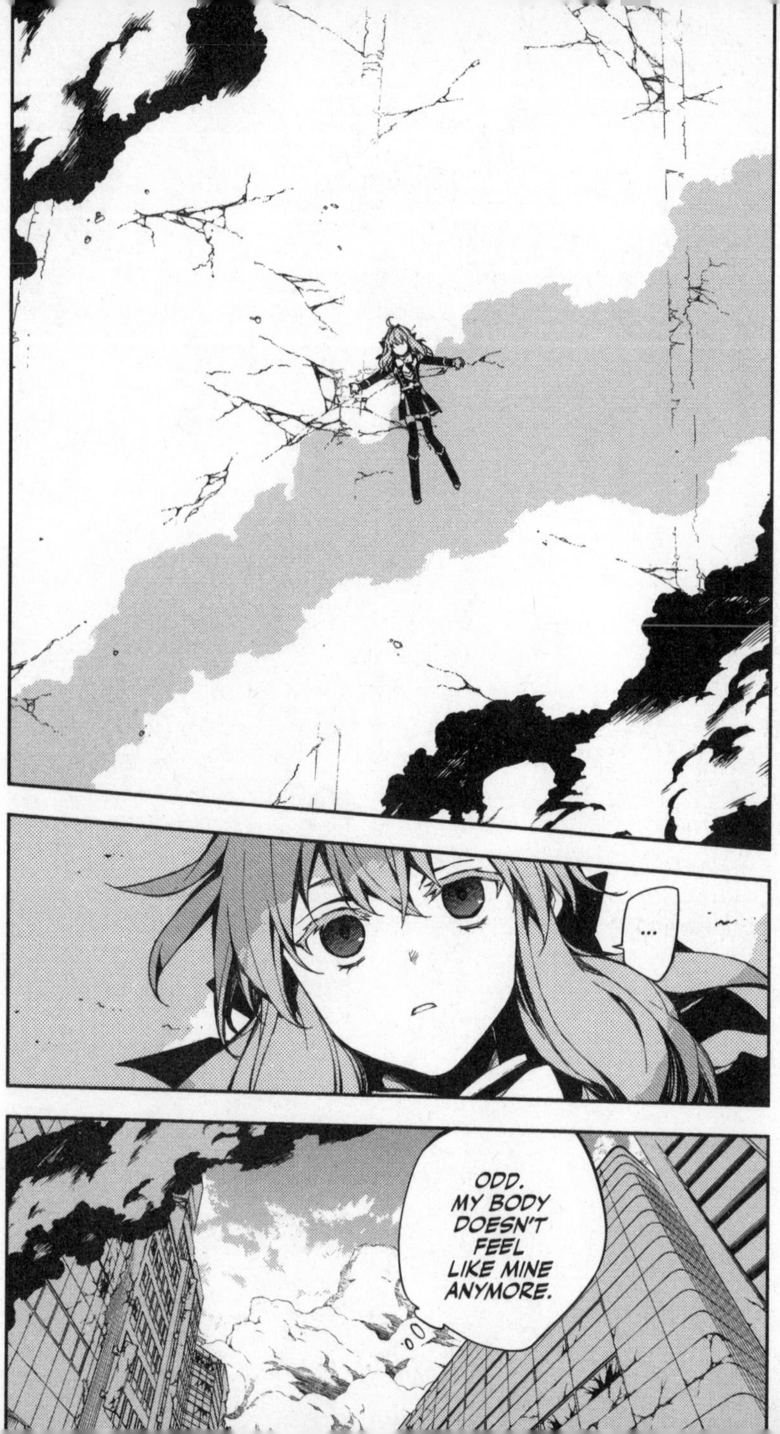
...
ODD. MY BODY DOESN'T FEEL LIKE MINE ANYMORE.

OW.

twch

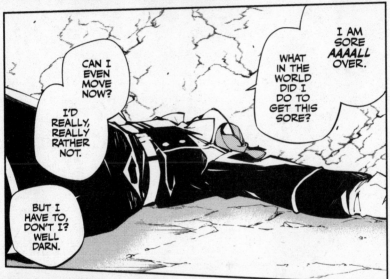

I AM SORE *AAAALL* OVER.

WHAT IN THE WORLD DID I DO TO GET THIS SORE?

CAN I EVEN MOVE NOW?

I'D REALLY, REALLY RATHER NOT.

BUT I HAVE TO, DON'T I? WELL DARN.

OOH OW OW.

OW.

OW OW OW OW OW.

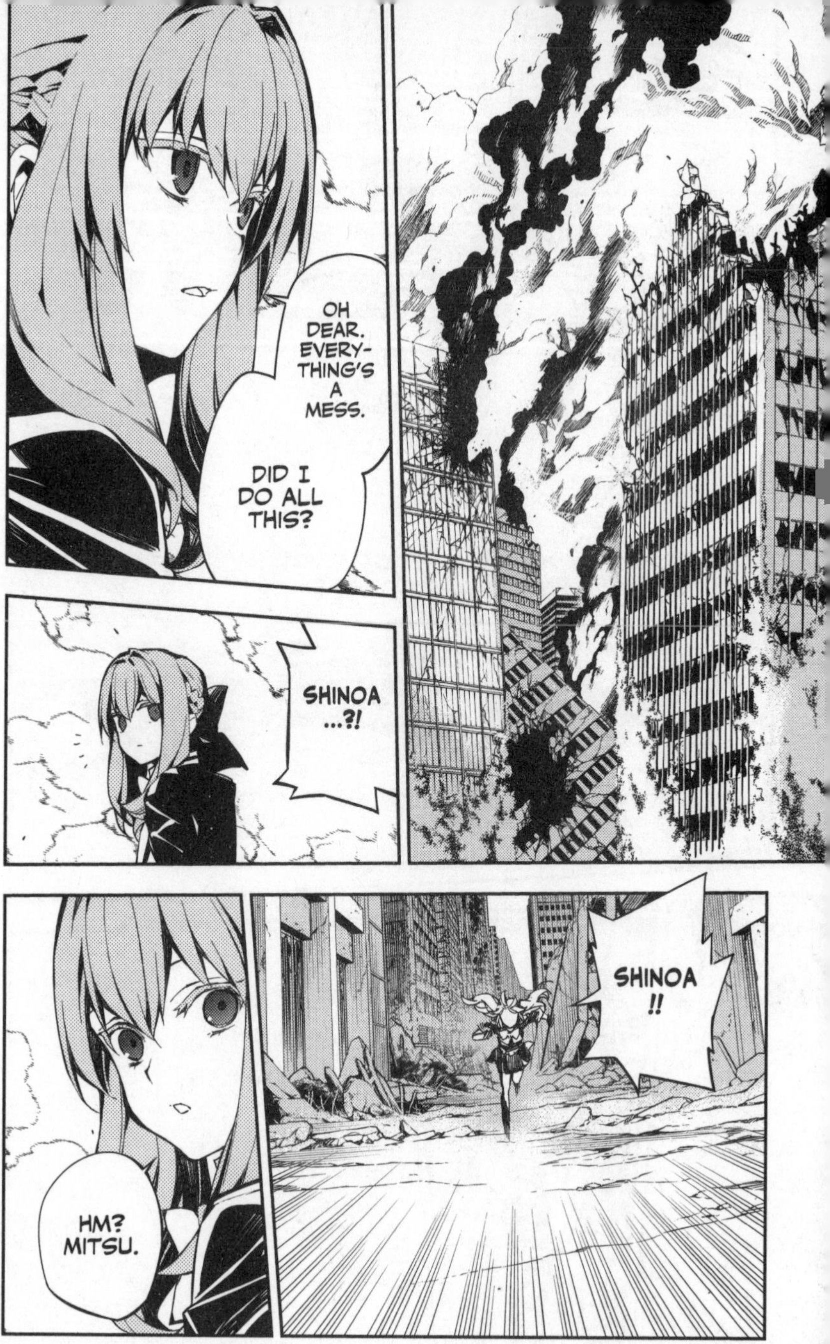
OH DEAR. EVERYTHING'S A MESS.
DID I DO ALL THIS?
SHINOA ...?!
SHINOA !!
HM? MITSU.

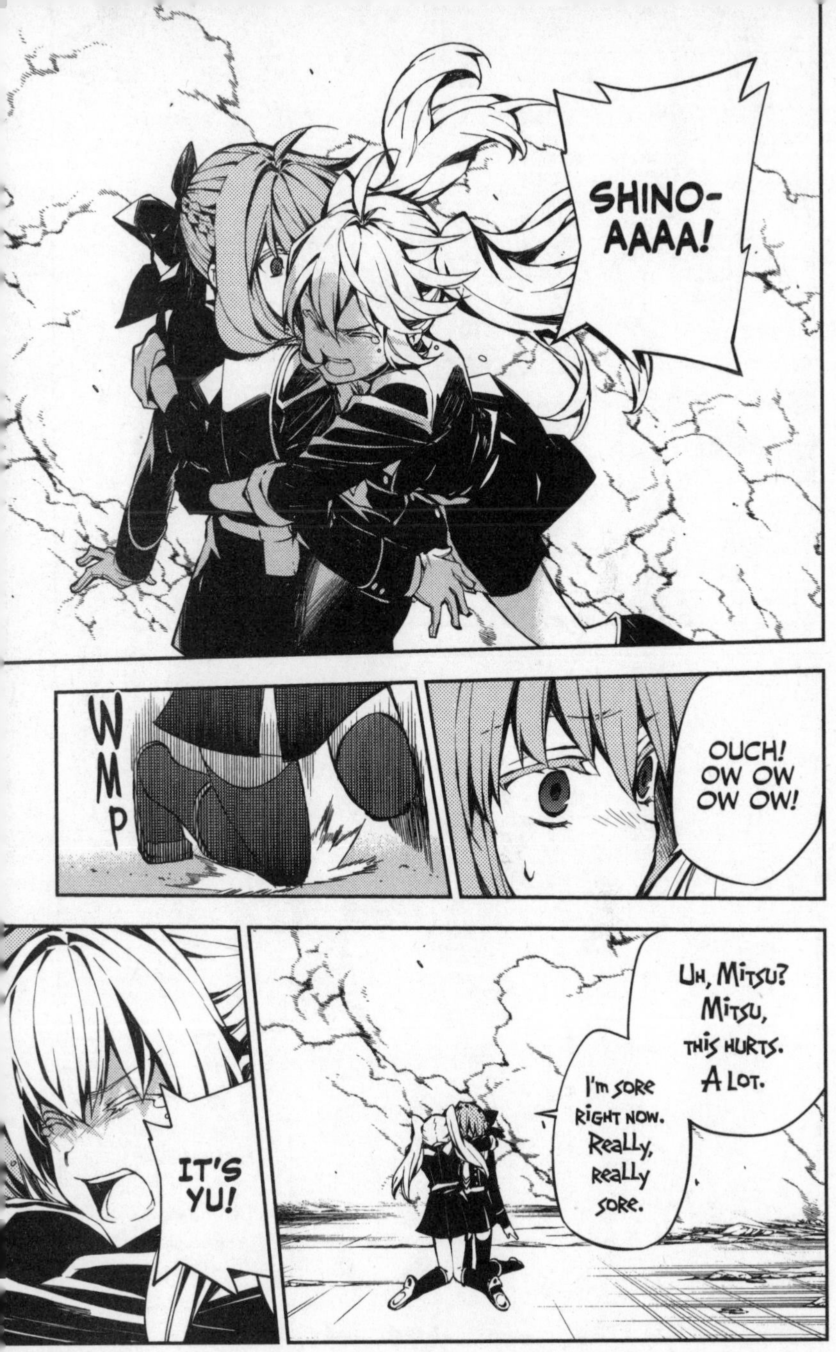
SHINO-AAAA!
OUCH! OW OW OW OW!
WMP
Uh, Mitsu? Mitsu, this hurts. A lot.
I'm sore right now. Really, really sore.
IT'S YU!

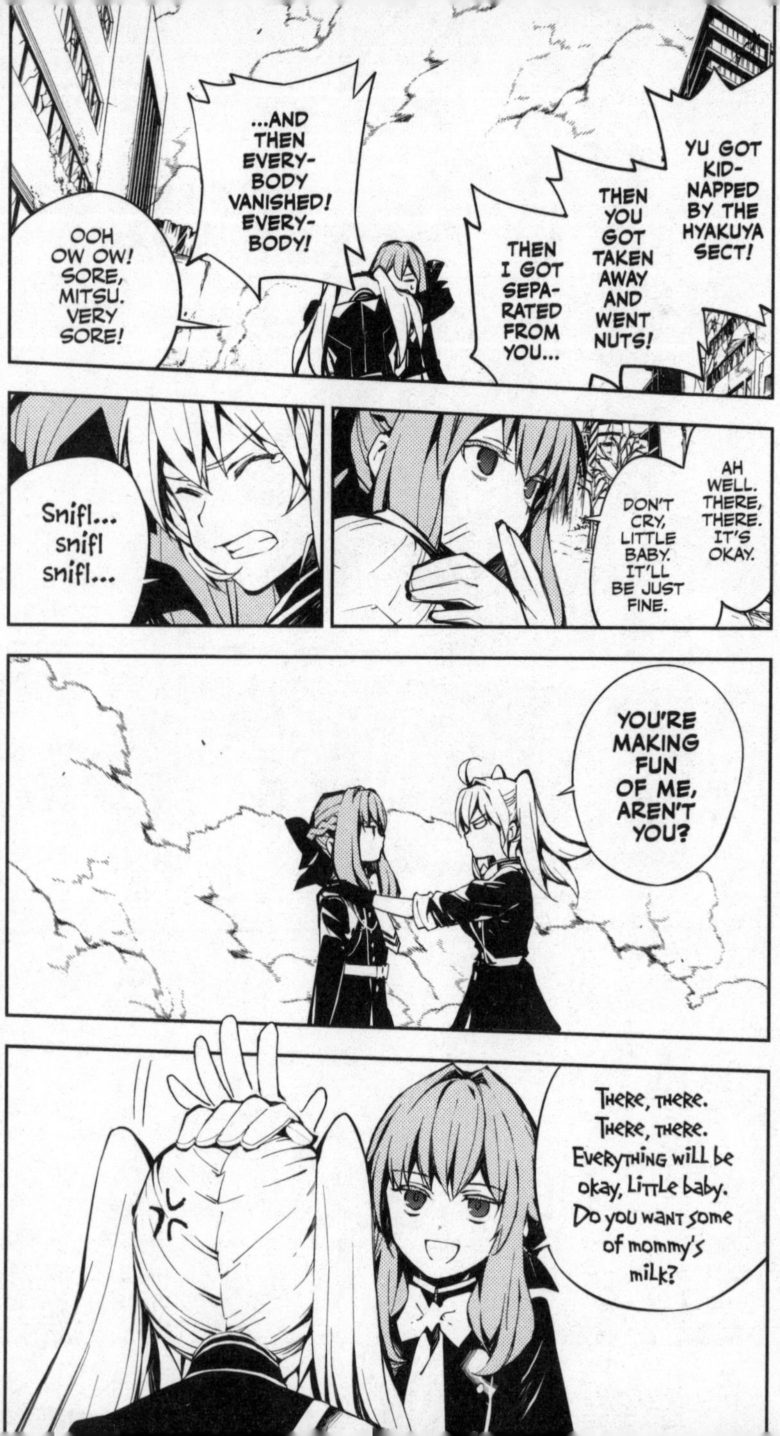
YU GOT KIDNAPPED BY THE HYAKUYA SECT!
THEN YOU GOT TAKEN AWAY AND WENT NUTS!
THEN I GOT SEPARATED FROM YOU...
...AND THEN EVERYBODY VANISHED! EVERYBODY!
OOH OW OW! SORE, MITSU. VERY SORE!
AH WELL. THERE, THERE. IT'S OKAY.
DON'T CRY, LITTLE BABY. IT'LL BE JUST FINE.
Snifl... snifl snifl...
YOU'RE MAKING FUN OF ME, AREN'T YOU?
There, there. There, there. Everything will be okay, Little baby. Do you want some of mommy's milk?

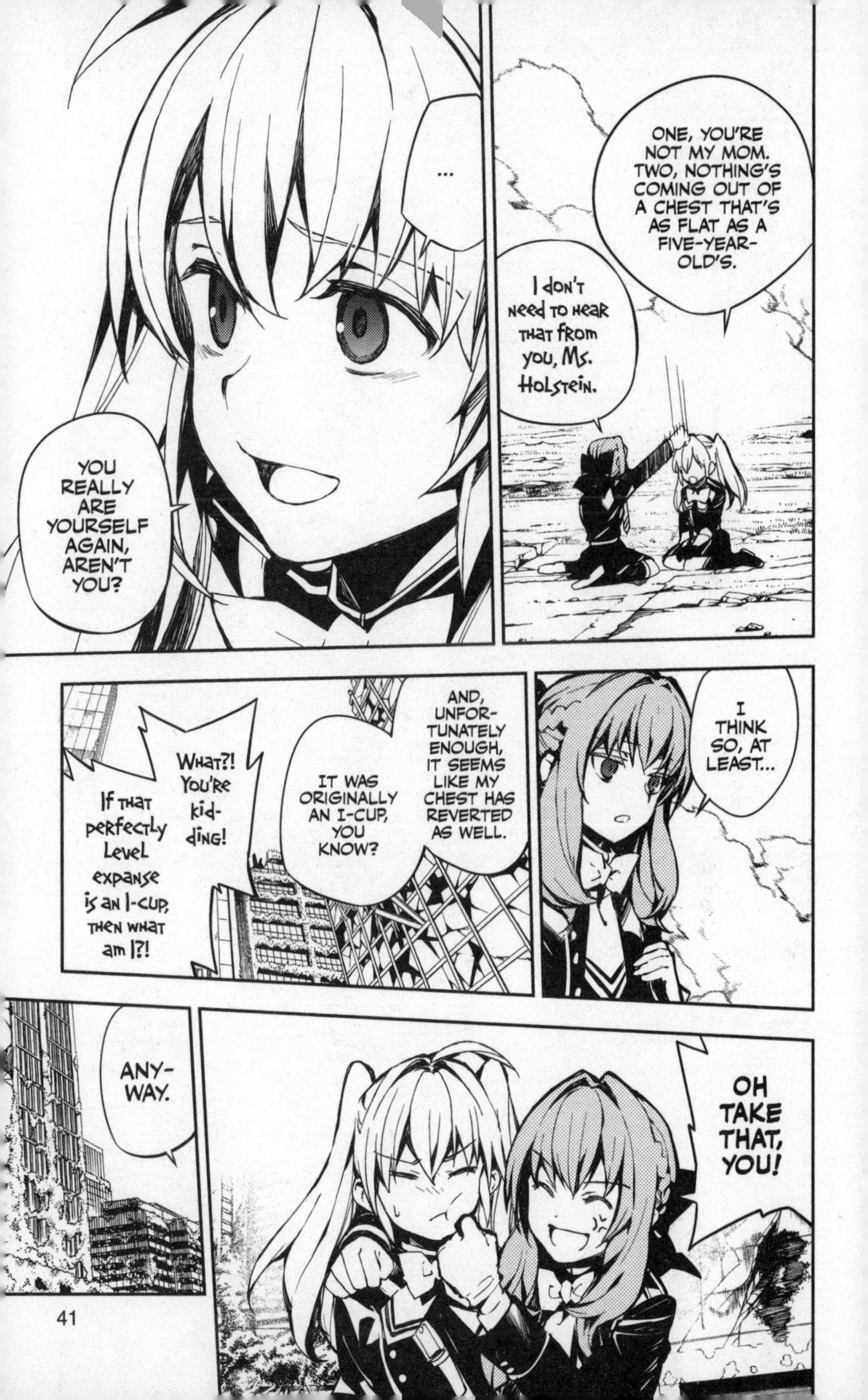
ONE, YOU'RE NOT MY MOM. TWO, NOTHING'S COMING OUT OF A CHEST THAT'S AS FLAT AS A FIVE-YEAR-OLD'S.
I don't need to hear that from you, Ms. Holstein.
...
YOU REALLY ARE YOURSELF AGAIN, AREN'T YOU?
I THINK SO, AT LEAST...
AND, UNFORTUNATELY ENOUGH, IT SEEMS LIKE MY CHEST HAS REVERTED AS WELL.
IT WAS ORIGINALLY AN I-CUP, YOU KNOW?
WHAT?! You're kid-ding!
If that perfectly Level expanse is an I-cup, then what am I?!
OH TAKE THAT, YOU!
ANY-WAY.

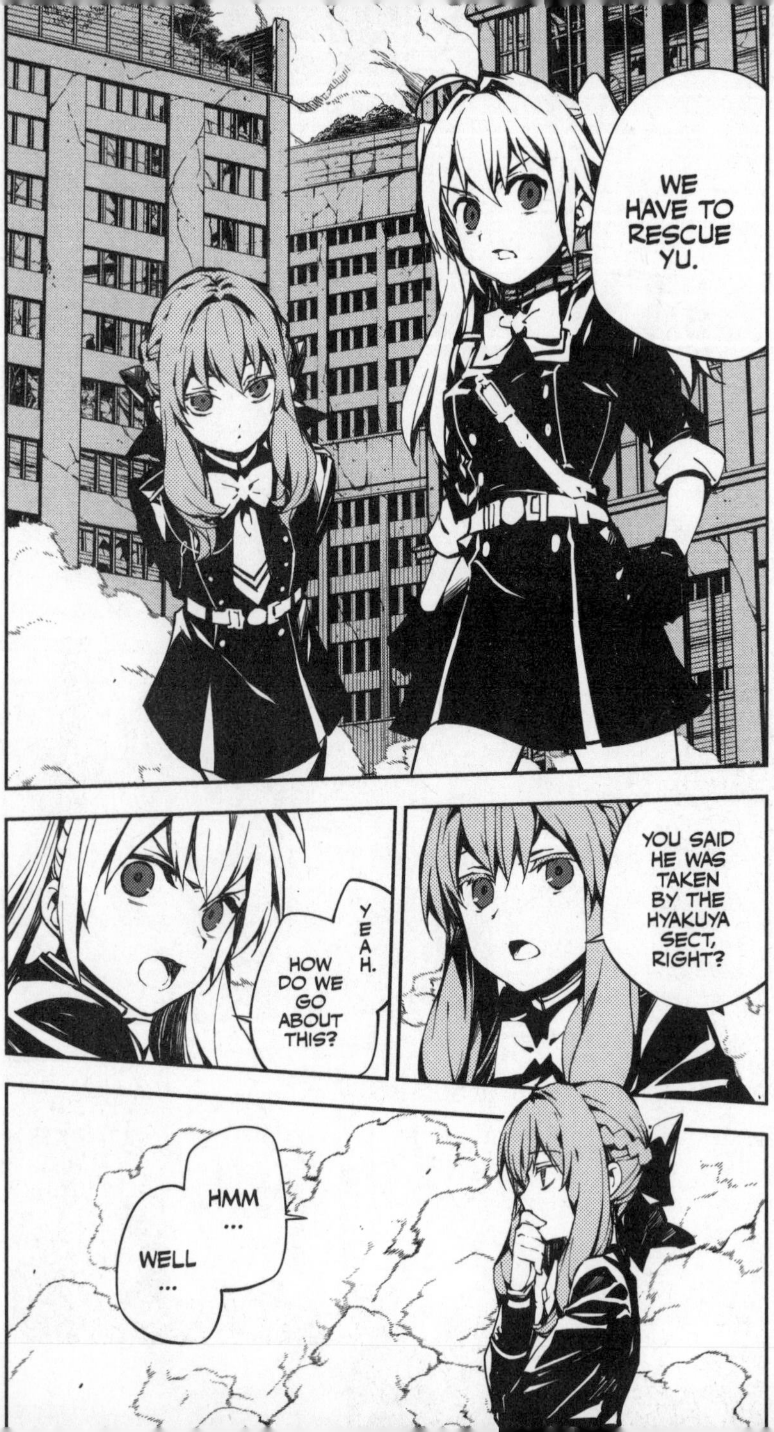
WE HAVE TO RESCUE YU.
YOU SAID HE WAS TAKEN BY THE HYAKUYA SECT, RIGHT?
YEAH.
HOW DO WE GO ABOUT THIS?
HMM...
WELL...

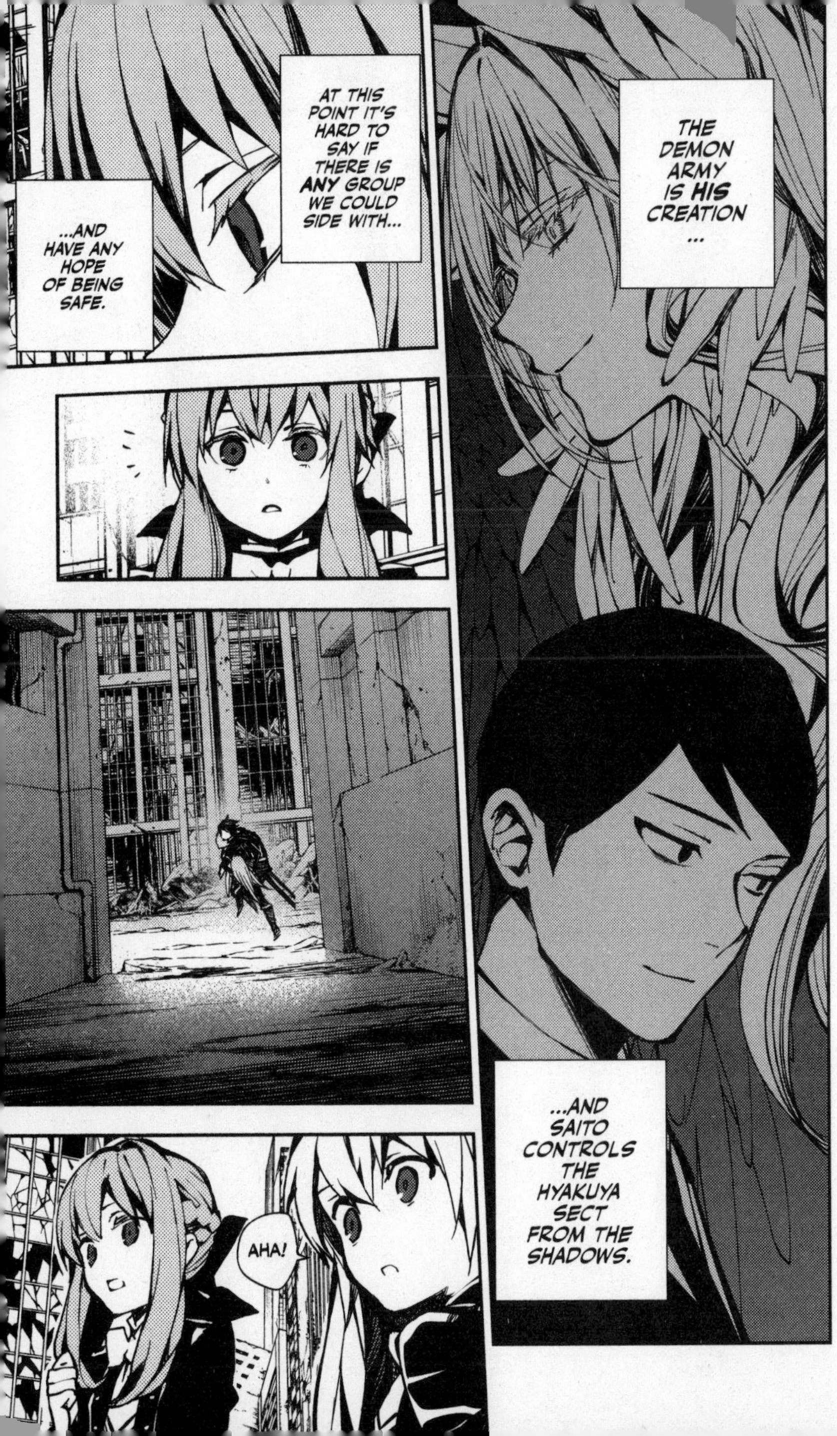
THE DEMON ARMY IS **HIS** CREATION ...
...AND SAITO CONTROLS THE HYAKUYA SECT FROM THE SHADOWS.
AT THIS POINT IT'S HARD TO SAY IF THERE IS **ANY** GROUP WE COULD SIDE WITH...
...AND HAVE ANY HOPE OF BEING SAFE.
AHA!

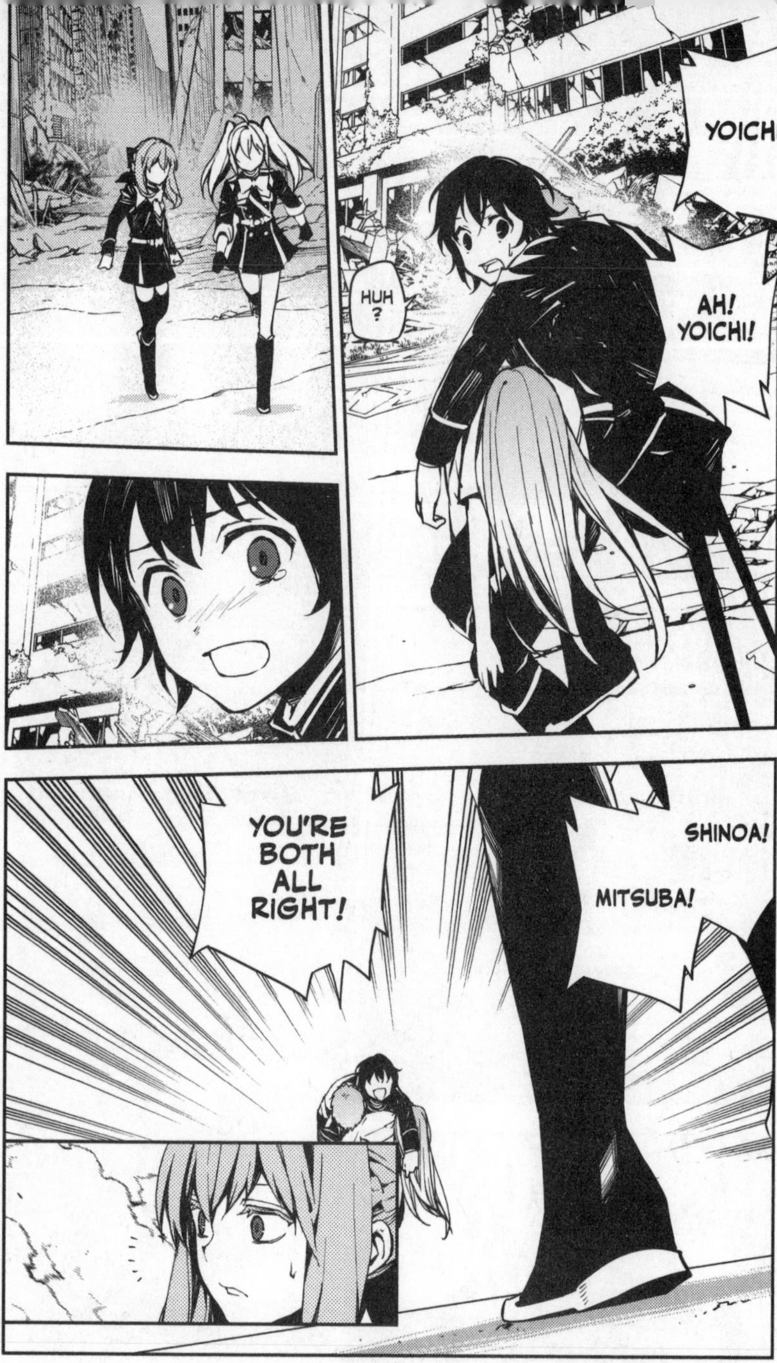
YOICHI!
HUH?
AH! YOICHI!
SHINOA!
MITSUBA!
YOU'RE BOTH ALL RIGHT!

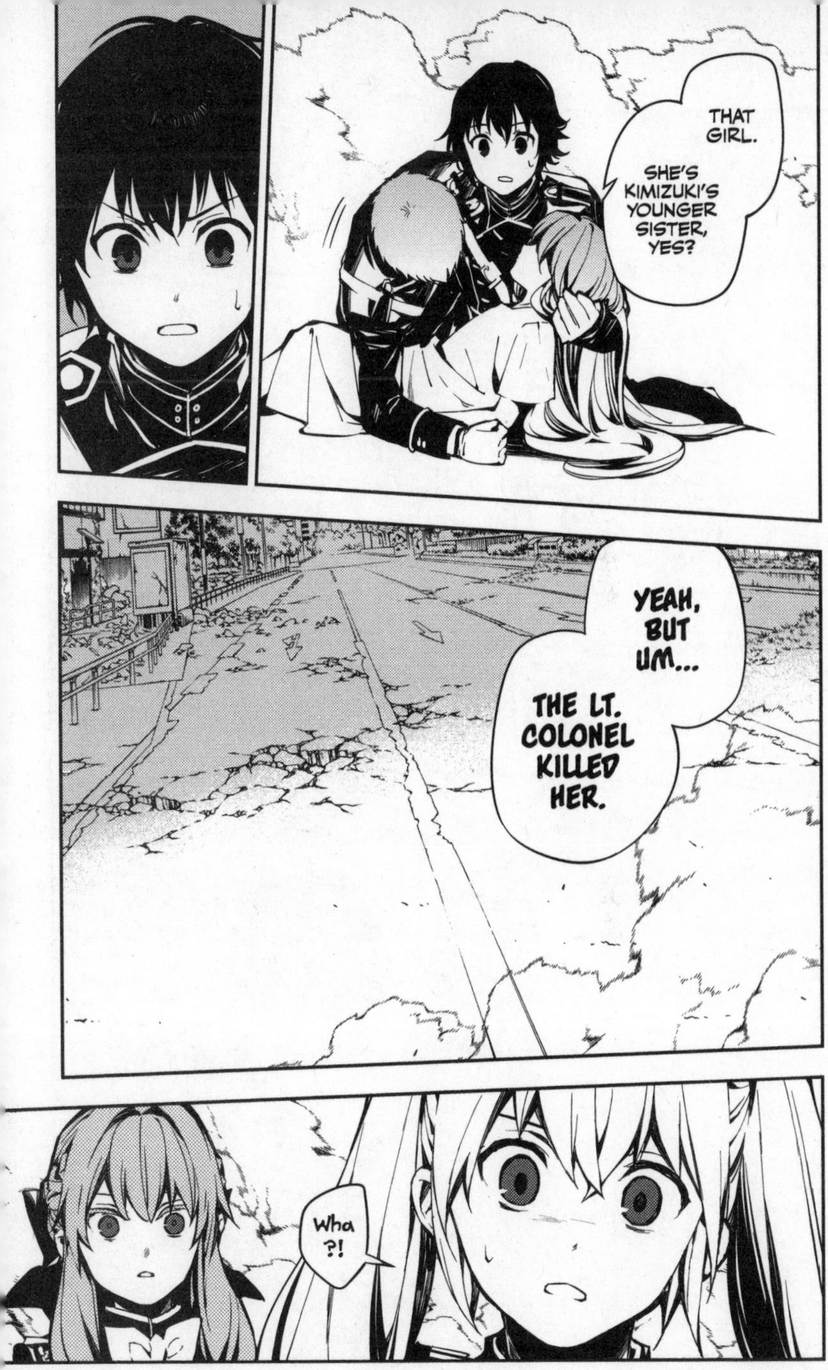
THAT GIRL.
SHE'S KIMIZUKI'S YOUNGER SISTER, YES?
YEAH, BUT UM...
THE LT. COLONEL KILLED HER.
Wha ?!

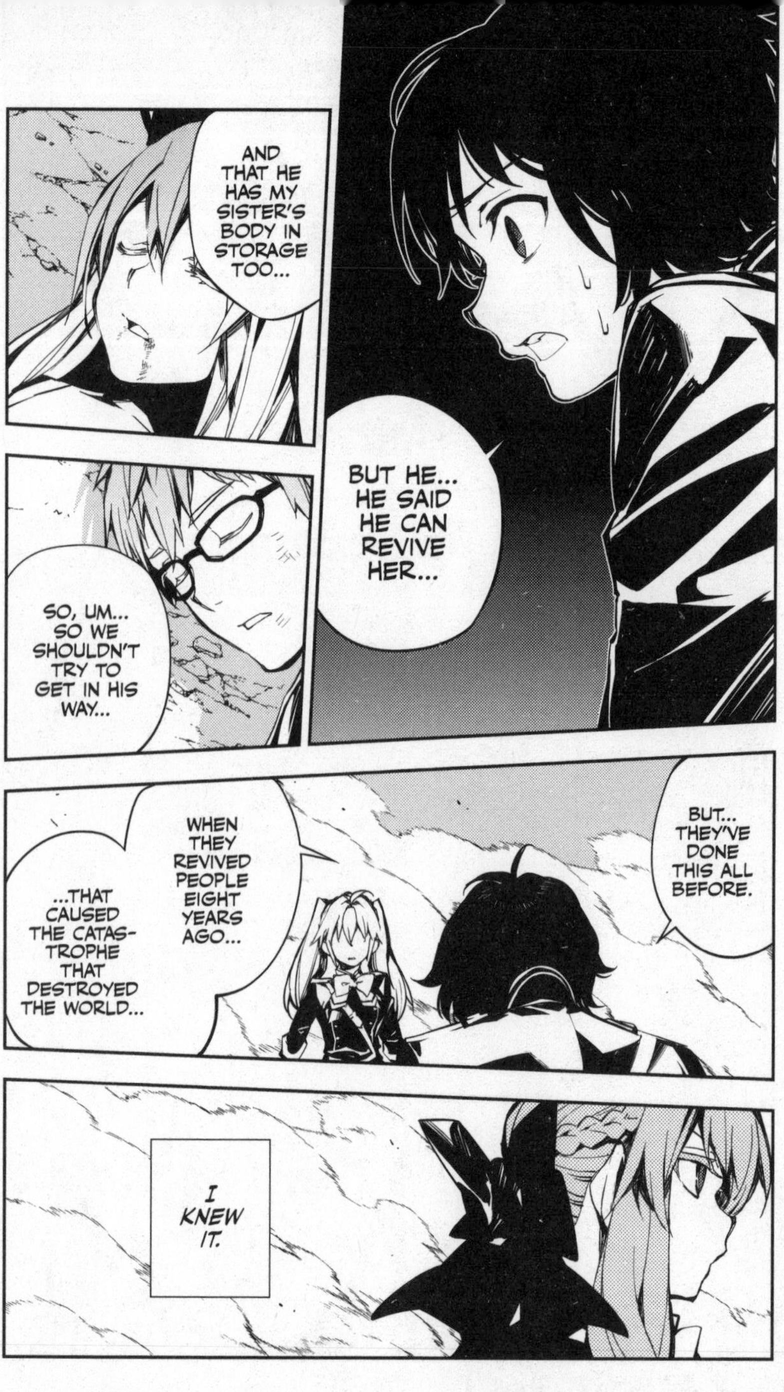
BUT HE... HE SAID HE CAN REVIVE HER...
AND THAT HE HAS MY SISTER'S BODY IN STORAGE TOO...
SO, UM... SO WE SHOULDN'T TRY TO GET IN HIS WAY...
BUT... THEY'VE DONE THIS ALL BEFORE.
WHEN THEY REVIVED PEOPLE EIGHT YEARS AGO...
...THAT CAUSED THE CATASTROPHE THAT DESTROYED THE WORLD...
I KNEW IT.

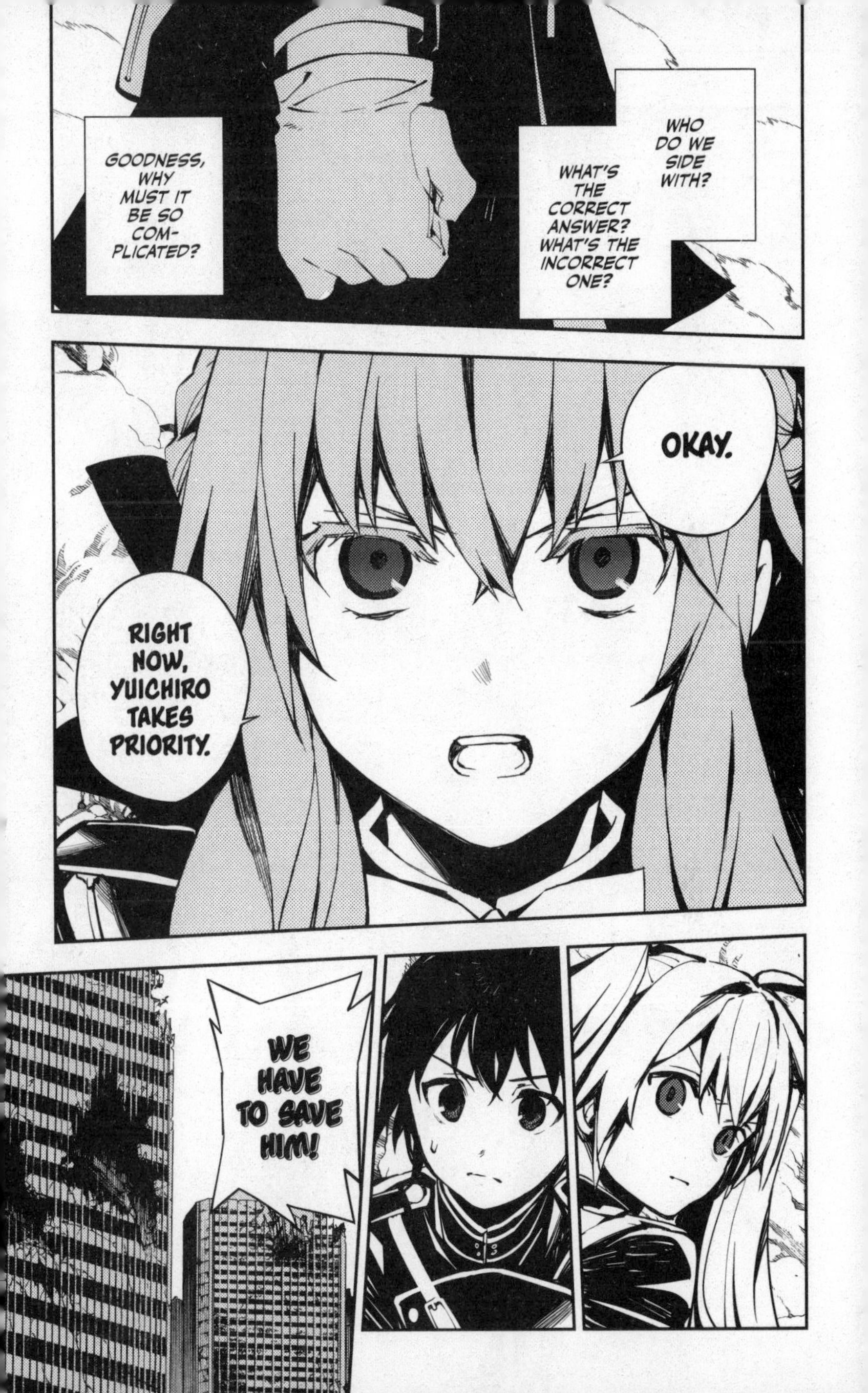
WHO DO WE SIDE WITH?
WHAT'S THE CORRECT ANSWER? WHAT'S THE INCORRECT ONE?
GOODNESS, WHY MUST IT BE SO COM-PLICATED?
OKAY.
RIGHT NOW, YUICHIRO TAKES PRIORITY.
WE HAVE TO SAVE HIM!

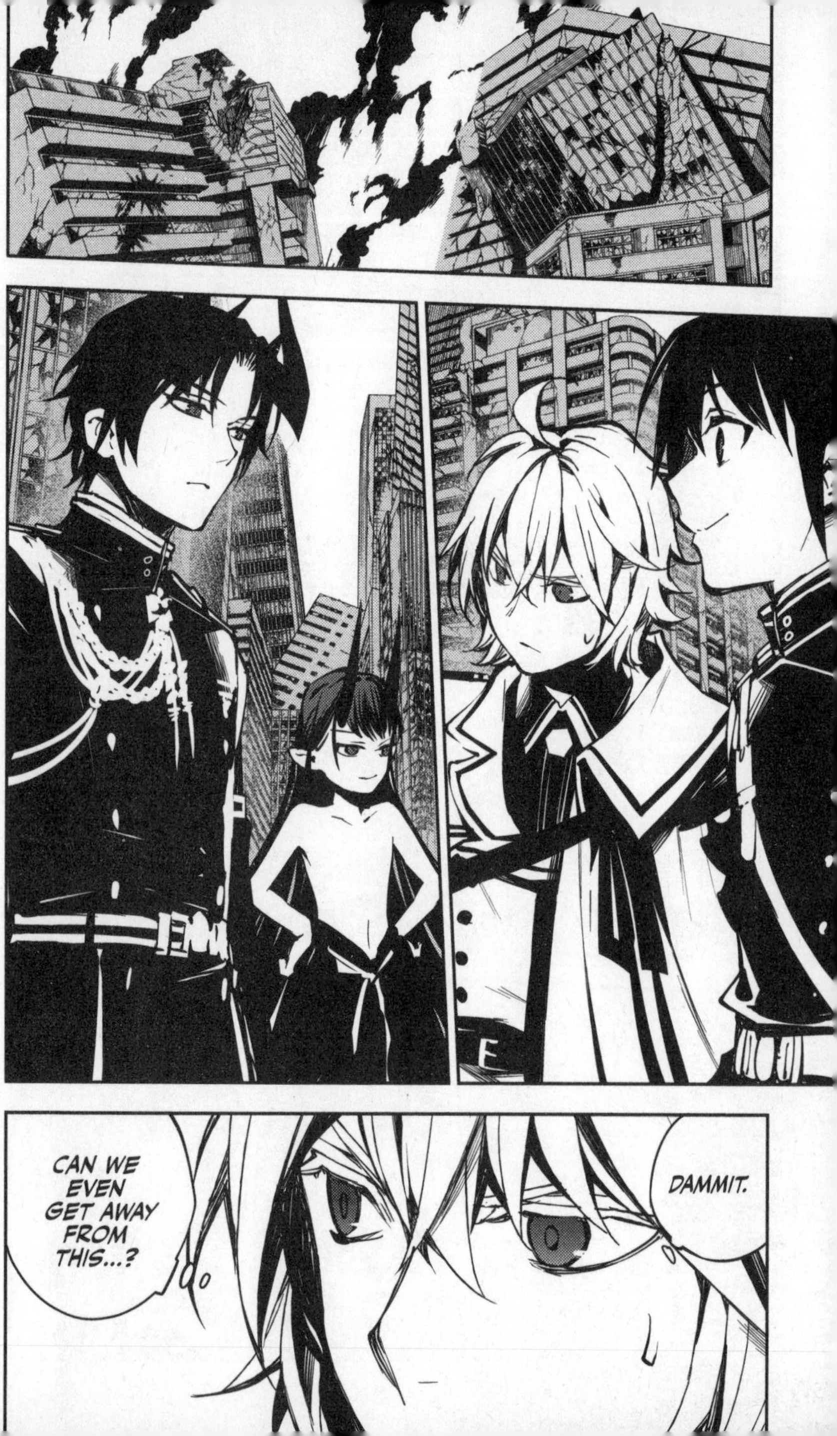
DAMMIT.
CAN WE EVEN GET AWAY FROM THIS...?

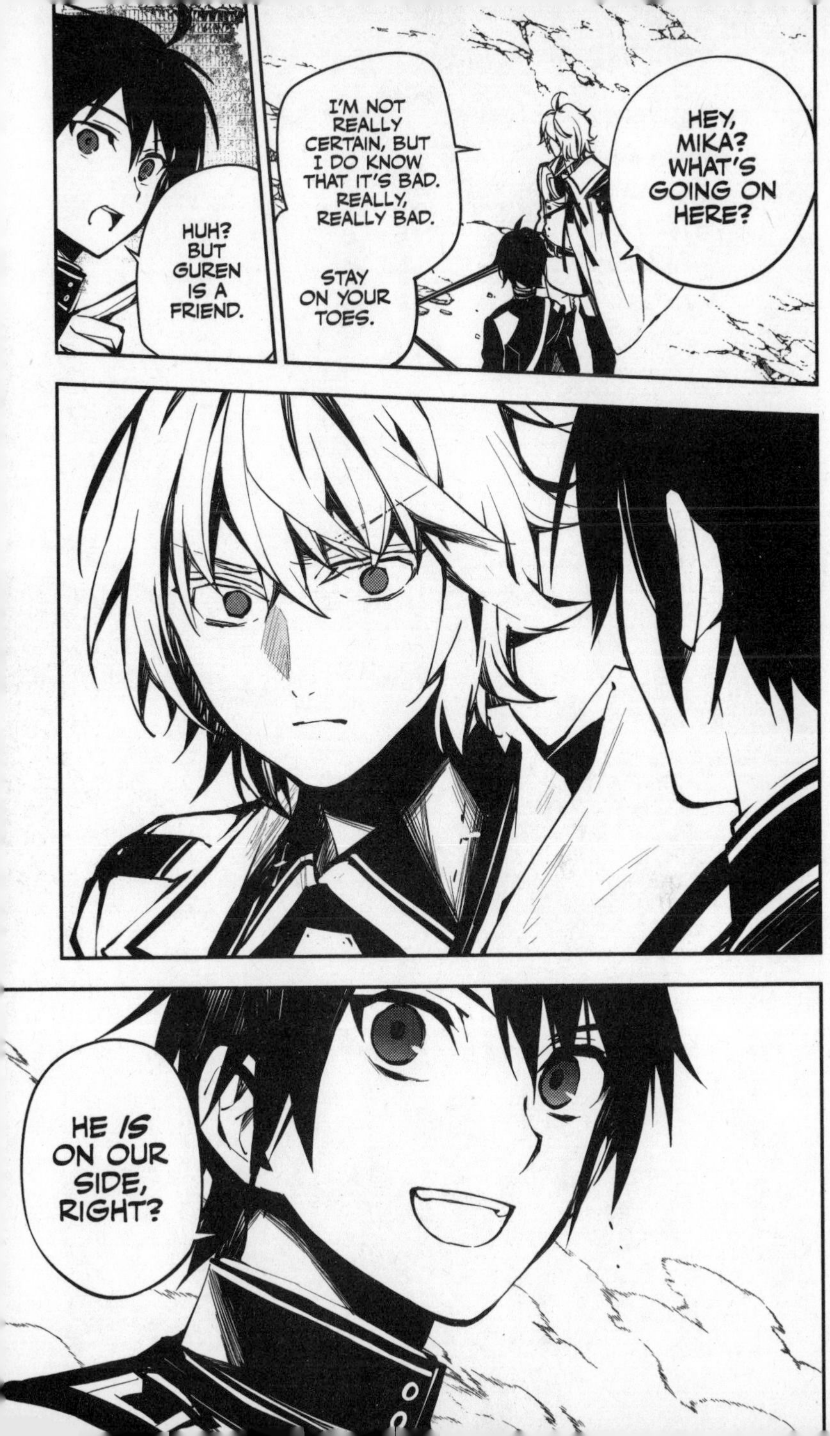
HEY, MIKA? WHAT'S GOING ON HERE?
I'M NOT REALLY CERTAIN, BUT I DO KNOW THAT IT'S BAD. REALLY, REALLY BAD.
STAY ON YOUR TOES.
HUH? BUT GUREN IS A FRIEND.
HE *IS* ON OUR SIDE, RIGHT?

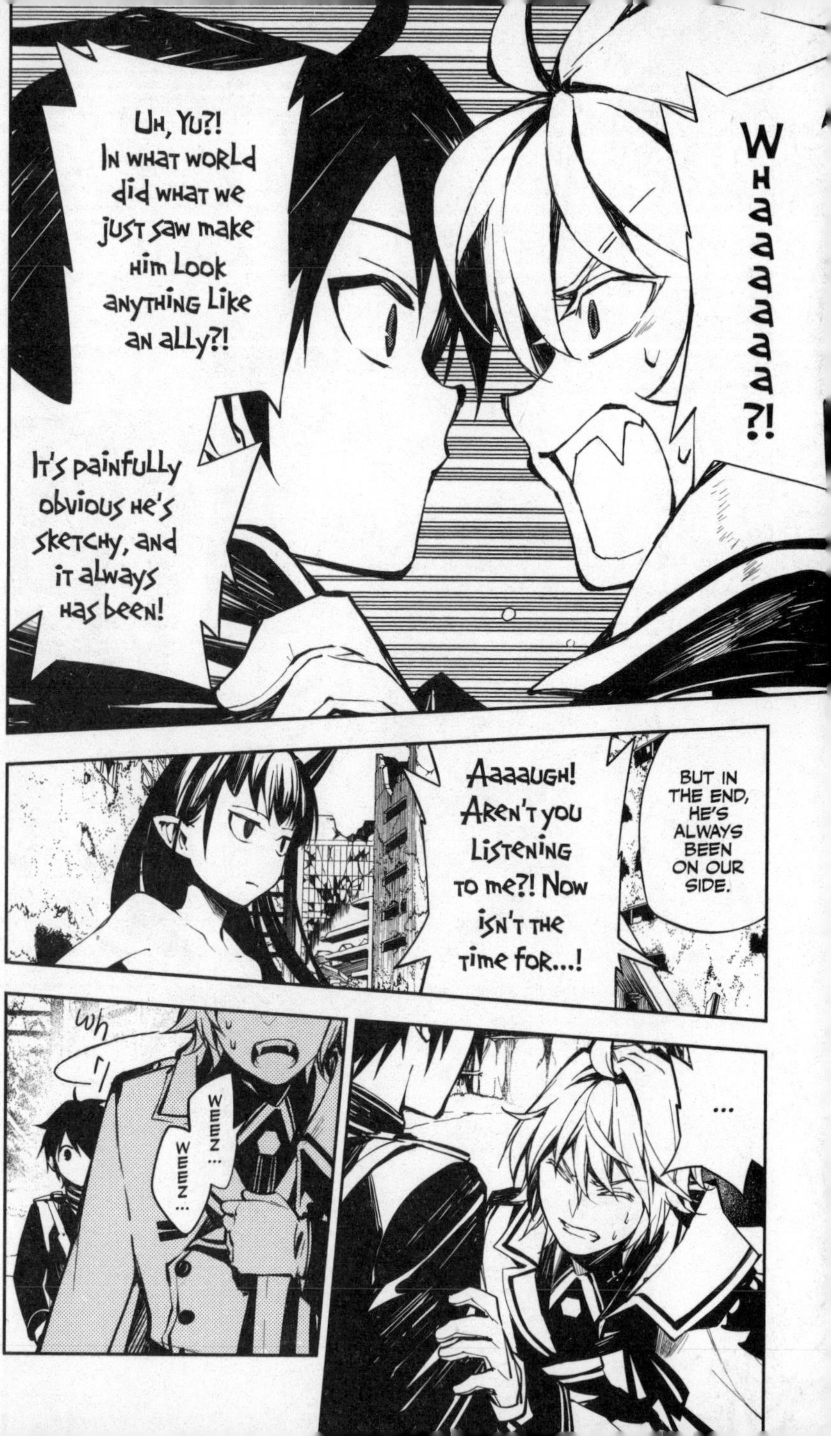
Whaaaaaaa?!
Uh, Yu?! In what world did what we just saw make him look anything like an ally?!
It's painfully obvious he's sketchy, and it always has been!
But in the end, he's always been on our side.
Aaaaugh! Aren't you listening to me?! Now isn't the time for...!
...
Wh
!
Weez...
Weez...

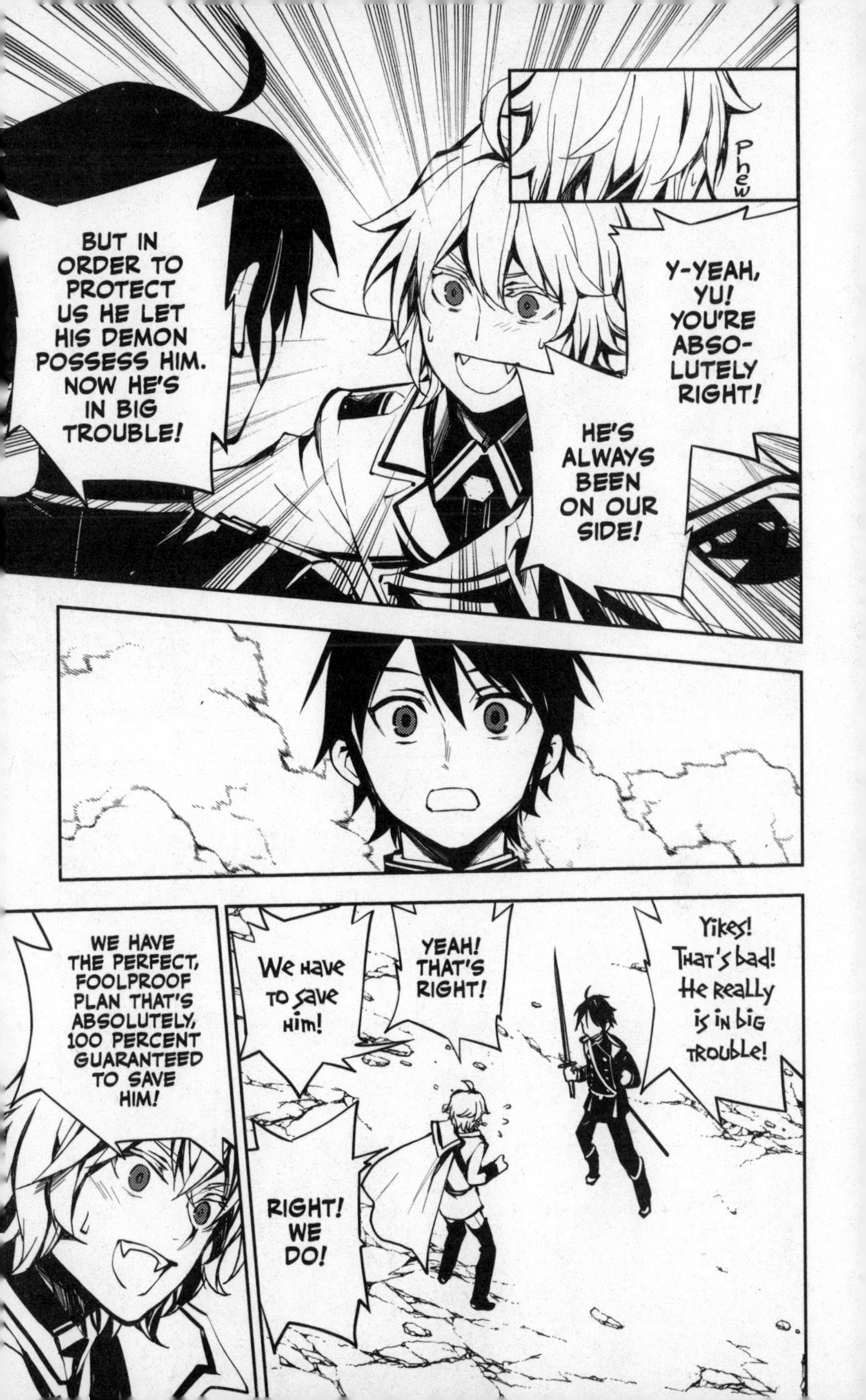
Phew
Y-YEAH, YU! YOU'RE ABSO-LUTELY RIGHT!
HE'S ALWAYS BEEN ON OUR SIDE!
BUT IN ORDER TO PROTECT US HE LET HIS DEMON POSSESS HIM. NOW HE'S IN BIG TROUBLE!
Yikes! That's bad! He really is in big trouble!
YEAH! THAT'S RIGHT!
We have to save him!
RIGHT! WE DO!
WE HAVE THE PERFECT, FOOLPROOF PLAN THAT'S ABSOLUTELY, 100 PERCENT GUARANTEED TO SAVE HIM!

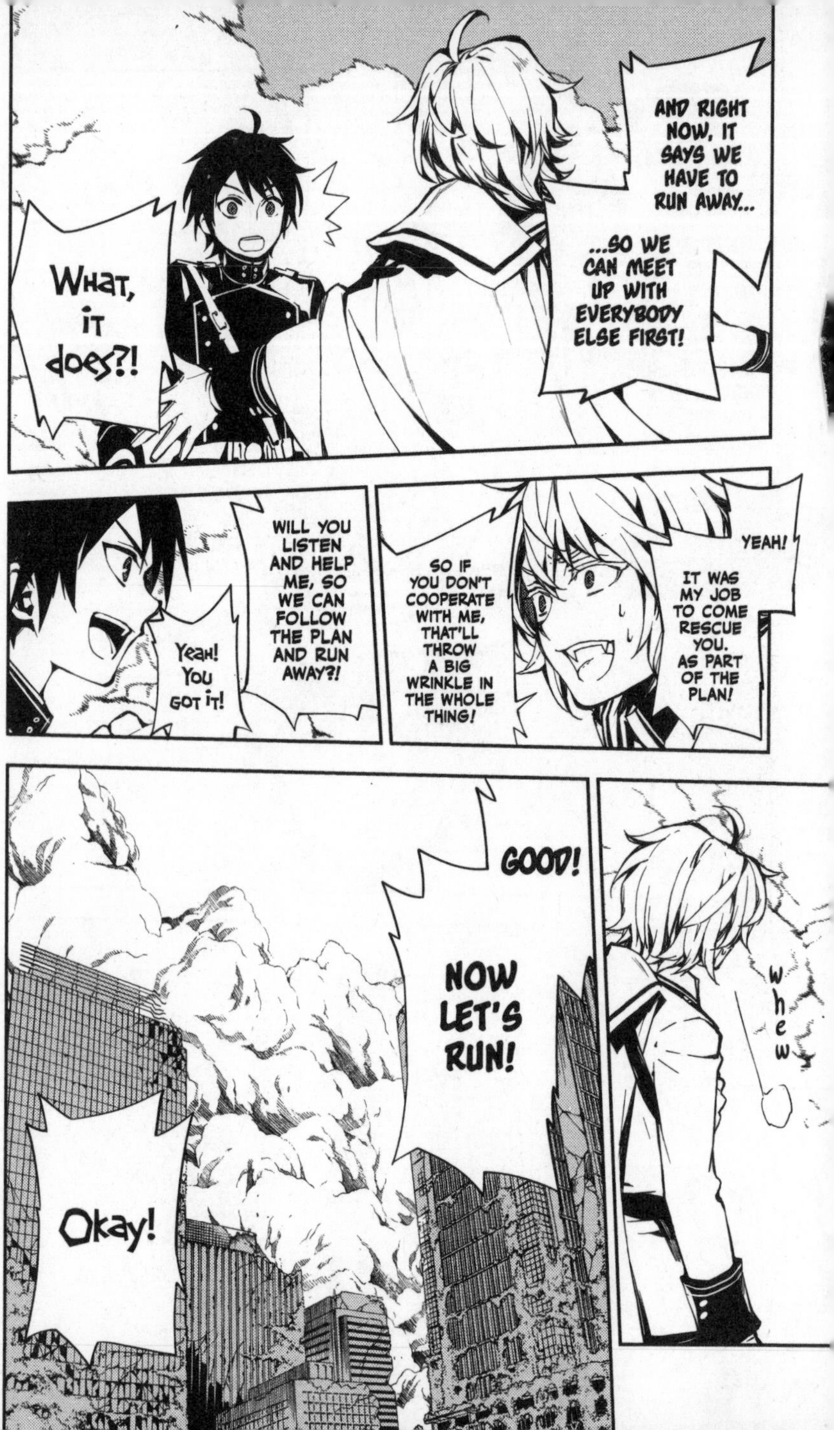
AND RIGHT NOW, IT SAYS WE HAVE TO RUN AWAY...
...SO WE CAN MEET UP WITH EVERYBODY ELSE FIRST!
WHAT, it does?!
YEAH!
IT WAS MY JOB TO COME RESCUE YOU. AS PART OF THE PLAN!
SO IF YOU DON'T COOPERATE WITH ME, THAT'LL THROW A BIG WRINKLE IN THE WHOLE THING!
WILL YOU LISTEN AND HELP ME, SO WE CAN FOLLOW THE PLAN AND RUN AWAY?!
Yeah! You got it!
whew
GOOD!
NOW LET'S RUN!
Okay!

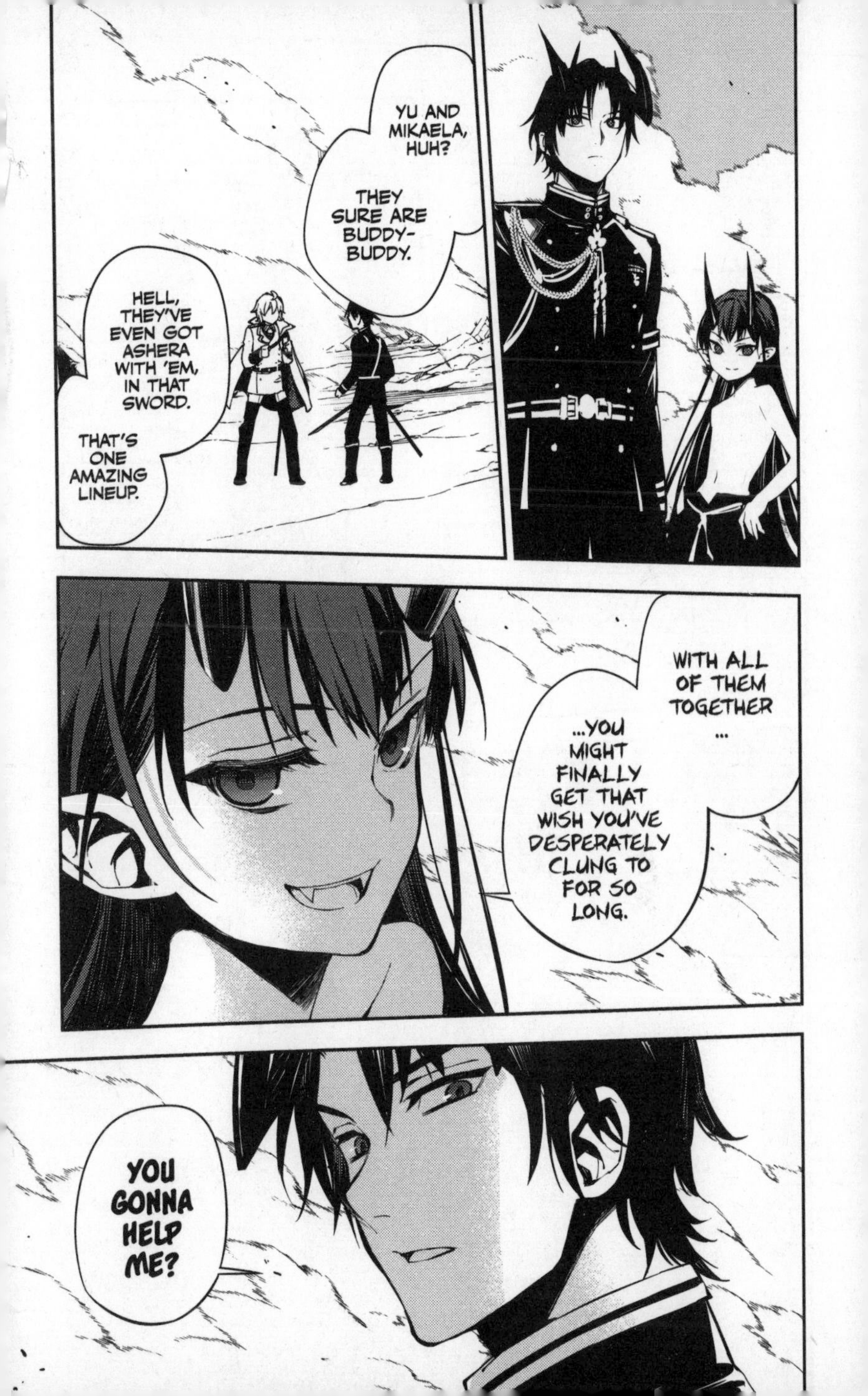
YU AND MIKAELA, HUH?
THEY SURE ARE BUDDY-BUDDY.
HELL, THEY'VE EVEN GOT ASHERA WITH 'EM, IN THAT SWORD.
THAT'S ONE AMAZING LINEUP.
WITH ALL OF THEM TOGETHER ...
...YOU MIGHT FINALLY GET THAT WISH YOU'VE DESPERATELY CLUNG TO FOR SO LONG.
YOU GONNA HELP ME?

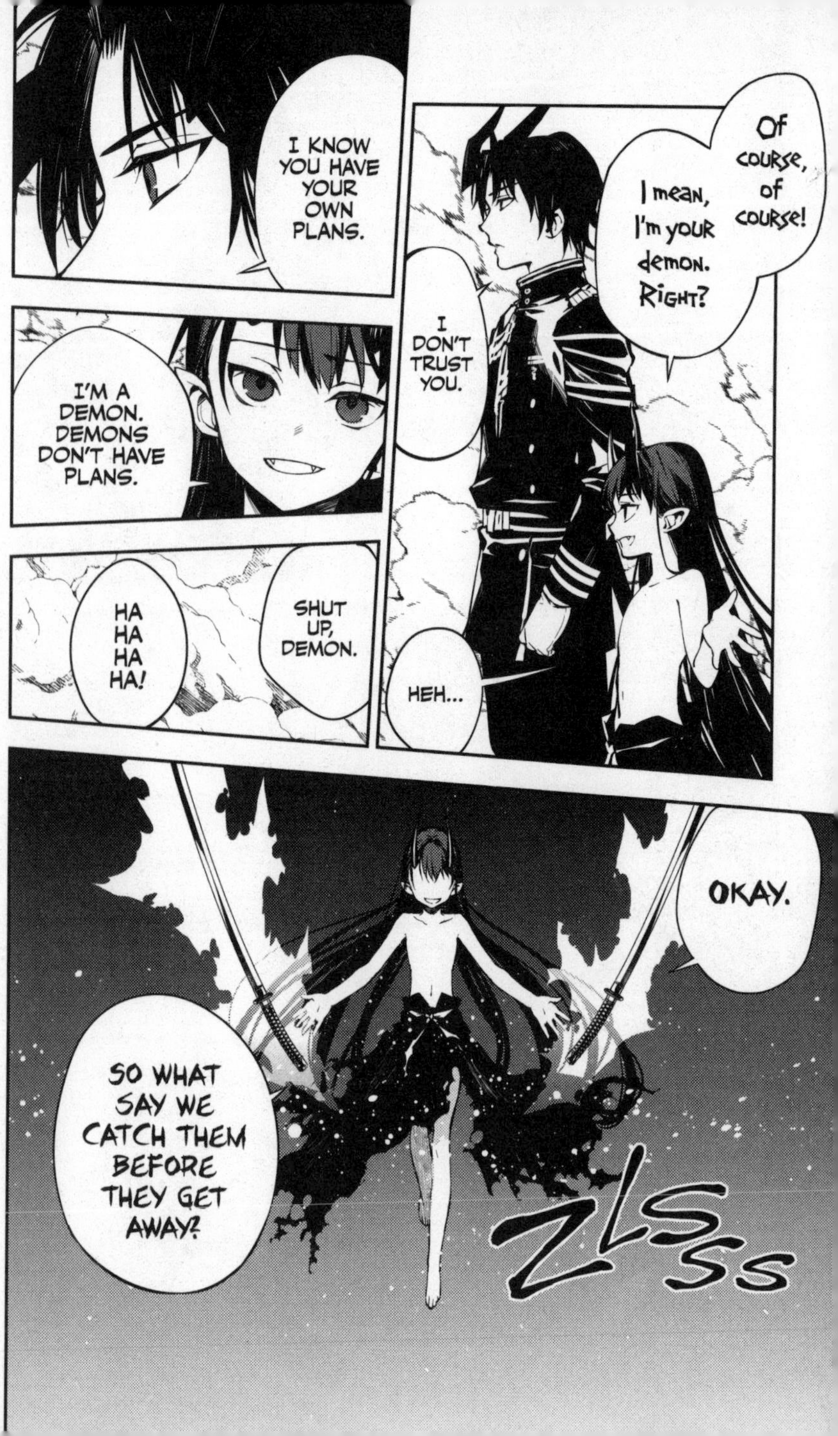
Of course, of course!
I mean, I'm your demon. Right?
I DON'T TRUST YOU.
HEH...
I KNOW YOU HAVE YOUR OWN PLANS.
I'M A DEMON. DEMONS DON'T HAVE PLANS.
SHUT UP, DEMON.
HA HA HA HA!
OKAY.
SO WHAT SAY WE CATCH THEM BEFORE THEY GET AWAY?
ZISSS

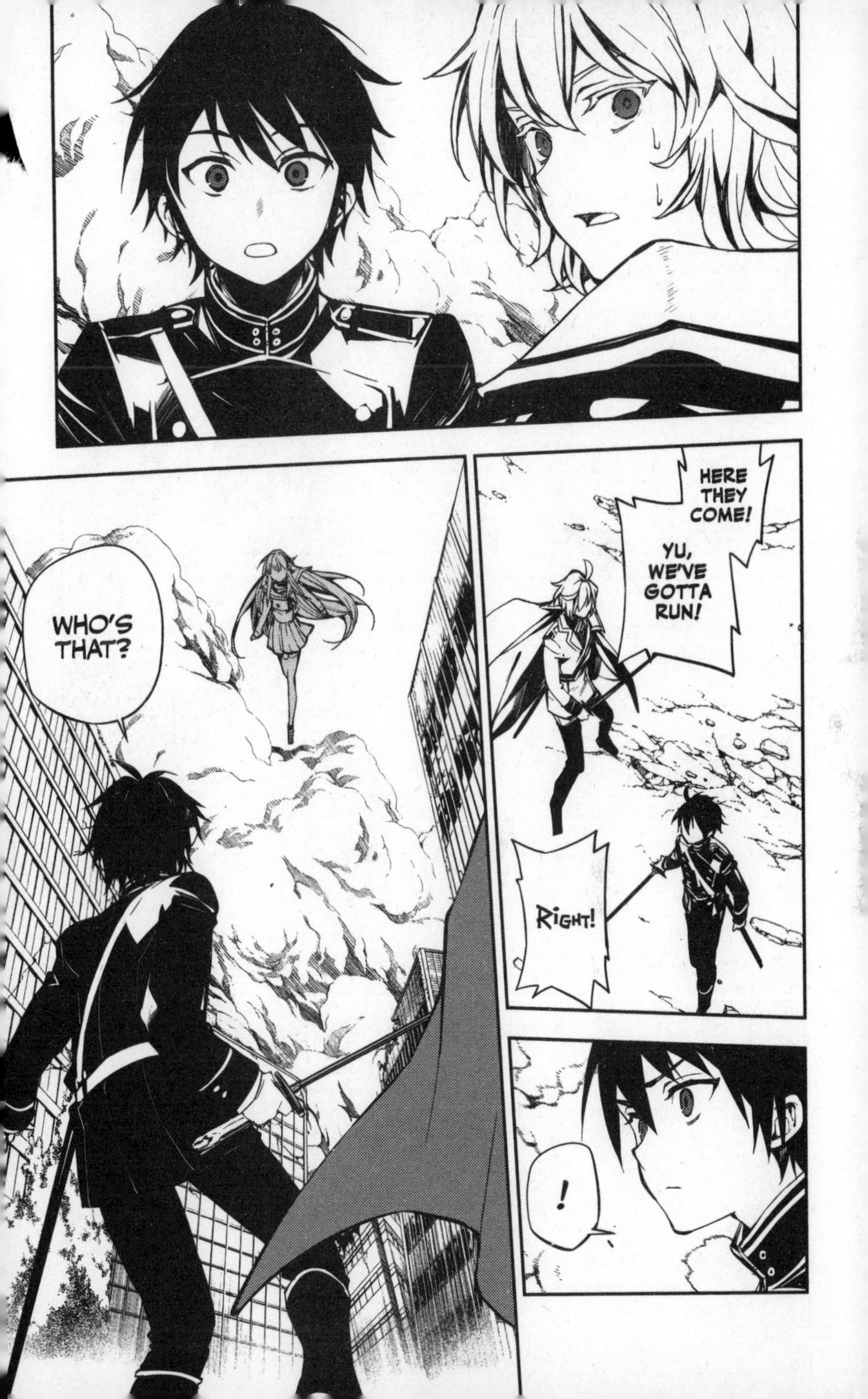
HERE THEY COME!
YU, WE'VE GOTTA RUN!
RIGHT!
!
WHO'S THAT?

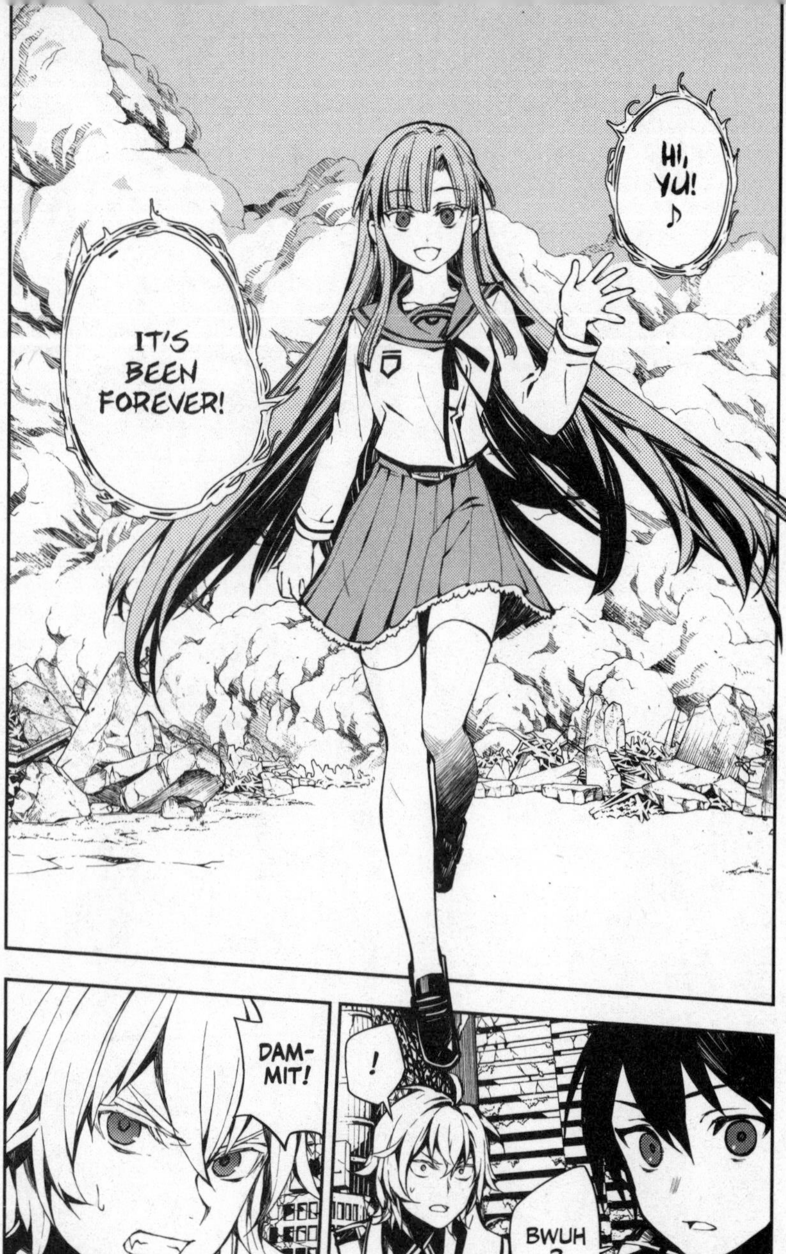
HI, YU! ♪
IT'S BEEN FOREVER!
BWUH?
!
DAM-MIT!

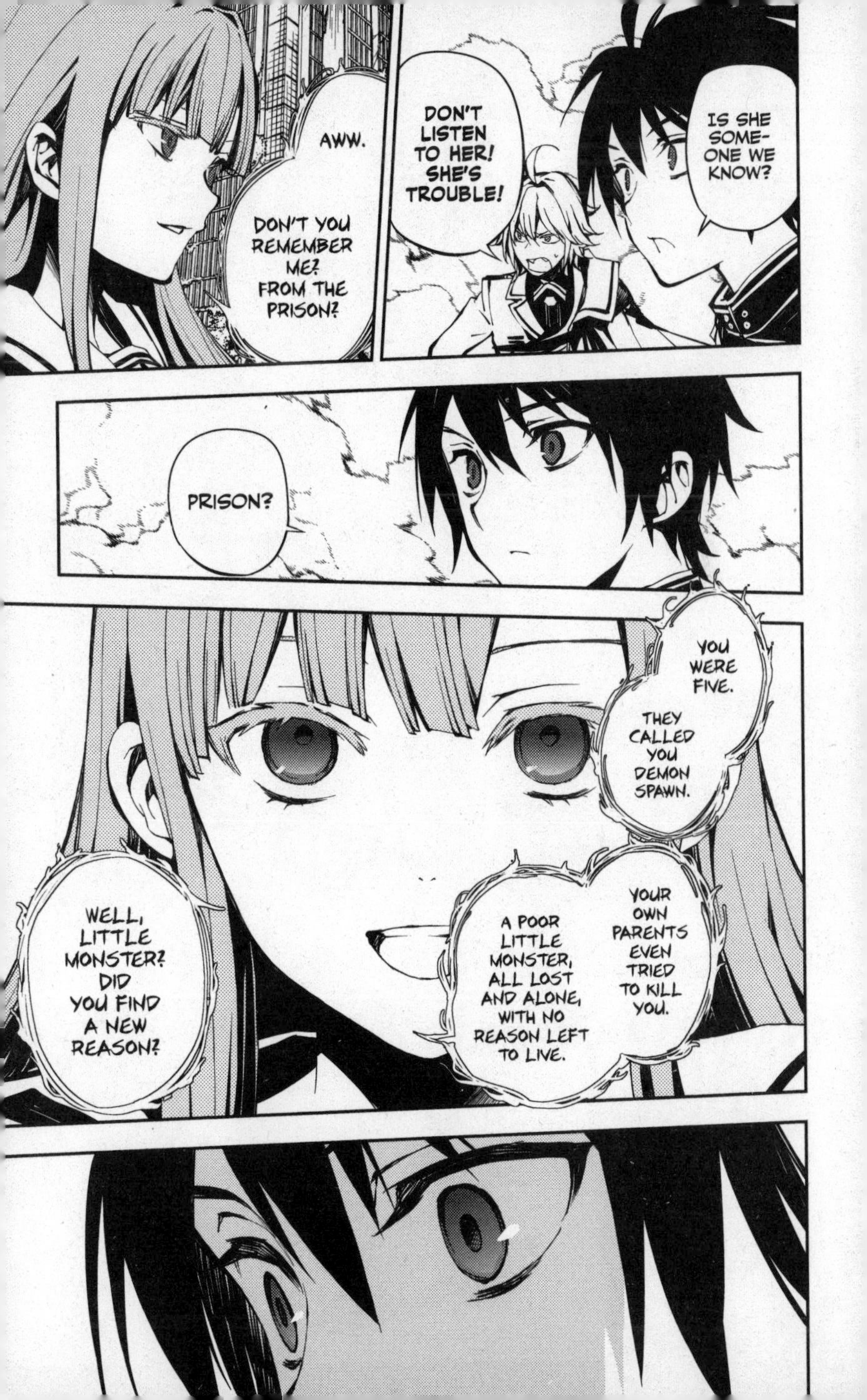
IS SHE SOMEONE WE KNOW?
DON'T LISTEN TO HER! SHE'S TROUBLE!
AWW.
DON'T YOU REMEMBER ME? FROM THE PRISON?
PRISON?
YOU WERE FIVE.
THEY CALLED YOU DEMON SPAWN.
YOUR OWN PARENTS EVEN TRIED TO KILL YOU.
A POOR LITTLE MONSTER, ALL LOST AND ALONE, WITH NO REASON LEFT TO LIVE.
WELL, LITTLE MONSTER? DID YOU FIND A NEW REASON?

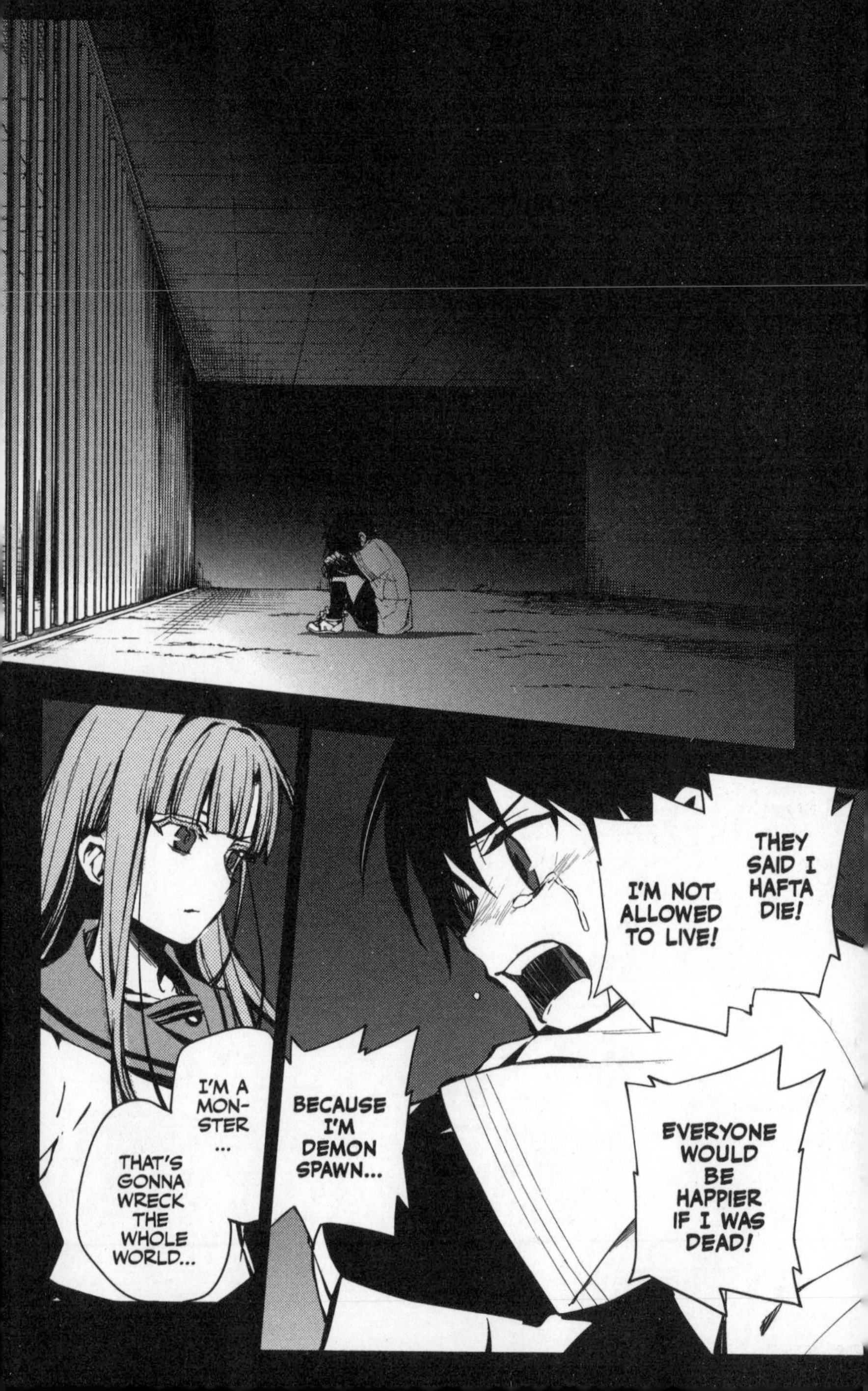
THEY SAID I HAFTA DIE!
I'M NOT ALLOWED TO LIVE!
EVERYONE WOULD BE HAPPIER IF I WAS DEAD!
BECAUSE I'M DEMON SPAWN...
I'M A MON-STER ...
THAT'S GONNA WRECK THE WHOLE WORLD...

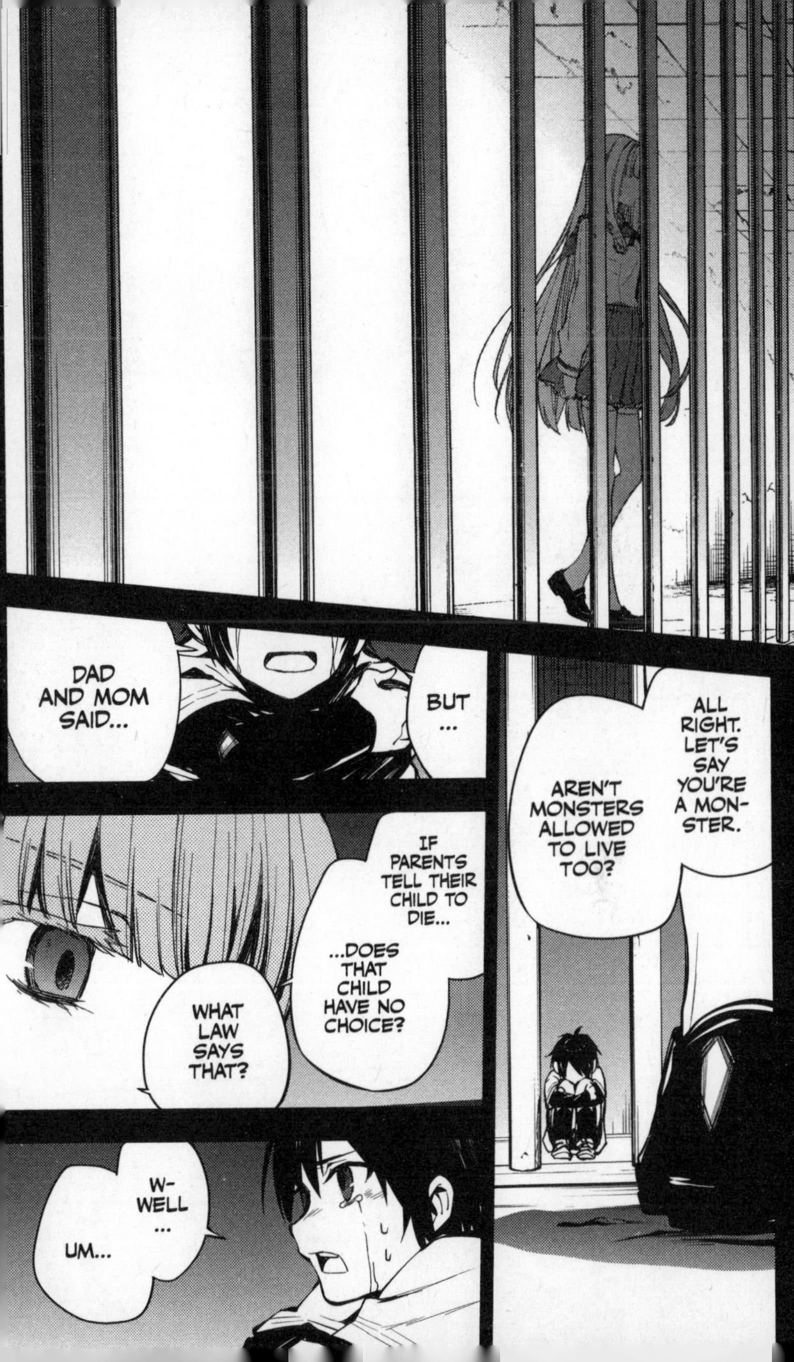
ALL RIGHT. LET'S SAY YOU'RE A MON- STER.
AREN'T MONSTERS ALLOWED TO LIVE TOO?
BUT ...
DAD AND MOM SAID...
IF PARENTS TELL THEIR CHILD TO DIE...
...DOES THAT CHILD HAVE NO CHOICE?
WHAT LAW SAYS THAT?
W- WELL ...
UM...

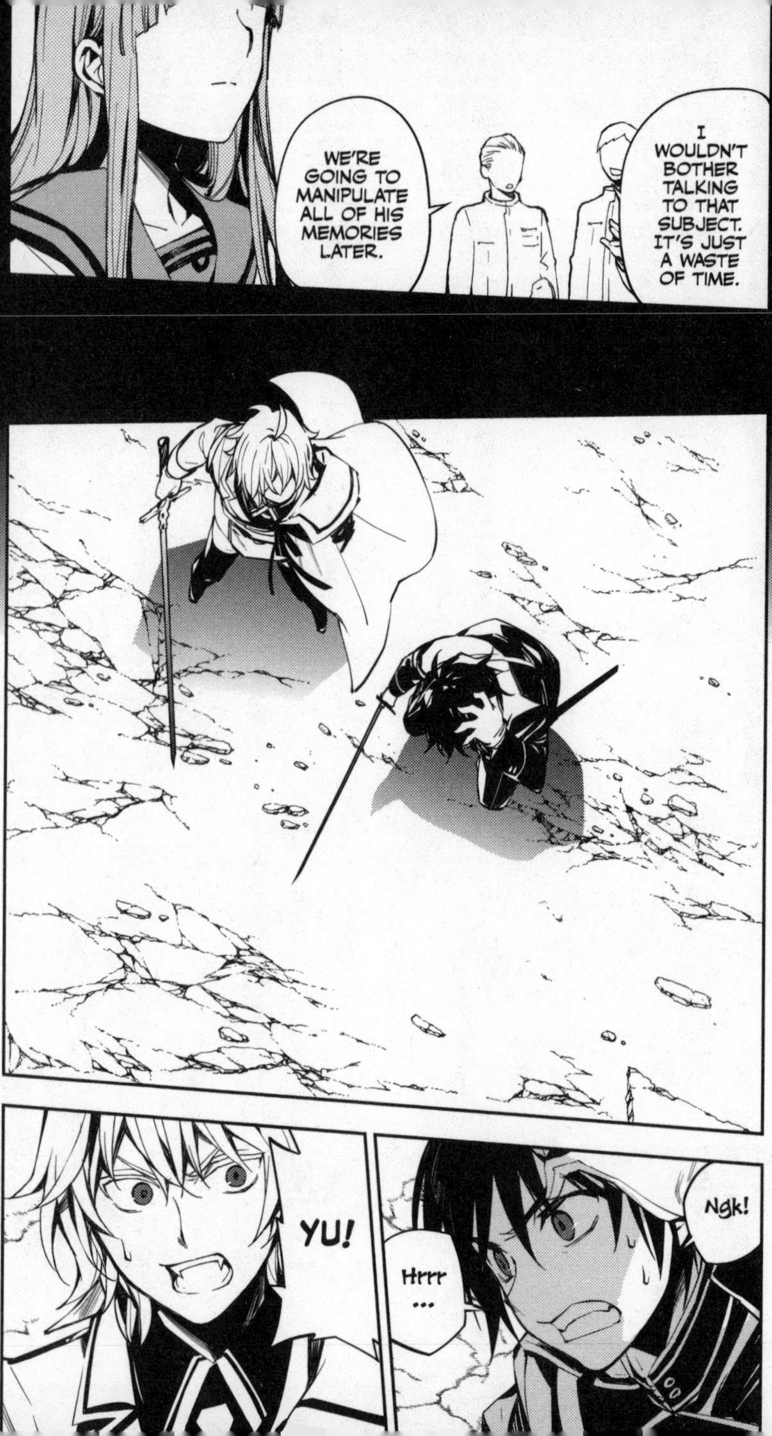
I WOULDN'T BOTHER TALKING TO THAT SUBJECT. IT'S JUST A WASTE OF TIME.
WE'RE GOING TO MANIPULATE ALL OF HIS MEMORIES LATER.
Ngk!
Hrrr...
YU!

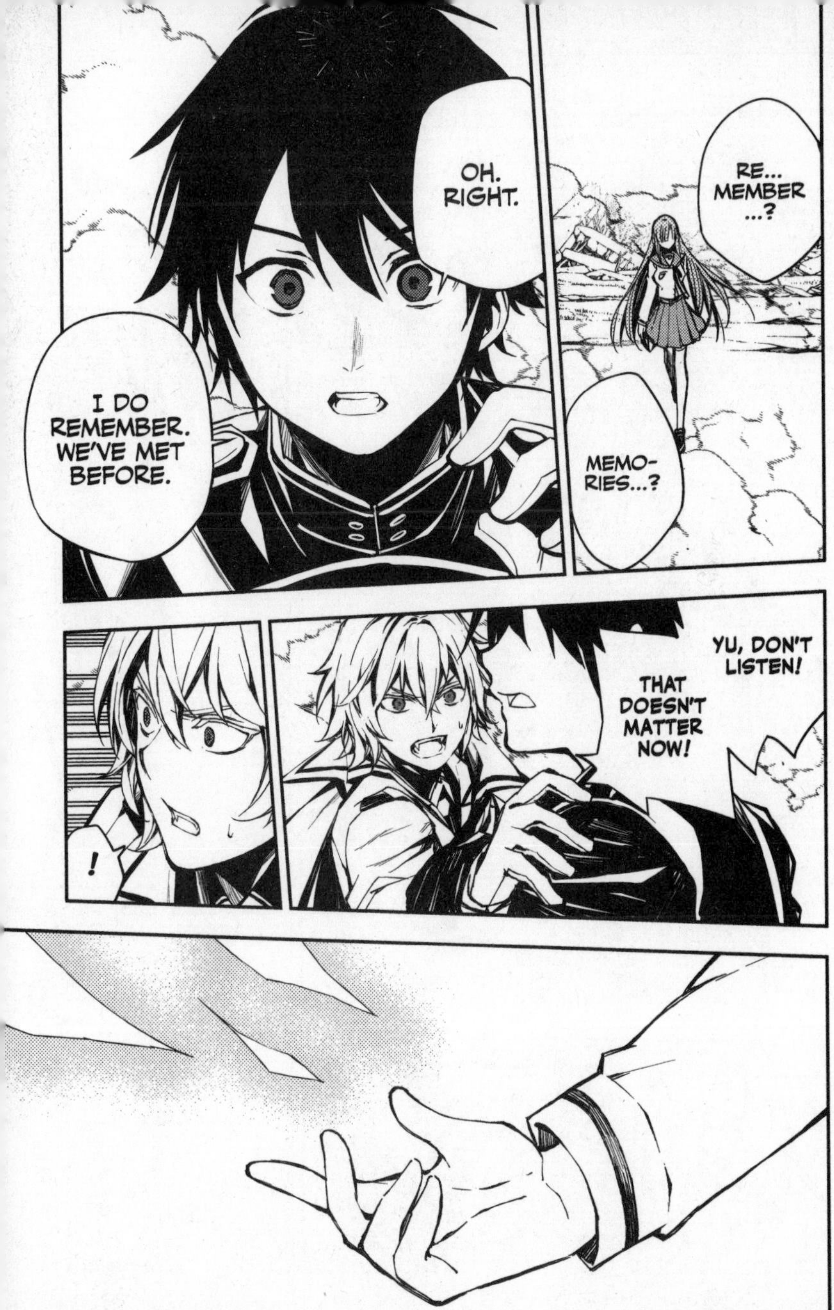
RE... MEMBER ...?
MEMORIES...?
OH. RIGHT.
I DO REMEMBER. WE'VE MET BEFORE.
YU, DON'T LISTEN!
THAT DOESN'T MATTER NOW!
!

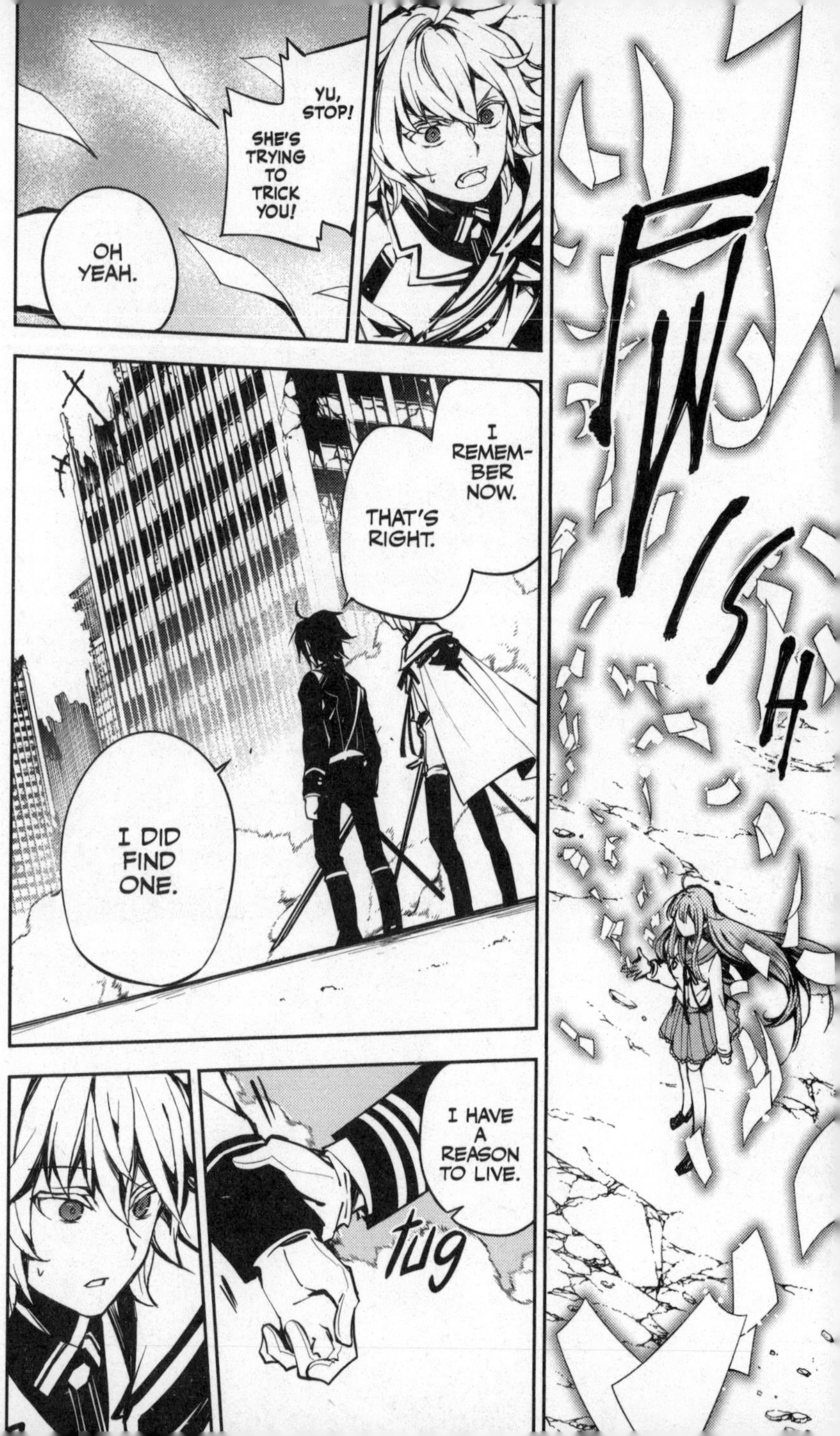
FWISH
YU, STOP!
SHE'S TRYING TO TRICK YOU!
OH YEAH.
I REMEMBER NOW.
THAT'S RIGHT.
I DID FIND ONE.
I HAVE A REASON TO LIVE.
tug

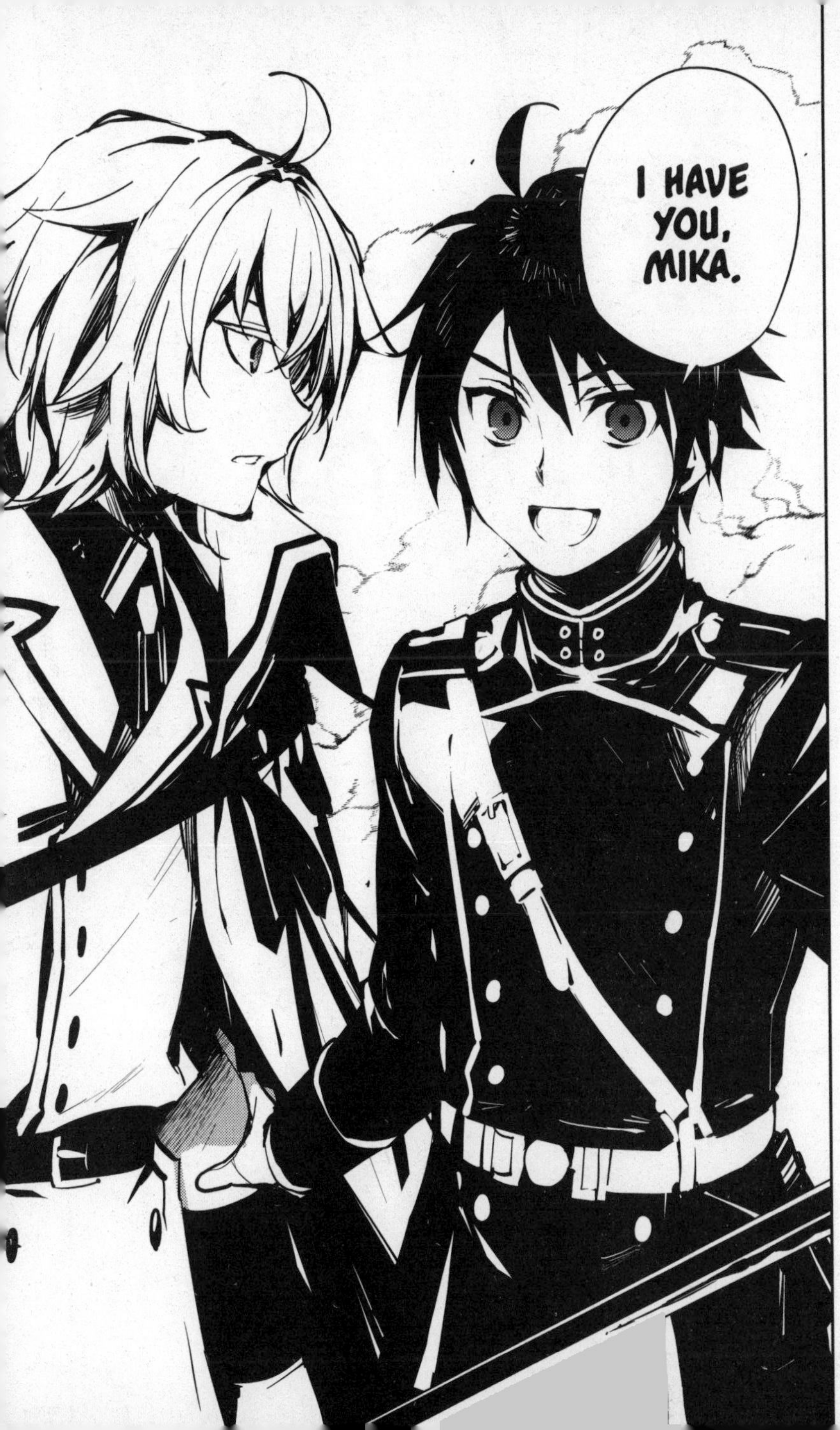
I HAVE YOU, MIKA.

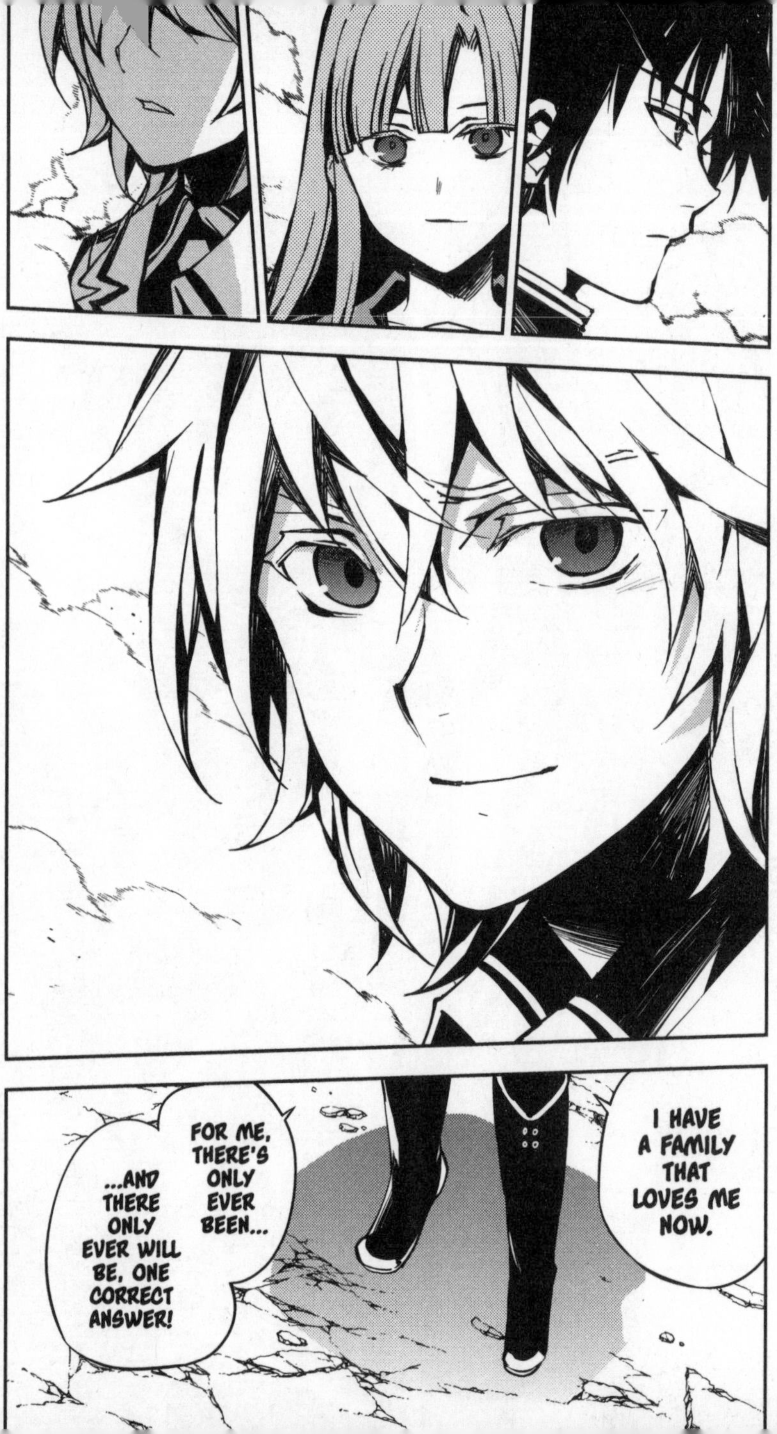
I HAVE A FAMILY THAT LOVES ME NOW.
FOR ME, THERE'S ONLY EVER BEEN...
...AND THERE ONLY EVER WILL BE, ONE CORRECT ANSWER!

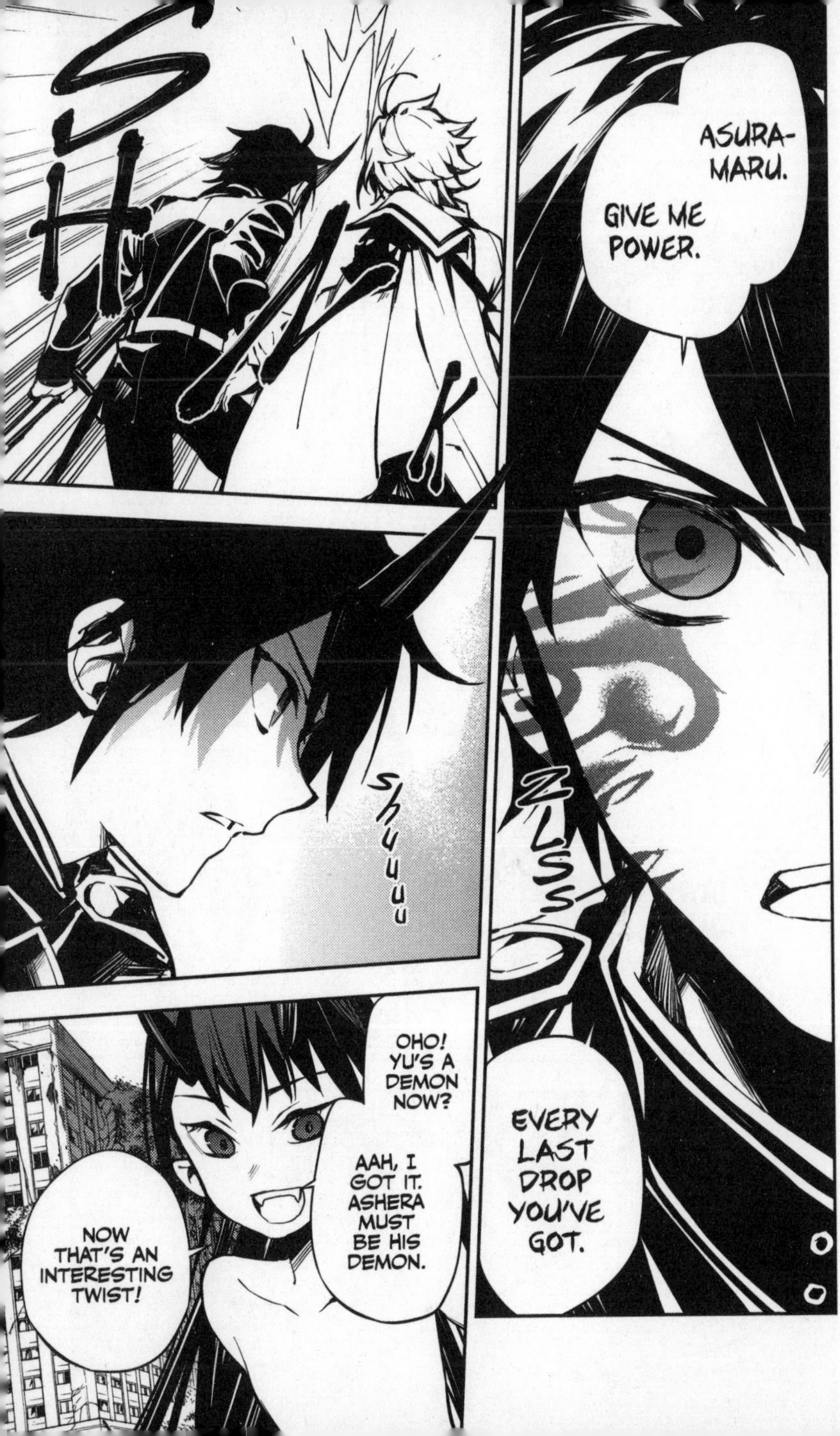
ASURA-MARU.
GIVE ME POWER.
ZLSS
EVERY LAST DROP YOU'VE GOT.
SHUUUU
OHO! YU'S A DEMON NOW?
AAH, I GOT IT. ASHERA MUST BE HIS DEMON.
NOW THAT'S AN INTERESTING TWIST!

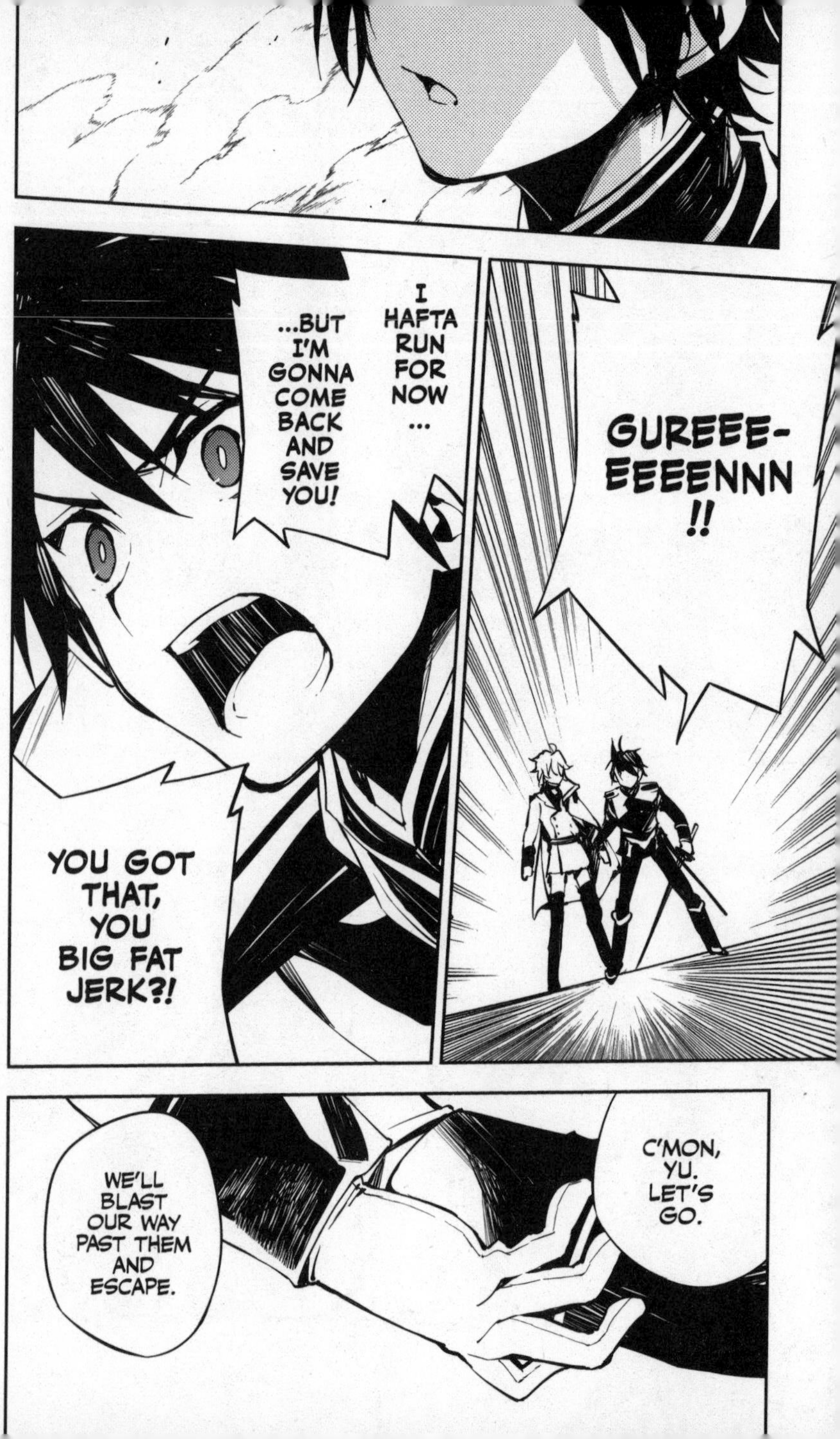
GUREEEE-EEEENNN!!
I HAFTA RUN FOR NOW...
...BUT I'M GONNA COME BACK AND SAVE YOU!
YOU GOT THAT, YOU BIG FAT JERK?!
C'MON, YU. LET'S GO.
WE'LL BLAST OUR WAY PAST THEM AND ESCAPE.

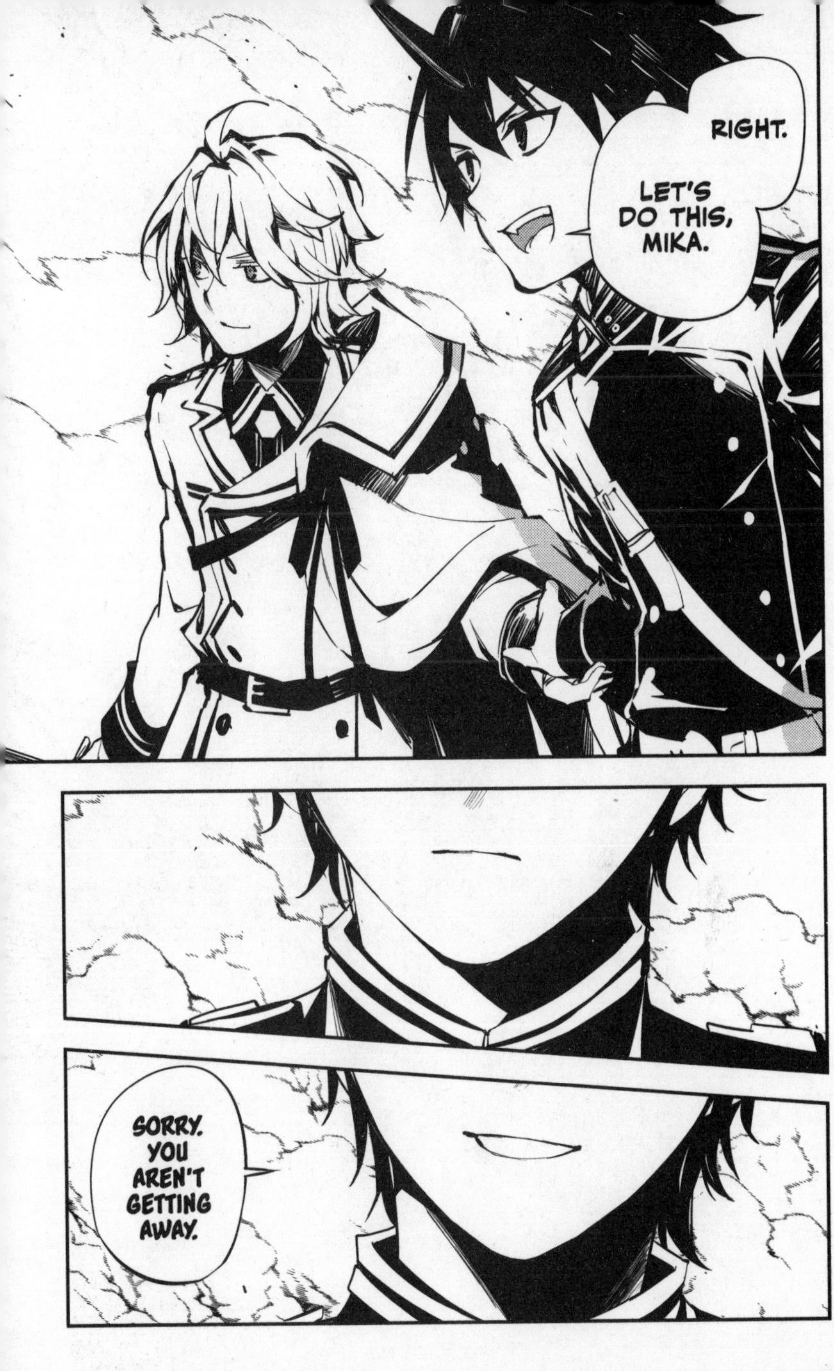
RIGHT.
LET'S DO THIS, MIKA.
SORRY. YOU AREN'T GETTING AWAY.

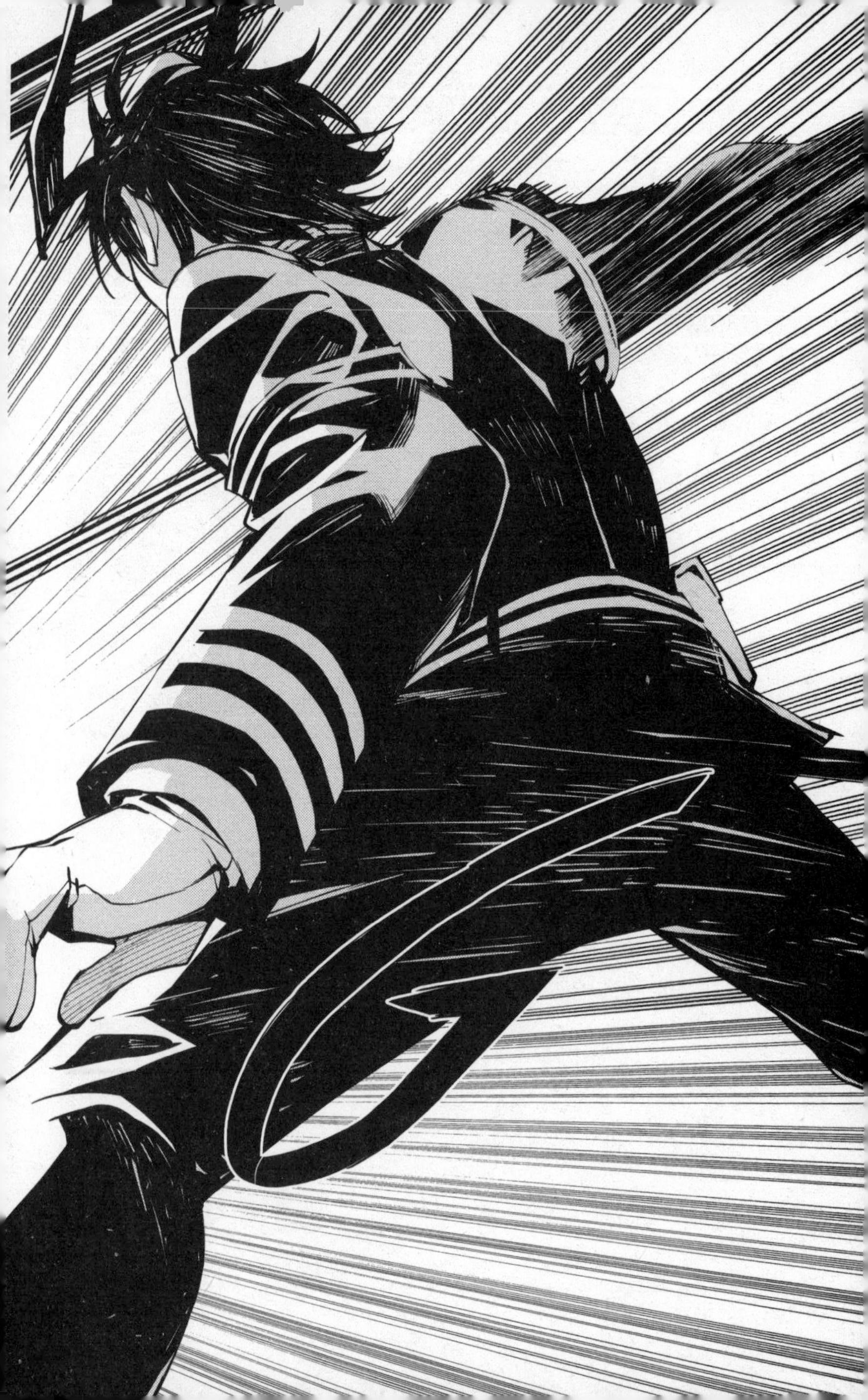

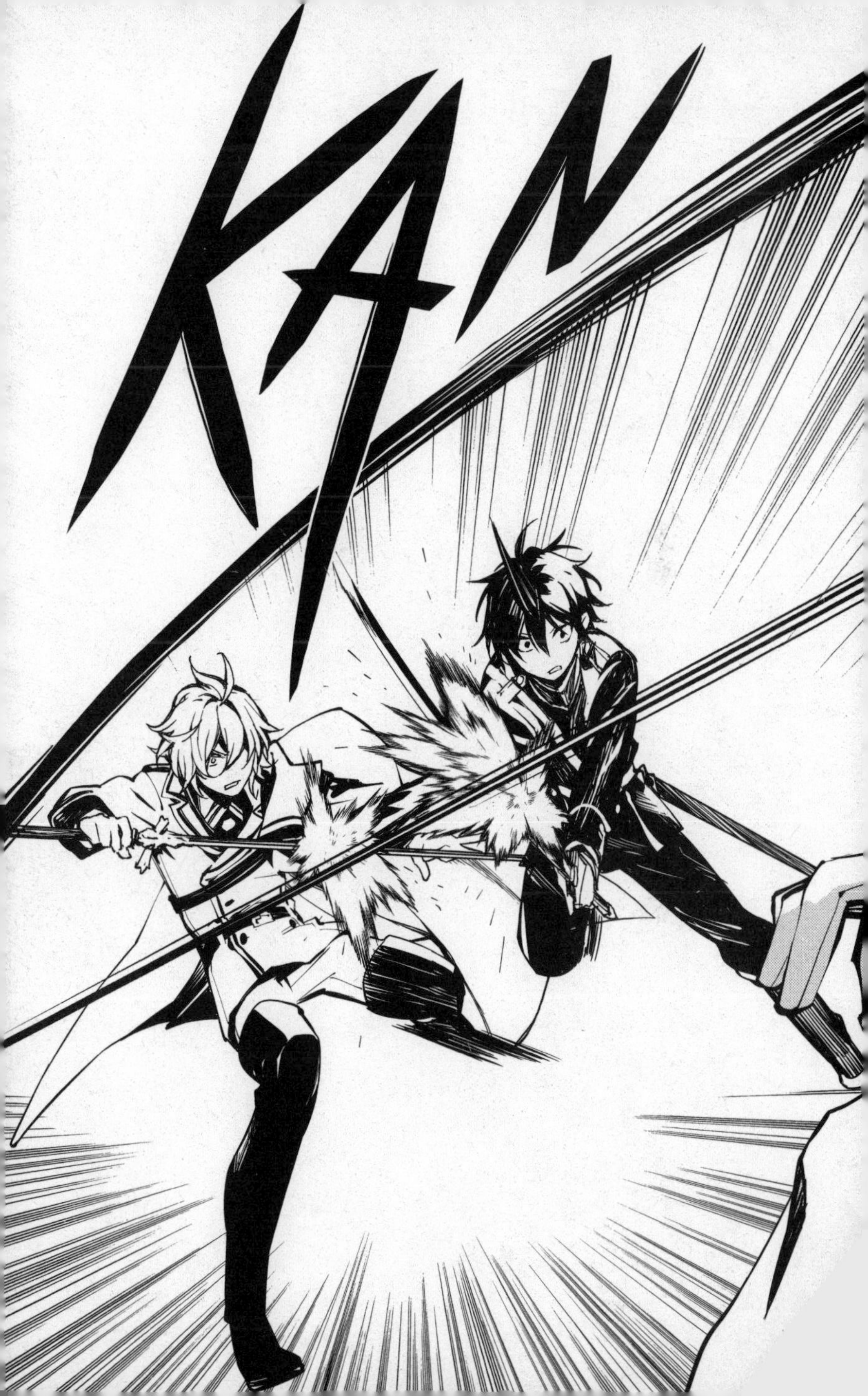
KAN

Seraph of the End

VAMPIRE REIGN

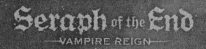

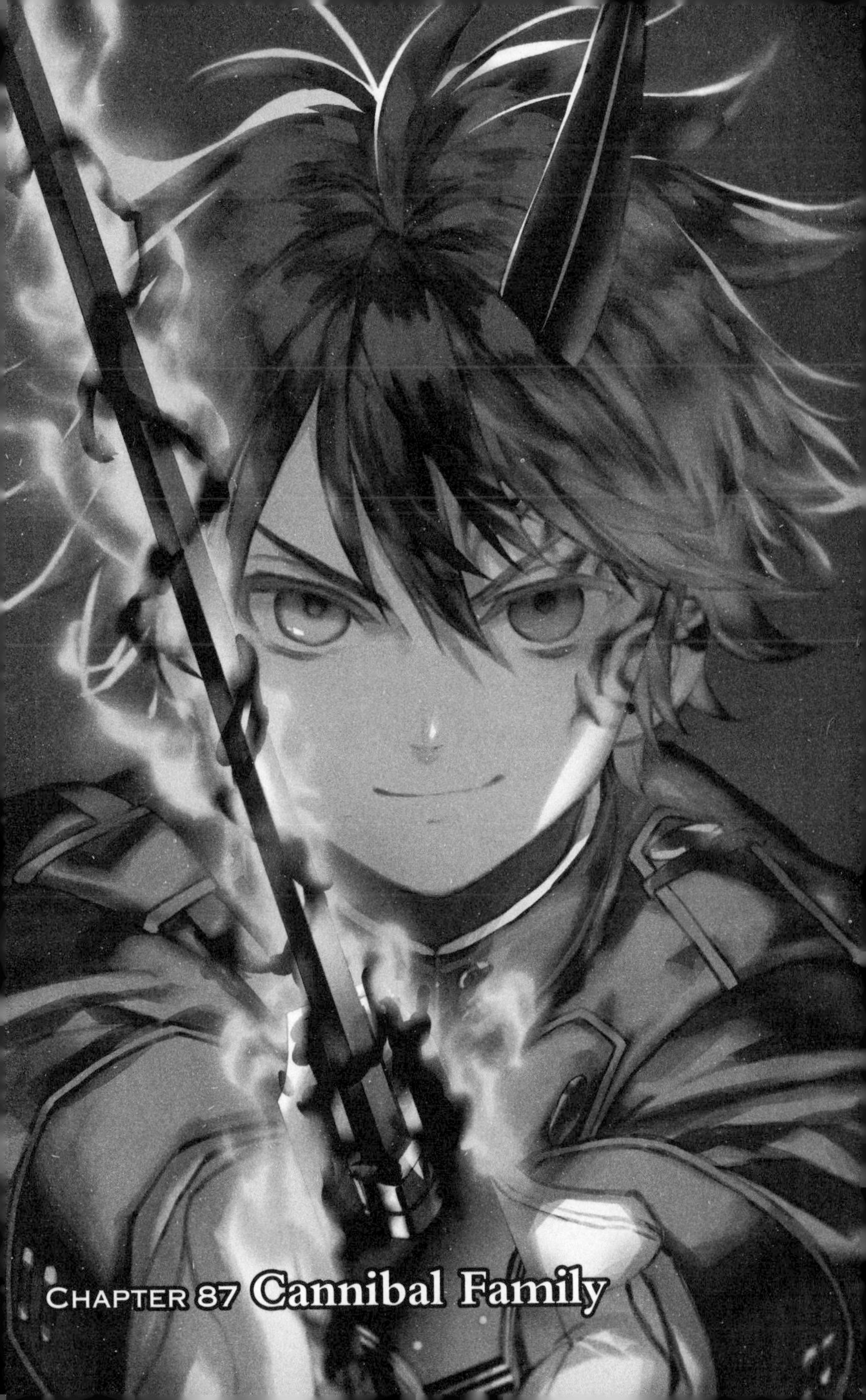
CHAPTER 87 Cannibal Family

Seraph of the End

VAMPIRE REIGN

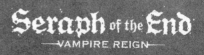

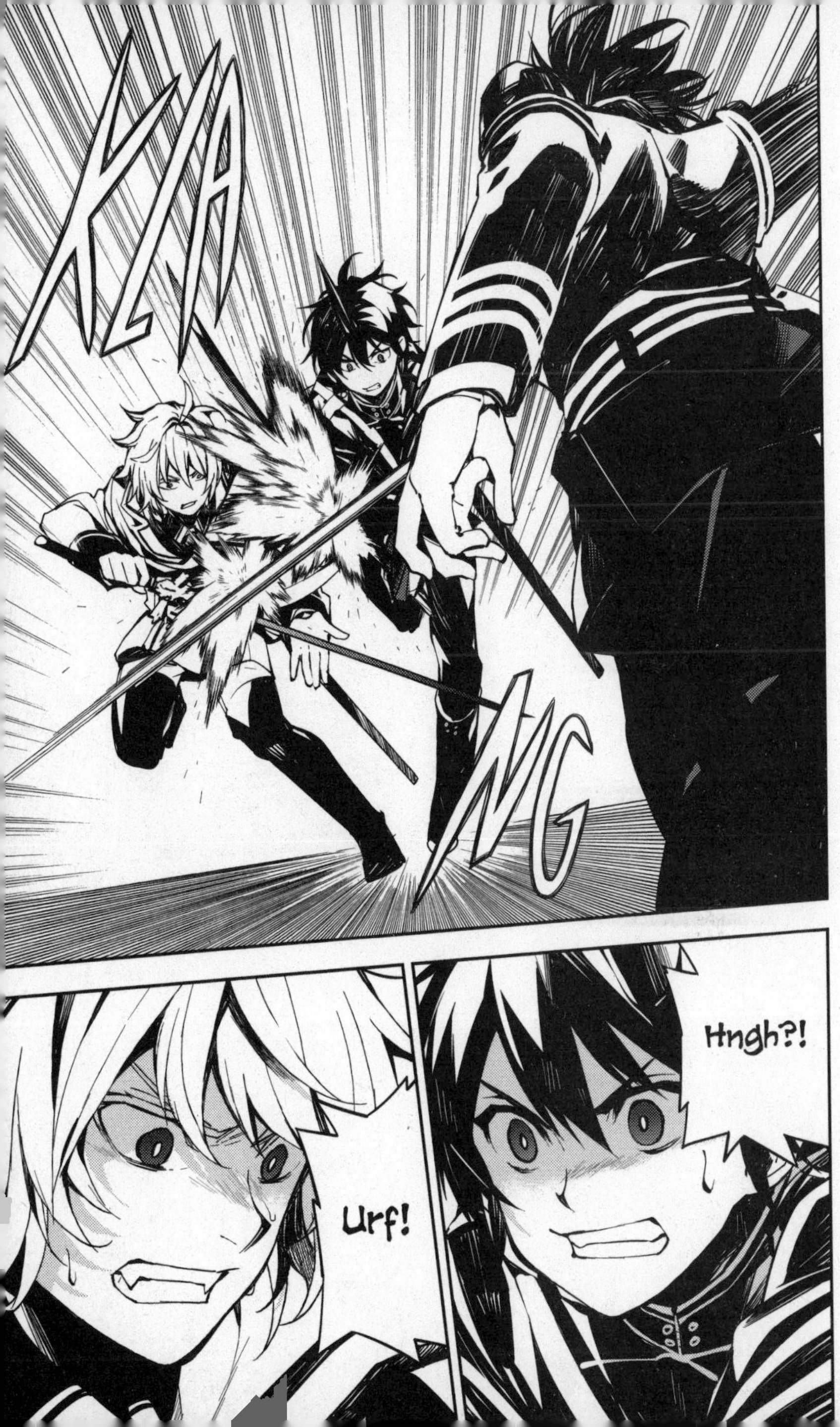
KLA
NG
Hngh?!
Urf!

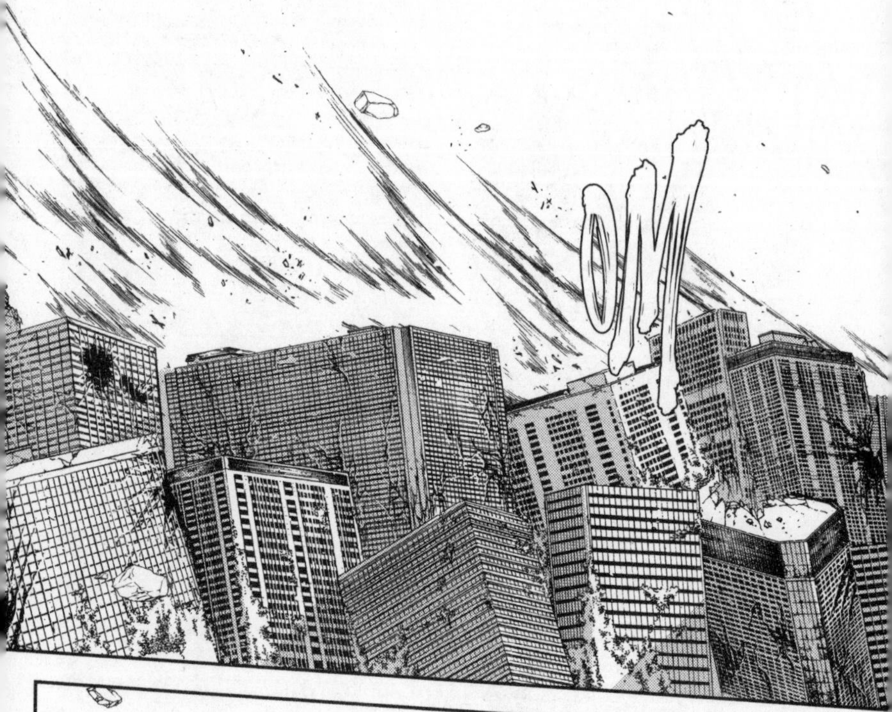
OM

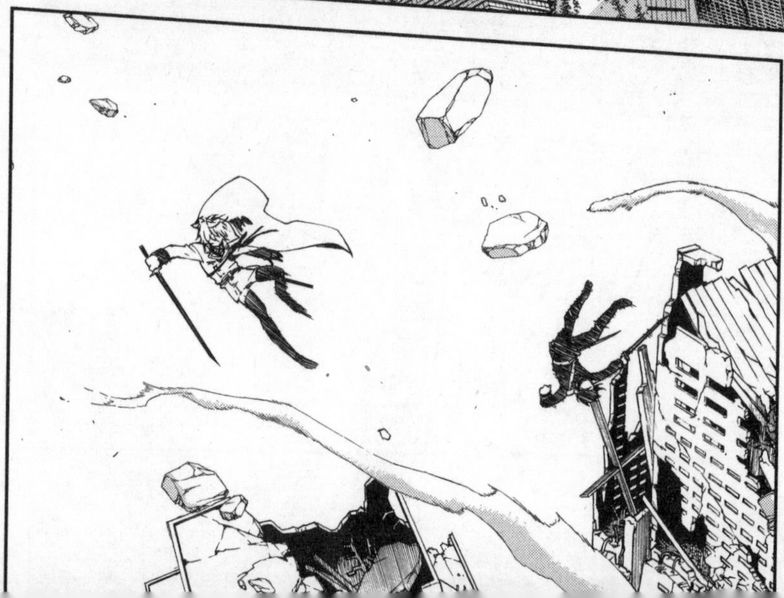

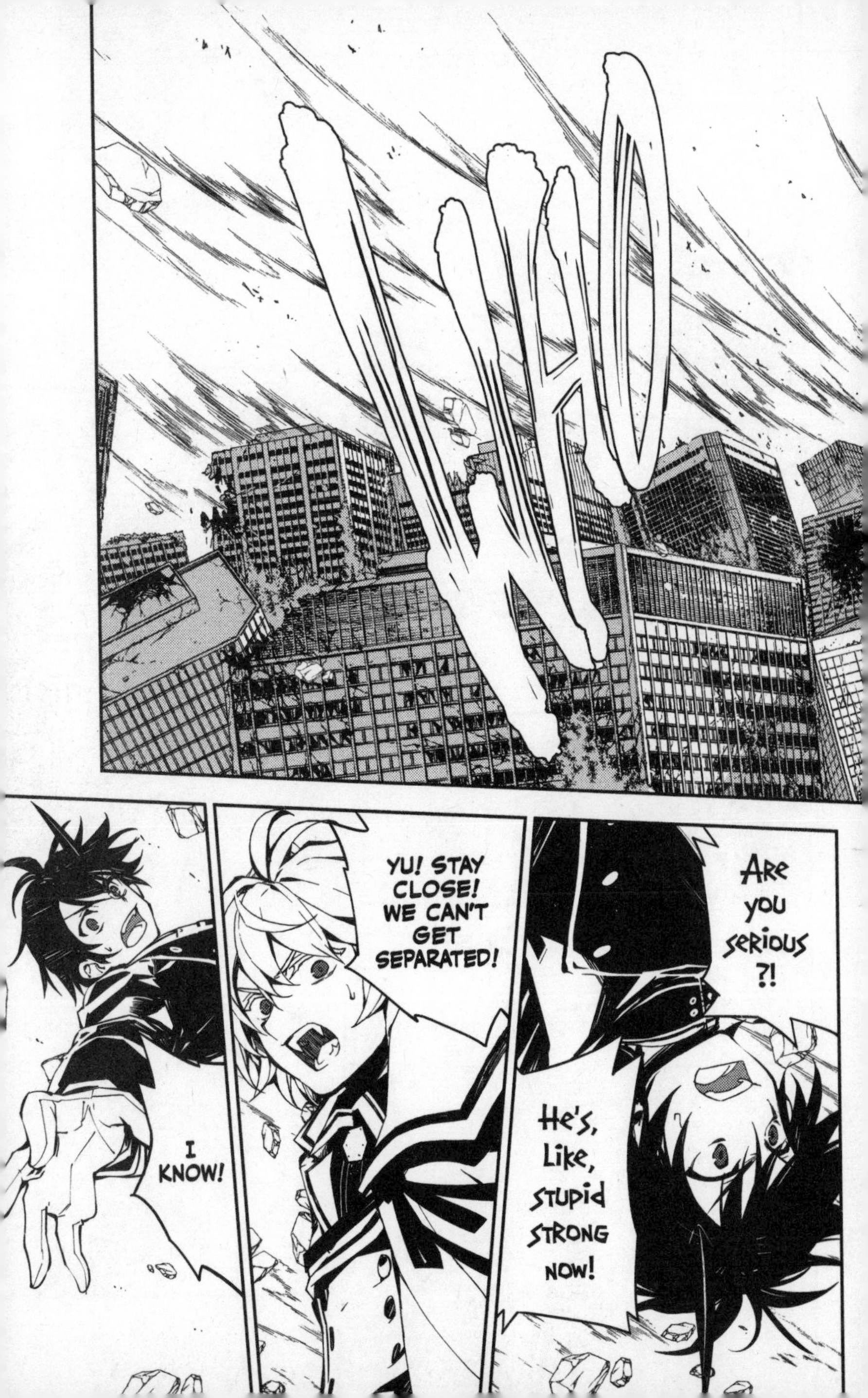
Are you serious?!
He's, like, stupid strong now!
YU! STAY CLOSE! WE CAN'T GET SEPARATED!
I KNOW!

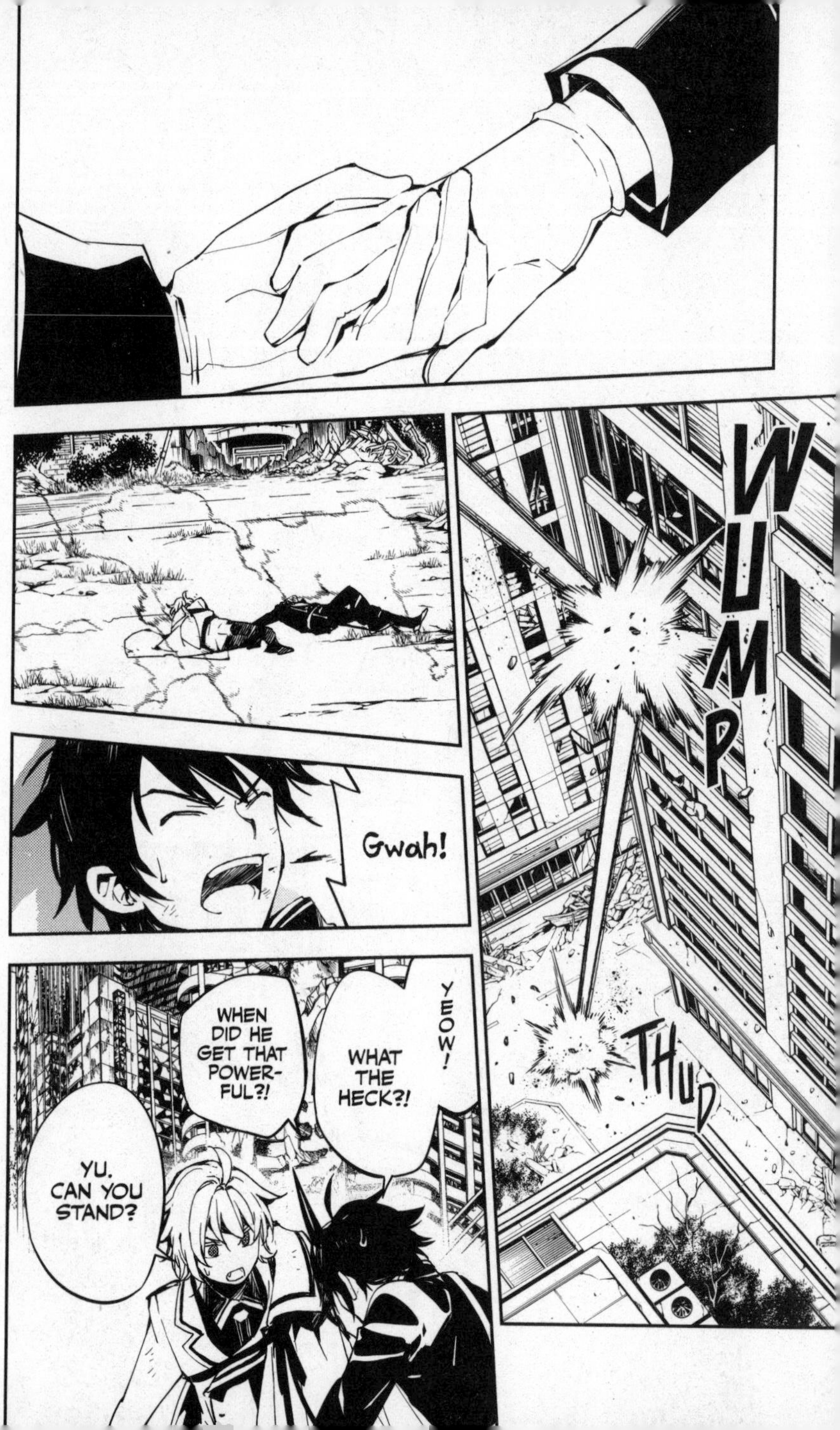
WUMP
THUD
Gwah!
YEOW!
WHAT THE HECK?!
WHEN DID HE GET THAT POWER-FUL?!
YU. CAN YOU STAND?

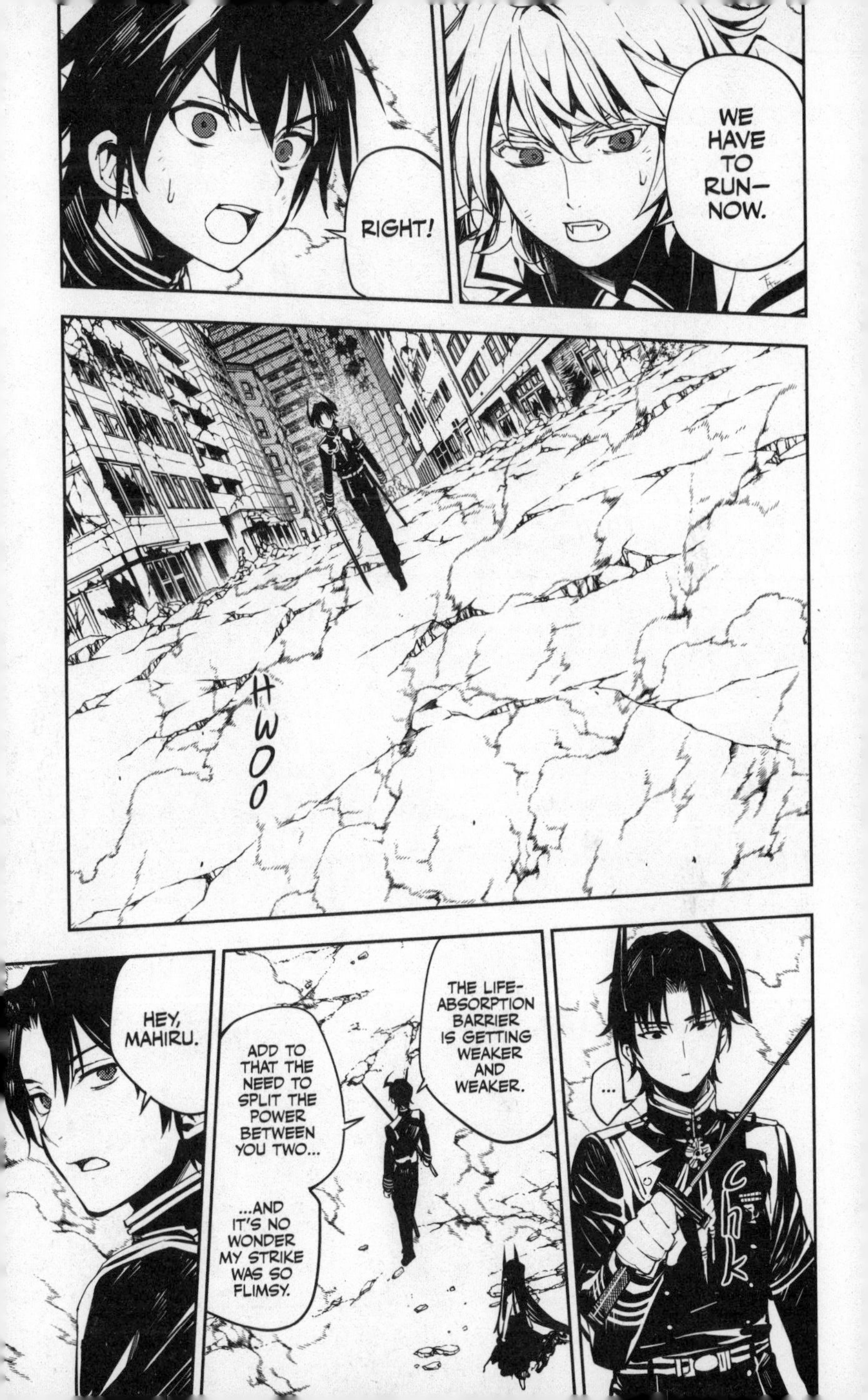

WE HAVE TO RUN— NOW.
RIGHT!
HWOO
...
chk
THE LIFE-ABSORPTION BARRIER IS GETTING WEAKER AND WEAKER.
ADD TO THAT THE NEED TO SPLIT THE POWER BETWEEN YOU TWO...
...AND IT'S NO WONDER MY STRIKE WAS SO FLIMSY.
HEY, MAHIRU.

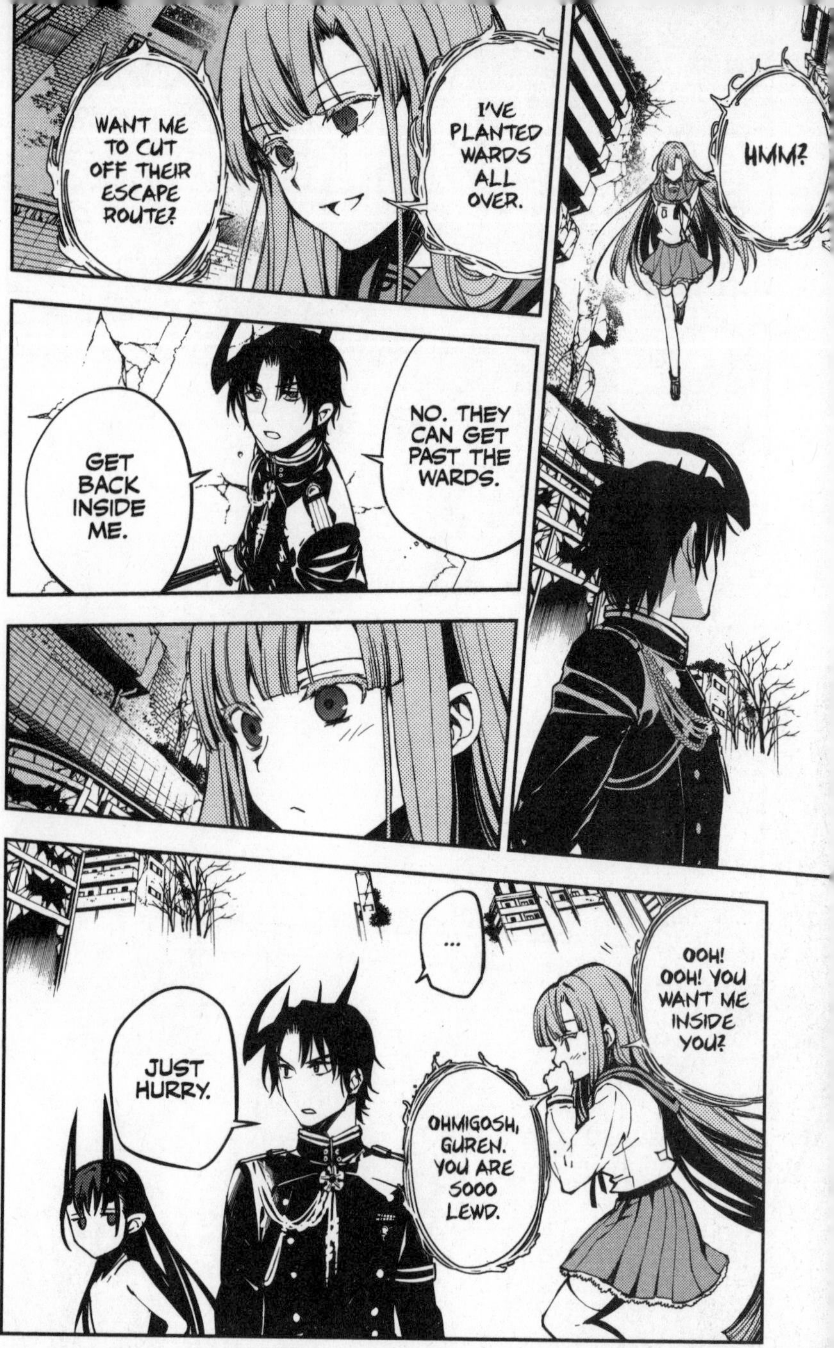
HMM?
I'VE PLANTED WARDS ALL OVER.
WANT ME TO CUT OFF THEIR ESCAPE ROUTE?
NO. THEY CAN GET PAST THE WARDS.
GET BACK INSIDE ME.
OOH! OOH! YOU WANT ME INSIDE YOU?
...
OHMIGOSH, GUREN. YOU ARE SOOO LEWD.
JUST HURRY.

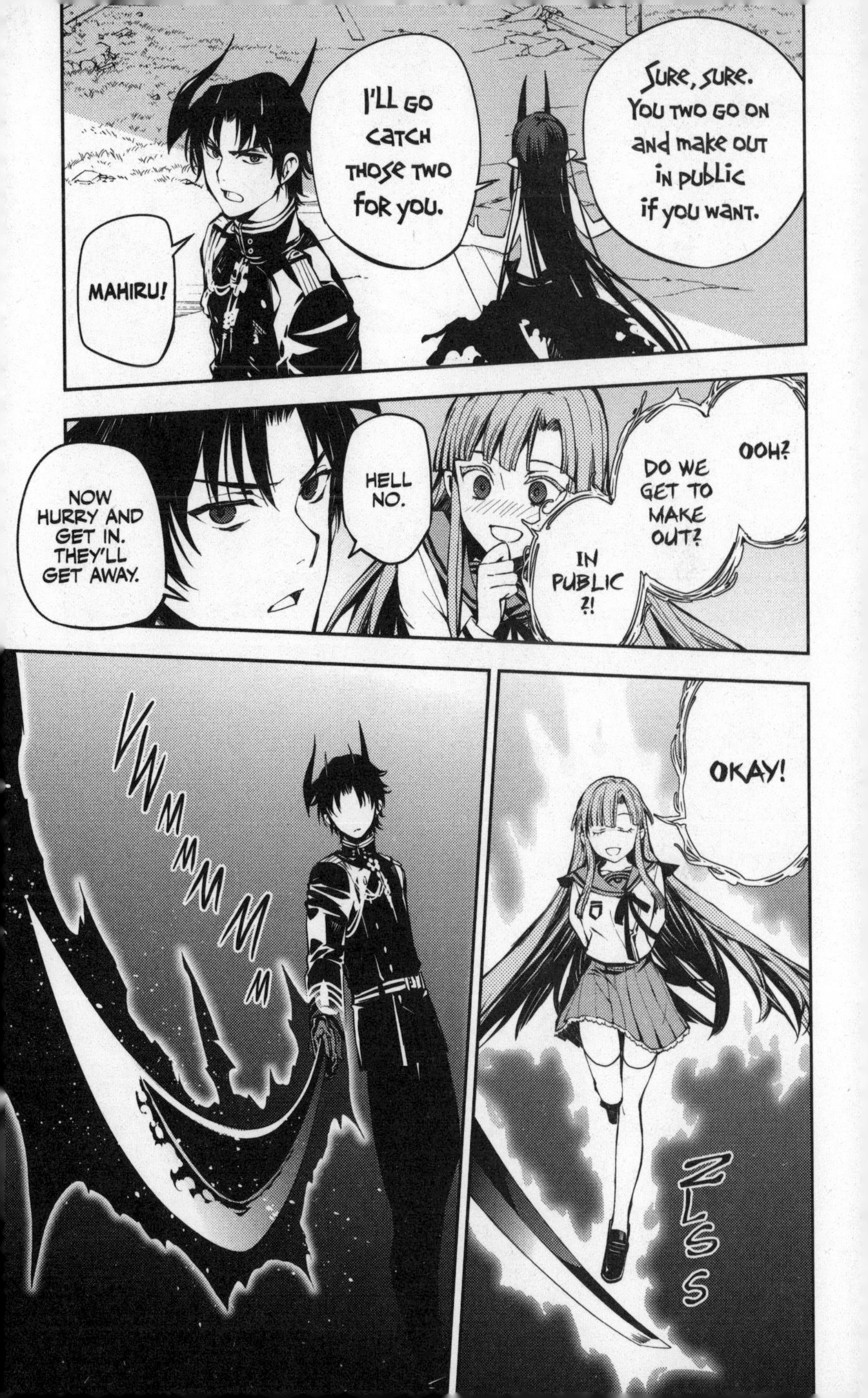
Sure, sure. You two go on and make out in public if you want.
I'LL GO CATCH THOSE TWO FOR YOU.
MAHIRU!
OOH? DO WE GET TO MAKE OUT?
IN PUBLIC?!
HELL NO.
NOW HURRY AND GET IN. THEY'LL GET AWAY.
OKAY!
ZLSS
VWMMMMM

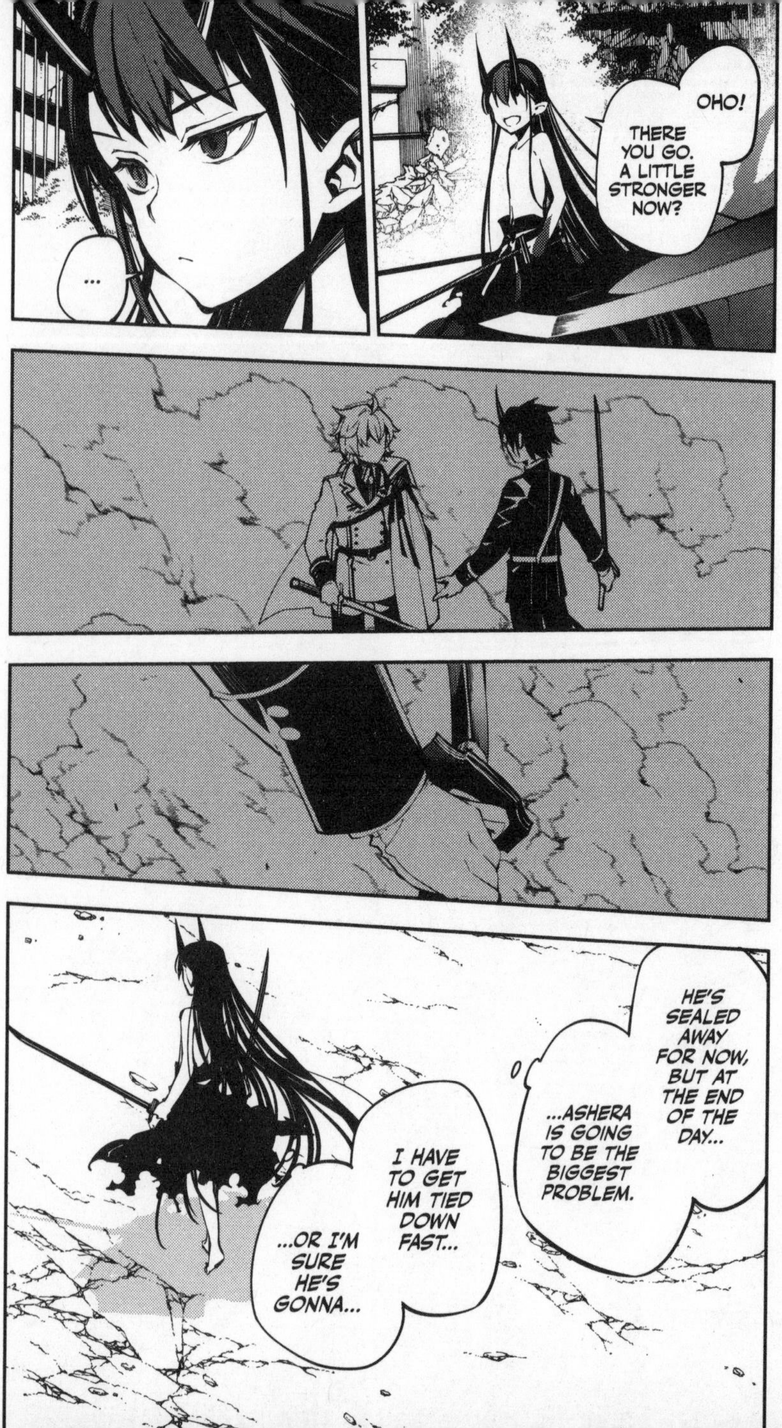
OHO!
THERE YOU GO. A LITTLE STRONGER NOW?
...
HE'S SEALED AWAY FOR NOW, BUT AT THE END OF THE DAY...
...ASHERA IS GOING TO BE THE BIGGEST PROBLEM.
I HAVE TO GET HIM TIED DOWN FAST...
...OR I'M SURE HE'S GONNA...

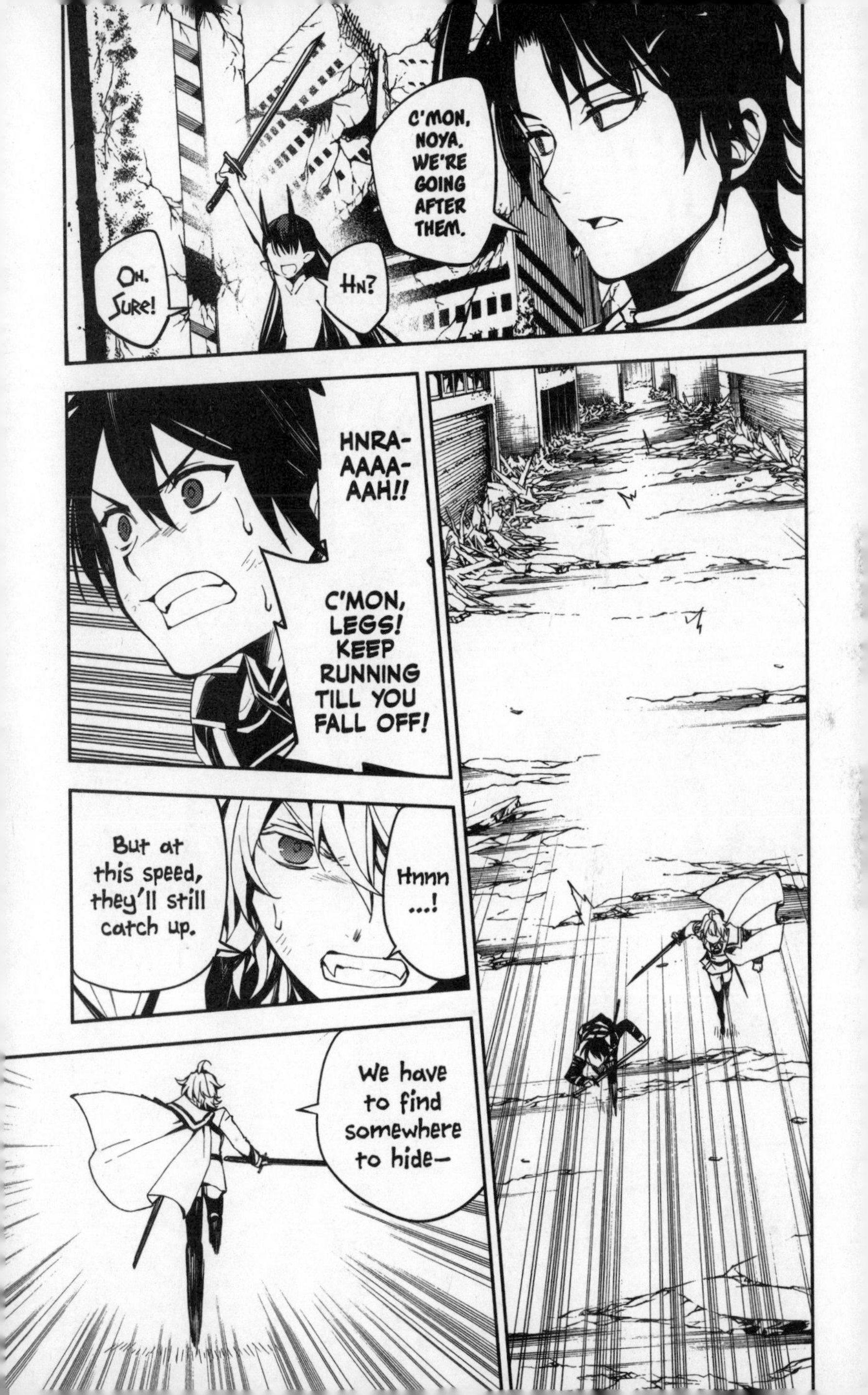
C'MON, NOYA. WE'RE GOING AFTER THEM.
Hn?
Oh. Sure!
HNRA-AAAAA-AAH!!
C'MON, LEGS! KEEP RUNNING TILL YOU FALL OFF!
Hnnn ...!
But at this speed, they'll still catch up.
We have to find somewhere to hide—

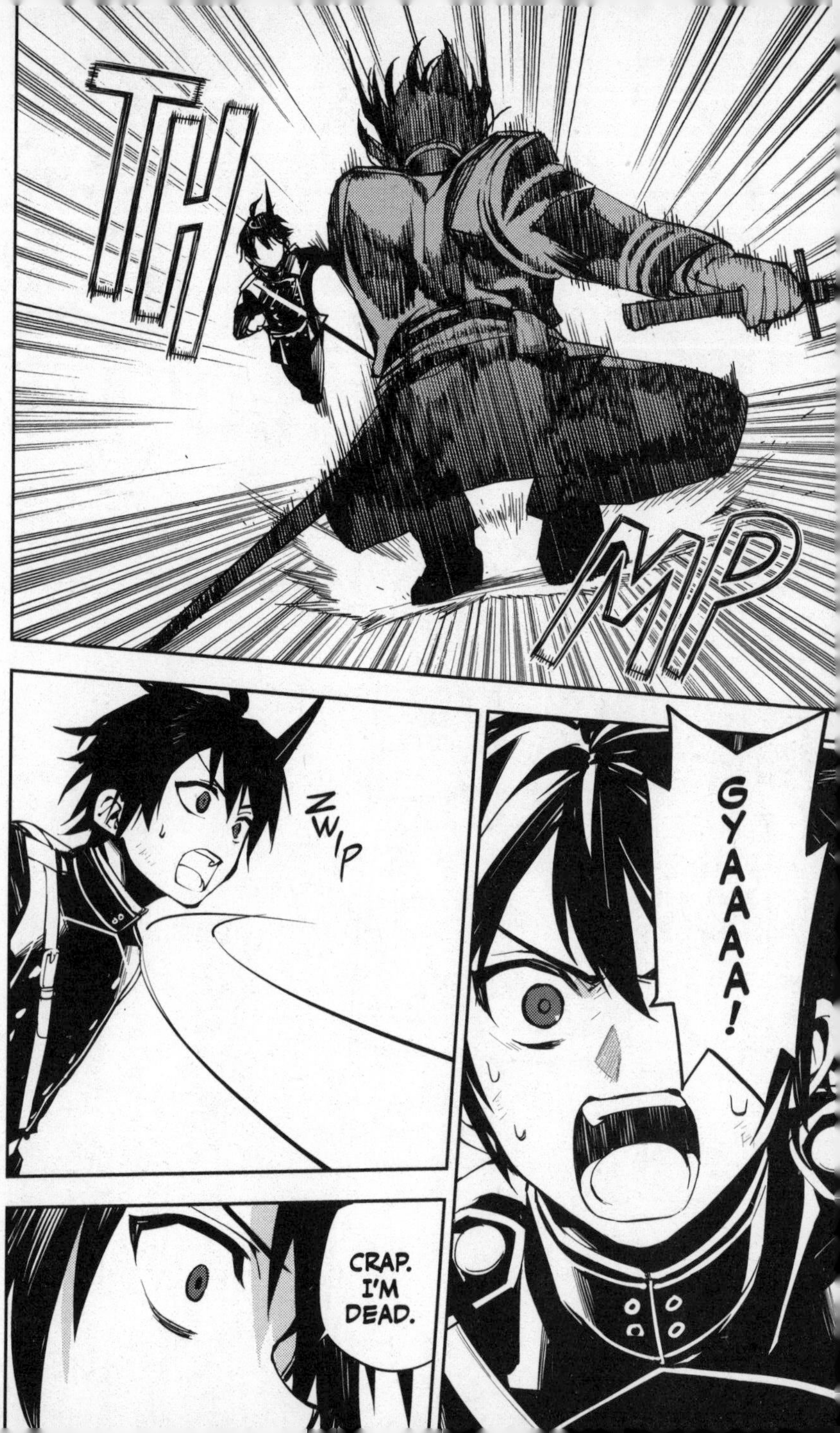
THMP
GYAAAAA!
ZWIP
CRAP. I'M DEAD.

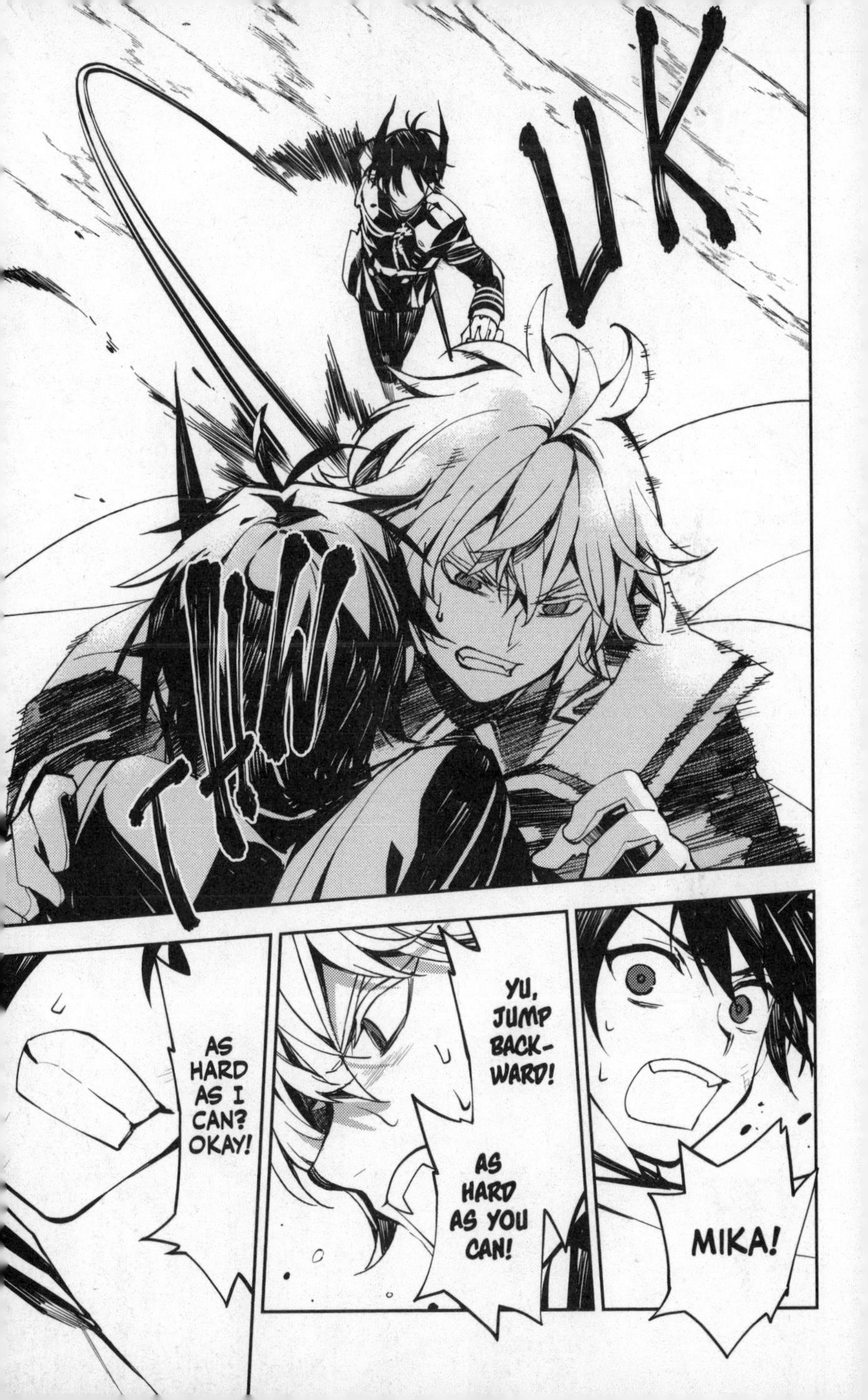
THWUK
MIKA!
YU, JUMP BACK-WARD!
AS HARD AS YOU CAN!
AS HARD AS I CAN? OKAY!

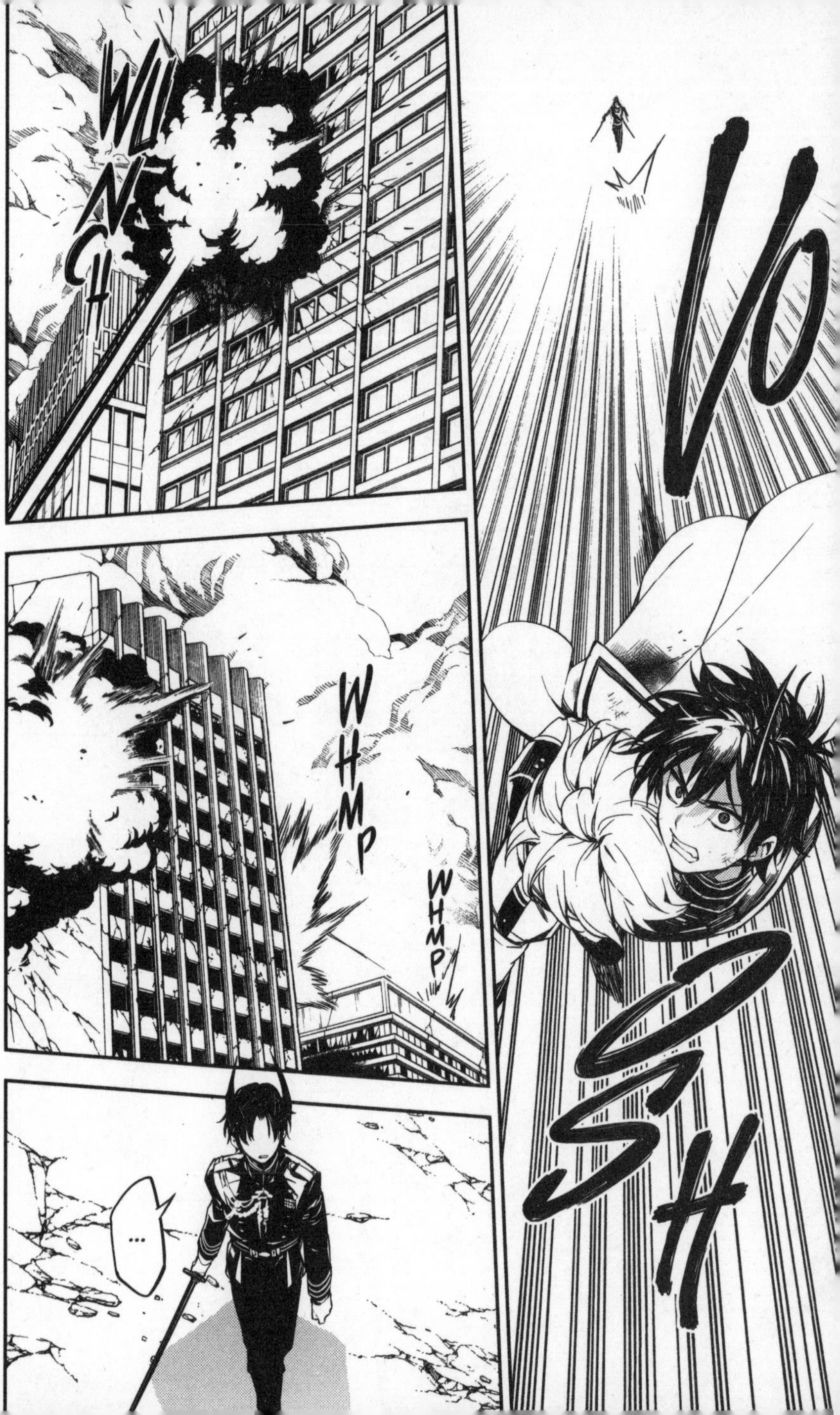
VOOSH
WUNCH
WHMP
WHMP
...

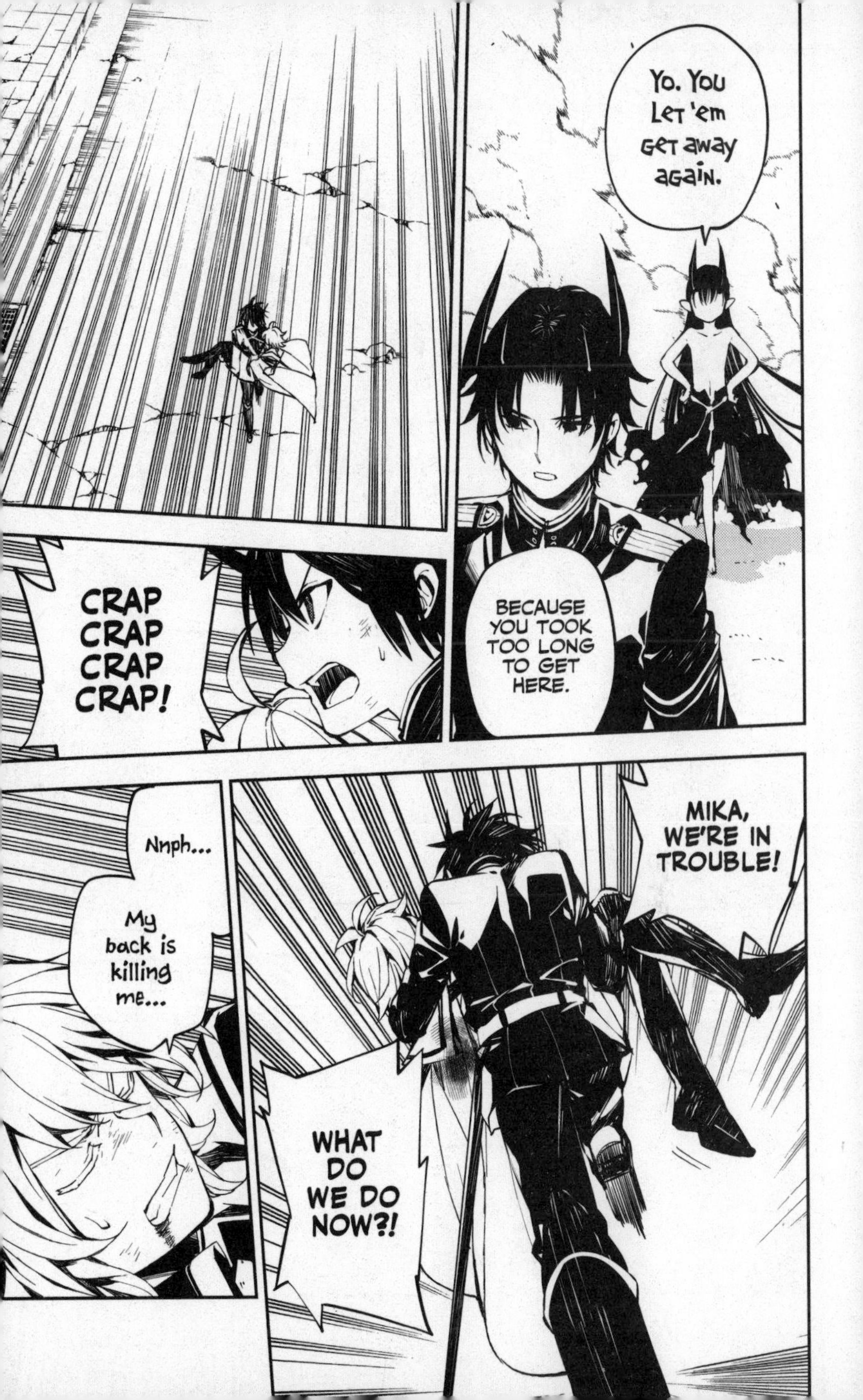
Yo. You Let 'em get away again.
BECAUSE YOU TOOK TOO LONG TO GET HERE.
CRAP CRAP CRAP CRAP!
MIKA, WE'RE IN TROUBLE!
WHAT DO WE DO NOW?!
Nnph...
My back is killing me...

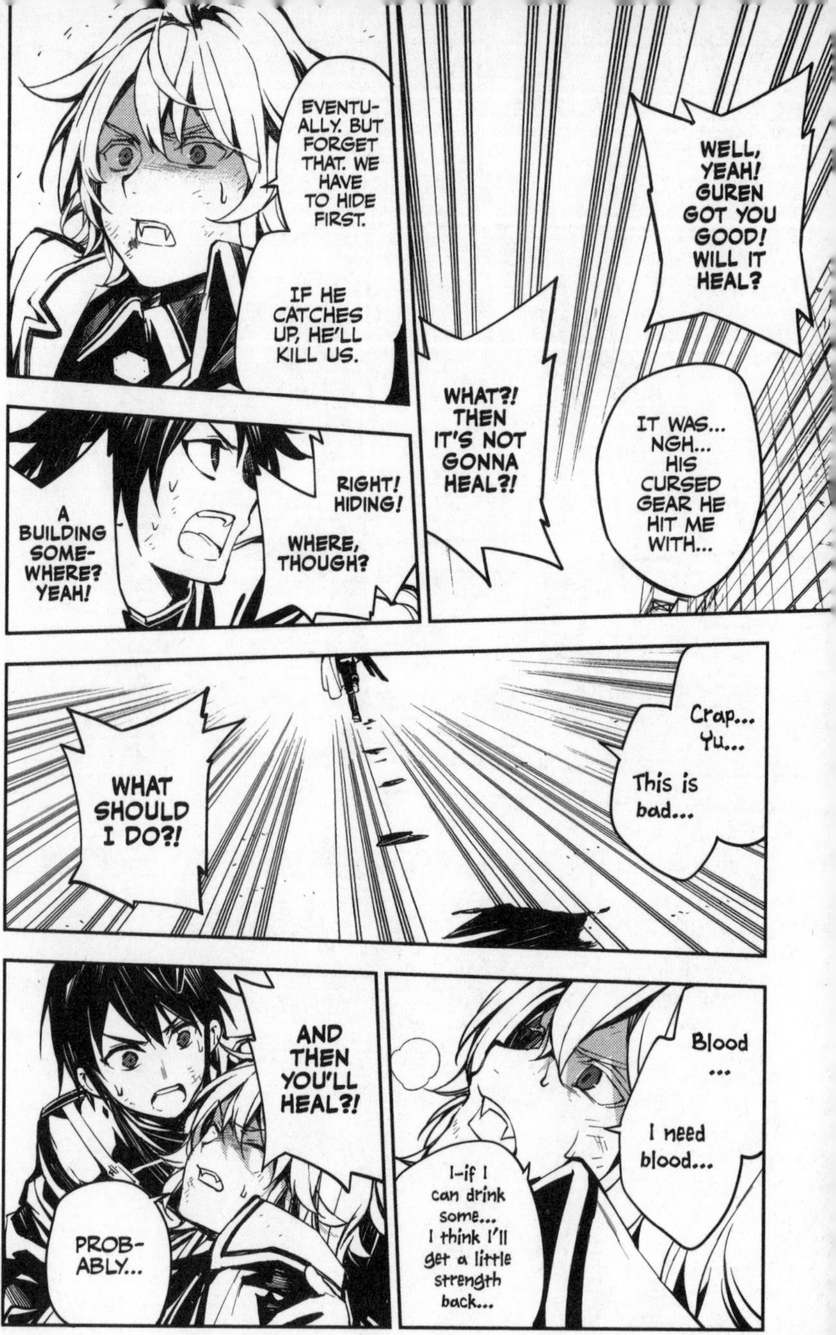
WELL, YEAH! GUREN GOT YOU GOOD! WILL IT HEAL?
IT WAS... NGH... HIS CURSED GEAR HE HIT ME WITH...
WHAT?! THEN IT'S NOT GONNA HEAL?!
EVENTU-ALLY. BUT FORGET THAT. WE HAVE TO HIDE FIRST.
IF HE CATCHES UP, HE'LL KILL US.
RIGHT! HIDING!
WHERE, THOUGH?
A BUILDING SOME-WHERE? YEAH!
Crap... Yu...
This is bad...
WHAT SHOULD I DO?!
Blood...
I need blood...
I-if I can drink some... I think I'll get a little strength back...
AND THEN YOU'LL HEAL?!
PROB-ABLY...

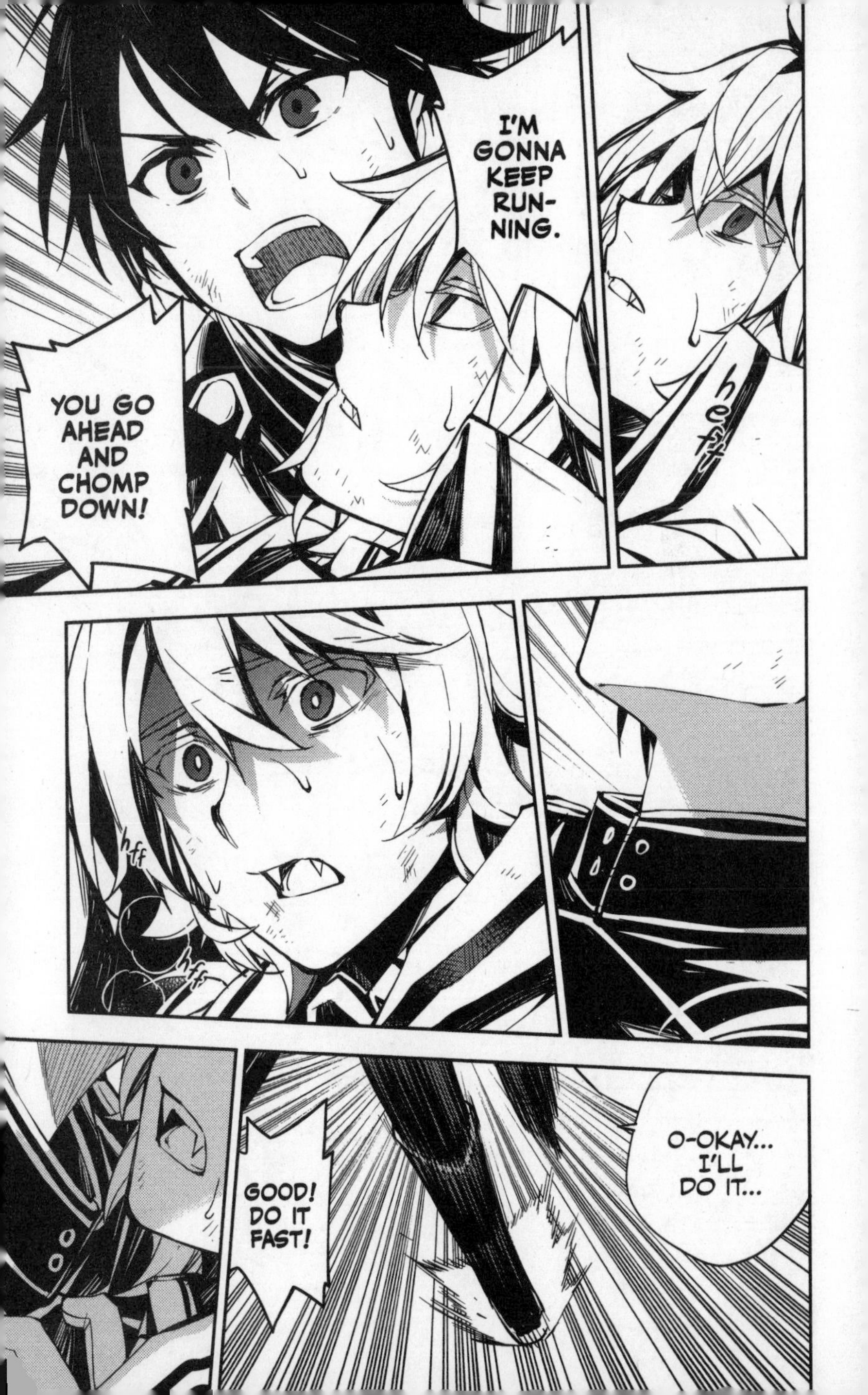
heft
I'M GONNA KEEP RUN-NING.
YOU GO AHEAD AND CHOMP DOWN!
hff
hff
O-OKAY... I'LL DO IT...
GOOD! DO IT FAST!

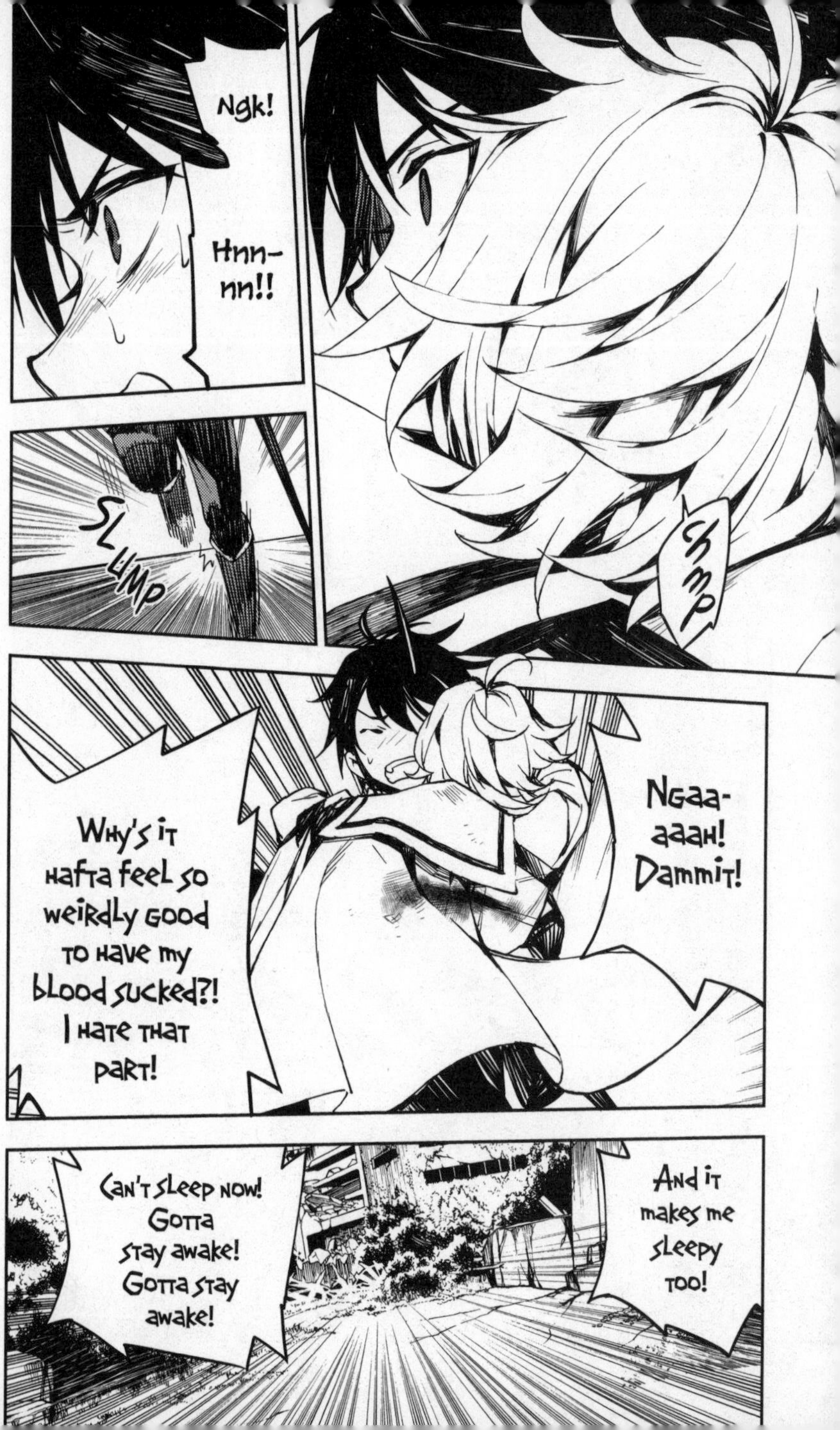
CHMP
Ngk!
Hnnn-nn!!
SLUMP
Ngaa-aaah! Dammit!
Why's it hafta feel so weirdly good to have my blood sucked?! I hate that part!
And it makes me sleepy too!
Can't sleep now! Gotta stay awake! Gotta stay awake!

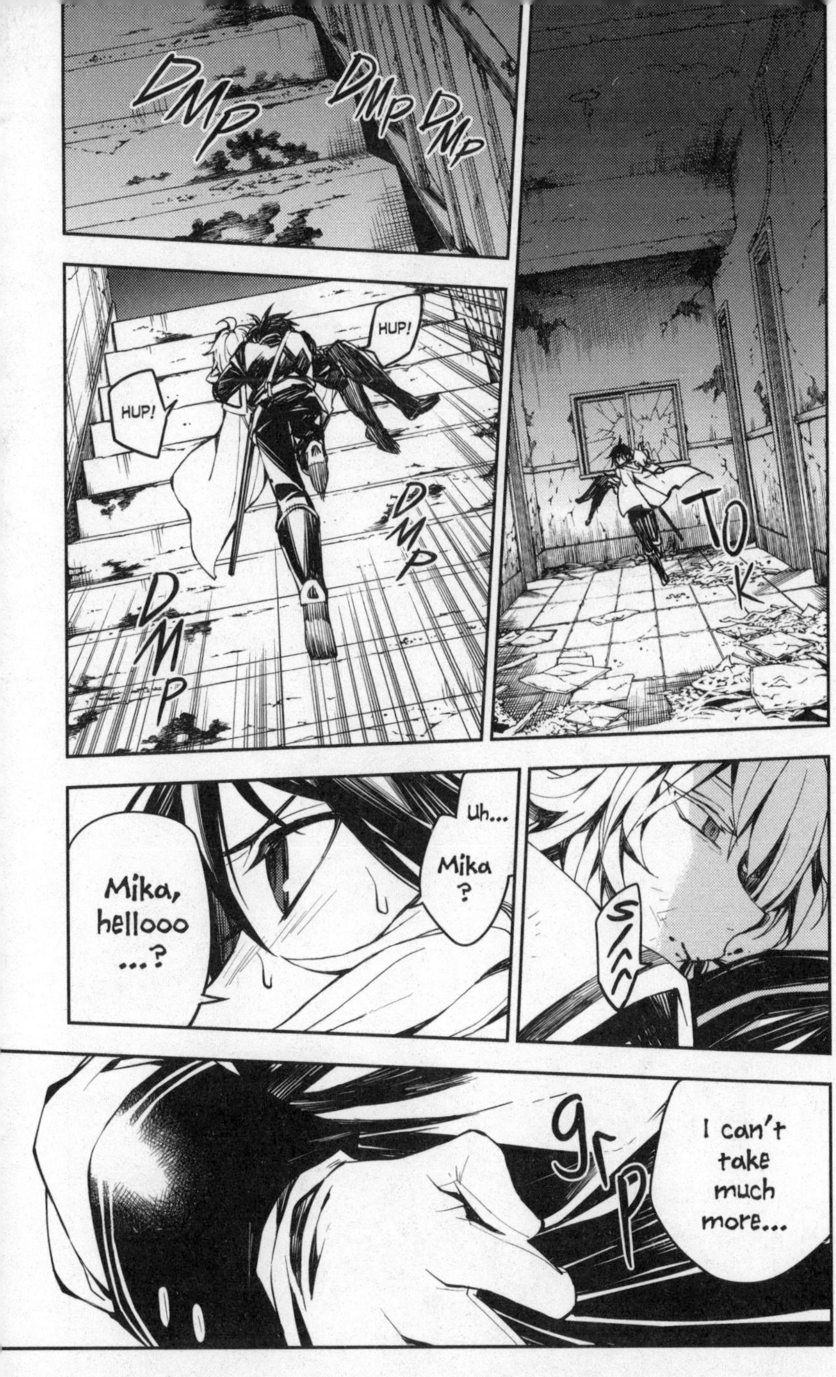
TOK
DMP DMP DMP
HUP!
HUP!
DMP
DMP
SLRR
Uh... Mika?
Mika, hellooo ...?
grp
I can't take much more...

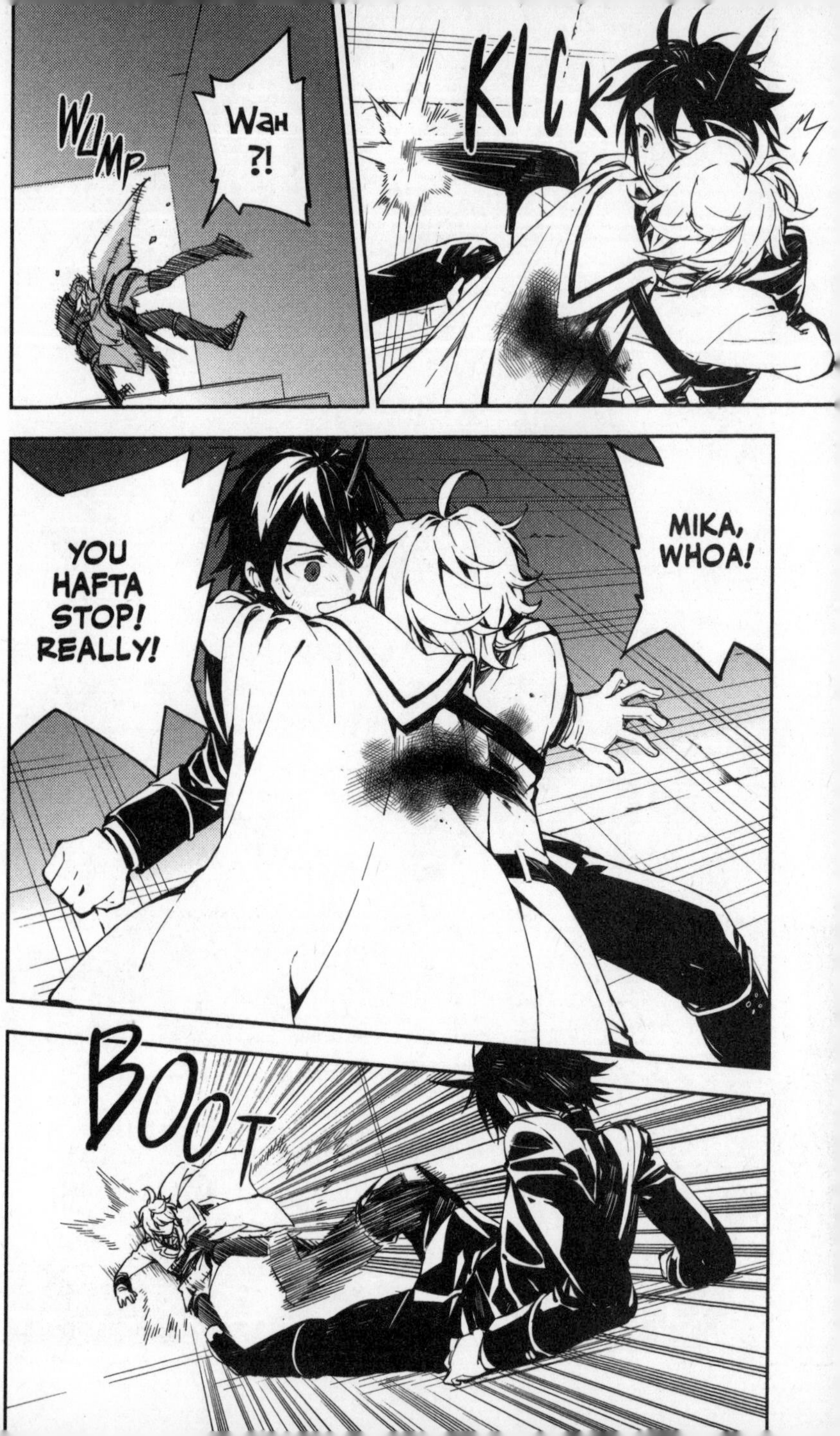
KICK
WAH ?!
WUMP
MIKA, WHOA!
YOU HAFTA STOP! REALLY!
BOOT

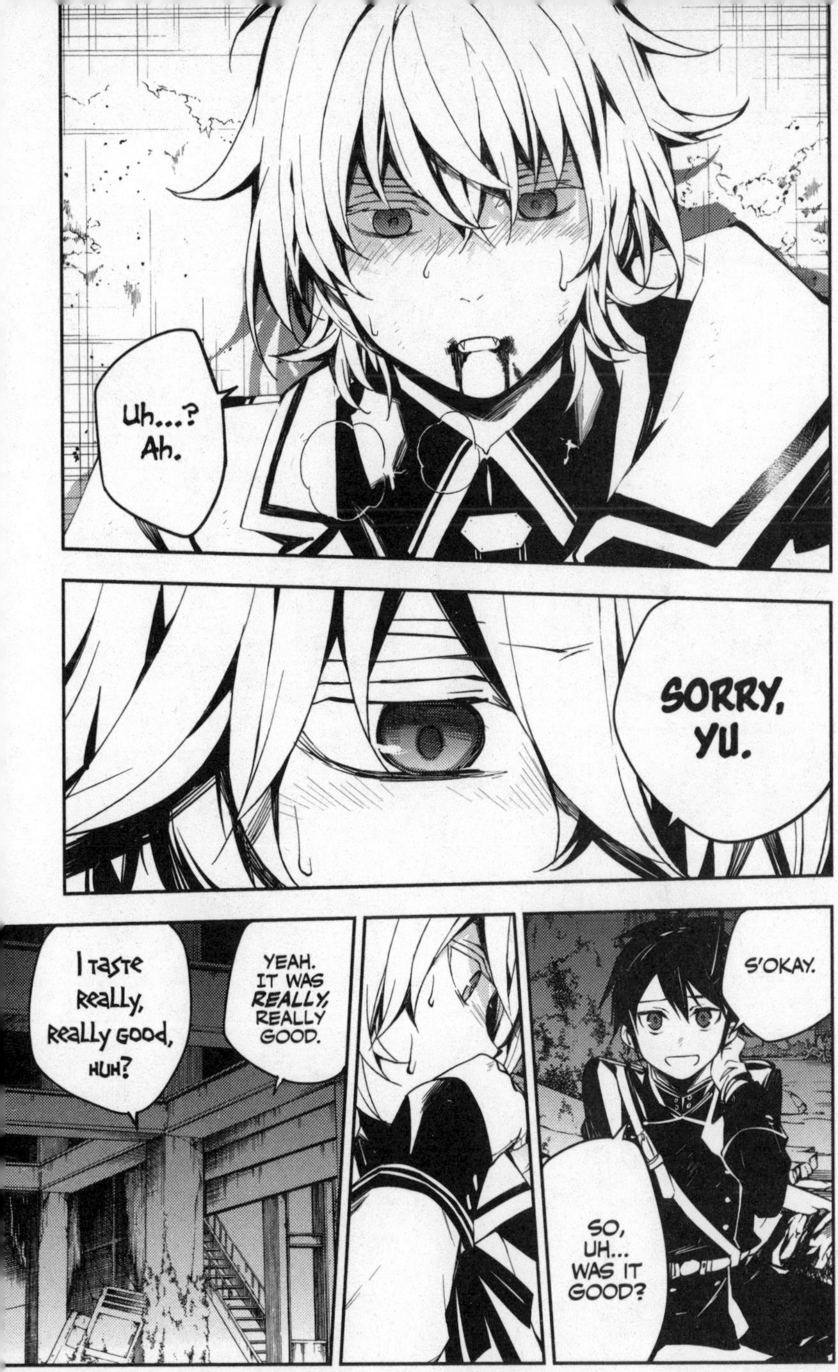
Uh...? Ah.
SORRY, YU.
S'OKAY.
SO, UH... WAS IT GOOD?
YEAH. IT WAS REALLY, REALLY GOOD.
I taste really, really good, huh?

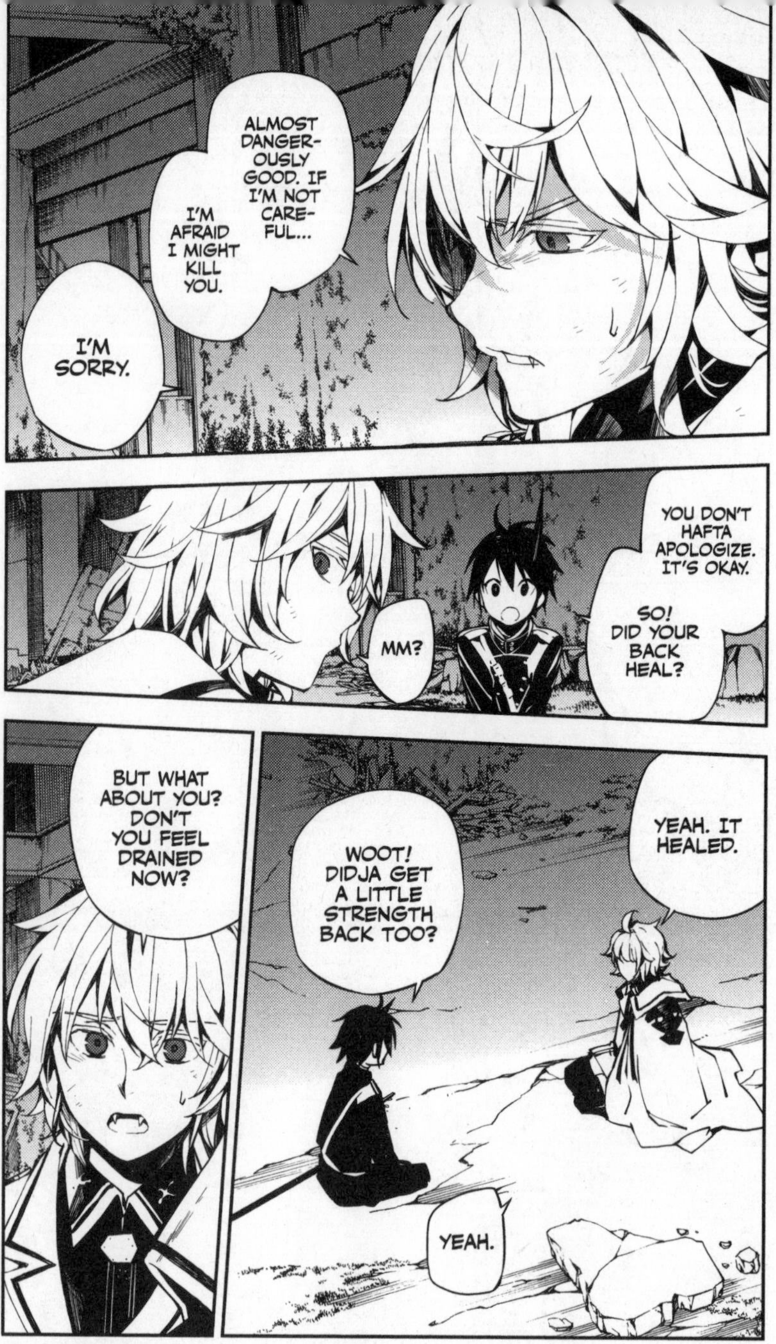
ALMOST DANGER-OUSLY GOOD. IF I'M NOT CARE-FUL...
I'M AFRAID I MIGHT KILL YOU.
I'M SORRY.
YOU DON'T HAFTA APOLOGIZE. IT'S OKAY.
SO! DID YOUR BACK HEAL?
MM?
YEAH. IT HEALED.
WOOT! DIDJA GET A LITTLE STRENGTH BACK TOO?
YEAH.
BUT WHAT ABOUT YOU? DON'T YOU FEEL DRAINED NOW?

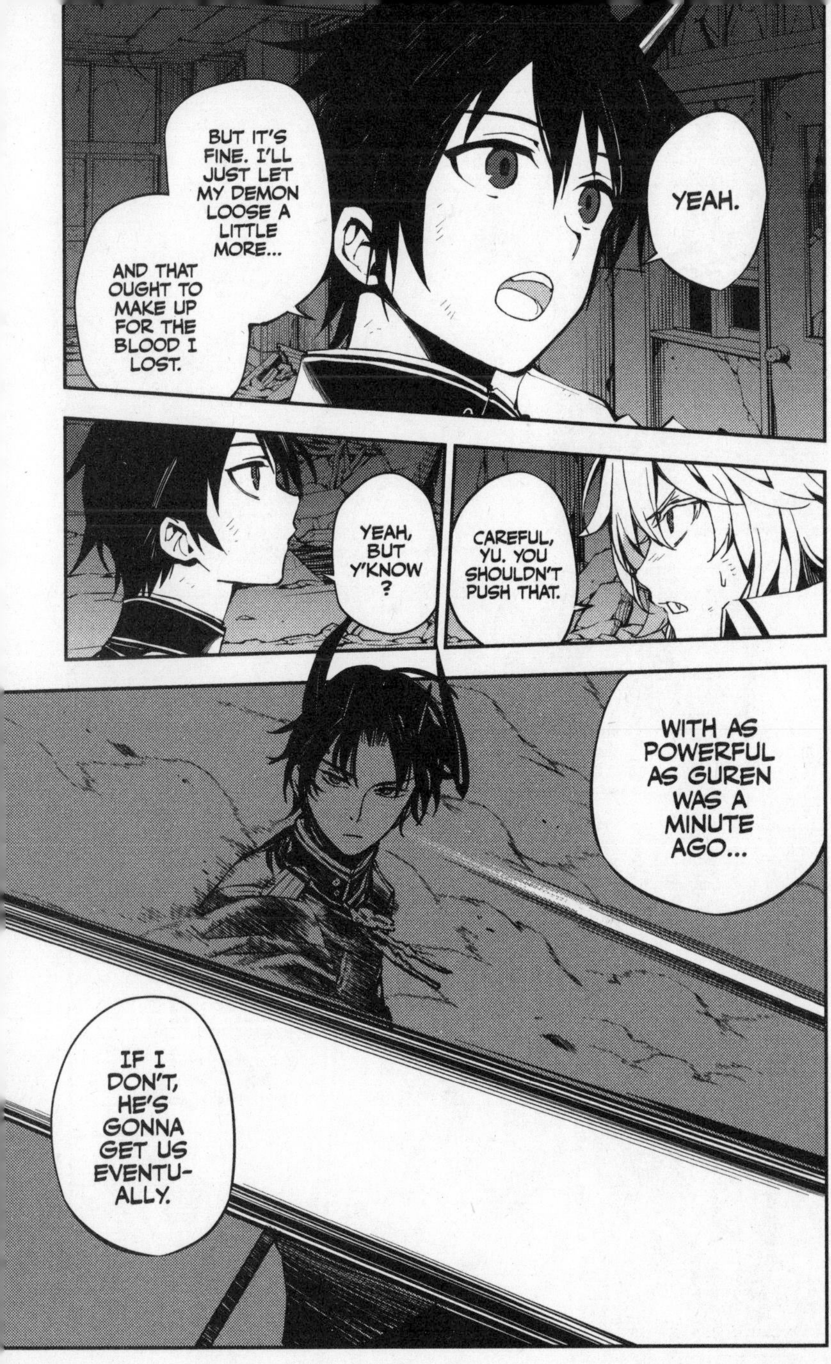
YEAH.
BUT IT'S FINE. I'LL JUST LET MY DEMON LOOSE A LITTLE MORE...
AND THAT OUGHT TO MAKE UP FOR THE BLOOD I LOST.
CAREFUL, YU. YOU SHOULDN'T PUSH THAT.
YEAH, BUT Y'KNOW?
WITH AS POWERFUL AS GUREN WAS A MINUTE AGO...
IF I DON'T, HE'S GONNA GET US EVENTU-ALLY.

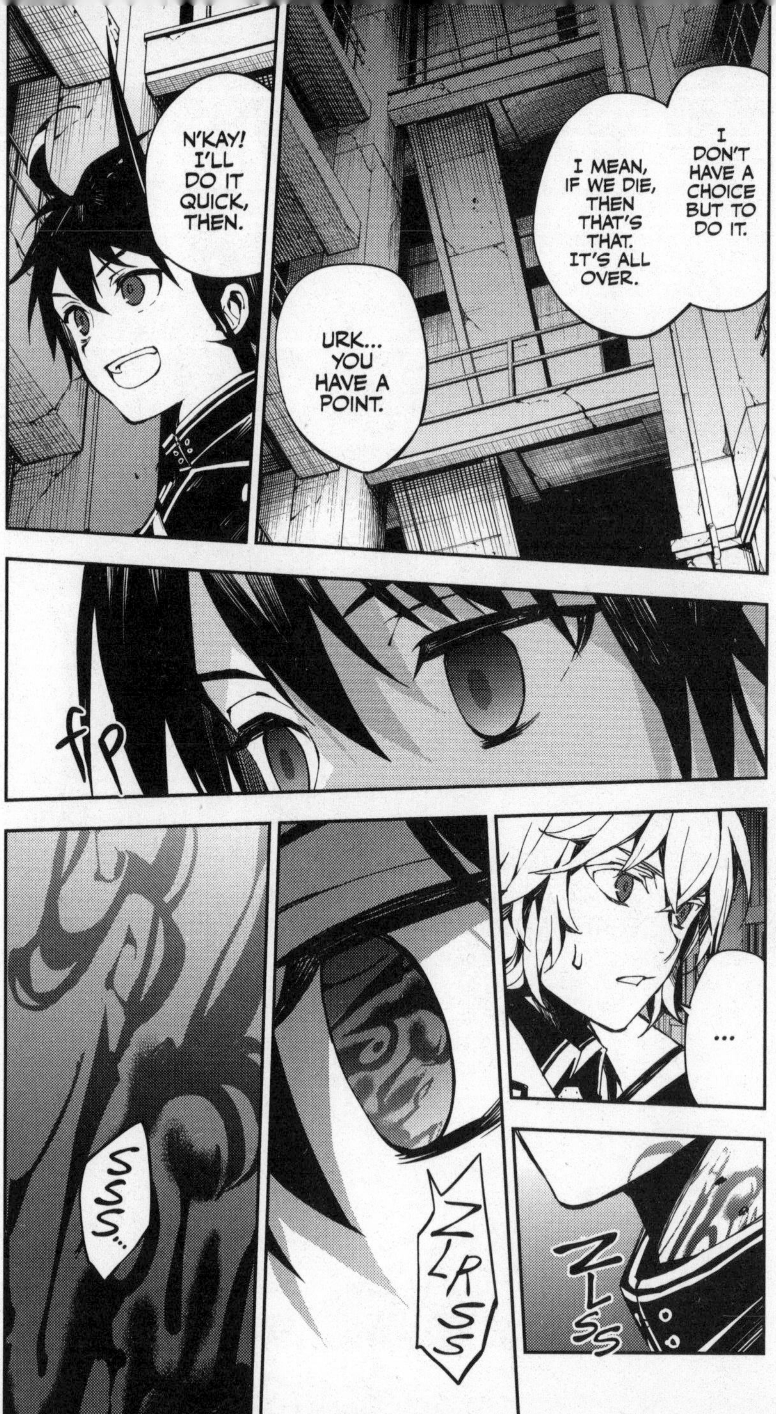
I DON'T HAVE A CHOICE BUT TO DO IT.
I MEAN, IF WE DIE, THEN THAT'S THAT. IT'S ALL OVER.
URK... YOU HAVE A POINT.
N'KAY! I'LL DO IT QUICK, THEN.
fp
...
ZLSS
ZLRSS
SSS...

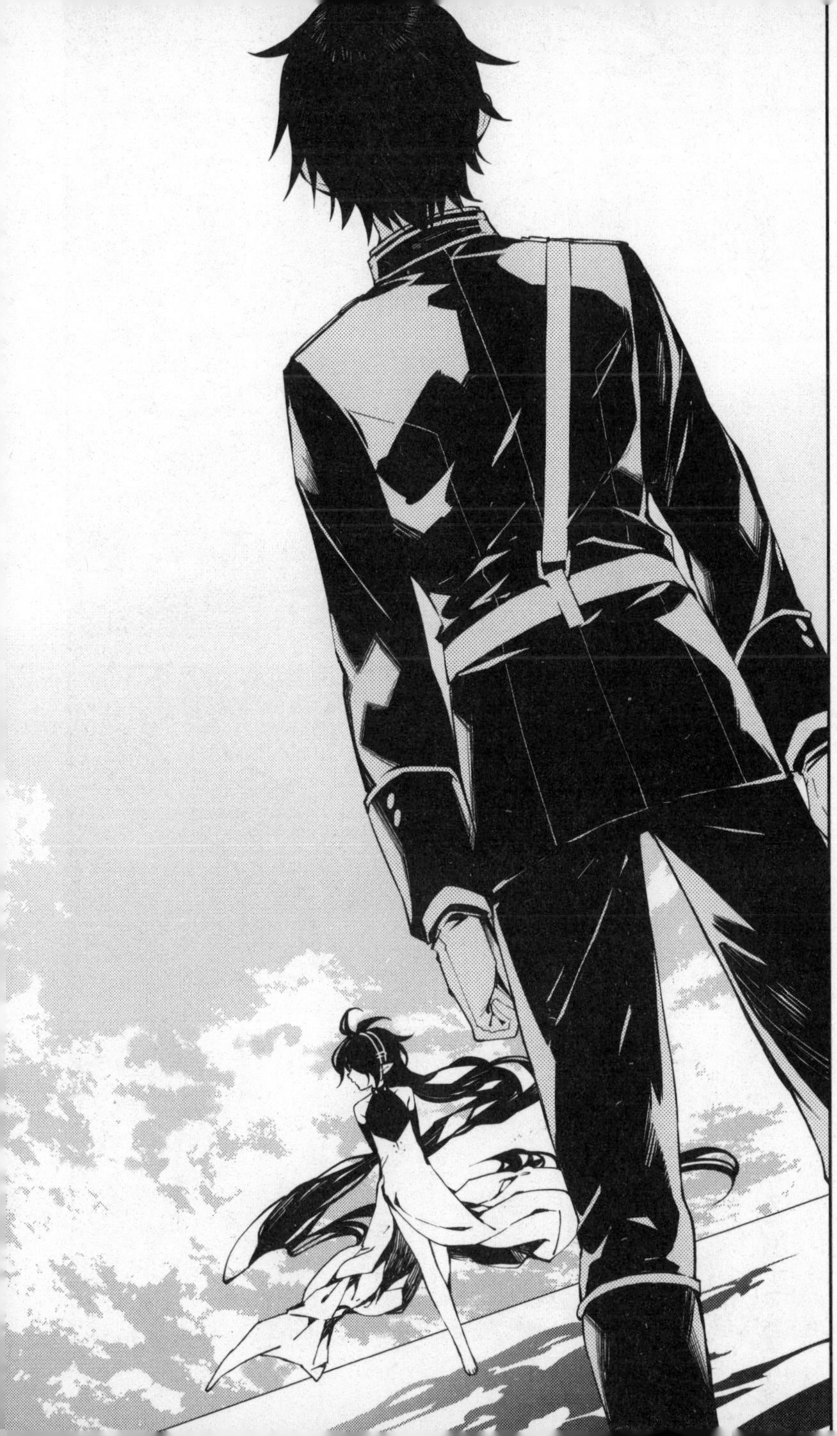

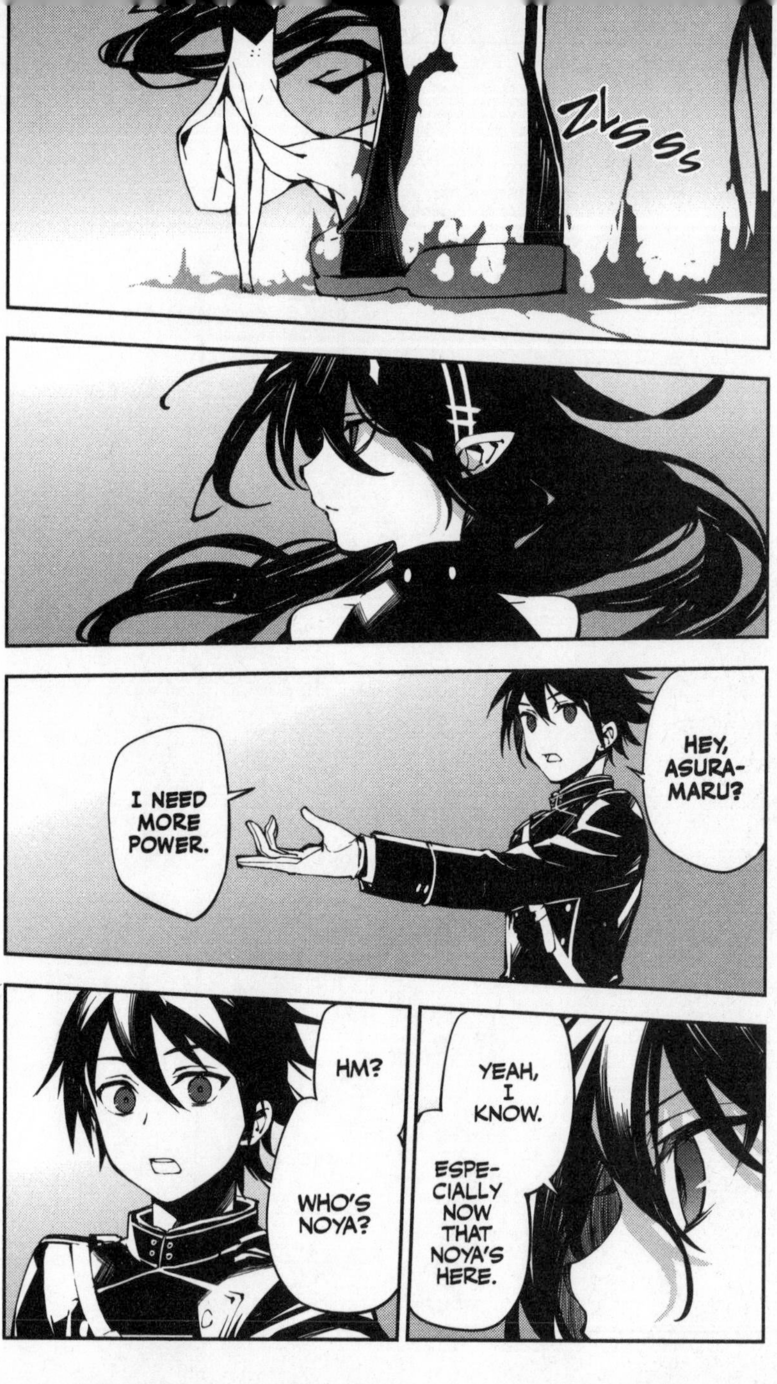
ZZSSSS
HEY, ASURA-MARU?
I NEED MORE POWER.
YEAH, I KNOW.
ESPECIALLY NOW THAT NOYA'S HERE.
HM?
WHO'S NOYA?

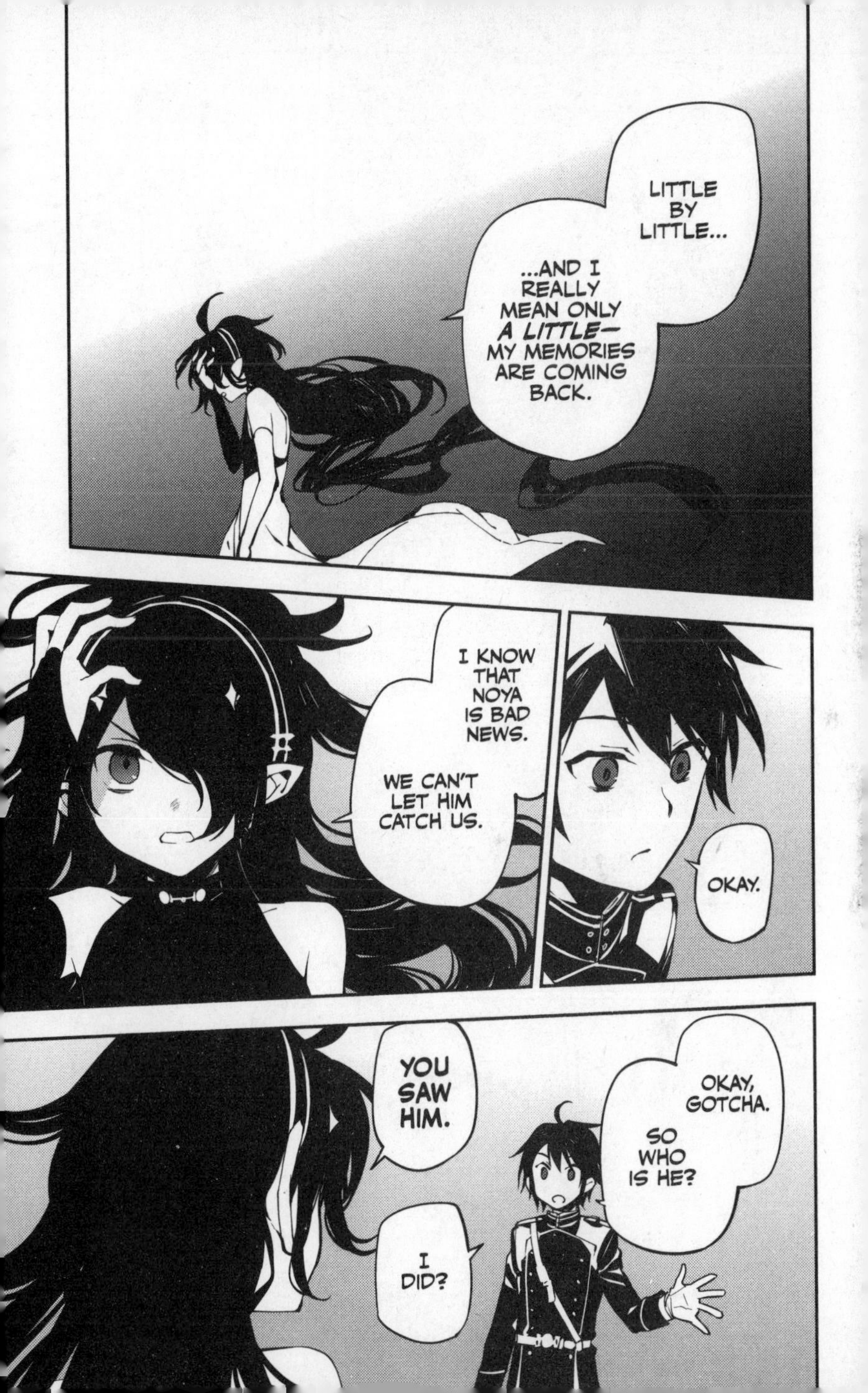
LITTLE BY LITTLE...
...AND I REALLY MEAN ONLY *A LITTLE*— MY MEMORIES ARE COMING BACK.
I KNOW THAT NOYA IS BAD NEWS.
WE CAN'T LET HIM CATCH US.
OKAY.
OKAY, GOTCHA.
SO WHO IS HE?
YOU SAW HIM.
I DID?

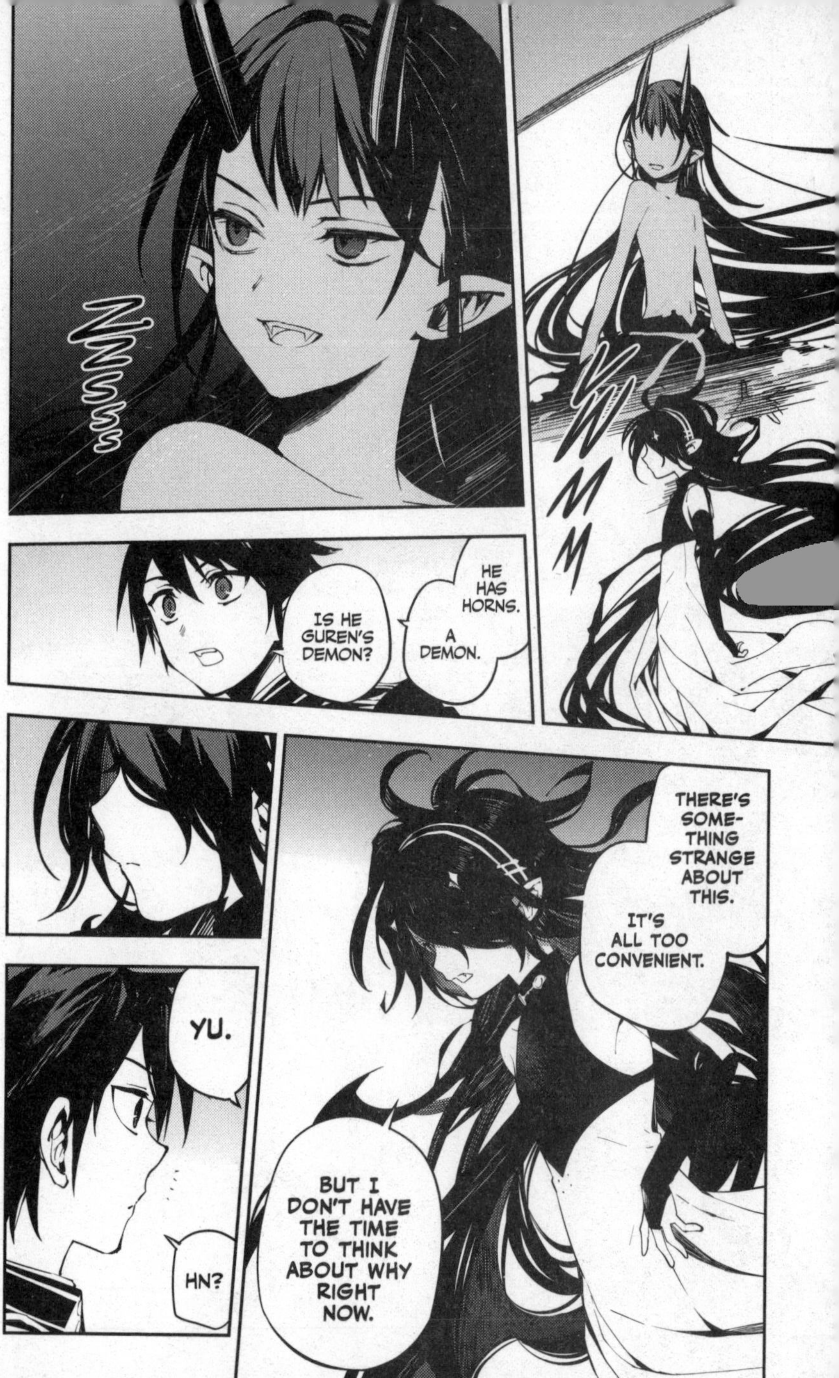

HE HAS HORNS.
A DEMON.
IS HE GUREN'S DEMON?
THERE'S SOME-THING STRANGE ABOUT THIS.
IT'S ALL TOO CONVENIENT.
BUT I DON'T HAVE THE TIME TO THINK ABOUT WHY RIGHT NOW.
YU.
HN?

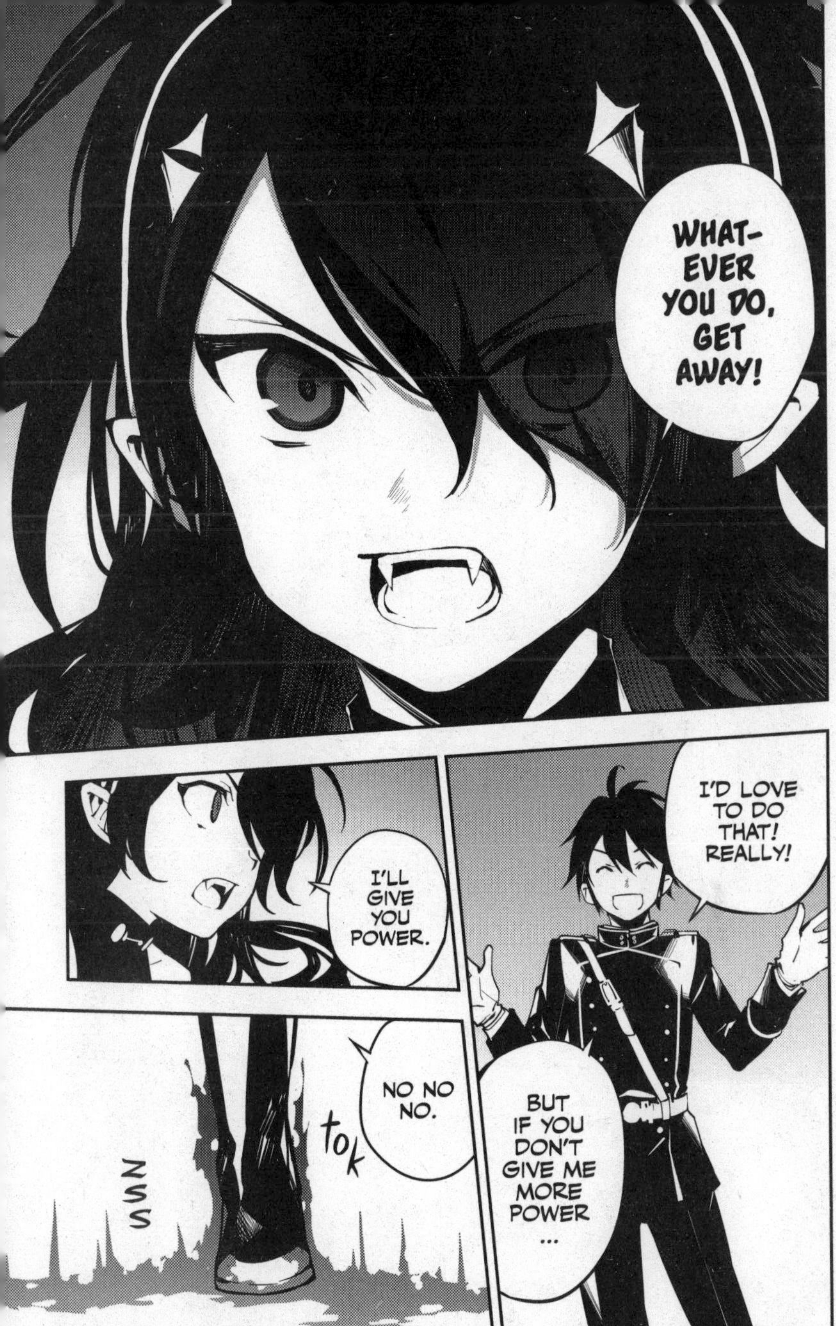
WHAT-EVER YOU DO, GET AWAY!
I'D LOVE TO DO THAT! REALLY!
BUT IF YOU DON'T GIVE ME MORE POWER ...
I'LL GIVE YOU POWER.
NO NO NO.
tok

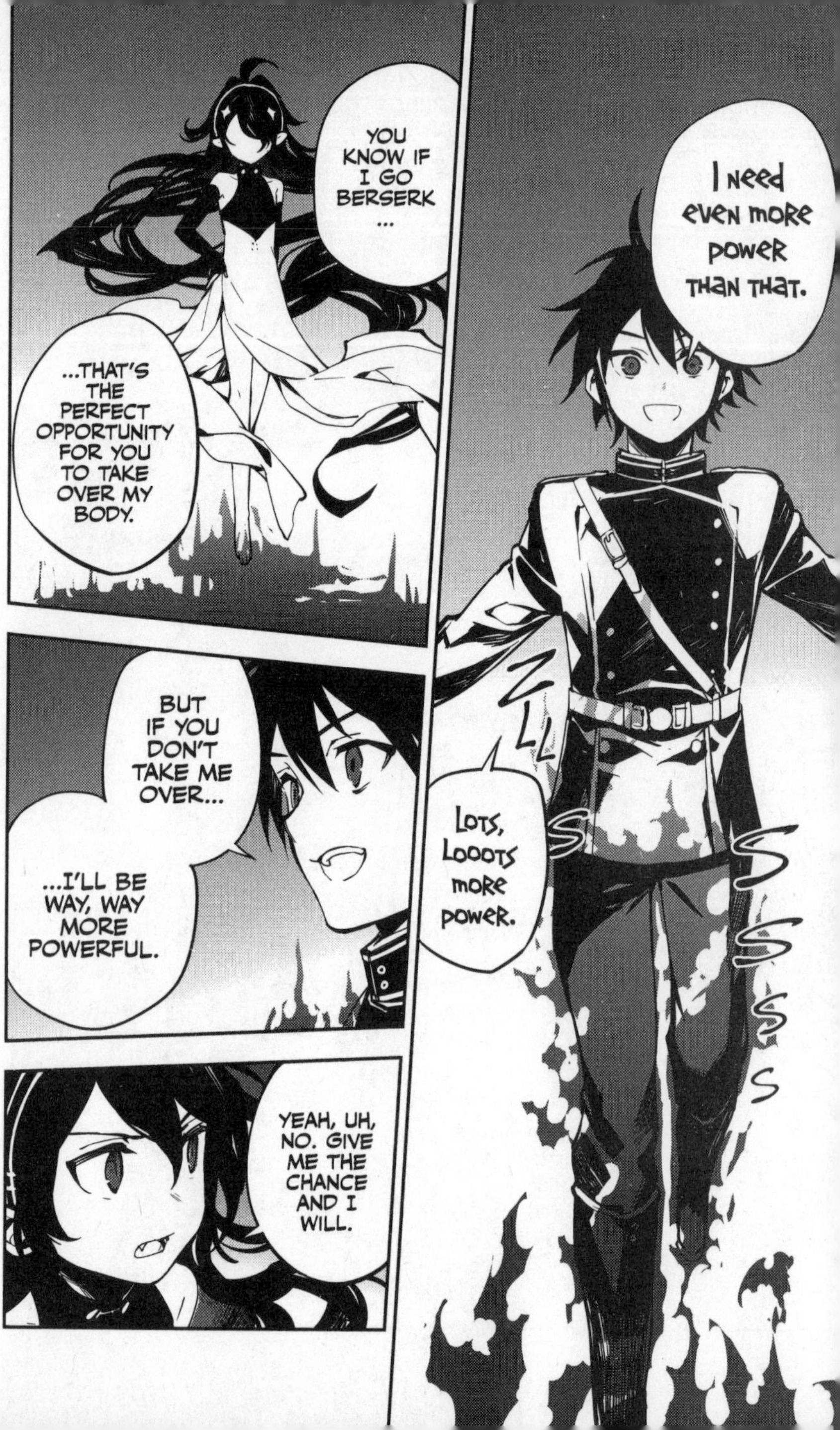
I need even more power than that.
Lots, looots more power.
YOU KNOW IF I GO BERSERK ...
...THAT'S THE PERFECT OPPORTUNITY FOR YOU TO TAKE OVER MY BODY.
BUT IF YOU DON'T TAKE ME OVER...
...I'LL BE WAY, WAY MORE POWERFUL.
YEAH, UH, NO. GIVE ME THE CHANCE AND I WILL.

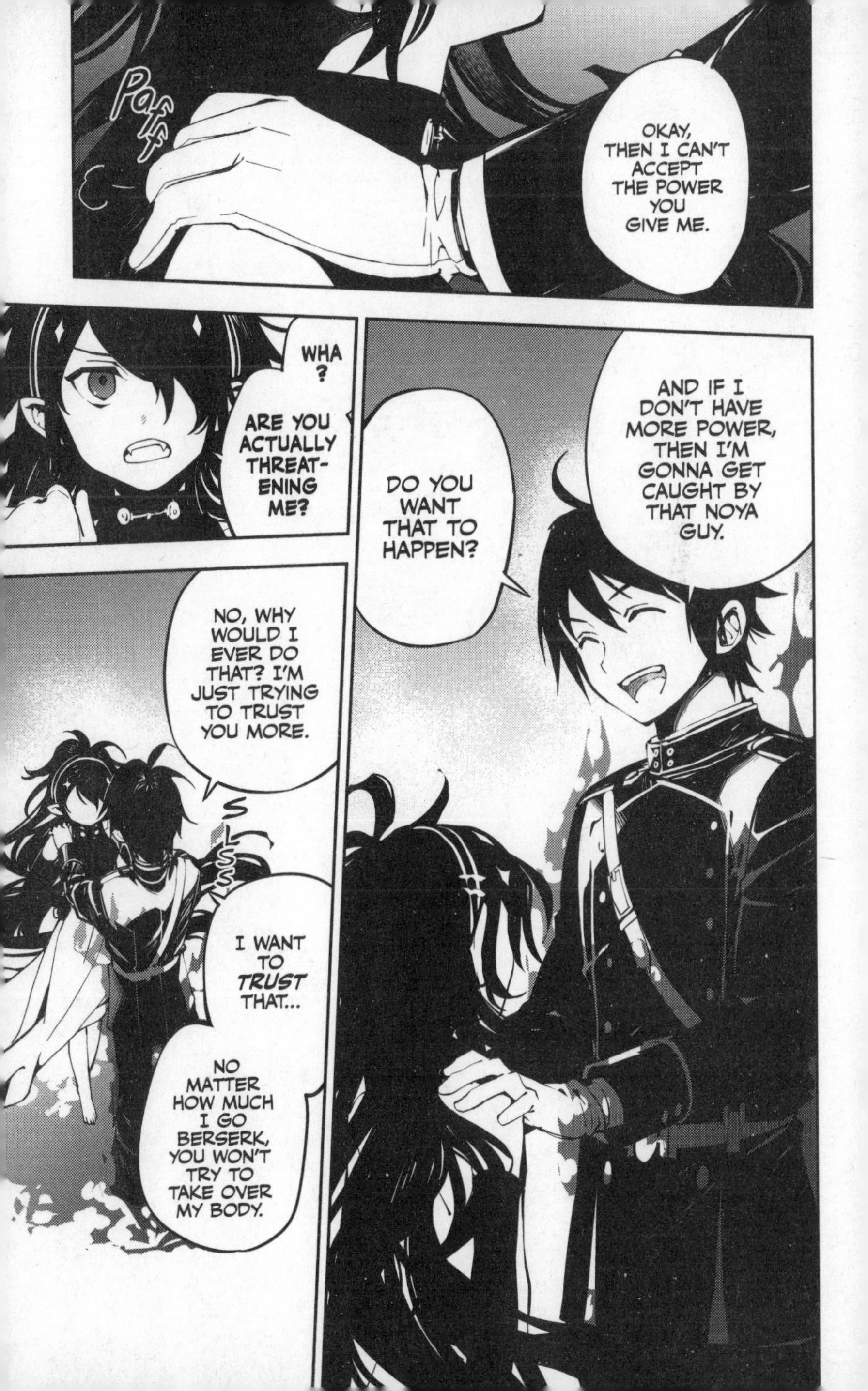
OKAY, THEN I CAN'T ACCEPT THE POWER YOU GIVE ME.
Paff
AND IF I DON'T HAVE MORE POWER, THEN I'M GONNA GET CAUGHT BY THAT NOYA GUY.
DO YOU WANT THAT TO HAPPEN?
WHA?
ARE YOU ACTUALLY THREATENING ME?
NO, WHY WOULD I EVER DO THAT? I'M JUST TRYING TO TRUST YOU MORE.
SLSS
I WANT TO *TRUST* THAT...
NO MATTER HOW MUCH I GO BERSERK, YOU WON'T TRY TO TAKE OVER MY BODY.

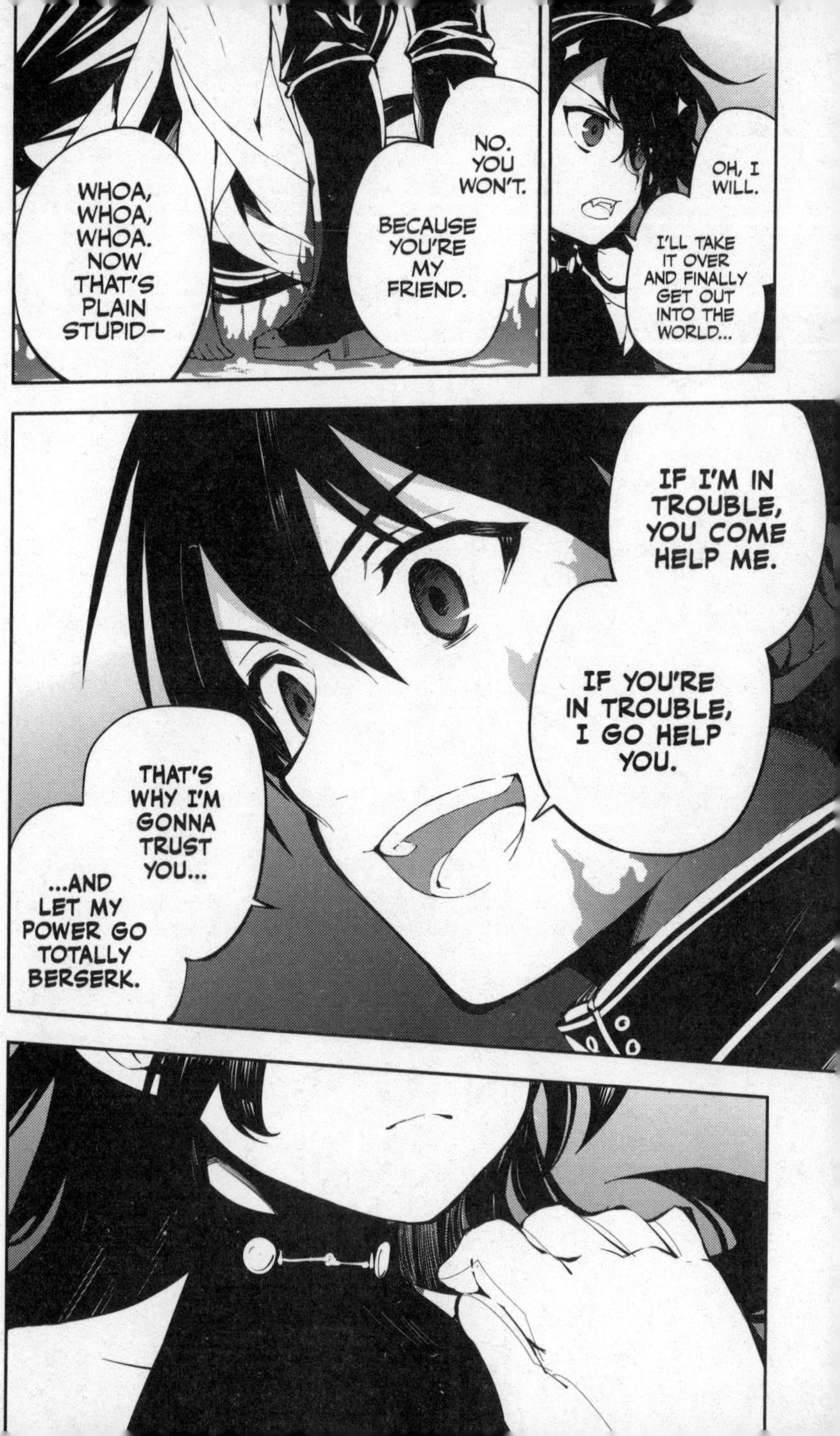
OH, I WILL.
I'LL TAKE IT OVER AND FINALLY GET OUT INTO THE WORLD...
NO. YOU WON'T.
BECAUSE YOU'RE MY FRIEND.
WHOA, WHOA, WHOA. NOW THAT'S PLAIN STUPID—
IF I'M IN TROUBLE, YOU COME HELP ME.
IF YOU'RE IN TROUBLE, I GO HELP YOU.
THAT'S WHY I'M GONNA TRUST YOU...
...AND LET MY POWER GO TOTALLY BERSERK.

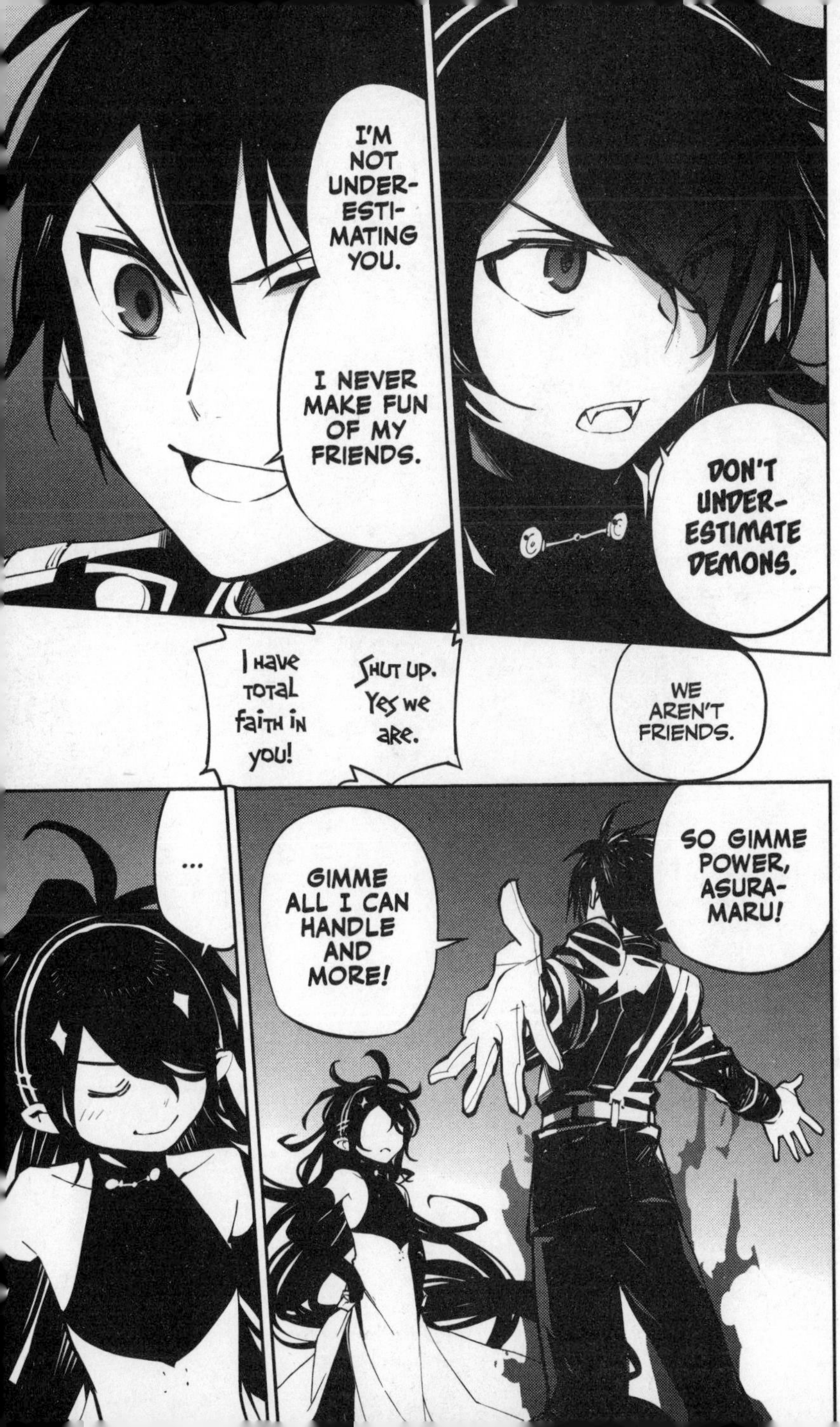
DON'T UNDER-ESTIMATE DEMONS.
I'M NOT UNDER-ESTI-MATING YOU.
I NEVER MAKE FUN OF MY FRIENDS.
WE AREN'T FRIENDS.
SHUT UP. YES WE ARE.
I HAVE TOTAL FAITH IN YOU!
SO GIMME POWER, ASURA-MARU!
GIMME ALL I CAN HANDLE AND MORE!
...

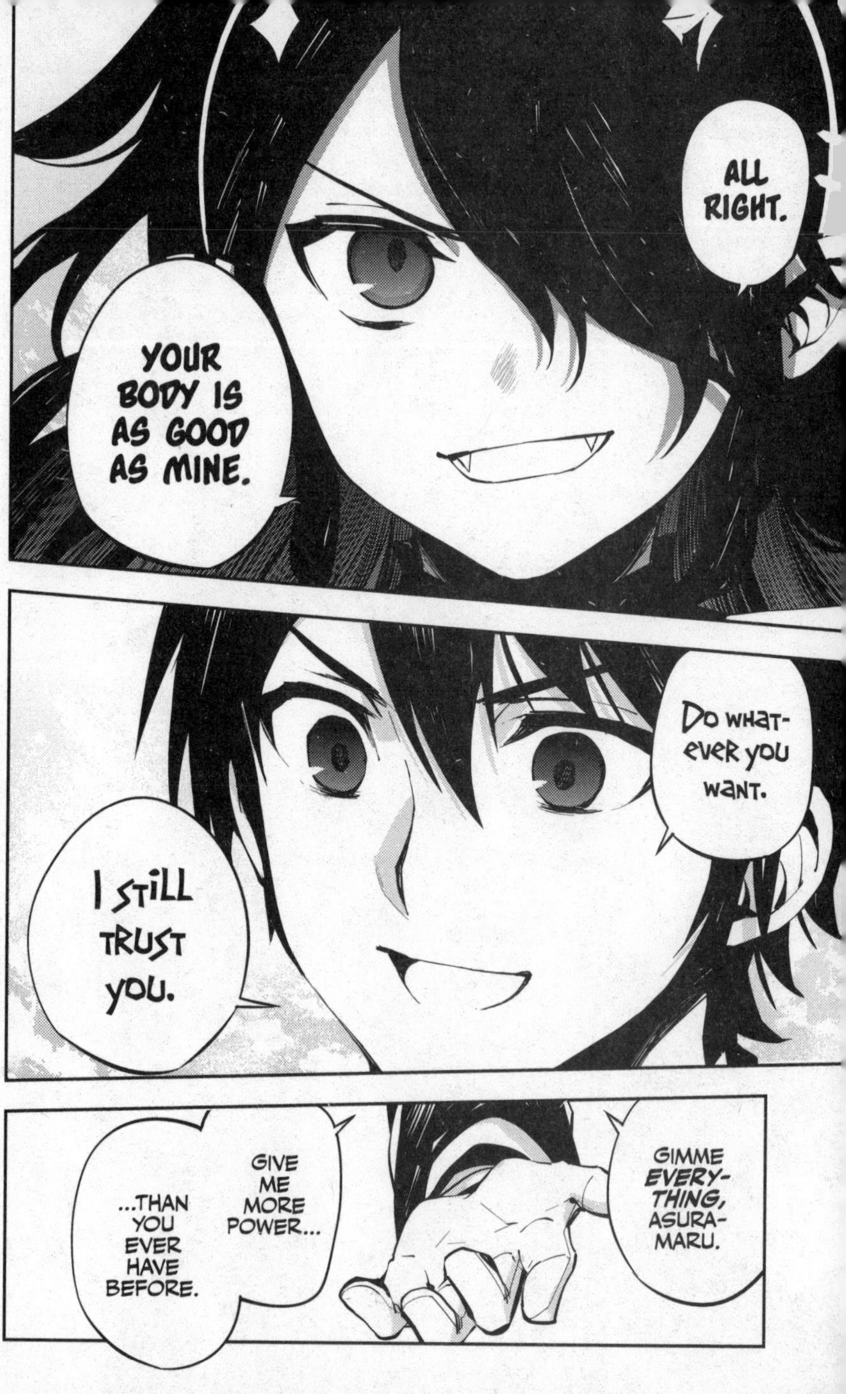
ALL RIGHT.
YOUR BODY IS AS GOOD AS MINE.
Do whatever you want.
I still trust you.
GIMME EVERYTHING, ASURA-MARU.
GIVE ME MORE POWER...
...THAN YOU EVER HAVE BEFORE.

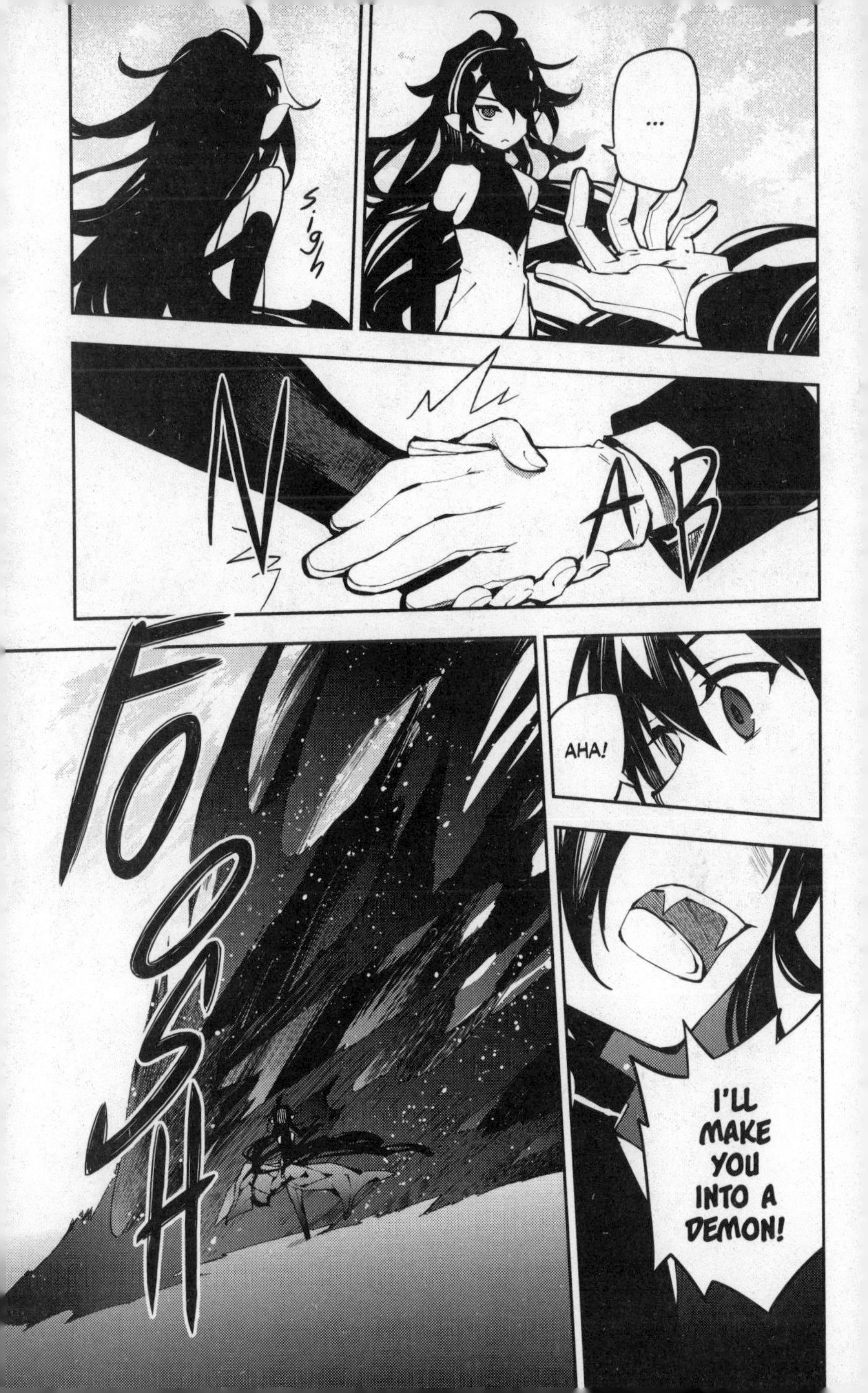
...
sigh
NAB
AHA!
I'LL MAKE YOU INTO A DEMON!
FOOSH

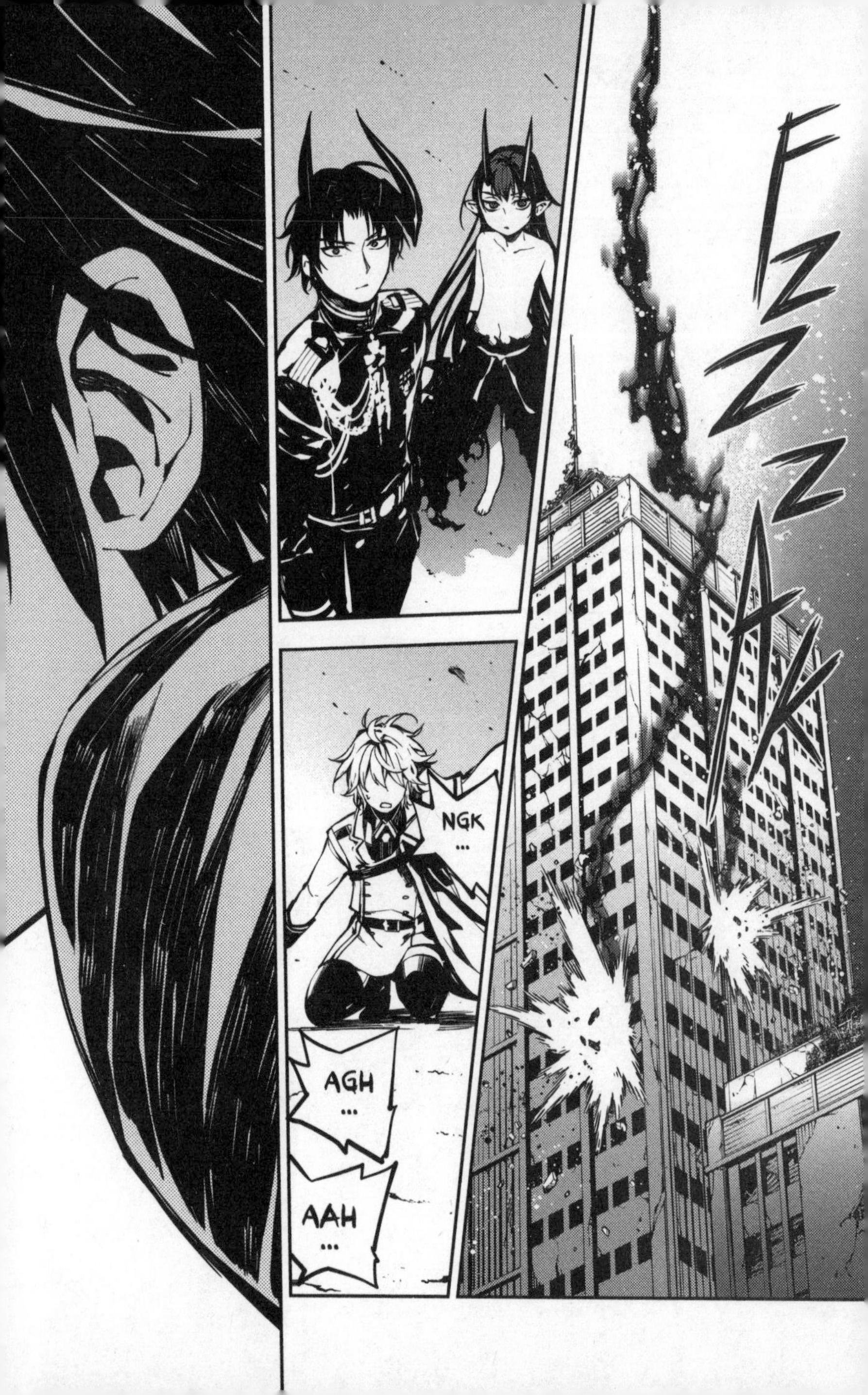
FZZZAK
NGK...
AGH...
AAH...

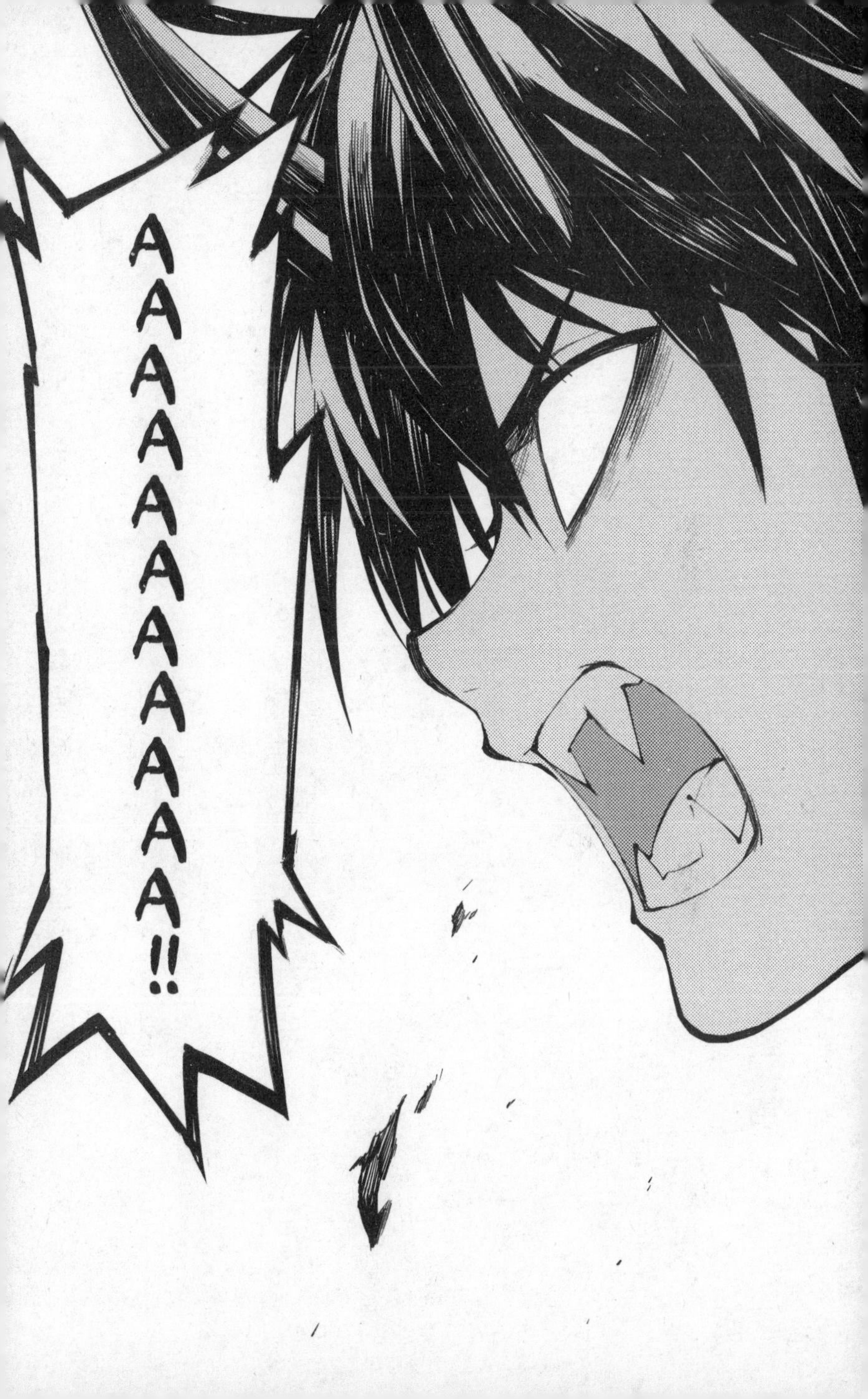
AAAAAAAAAAA!!

Seraph of the End
—VAMPIRE REIGN—

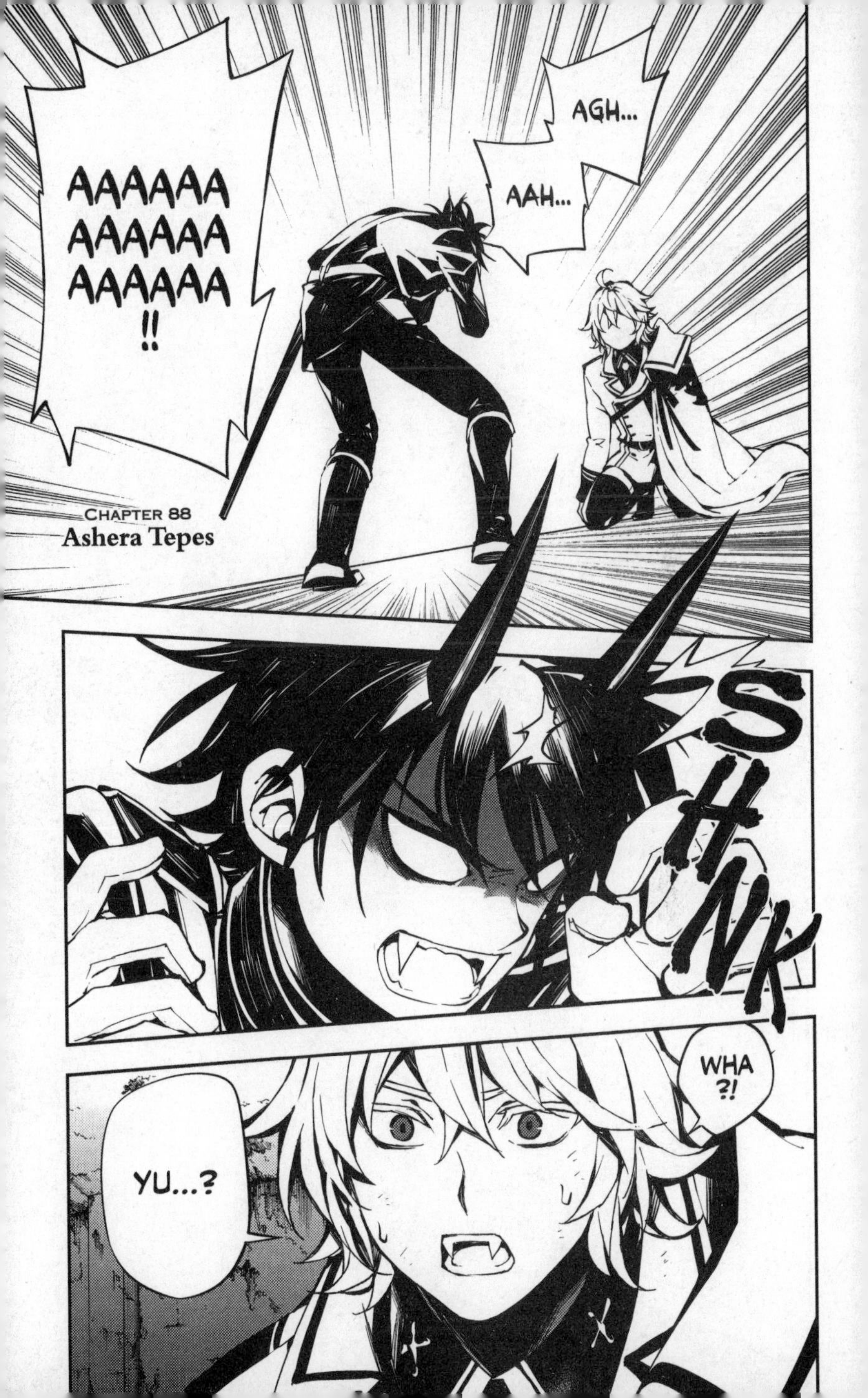
AGH...
AAH...
AAAAAA AAAAAA AAAAAA !!
CHAPTER 88
Ashera Tepes
SHINK
WHA ?!
YU...?

CHAPTER 88 Ashera Tepes

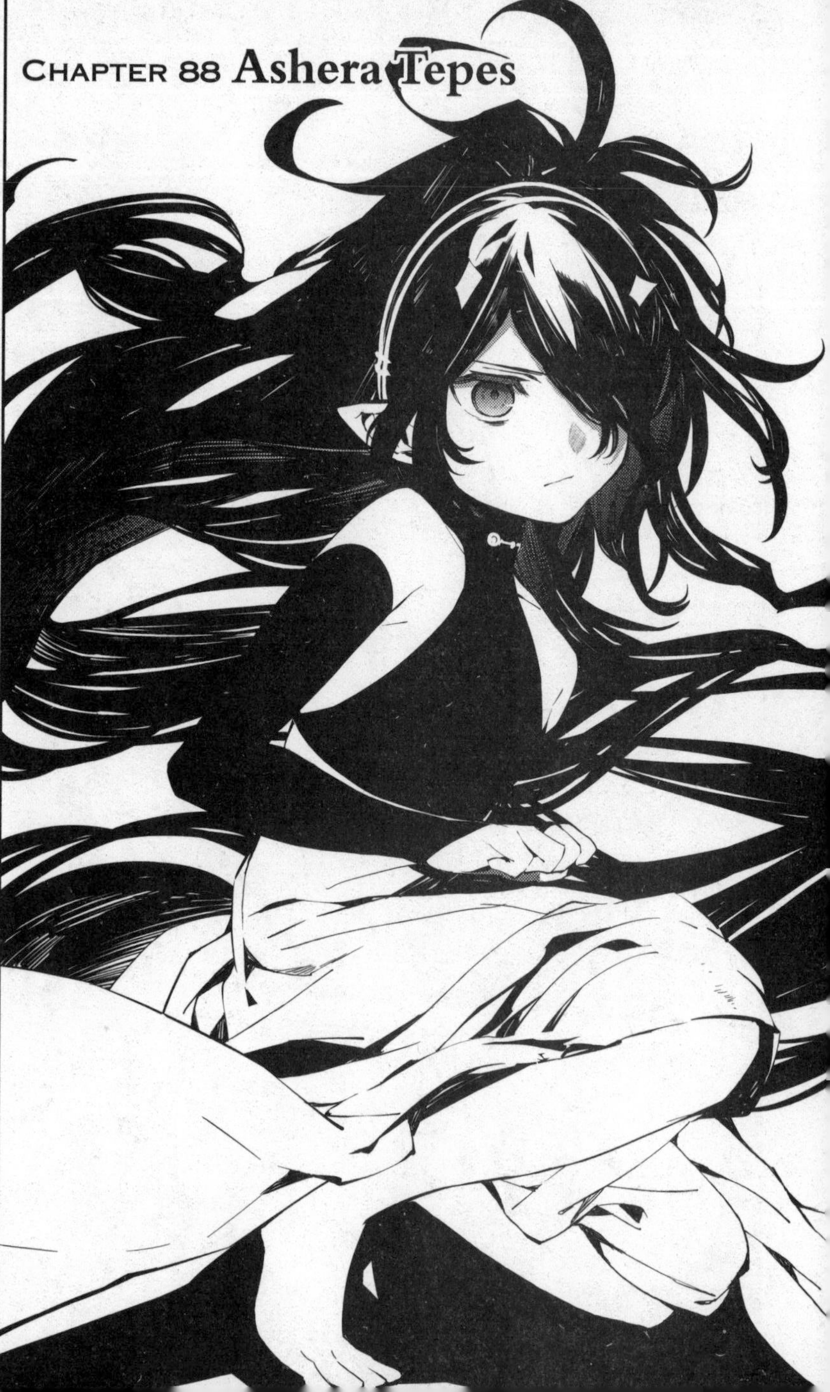

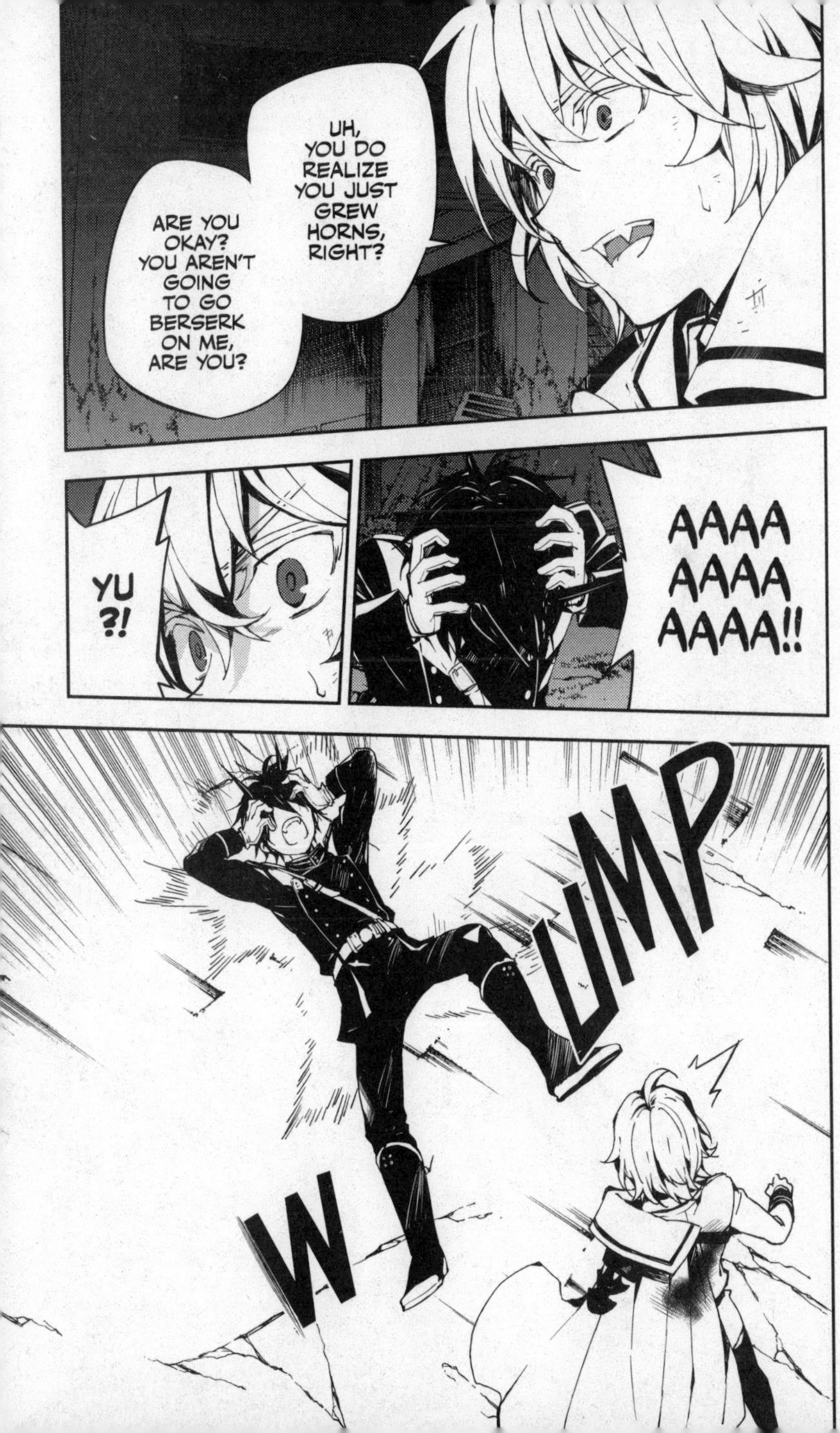
UH, YOU DO REALIZE YOU JUST GREW HORNS, RIGHT?
ARE YOU OKAY? YOU AREN'T GOING TO GO BERSERK ON ME, ARE YOU?
AAAAAAAAAAAA!!
YU ?!
WUMP

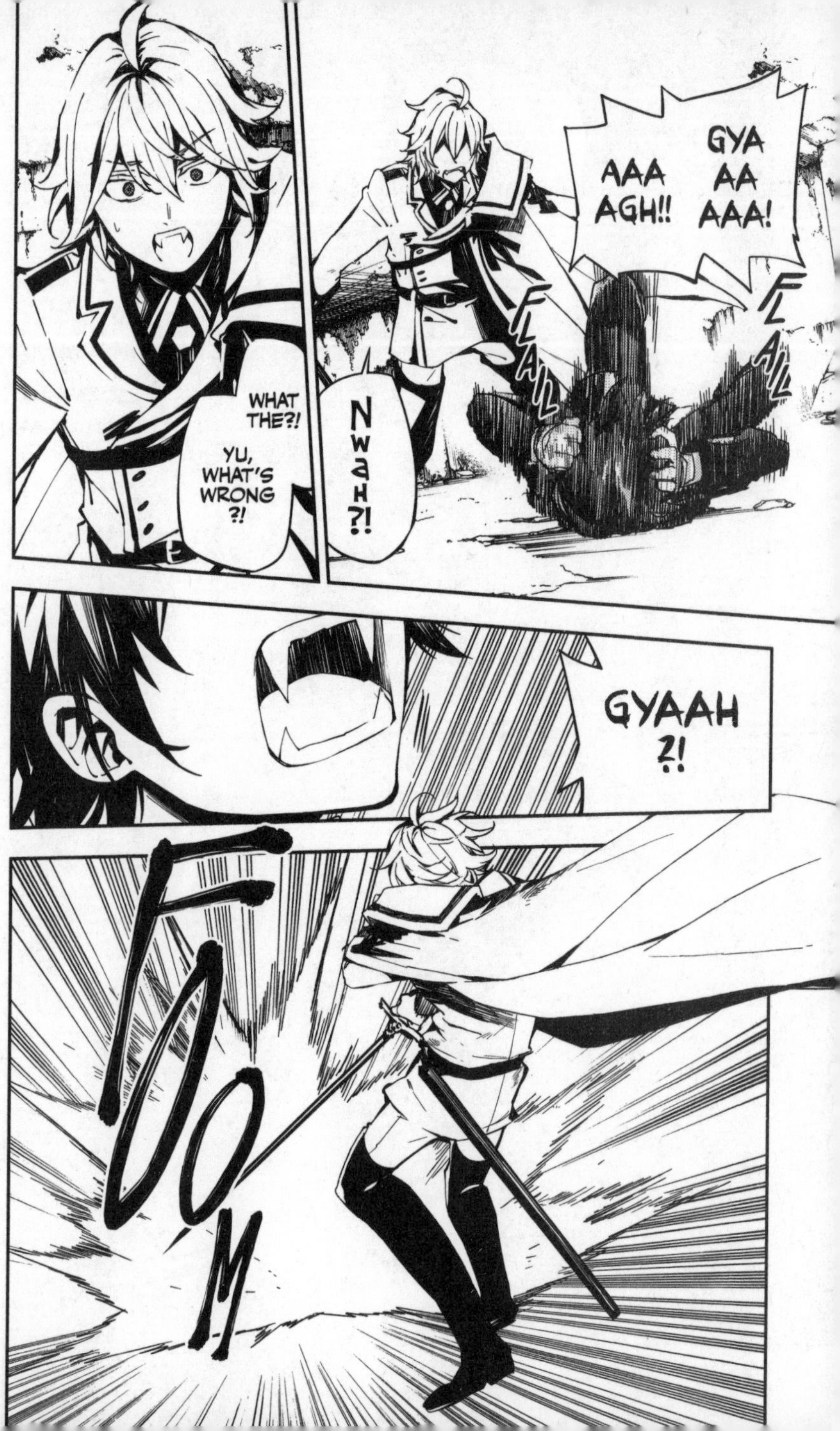
GYA AA AAA!
AAA AGH!!
FLAIL
FLAIL
Nwah?!
WHAT THE?!
YU, WHAT'S WRONG?!
GYAAH?!
FWOOM

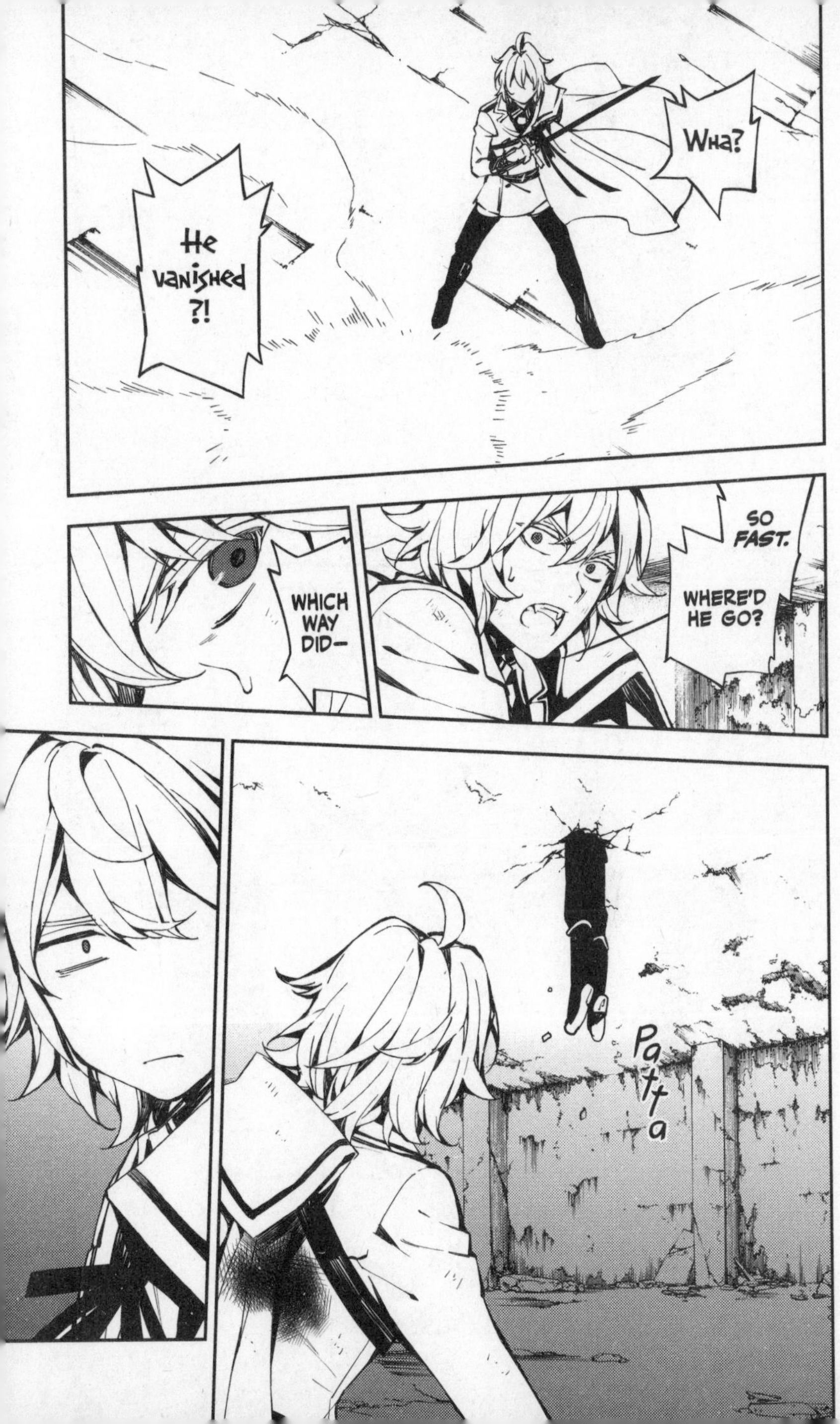
Wha?
He vanished ?!
SO FAST.
WHERE'D HE GO?
WHICH WAY DID-
Patta

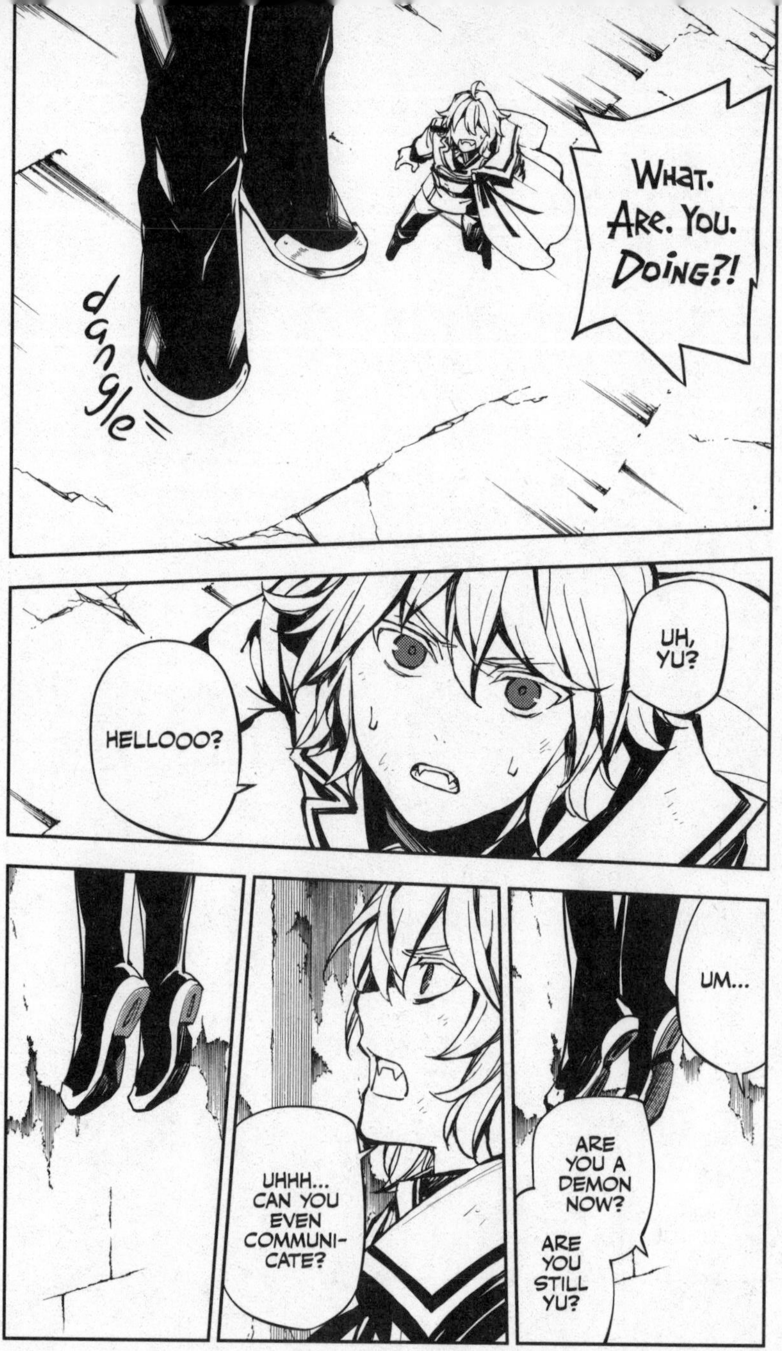
What. Are. You. Doing?!
dangle
UH, YU?
HELLOOO?
UM...
ARE YOU A DEMON NOW?
ARE YOU STILL YU?
UHHH... CAN YOU EVEN COMMUNICATE?

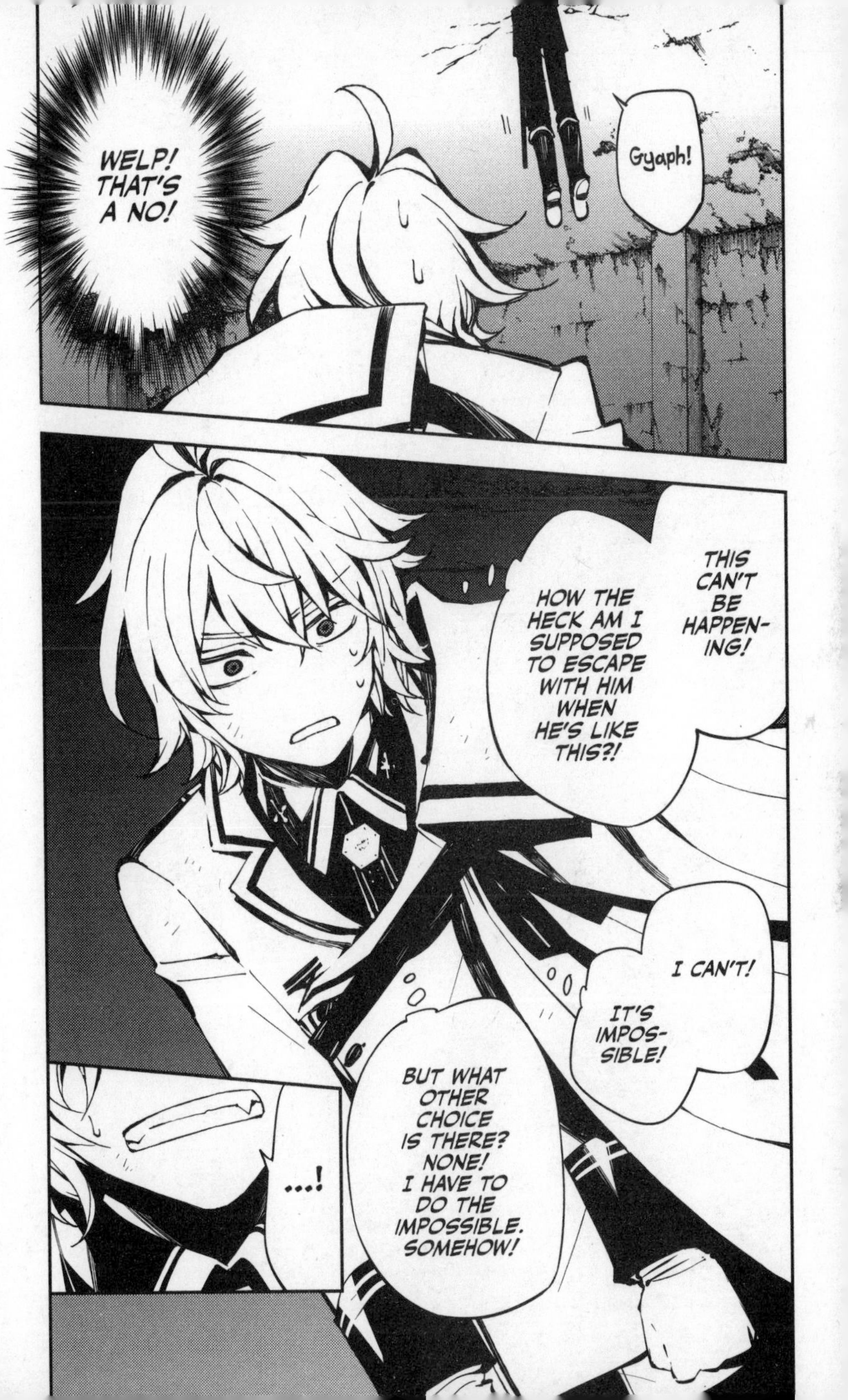
Gyaph!
WELP! THAT'S A NO!
THIS CAN'T BE HAPPENING!
HOW THE HECK AM I SUPPOSED TO ESCAPE WITH HIM WHEN HE'S LIKE THIS?!
I CAN'T!
IT'S IMPOSSIBLE!
BUT WHAT OTHER CHOICE IS THERE? NONE! I HAVE TO DO THE IMPOSSIBLE. SOMEHOW!
...!

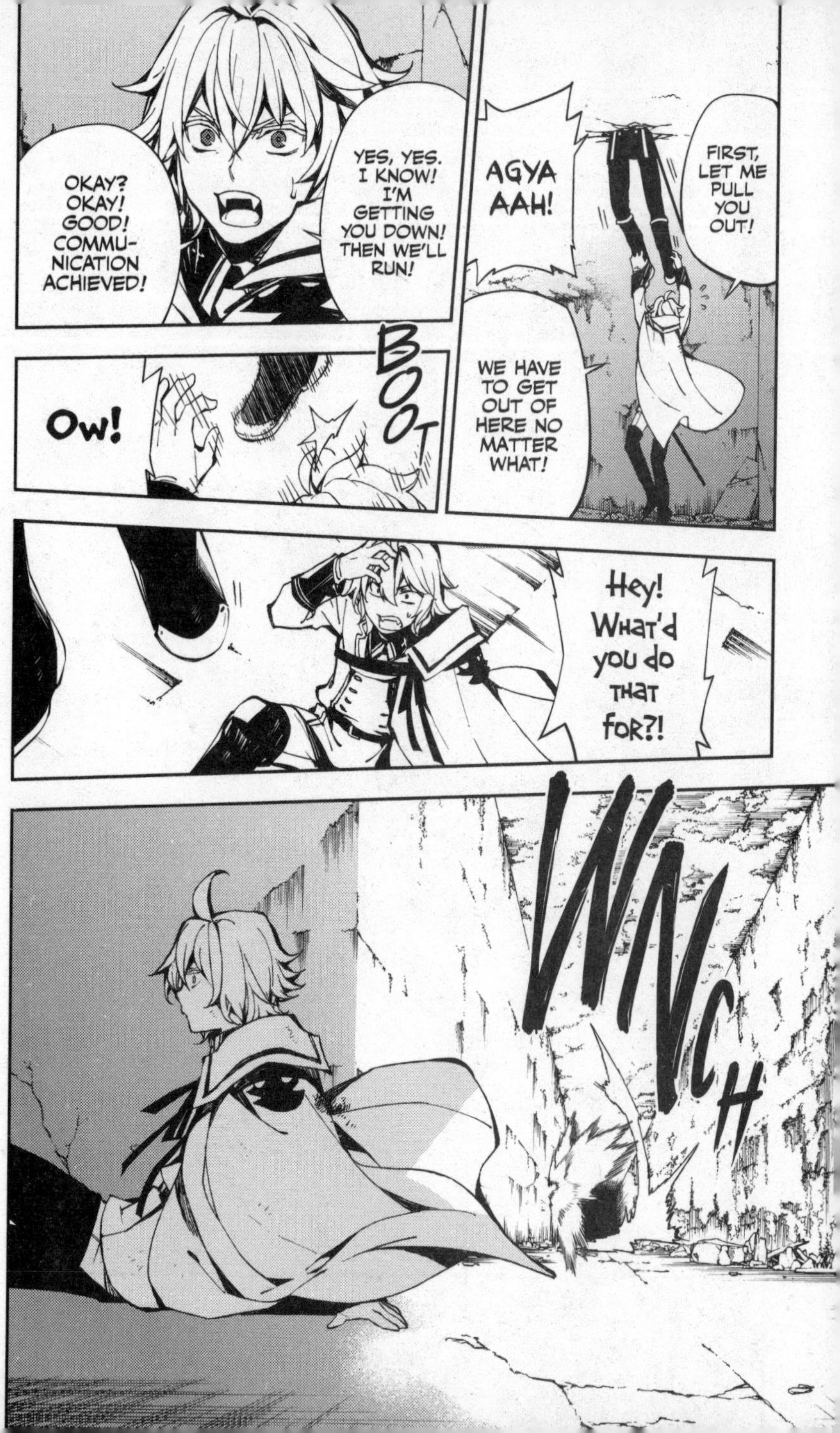

FIRST, LET ME PULL YOU OUT!
AGYA AAH!
WE HAVE TO GET OUT OF HERE NO MATTER WHAT!
YES, YES. I KNOW! I'M GETTING YOU DOWN! THEN WE'LL RUN!
OKAY? OKAY! GOOD! COMMUNICATION ACHIEVED!
BOOT
Ow!
Hey! What'd you do that for?!
WNCH

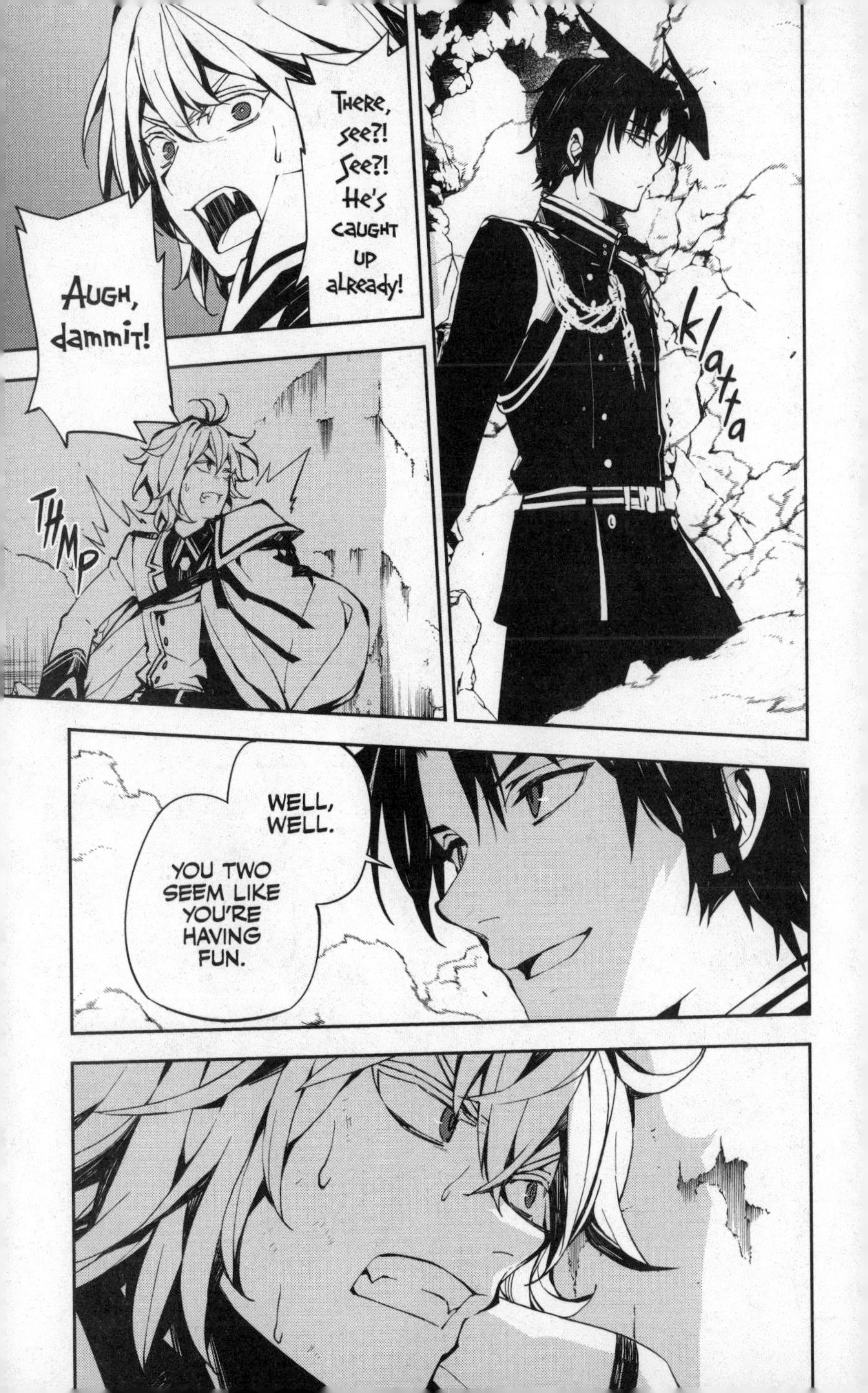
klatta
There, see?! See?! He's caught up already!
Augh, dammit!
THMP
WELL, WELL.
YOU TWO SEEM LIKE YOU'RE HAVING FUN.

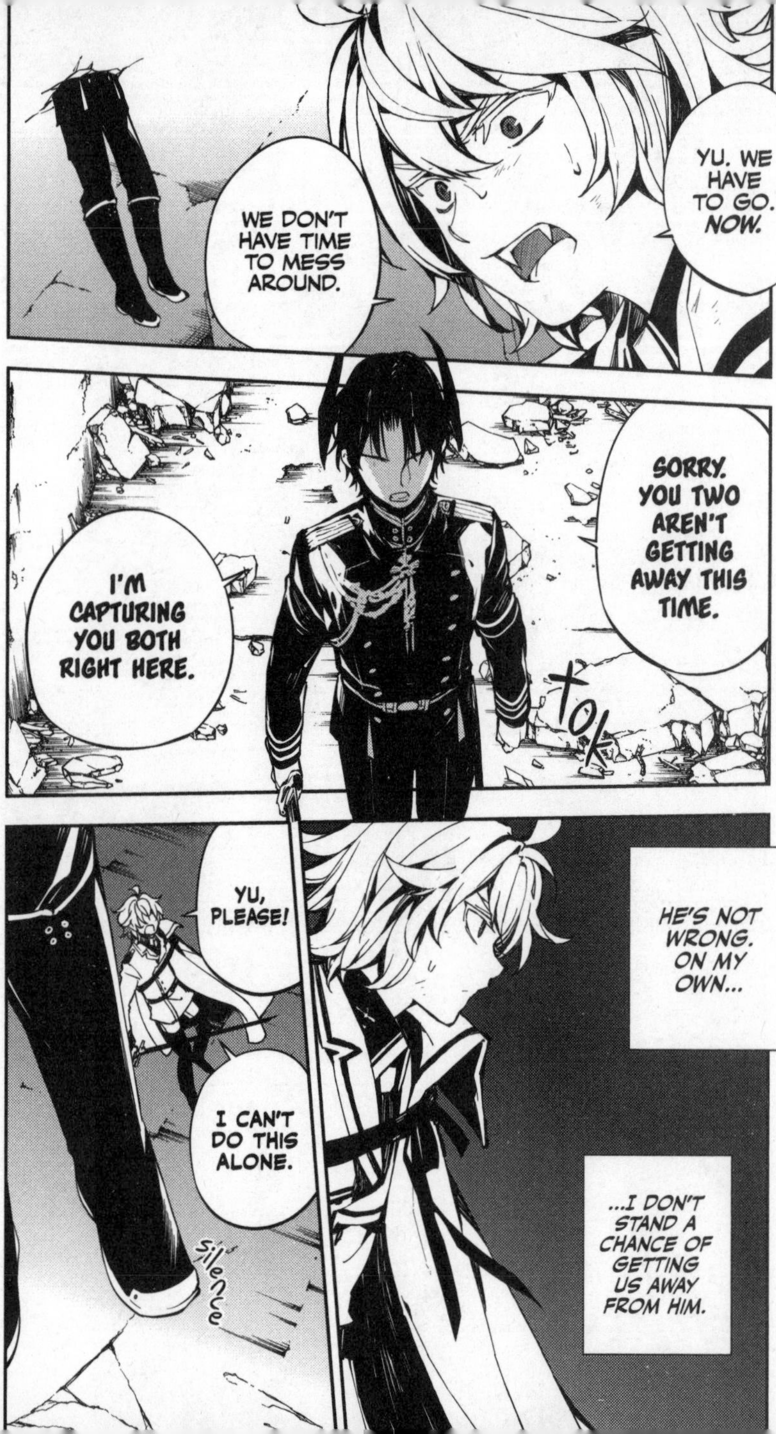
YU. WE HAVE TO GO. NOW.
WE DON'T HAVE TIME TO MESS AROUND.
SORRY. YOU TWO AREN'T GETTING AWAY THIS TIME.
TOK
I'M CAPTURING YOU BOTH RIGHT HERE.
HE'S NOT WRONG. ON MY OWN...
YU, PLEASE!
I CAN'T DO THIS ALONE.
...I DON'T STAND A CHANCE OF GETTING US AWAY FROM HIM.
silence

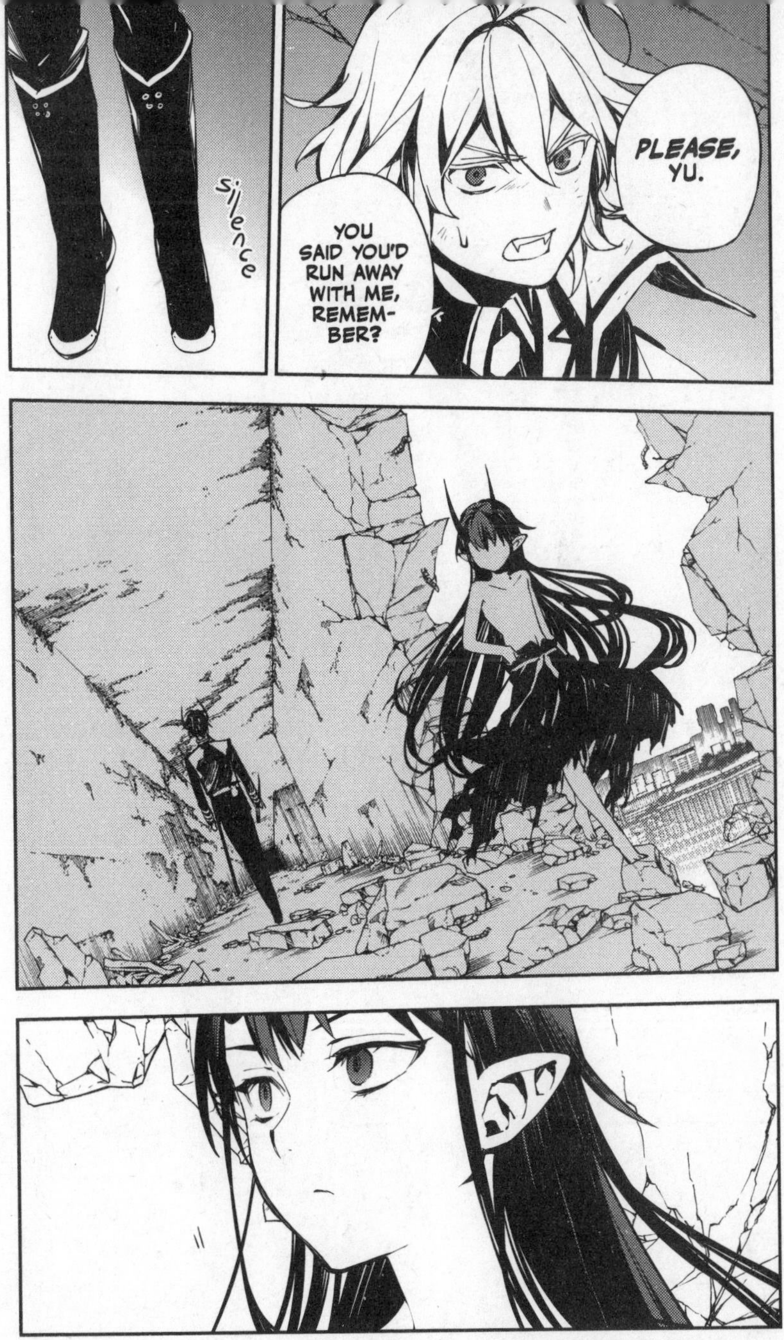
PLEASE, YU.
YOU SAID YOU'D RUN AWAY WITH ME, REMEMBER?
silence

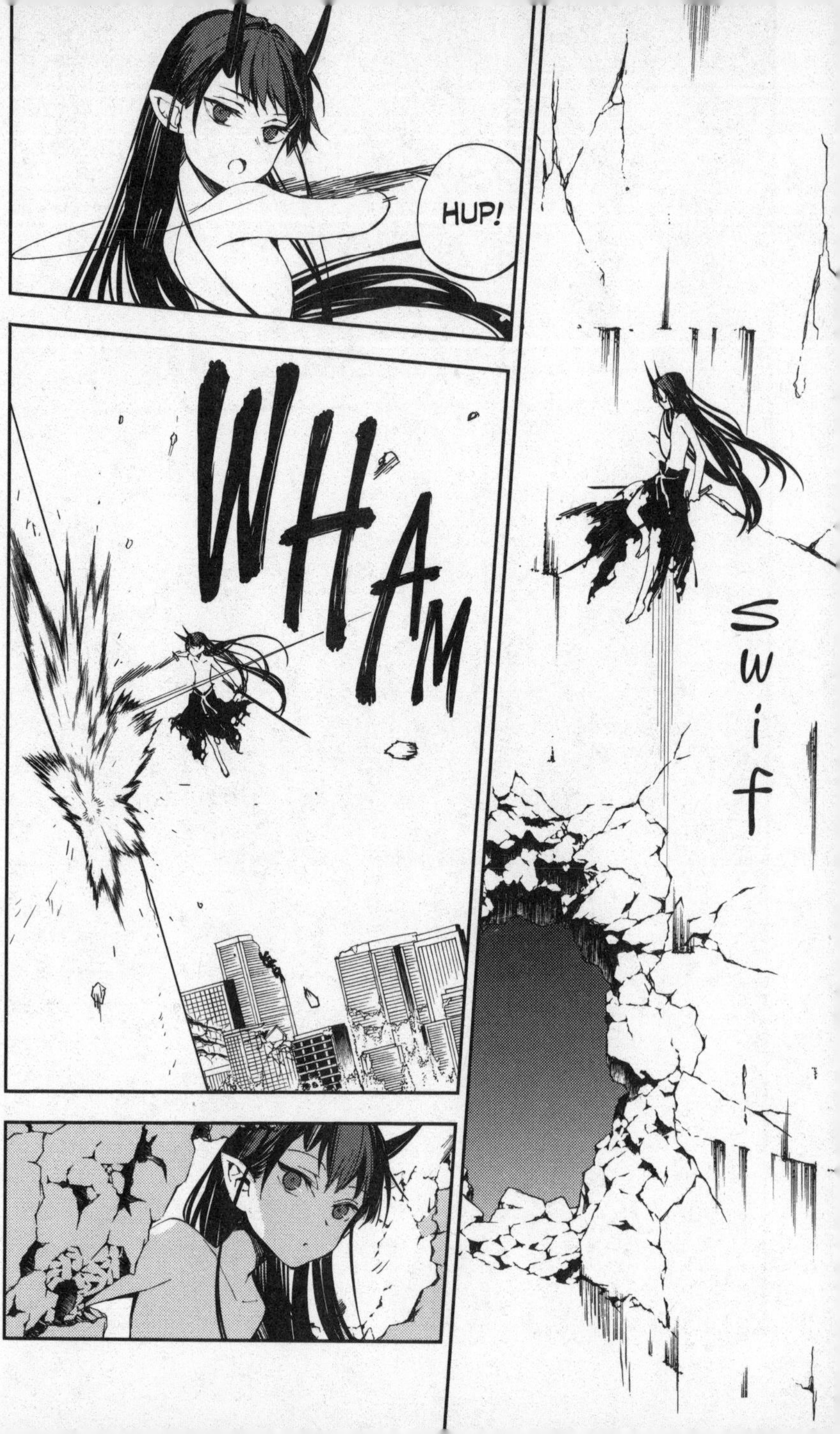
swif
HUP!
WHAM

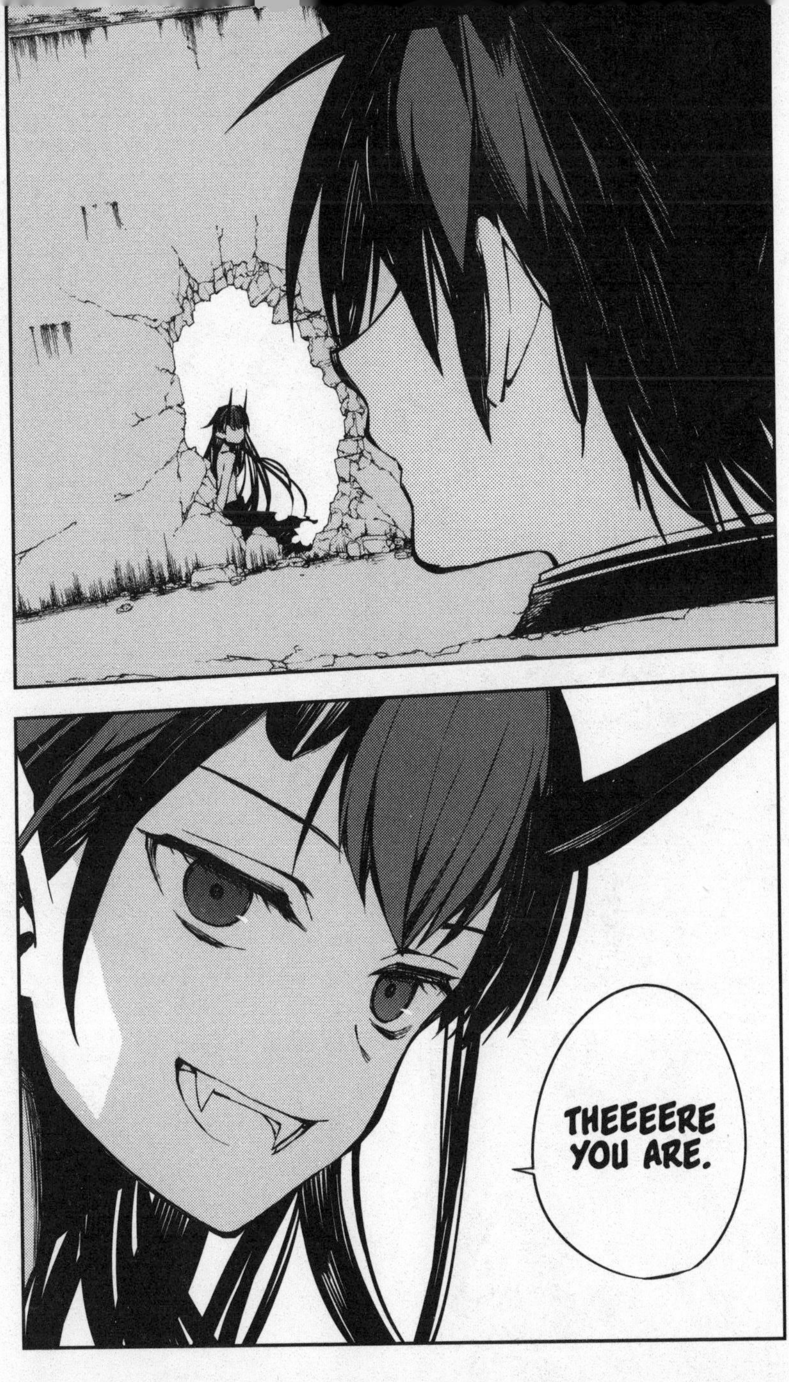
THEEEERE YOU ARE.

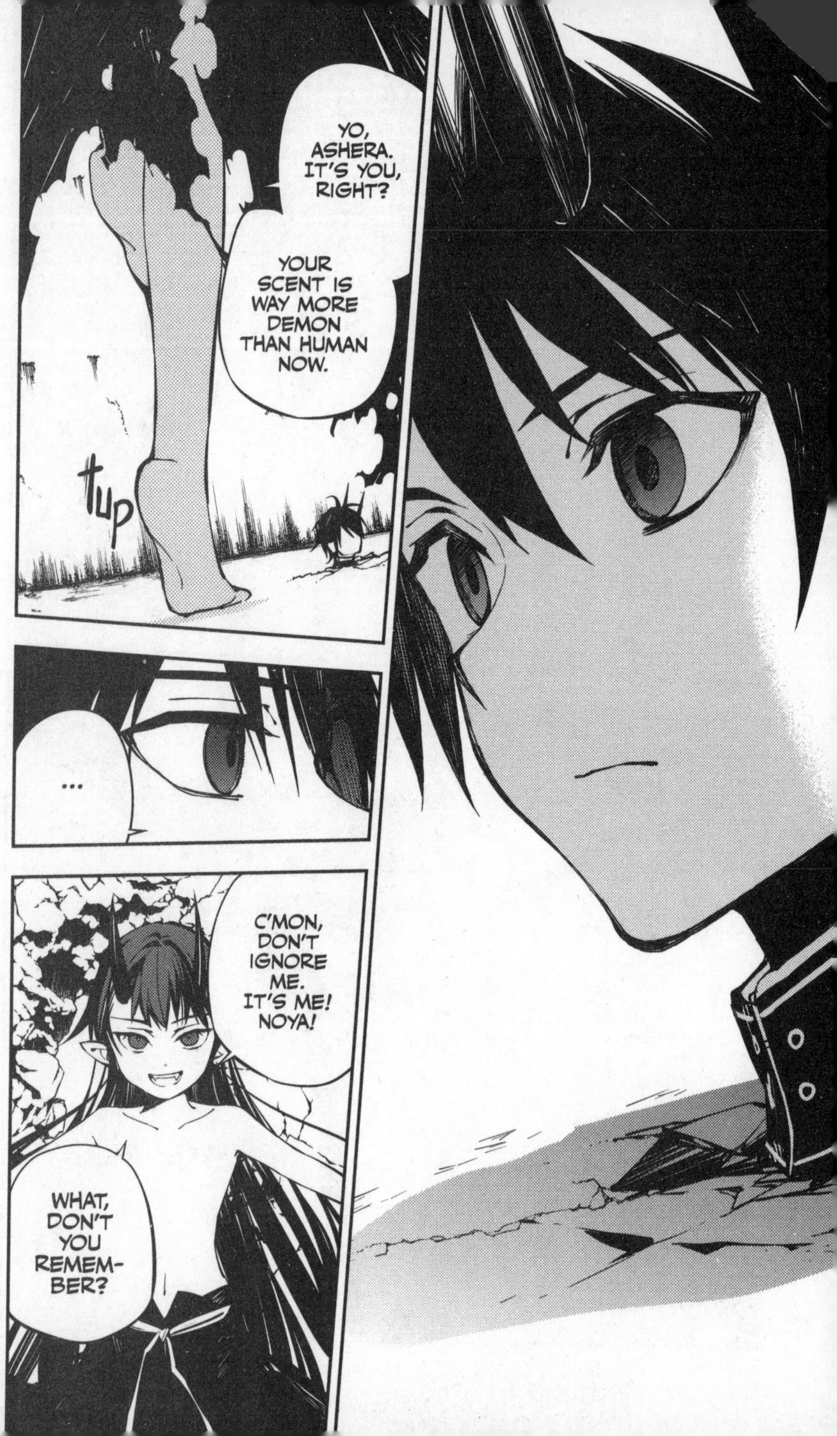
YO, ASHERA. IT'S YOU, RIGHT?
YOUR SCENT IS WAY MORE DEMON THAN HUMAN NOW.
TUP
...
C'MON, DON'T IGNORE ME. IT'S ME! NOYA!
WHAT, DON'T YOU REMEM-BER?

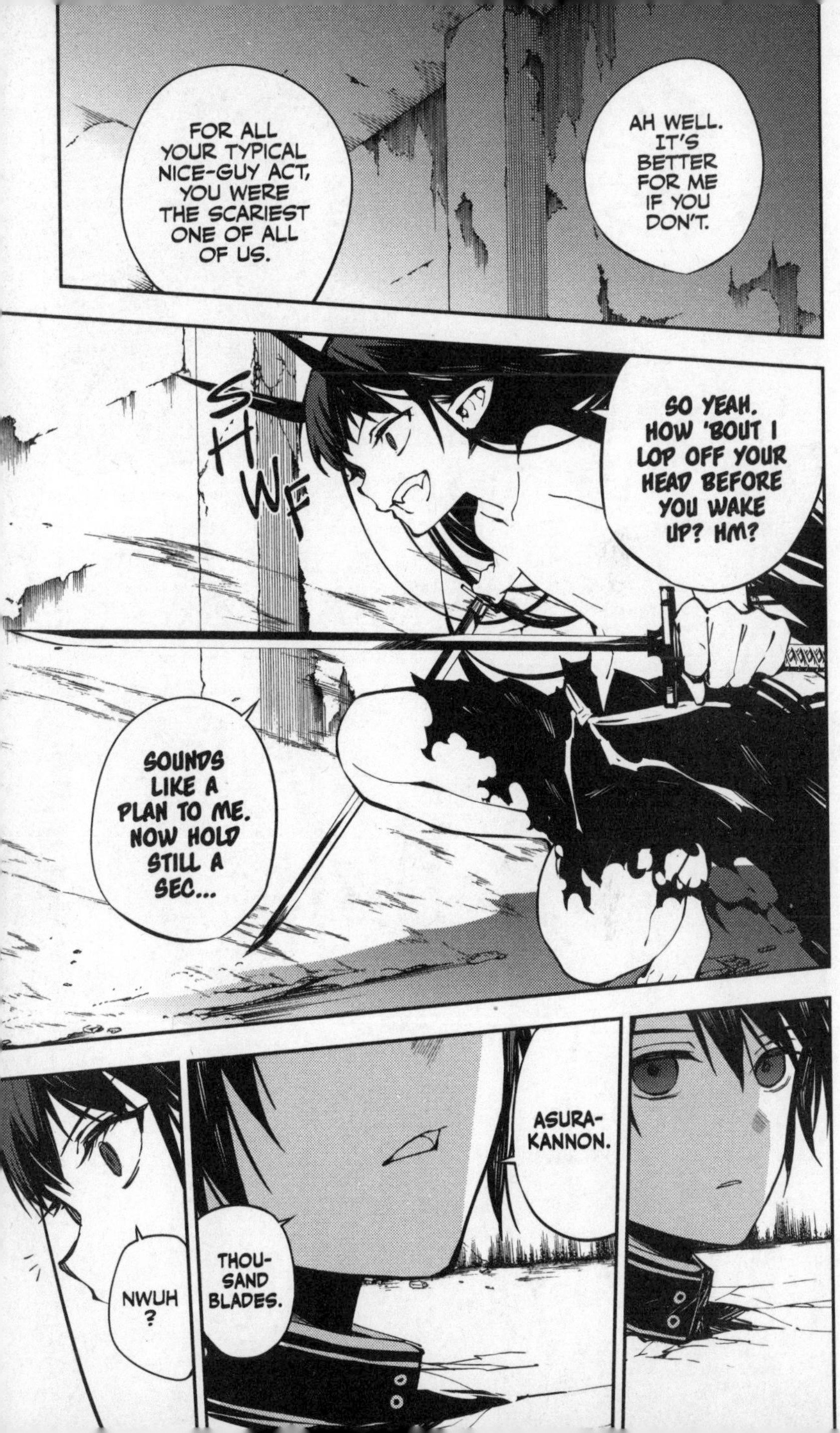
AH WELL. IT'S BETTER FOR ME IF YOU DON'T.
FOR ALL YOUR TYPICAL NICE-GUY ACT, YOU WERE THE SCARIEST ONE OF ALL OF US.
SO YEAH. HOW 'BOUT I LOP OFF YOUR HEAD BEFORE YOU WAKE UP? HM?
SHWF
SOUNDS LIKE A PLAN TO ME. NOW HOLD STILL A SEC...
ASURA-KANNON.
THOUSAND BLADES.
NWUH?

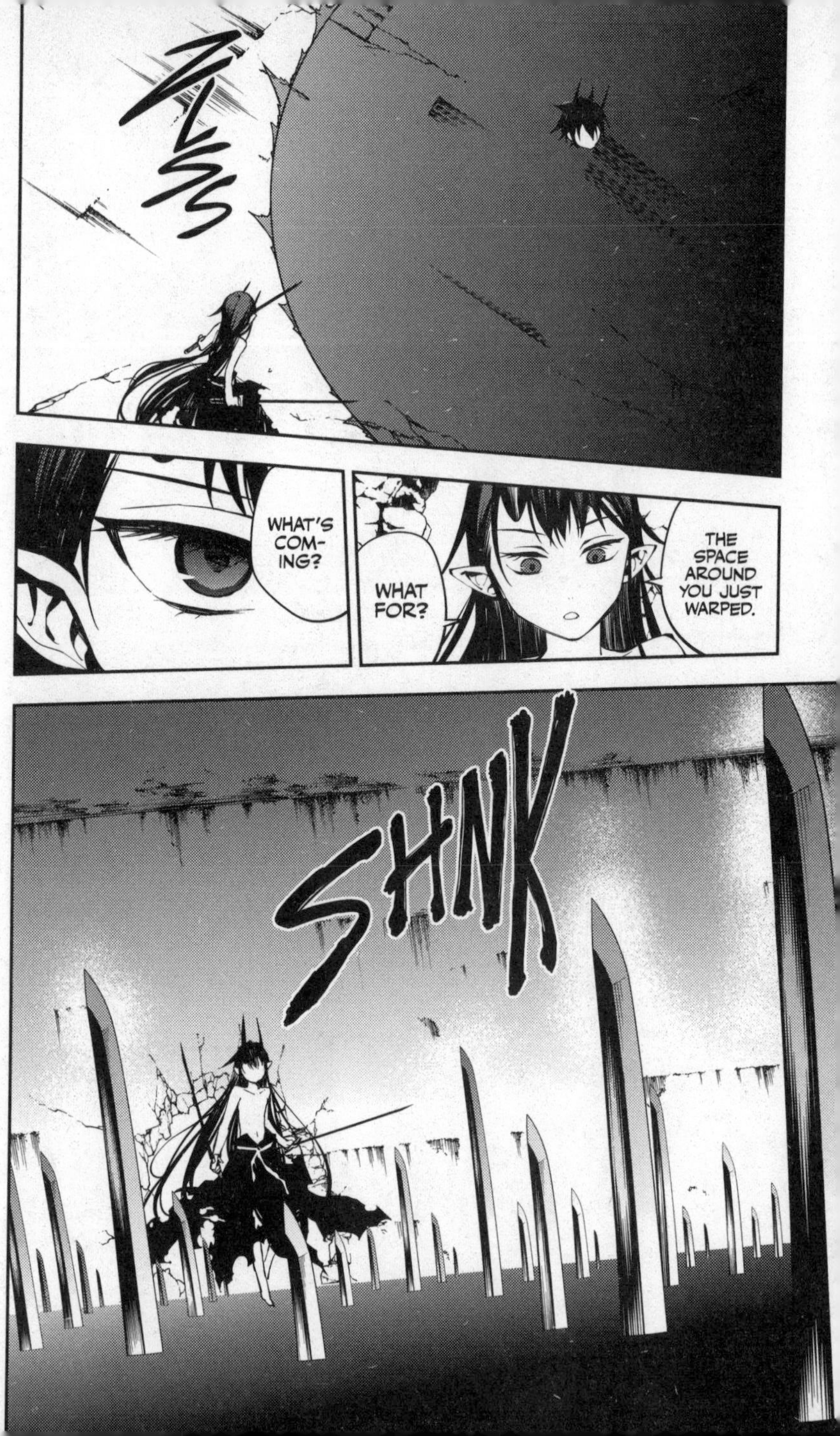
THE SPACE AROUND YOU JUST WARPED.
WHAT FOR?
WHAT'S COMING?
SHNK

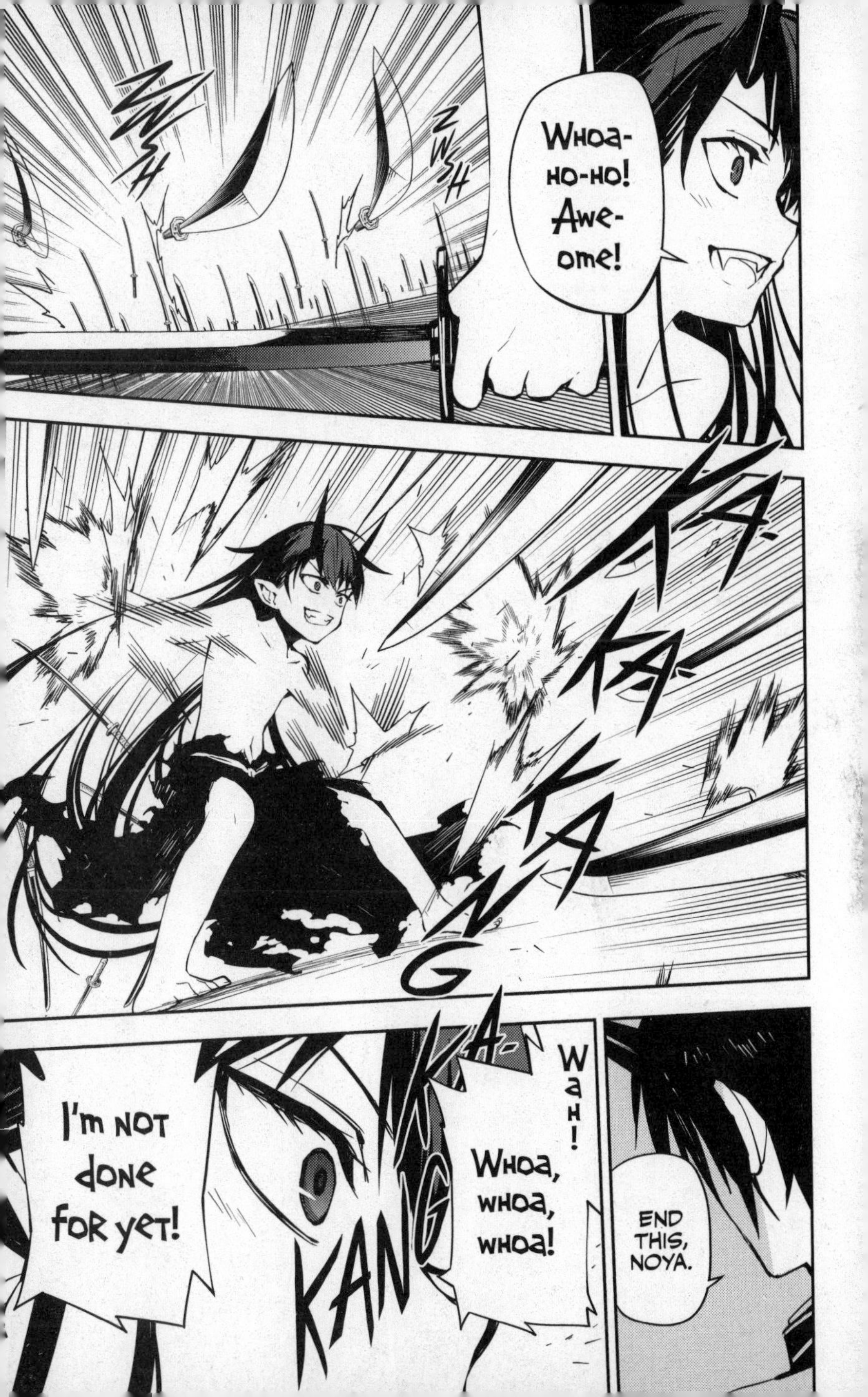
Whoa-ho-ho! Awe-ome!
ZWSH
ZWSH
KA-KA-KA-KANG
END THIS, NOYA.
WAH!
Whoa, whoa, whoa!
KA-KANG
I'm NOT done for yet!

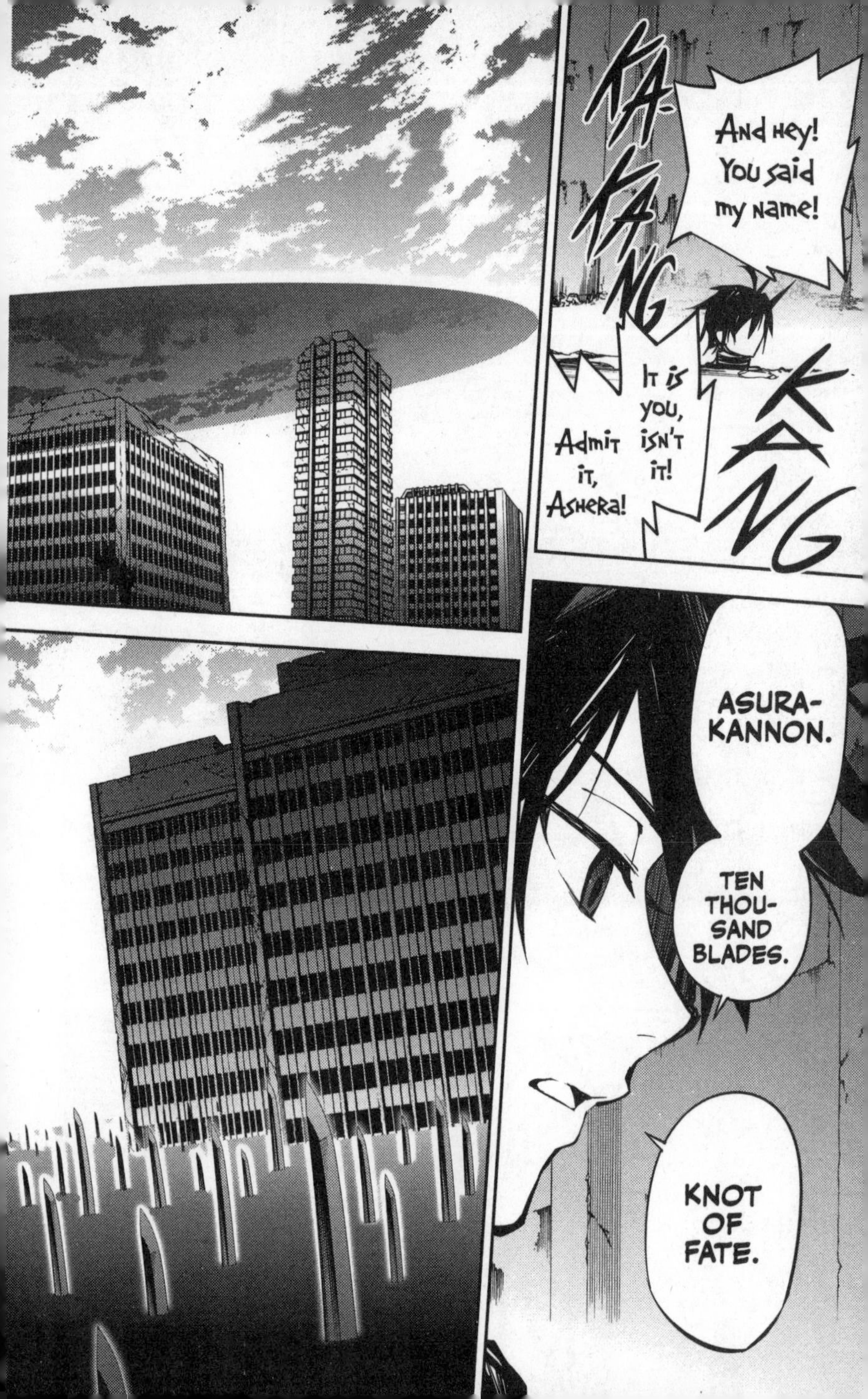
KA-KAKANG
And hey! You said my name!
It is you, isn't it!
Admit it, Ashera!
KANG
ASURA-KANNON.
TEN THOUSAND BLADES.
KNOT OF FATE.

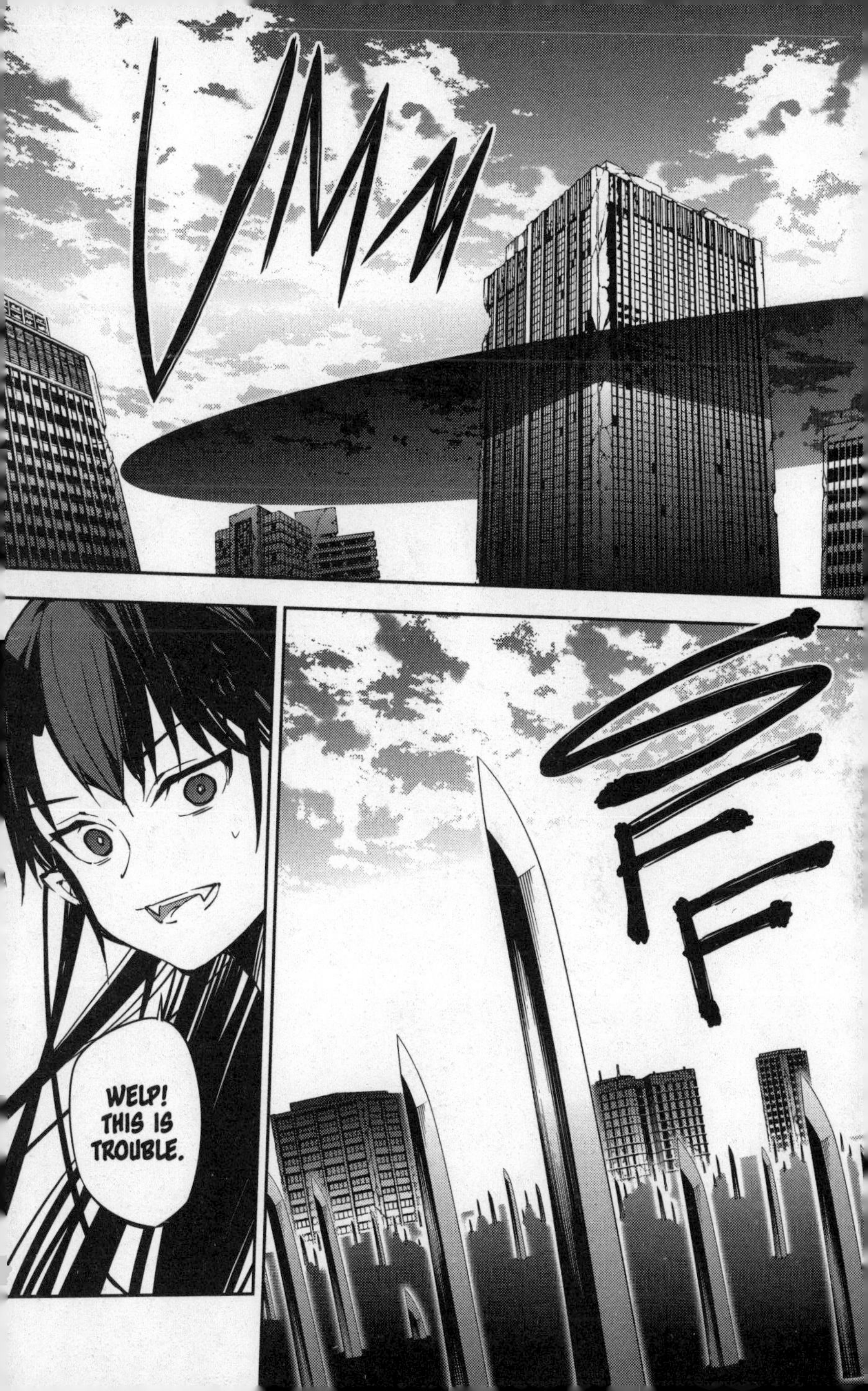
VMM
OOFF
WELP! THIS IS TROUBLE.

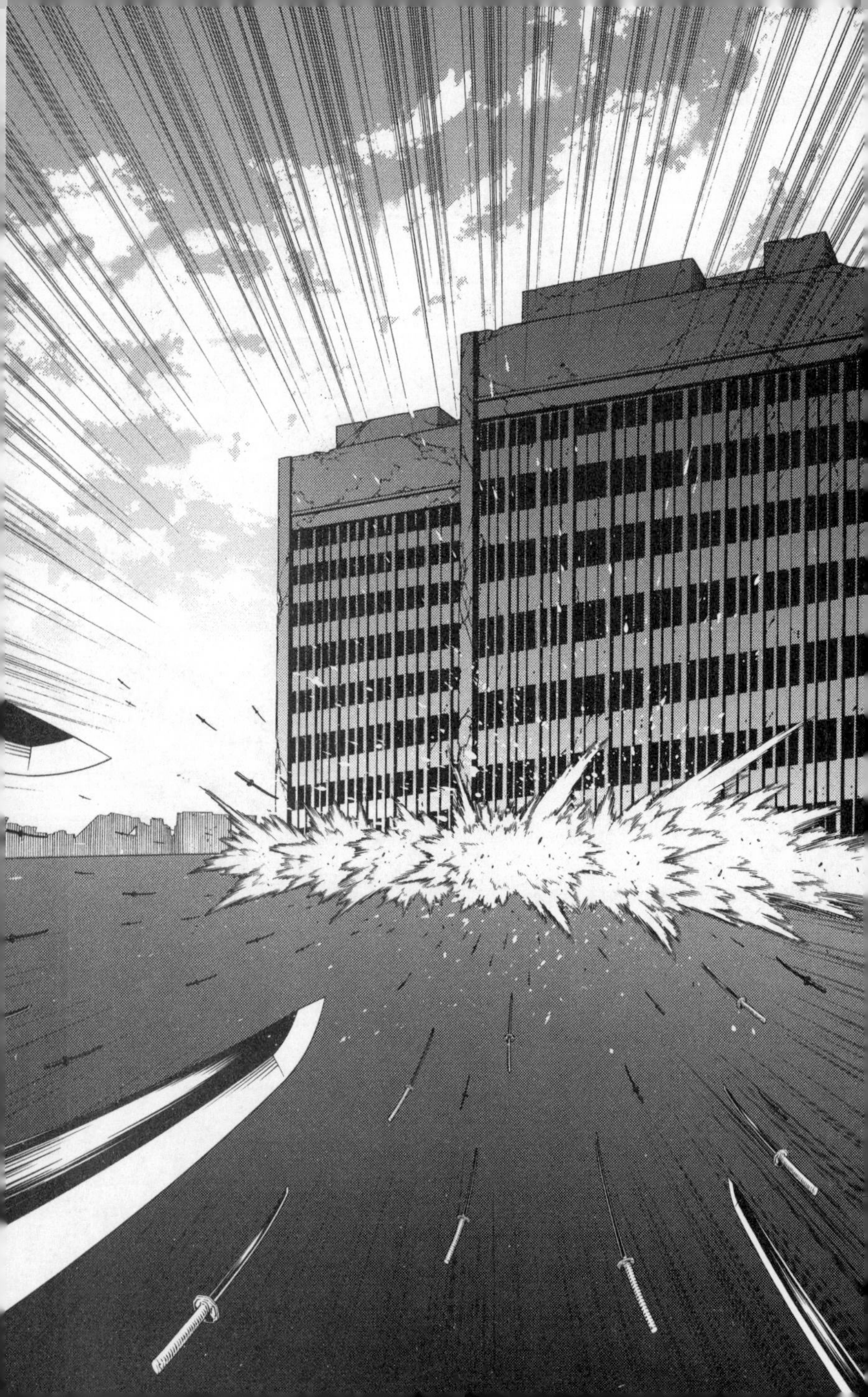

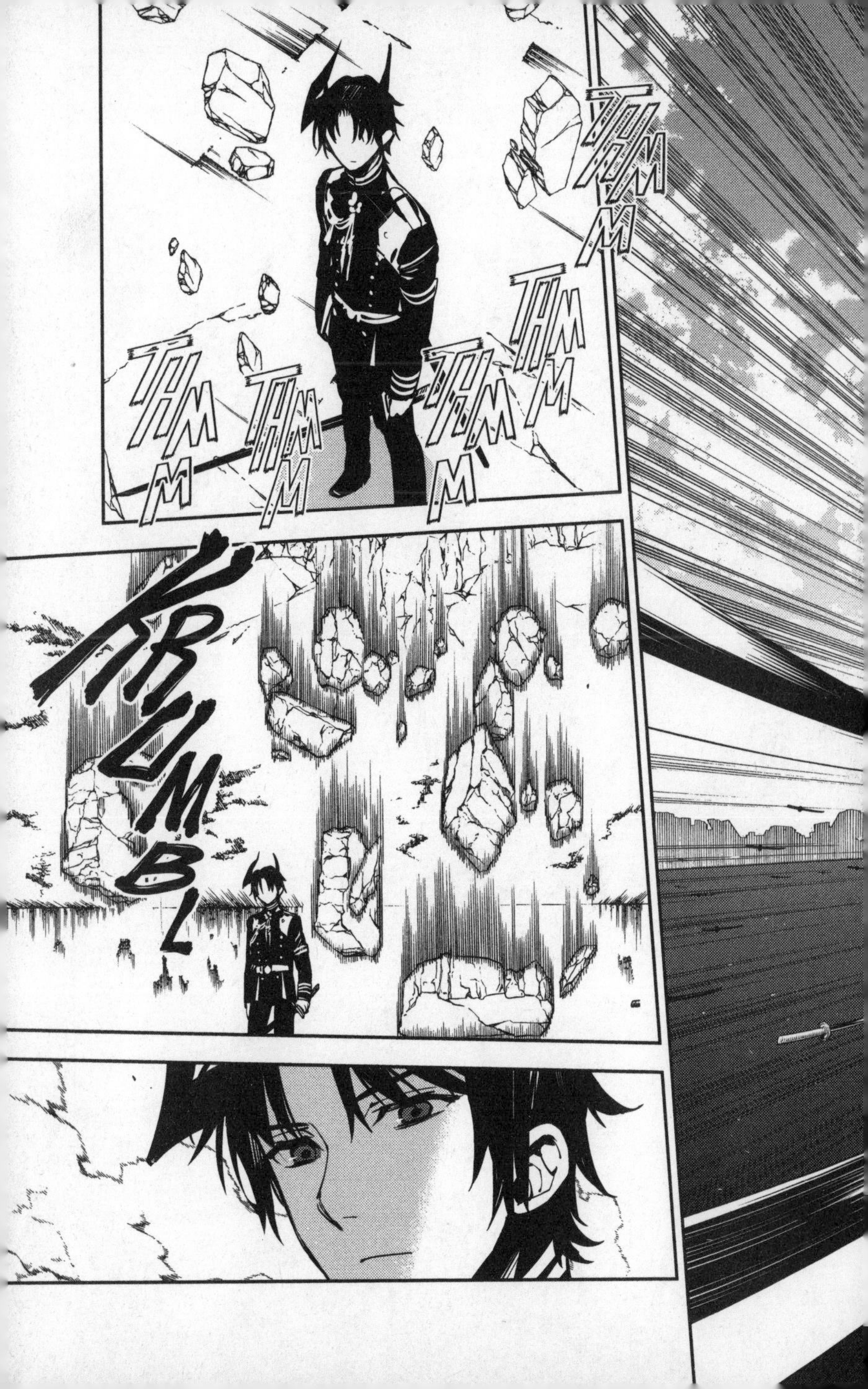
THMMM
THMMM
THMMM
THMMM
THMMM
KRUMBL

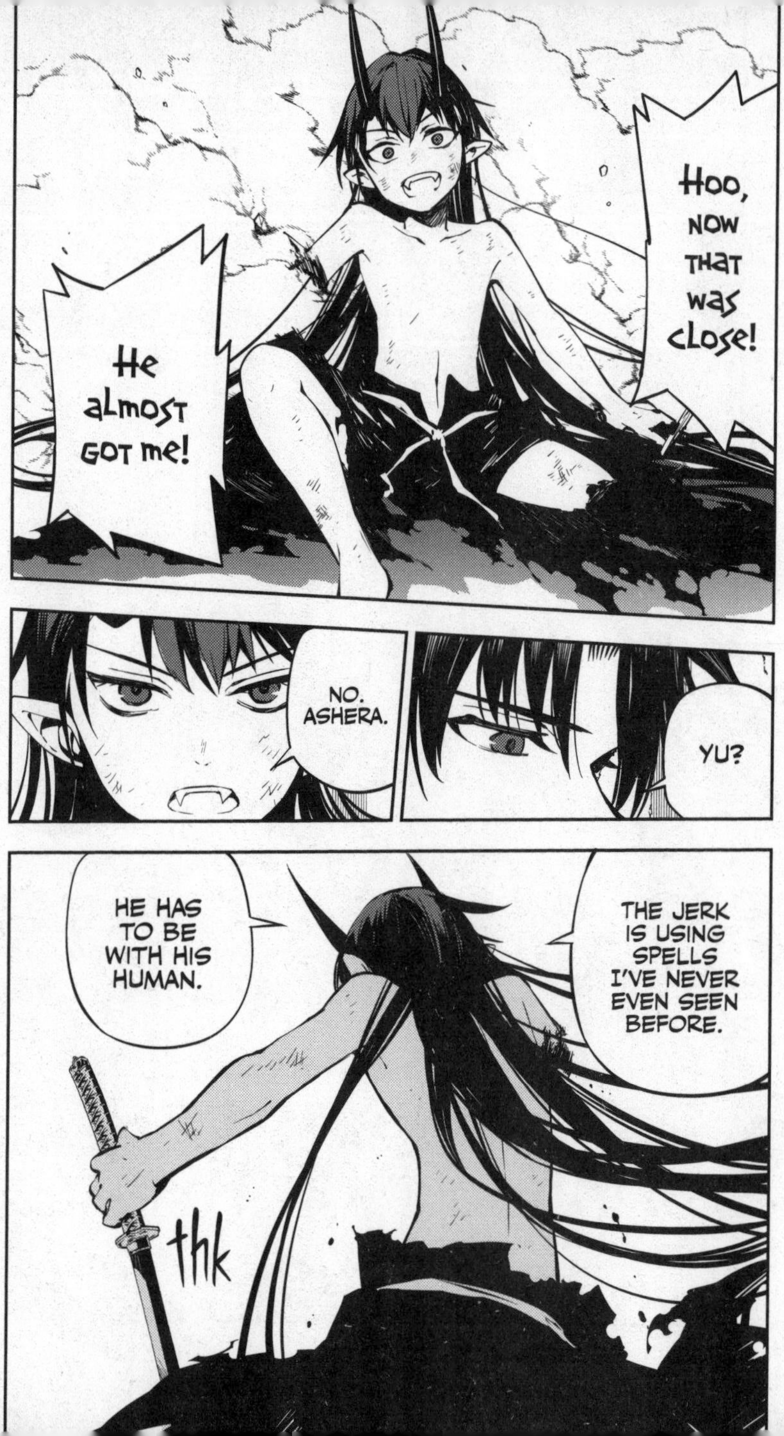
Hoo, now that was close!
He almost got me!
YU?
NO. ASHERA.
THE JERK IS USING SPELLS I'VE NEVER EVEN SEEN BEFORE.
HE HAS TO BE WITH HIS HUMAN.
thk

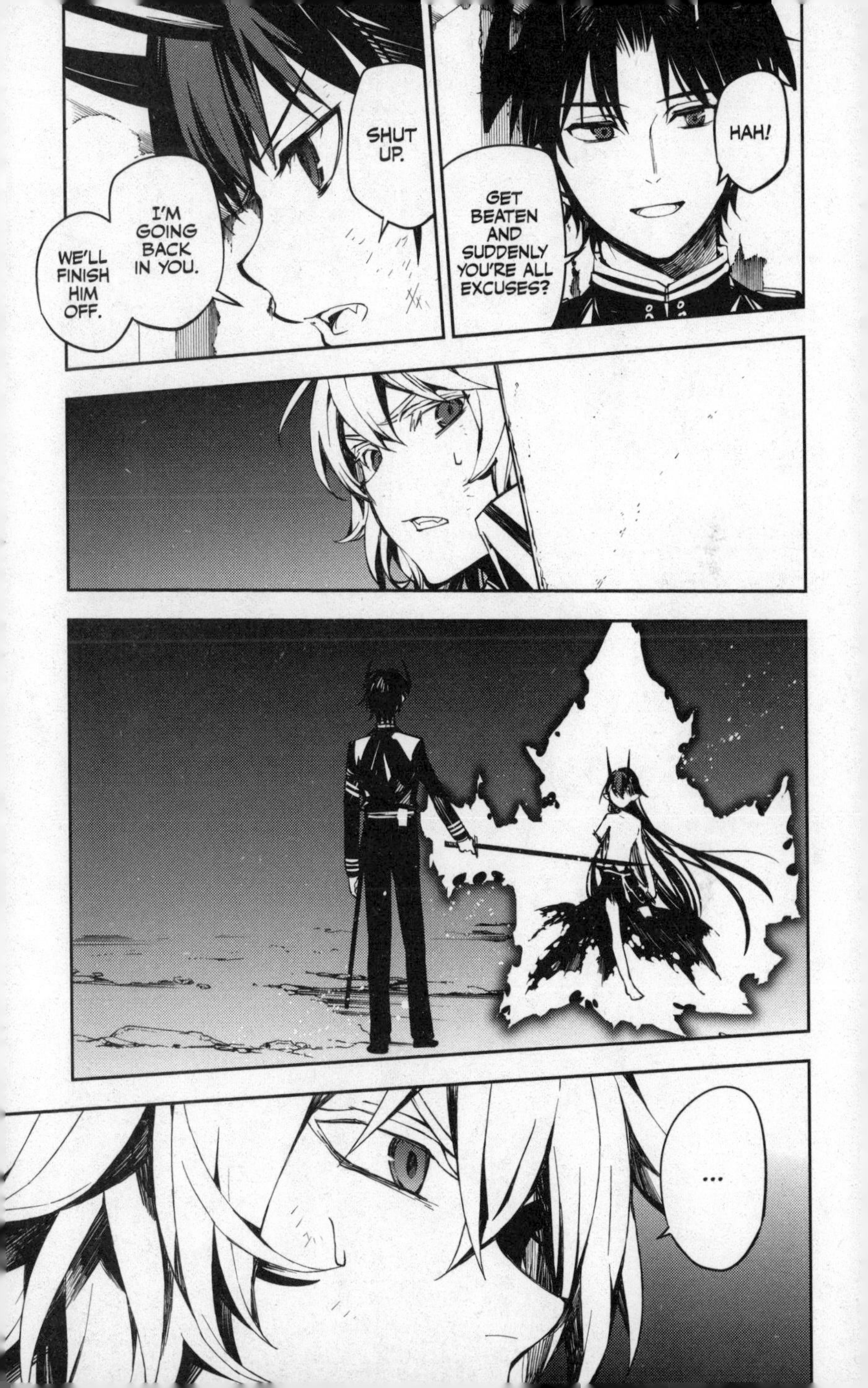
HAH!
GET BEATEN AND SUDDENLY YOU'RE ALL EXCUSES?
SHUT UP.
I'M GOING BACK IN YOU.
WE'LL FINISH HIM OFF.
...

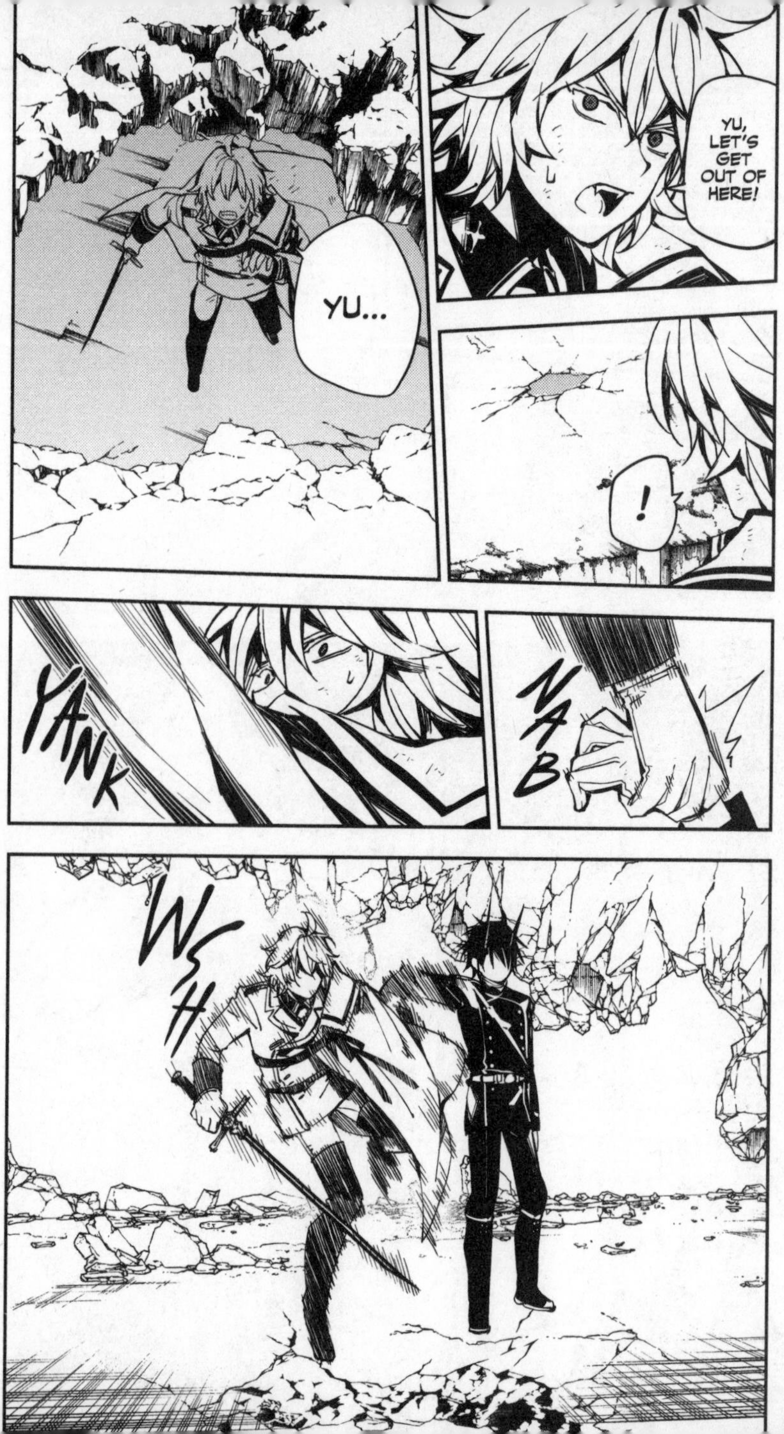
YU, LET'S GET OUT OF HERE!
!
YU...
NAB
YANK
WSH

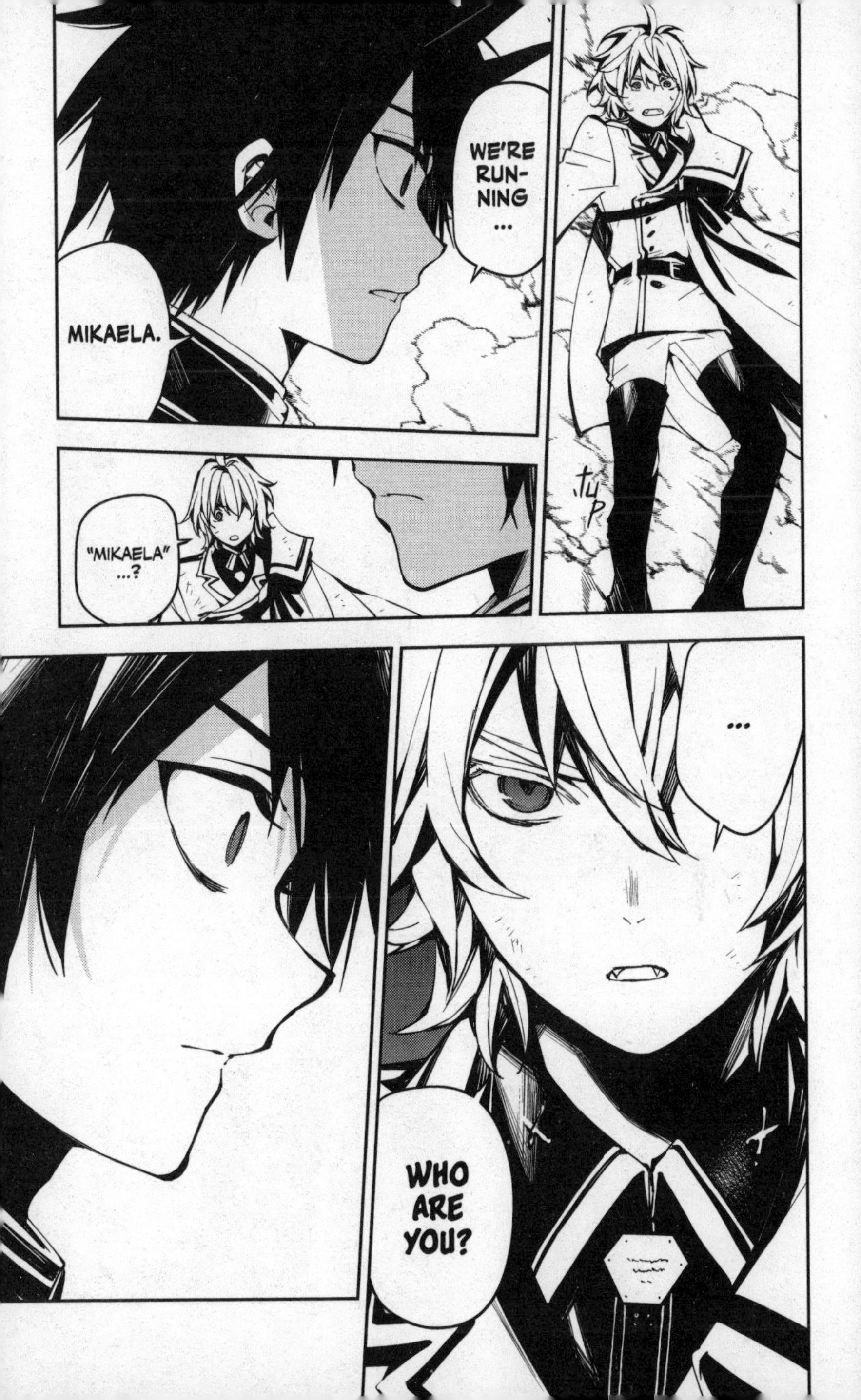
tup
WE'RE RUN-NING ...
MIKAELA.
"MIKAELA" ...?
...
WHO ARE YOU?

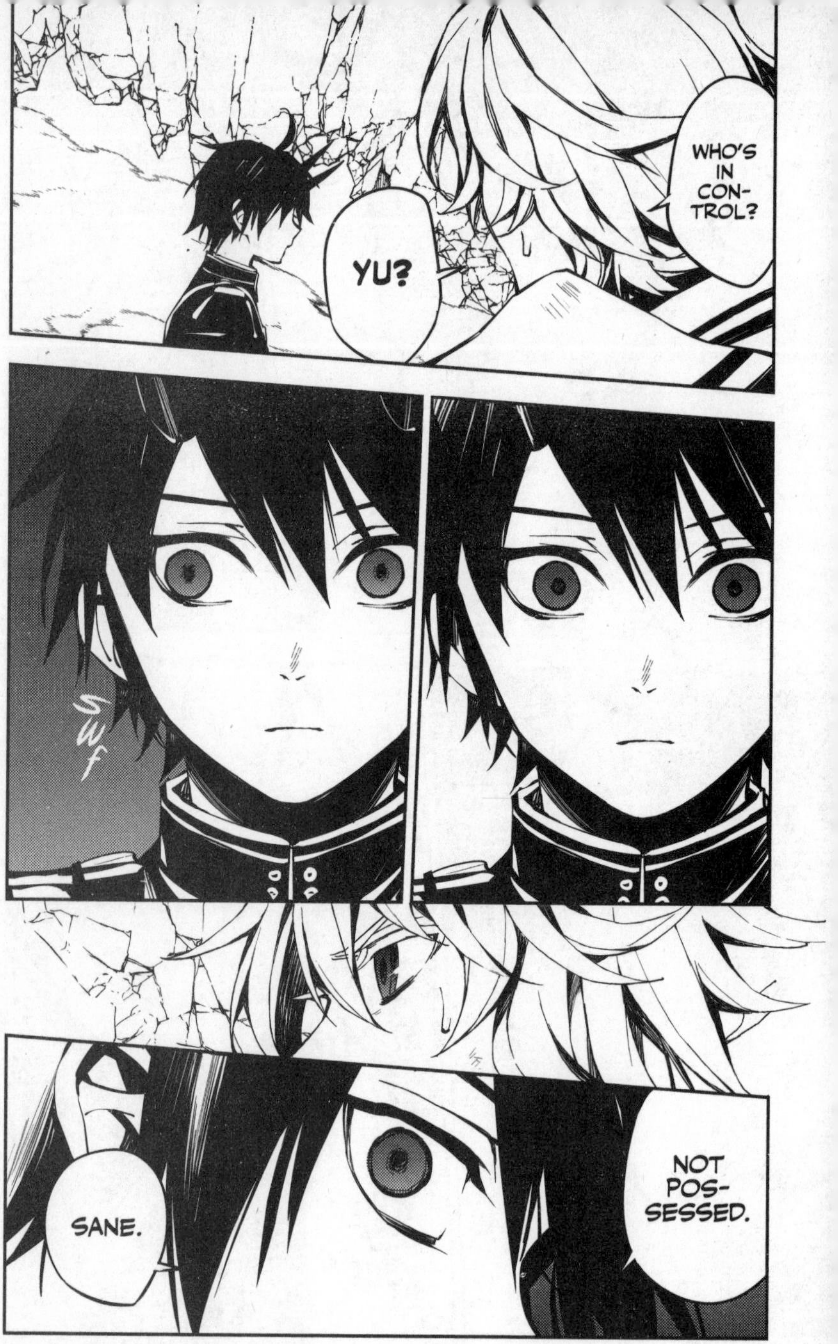
WHO'S IN CON-TROL?
YU?
SWF
NOT POS-SESSED.
SANE.

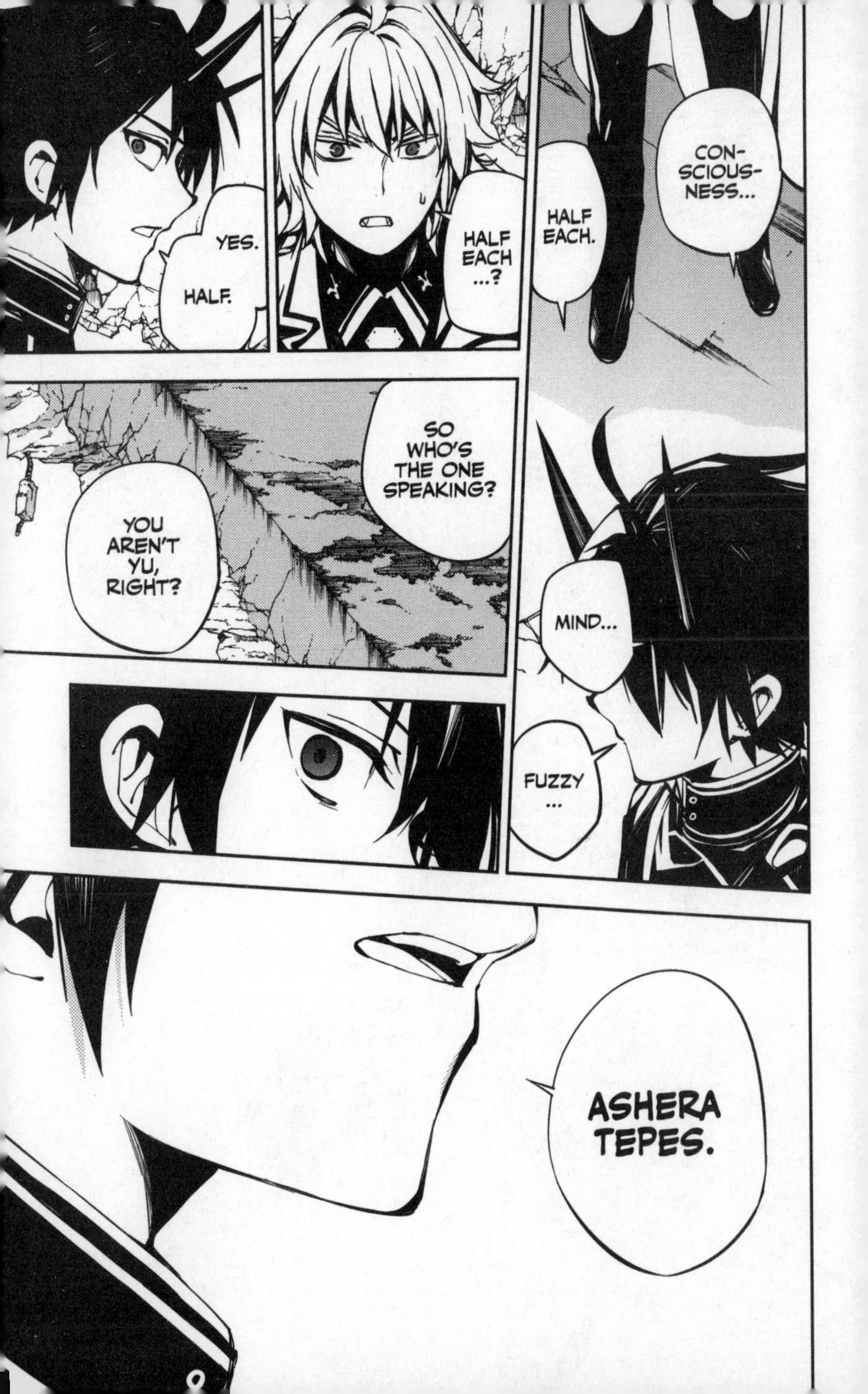
CON-SCIOUS-NESS...
HALF EACH.
HALF EACH ...?
YES.
HALF.
MIND...
FUZZY ...
SO WHO'S THE ONE SPEAKING?
YOU AREN'T YU, RIGHT?
ASHERA TEPES.

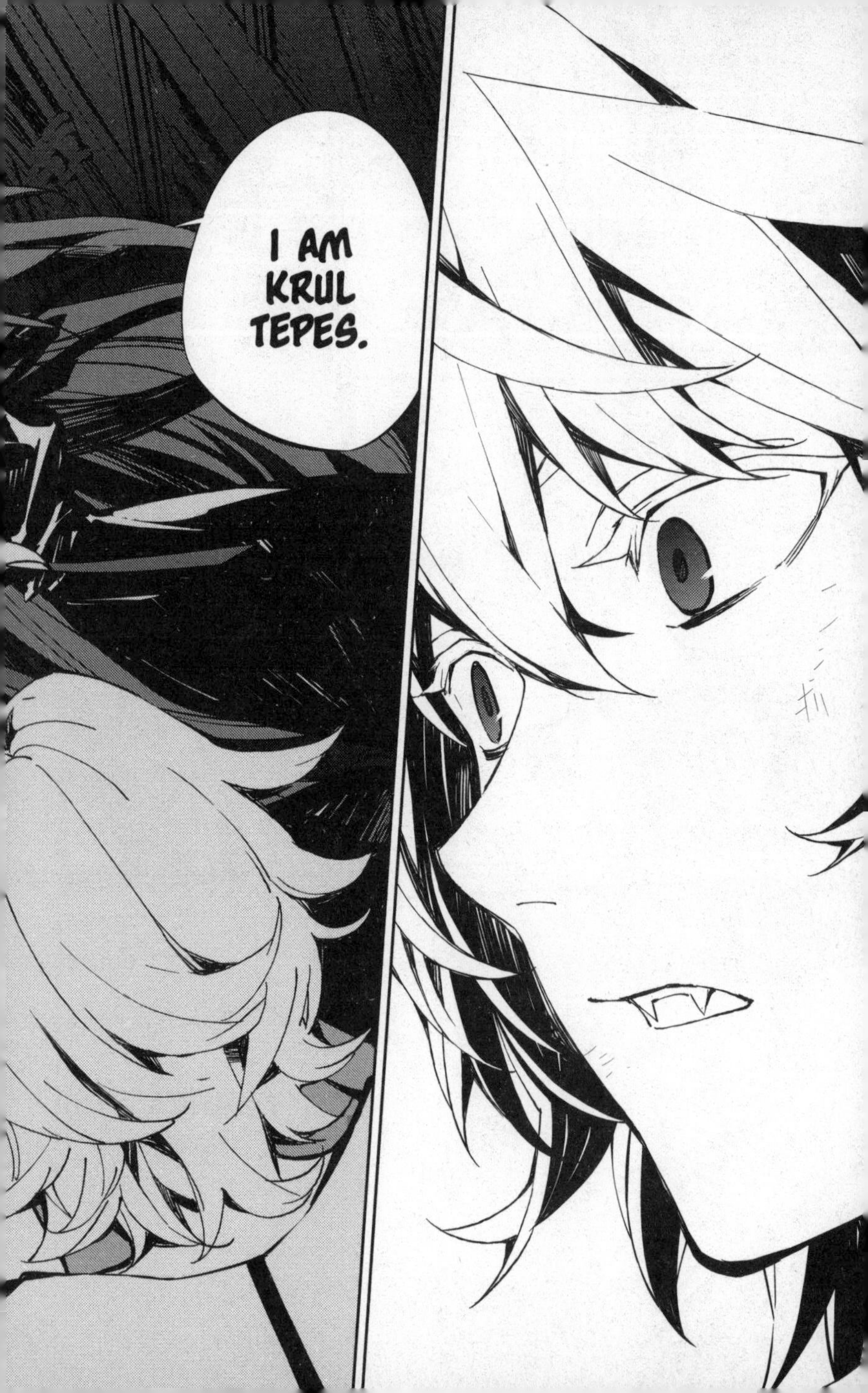
I AM KRUL TEPES.

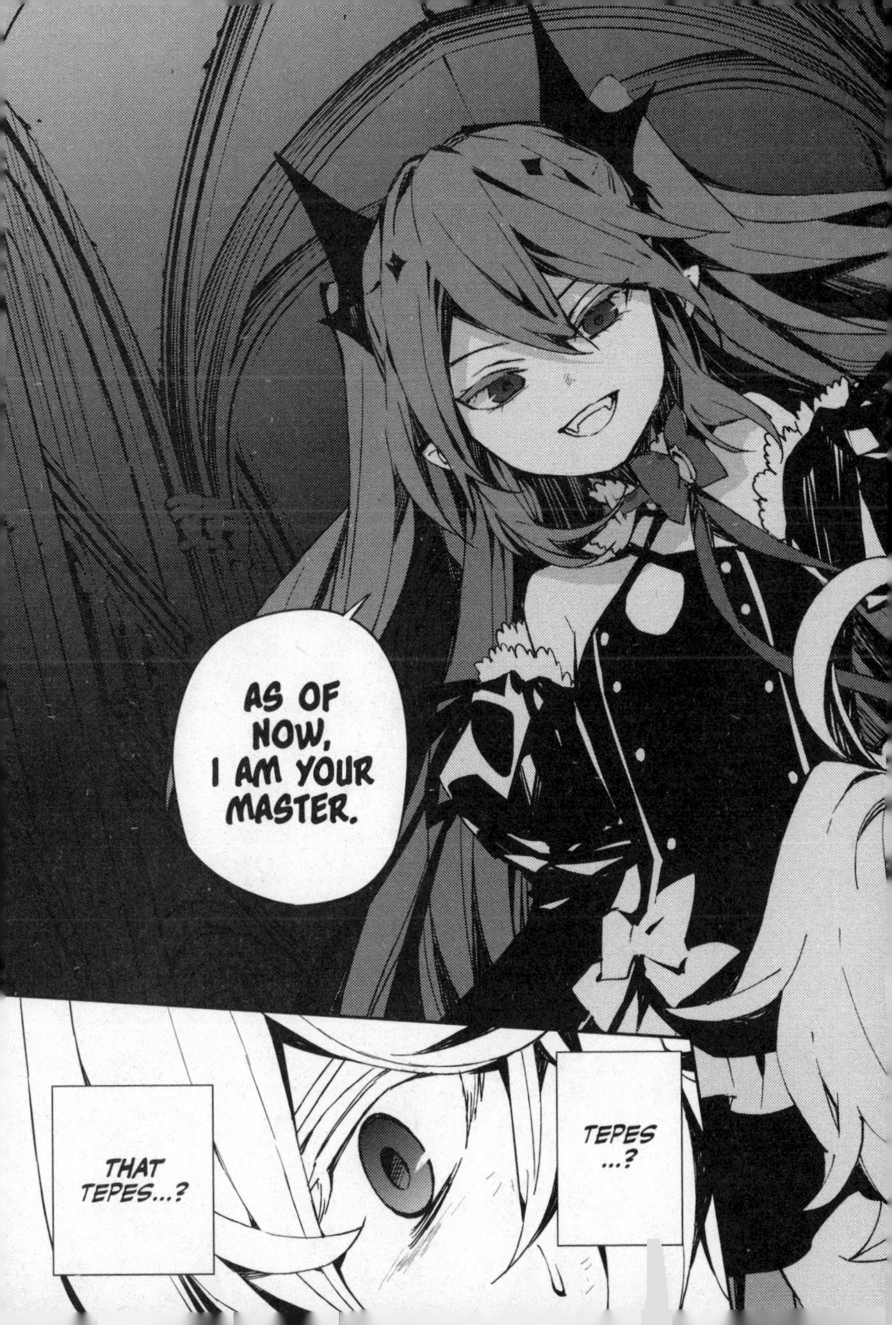
AS OF NOW, I AM YOUR MASTER.
TEPES ...?
THAT TEPES...?

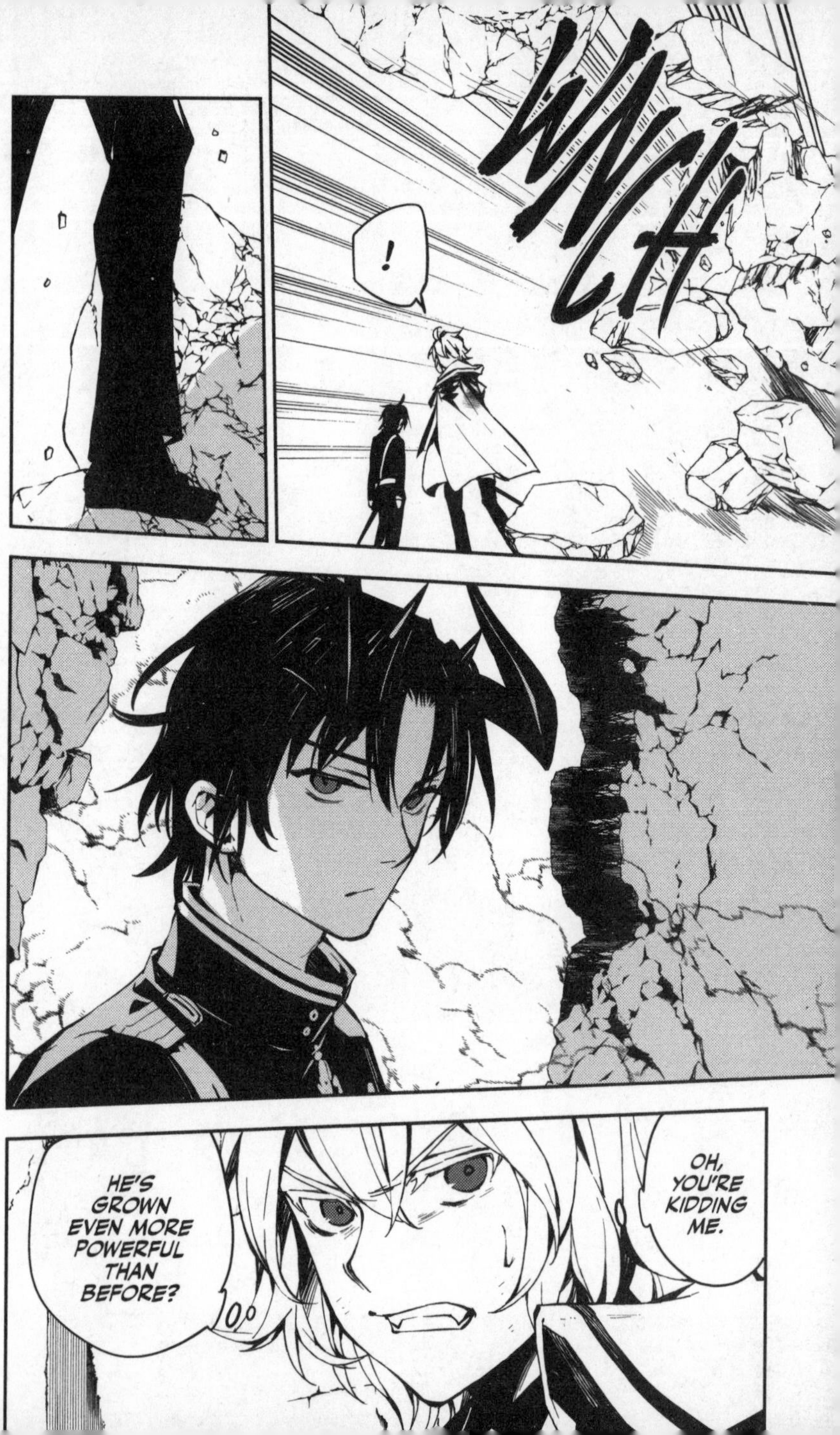
WNCH
!
OH, YOU'RE KIDDING ME.
HE'S GROWN EVEN MORE POWERFUL THAN BEFORE?

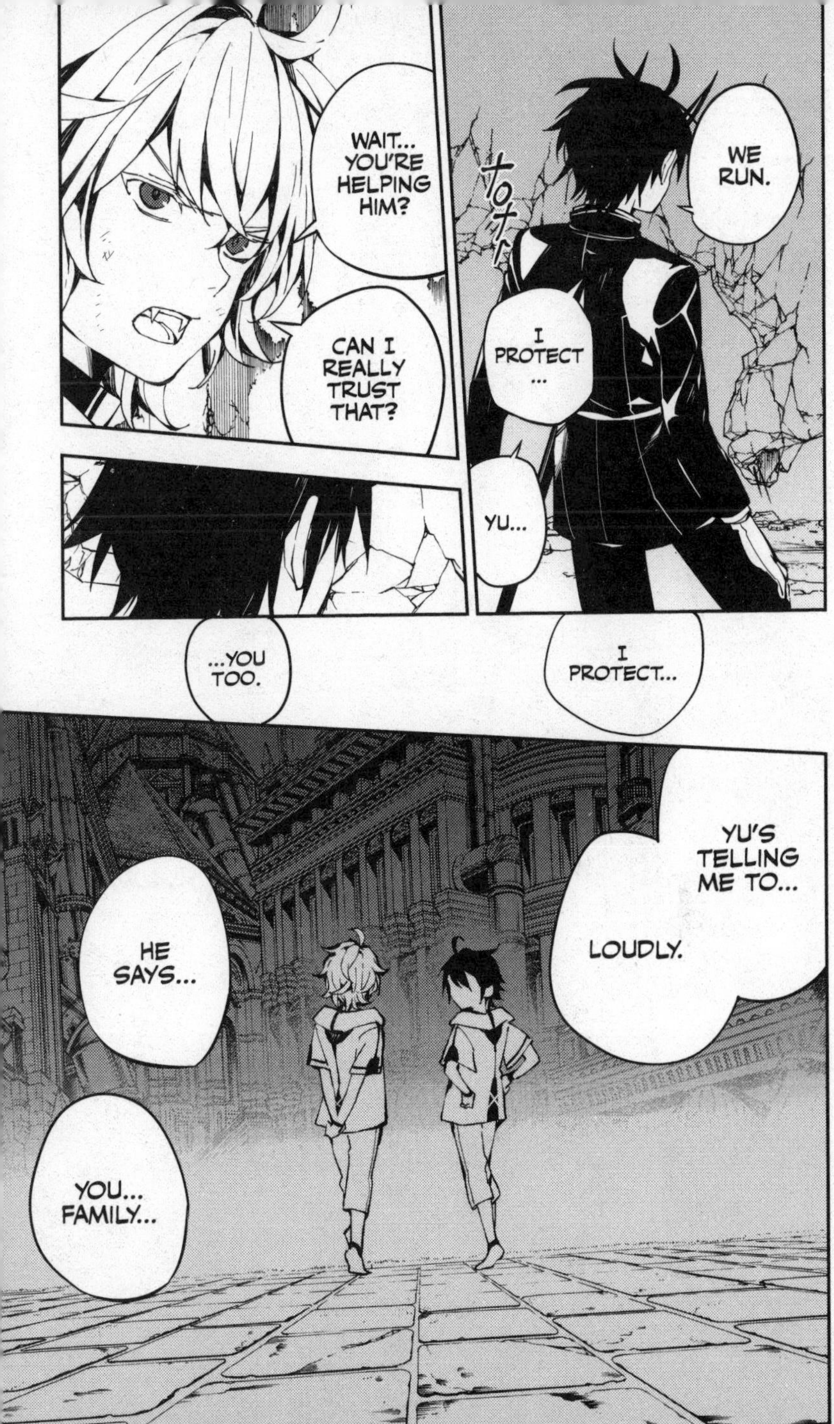
WE RUN.
I PROTECT ...
YU...
WAIT... YOU'RE HELPING HIM?
CAN I REALLY TRUST THAT?
I PROTECT...
...YOU TOO.
YU'S TELLING ME TO...
LOUDLY.
HE SAYS...
YOU... FAMILY...

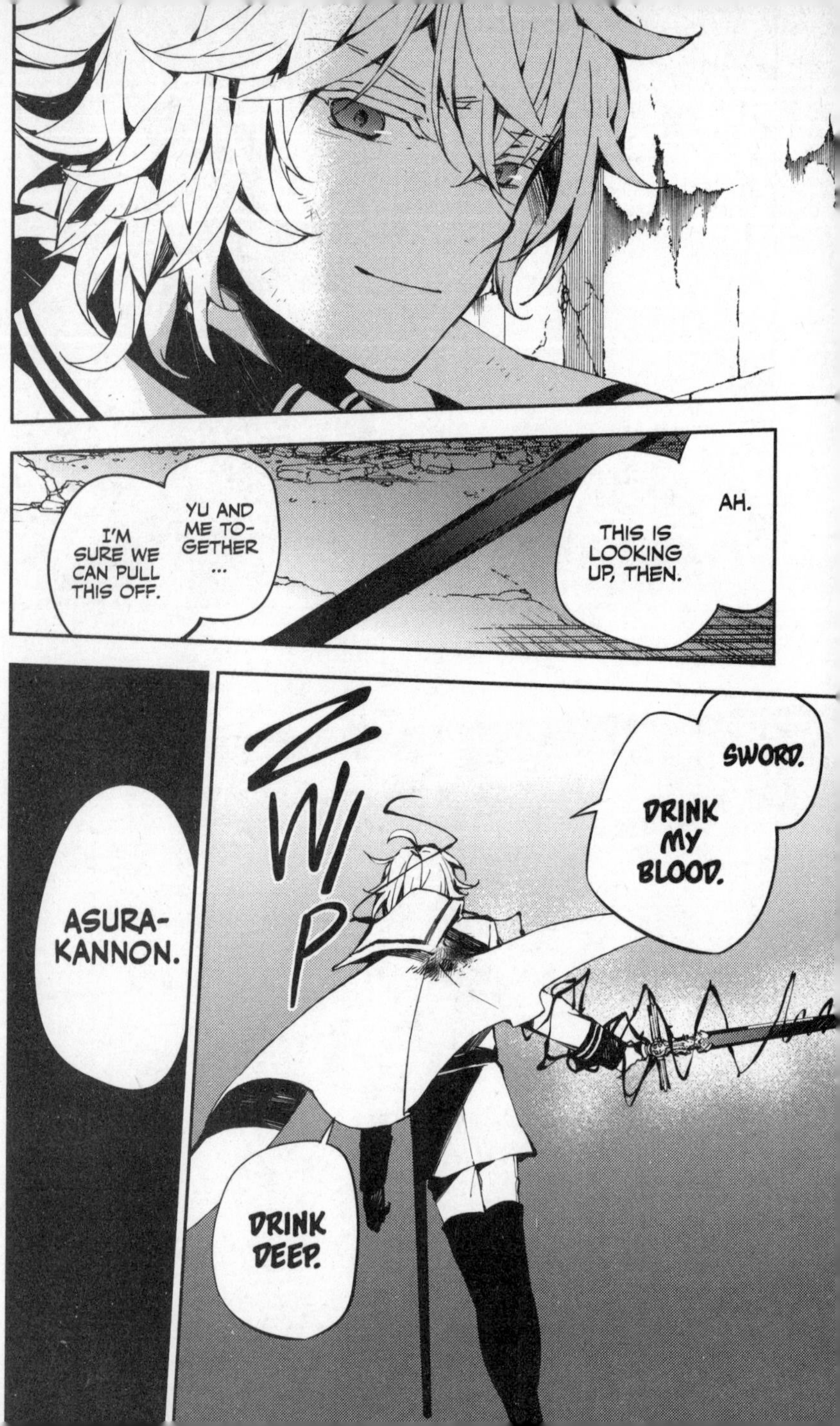
AH.
THIS IS LOOKING UP, THEN.
YU AND ME TO-GETHER ...
I'M SURE WE CAN PULL THIS OFF.
SWORD.
DRINK MY BLOOD.
ZWIP
DRINK DEEP.
ASURA-KANNON.

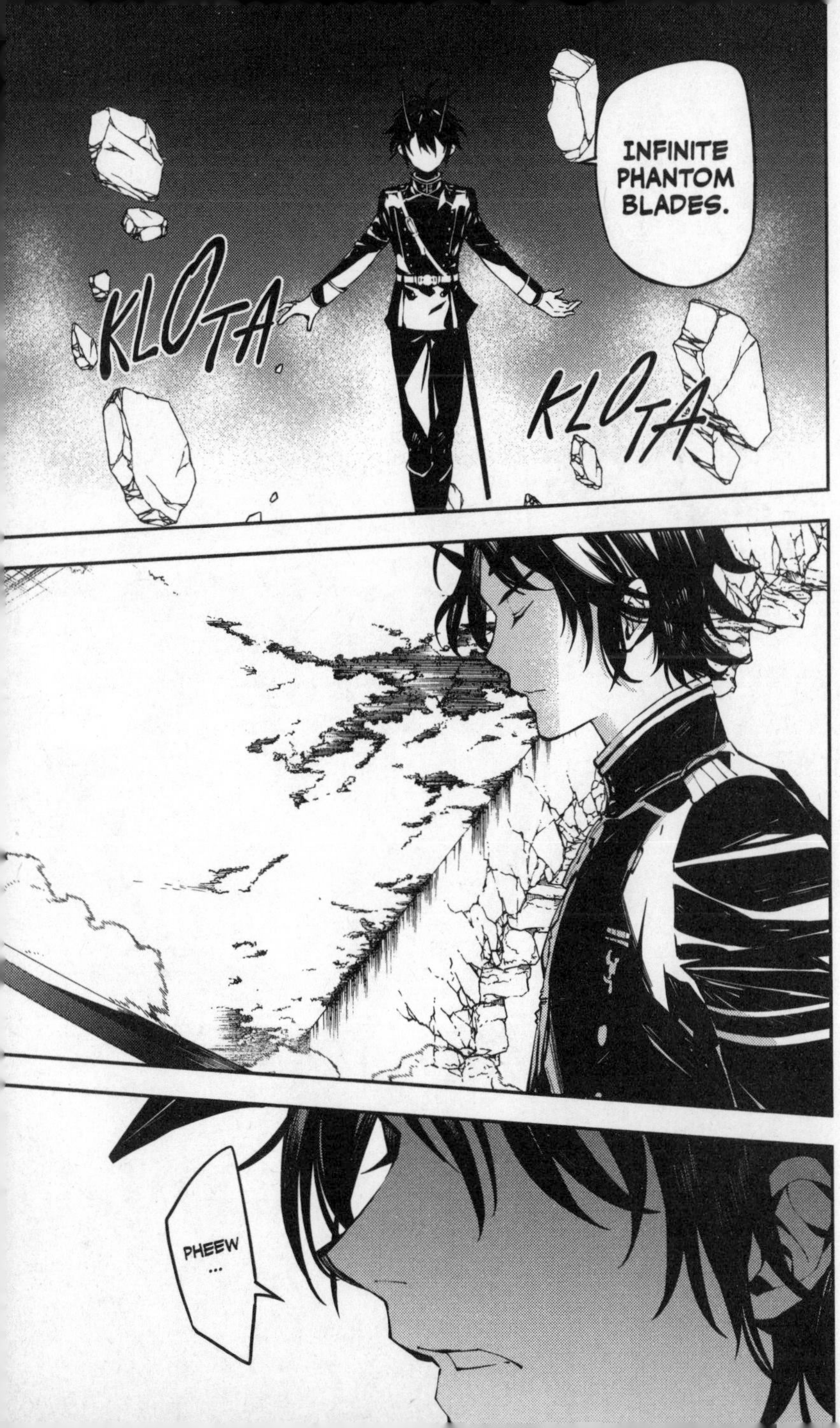
INFINITE PHANTOM BLADES.
KLOTA
KLOTA
PHEEW ...

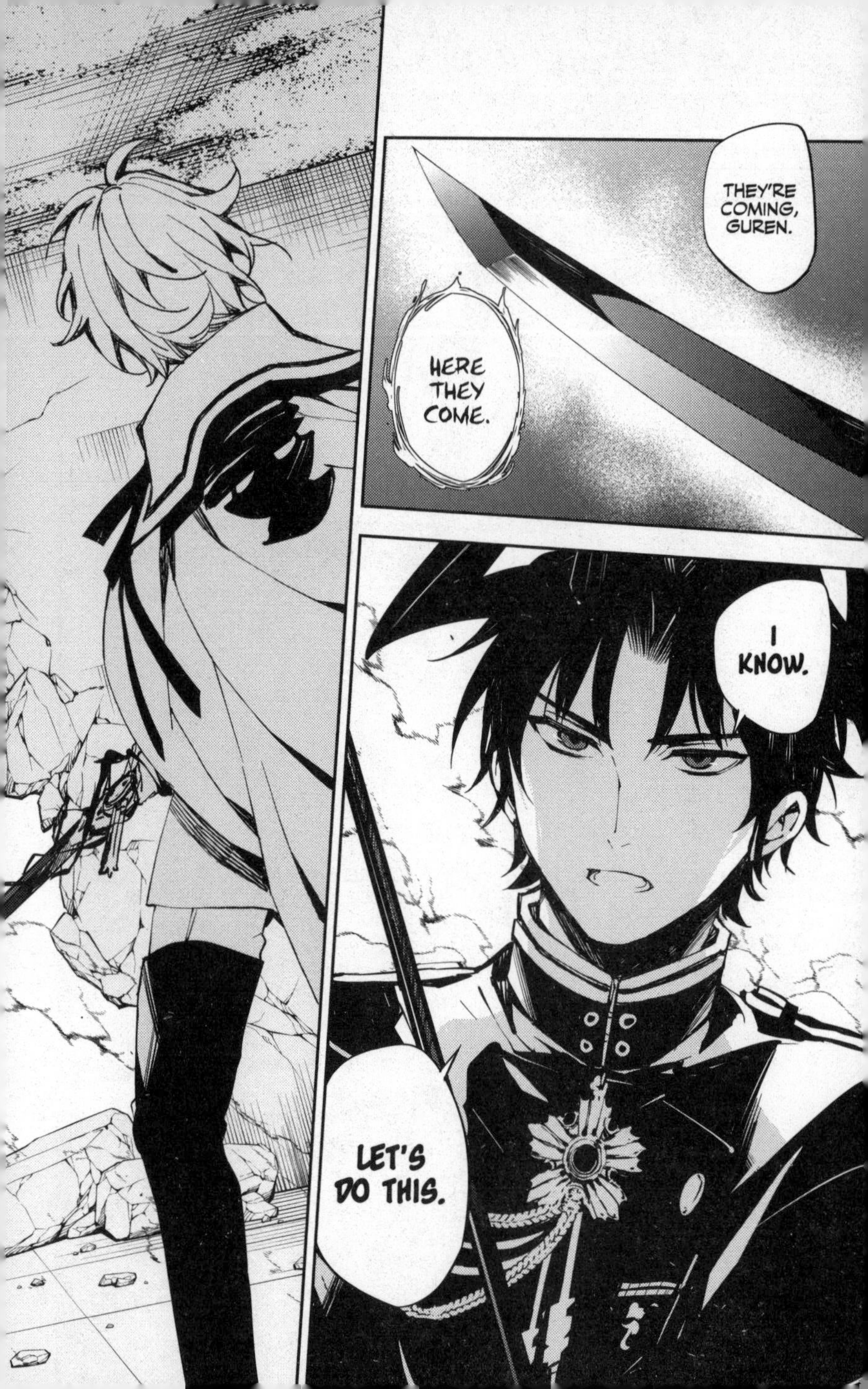
THEY'RE COMING, GUREN.
HERE THEY COME.
I KNOW.
LET'S DO THIS.

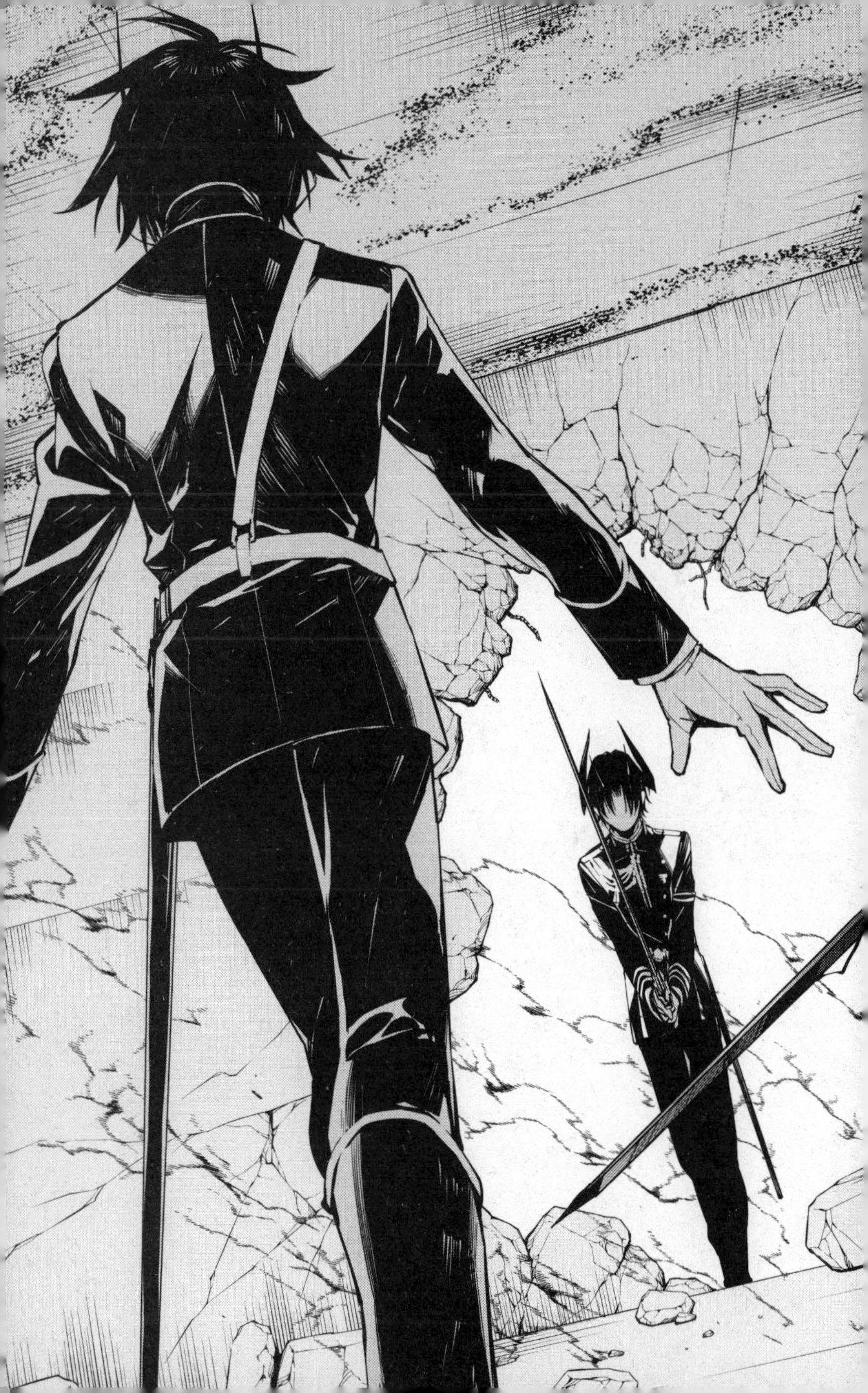

Seraph of the End
VAMPIRE REIGN

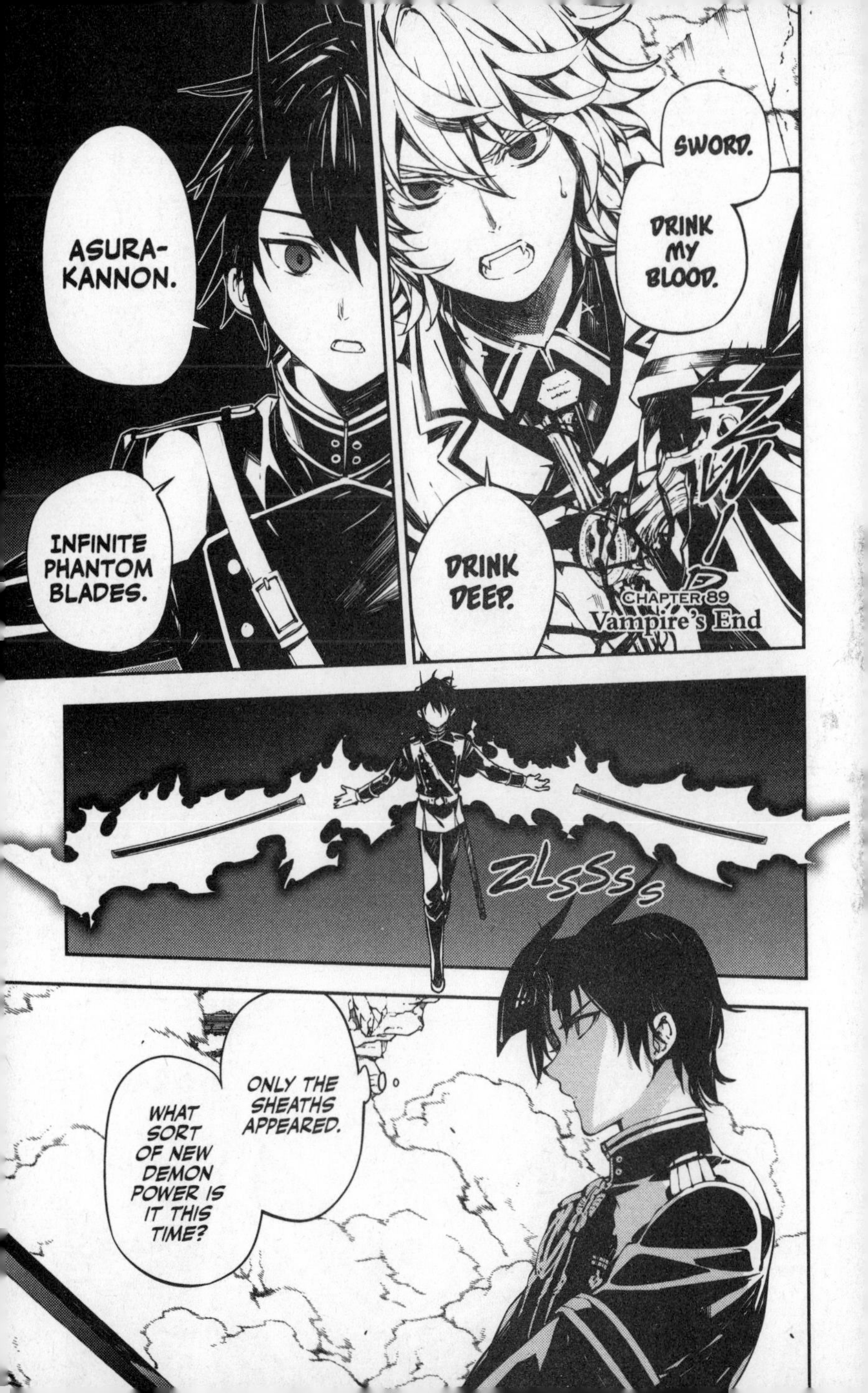
SWORD.
DRINK MY BLOOD.
DRINK DEEP.
CHAPTER 89
Vampire's End
ASURA-KANNON.
INFINITE PHANTOM BLADES.
ZLSSSS
ONLY THE SHEATHS APPEARED.
WHAT SORT OF NEW DEMON POWER IS IT THIS TIME?

Chapter 89 Vampire's End

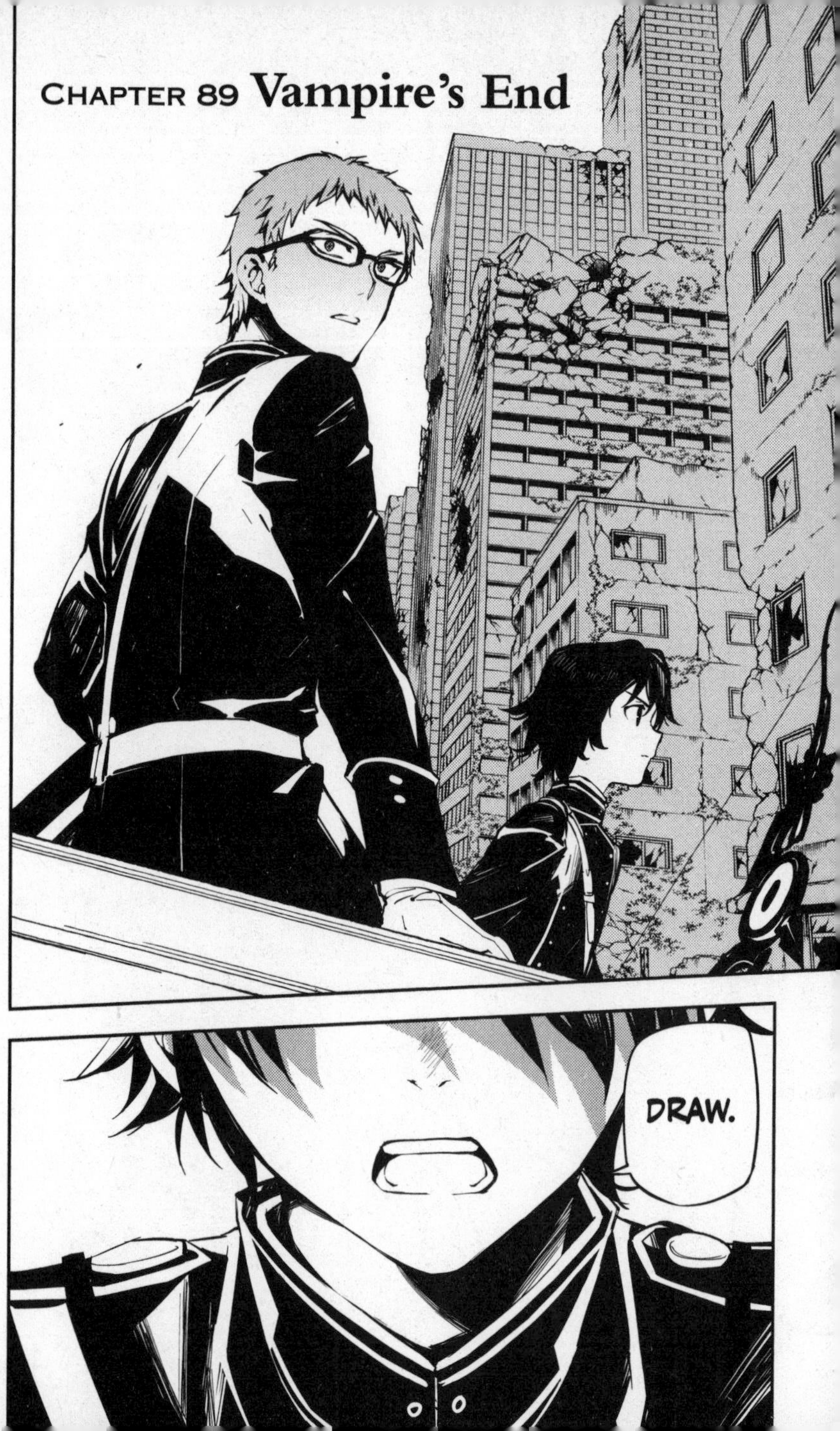
DRAW.

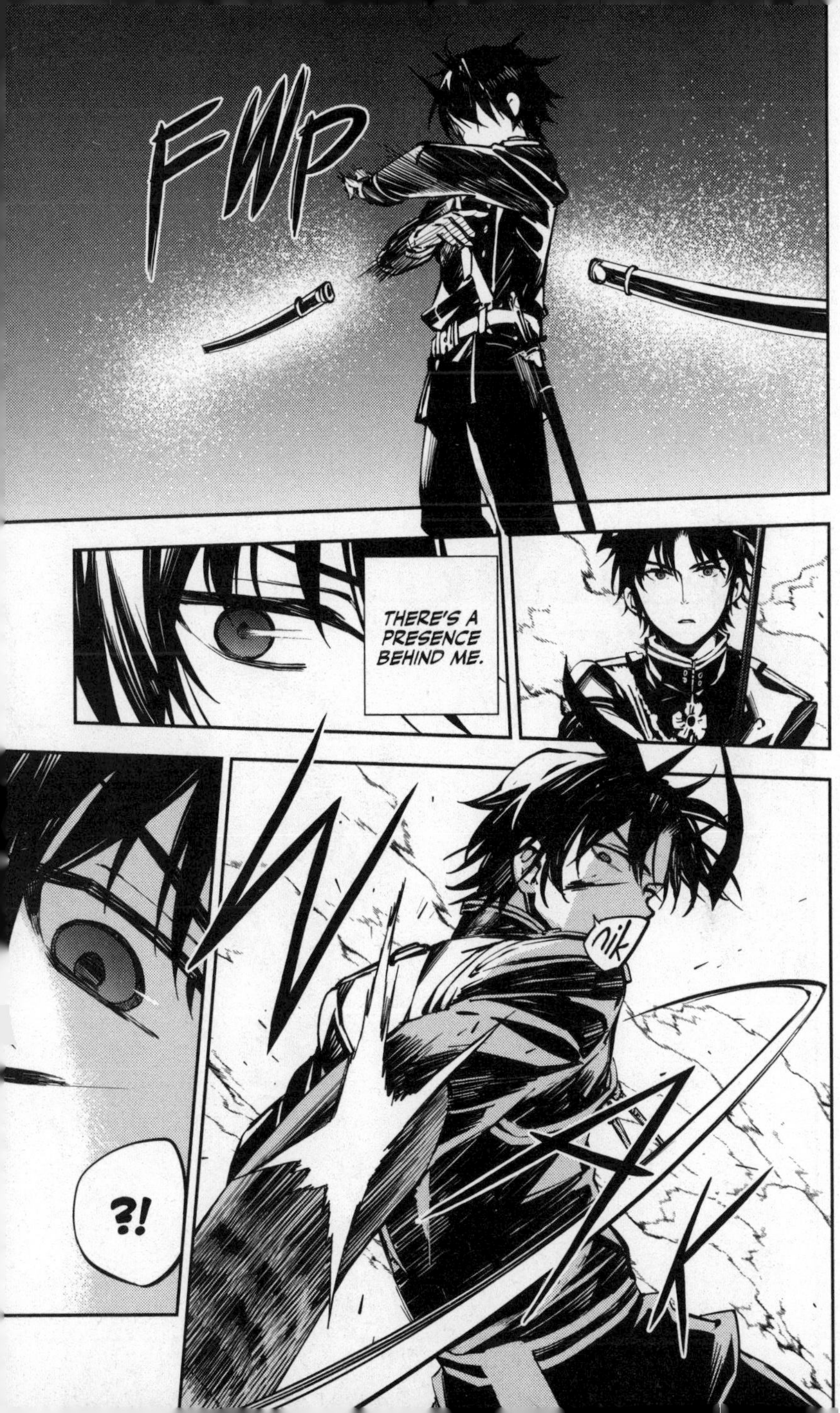
FWP
THERE'S A PRESENCE BEHIND ME.
NIK
?!

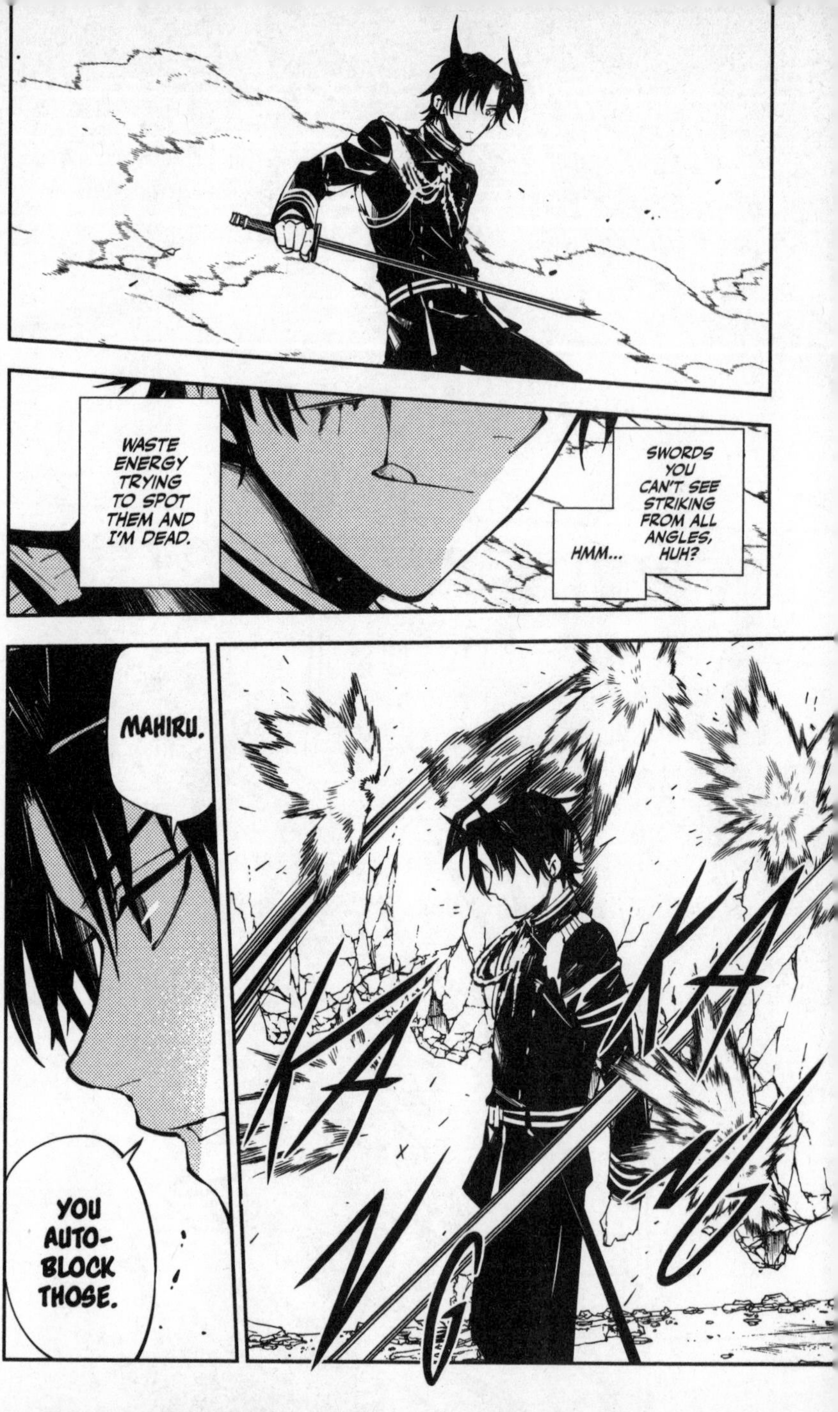
SWORDS YOU CAN'T SEE STRIKING FROM ALL ANGLES, HUH?
HMM...
WASTE ENERGY TRYING TO SPOT THEM AND I'M DEAD.
KANG
KANG
MAHIRU.
YOU AUTO-BLOCK THOSE.

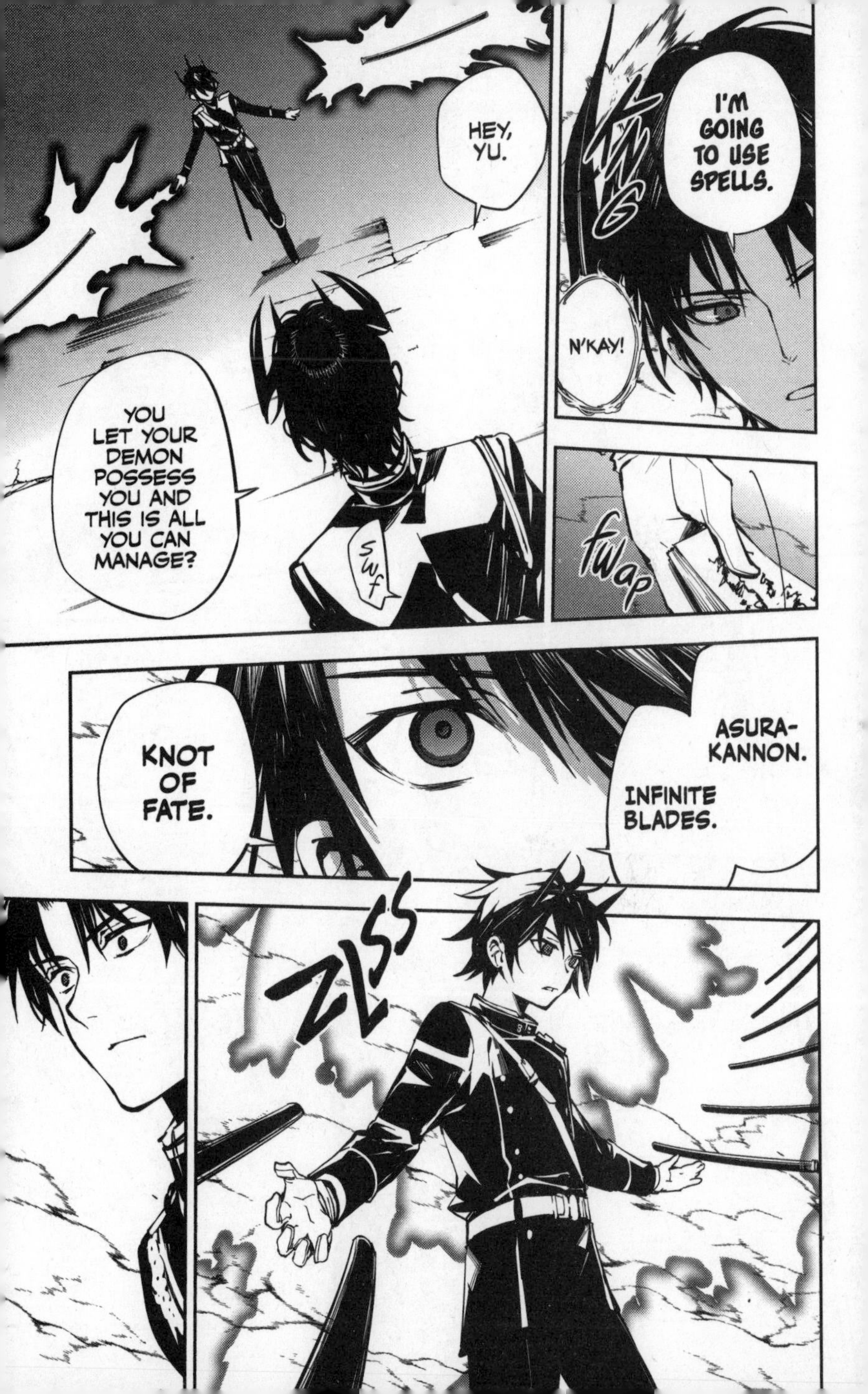

I'M GOING TO USE SPELLS.
N'KAY!
fwap
HEY, YU.
YOU LET YOUR DEMON POSSESS YOU AND THIS IS ALL YOU CAN MANAGE?
swf
ASURA-KANNON.
INFINITE BLADES.
KNOT OF FATE.
ZZSS

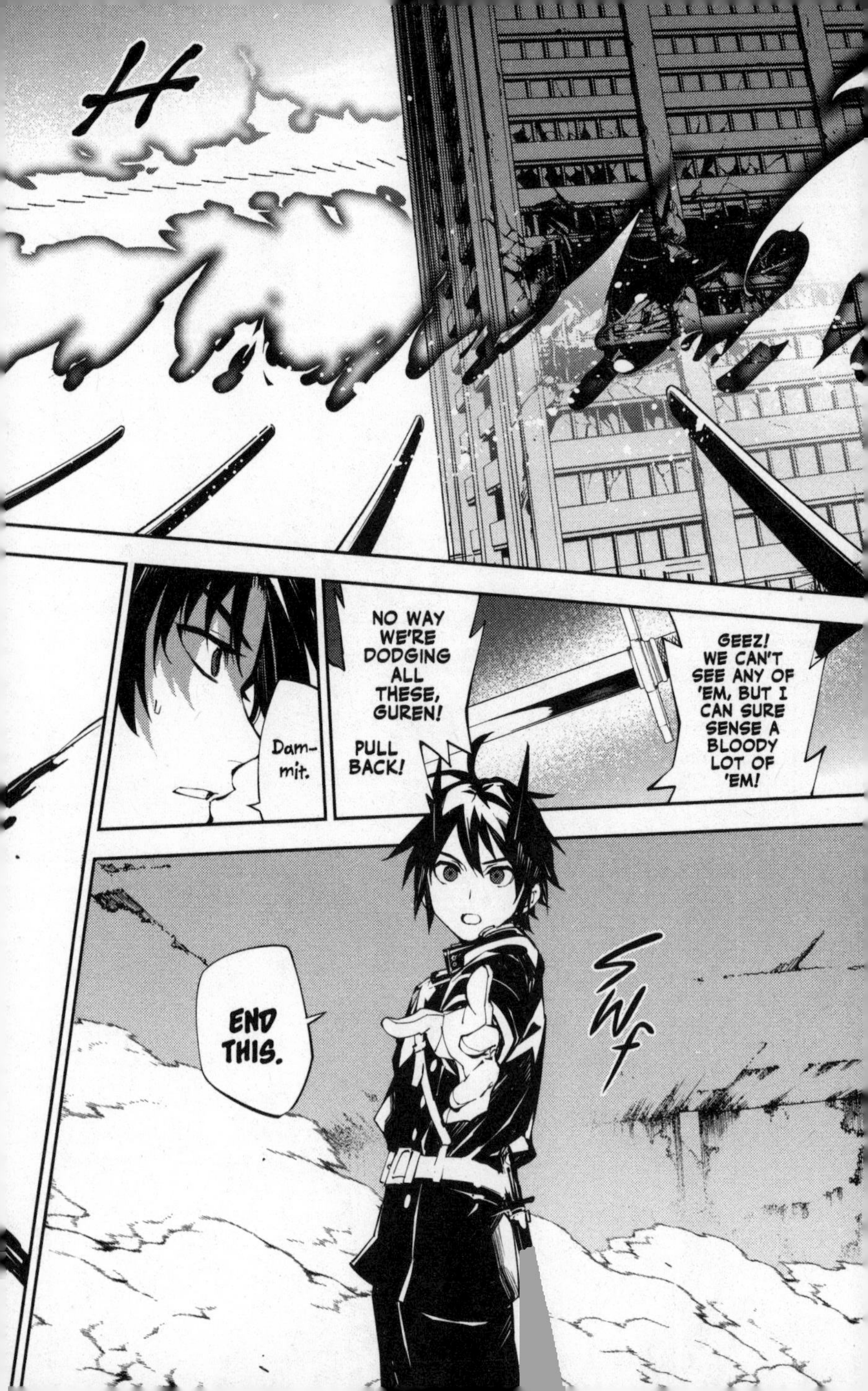
GEEZ! WE CAN'T SEE ANY OF 'EM, BUT I CAN SURE SENSE A BLOODY LOT OF 'EM!
NO WAY WE'RE DODGING ALL THESE, GUREN!
PULL BACK!
Dam-mit.
SWf
END THIS.

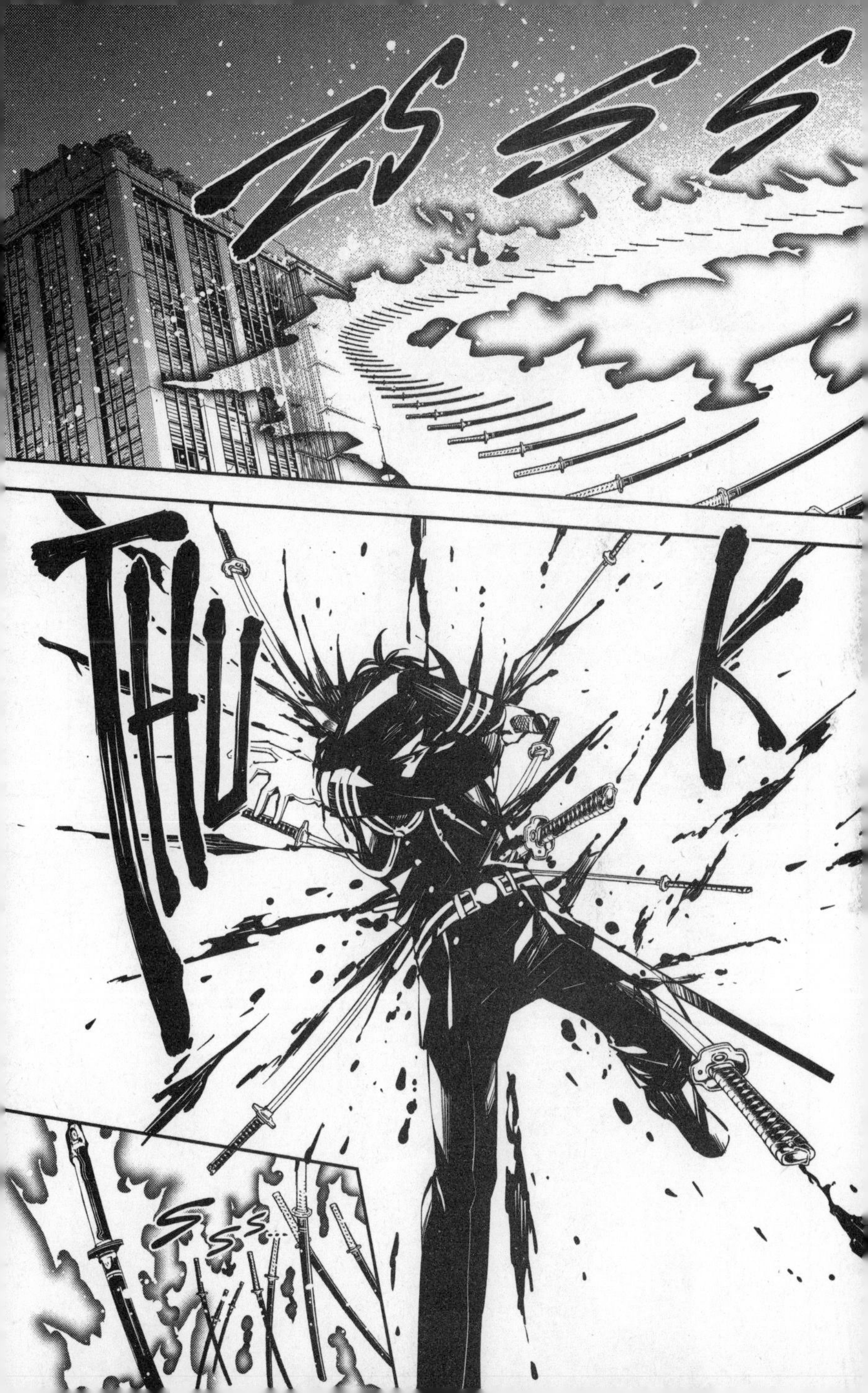
ZSSS
THUNK
SSS...

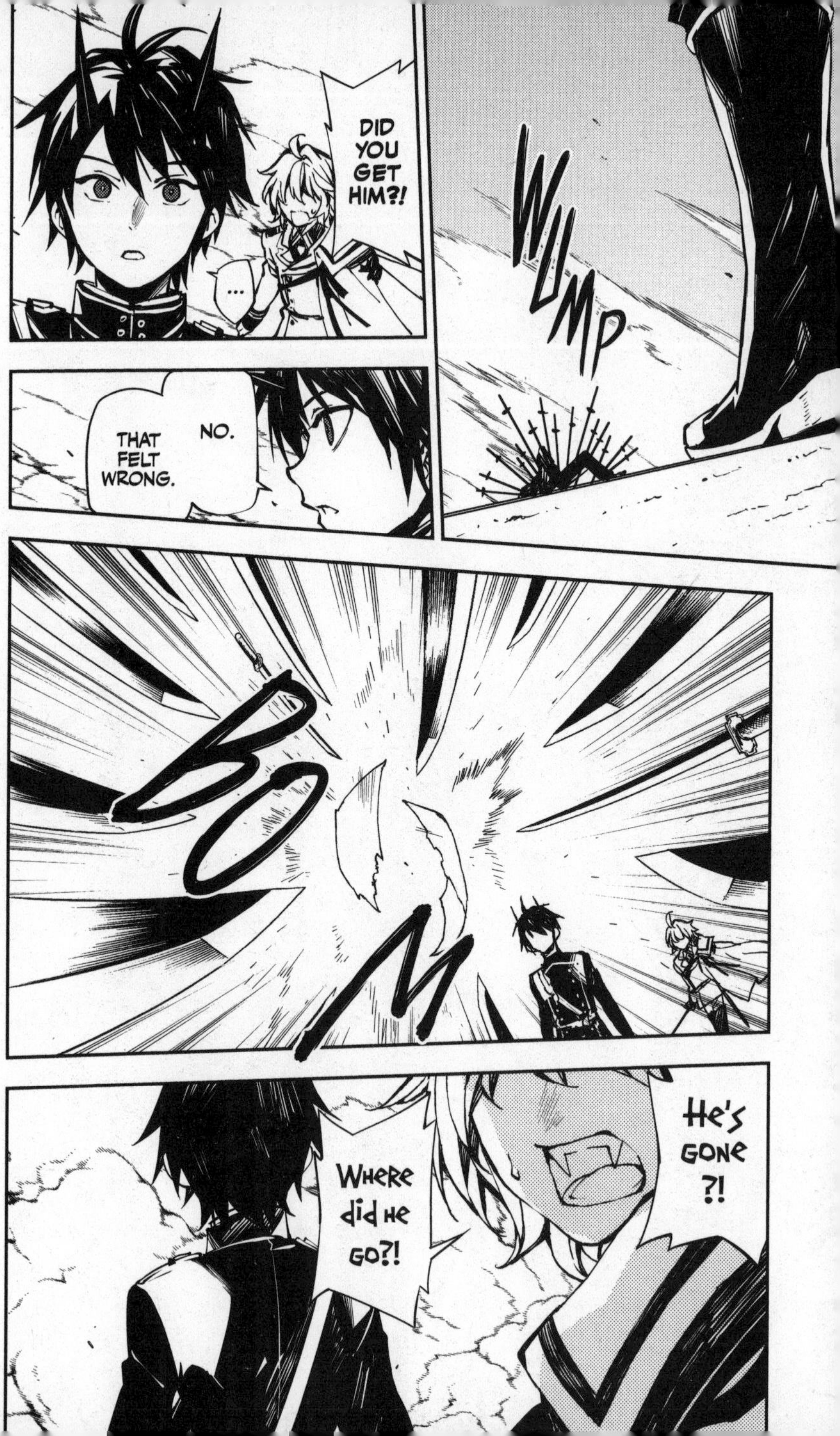
WUMP
DID YOU GET HIM?!
...
NO.
THAT FELT WRONG.
BOOM
He's GONE ?!
Where did He GO?!

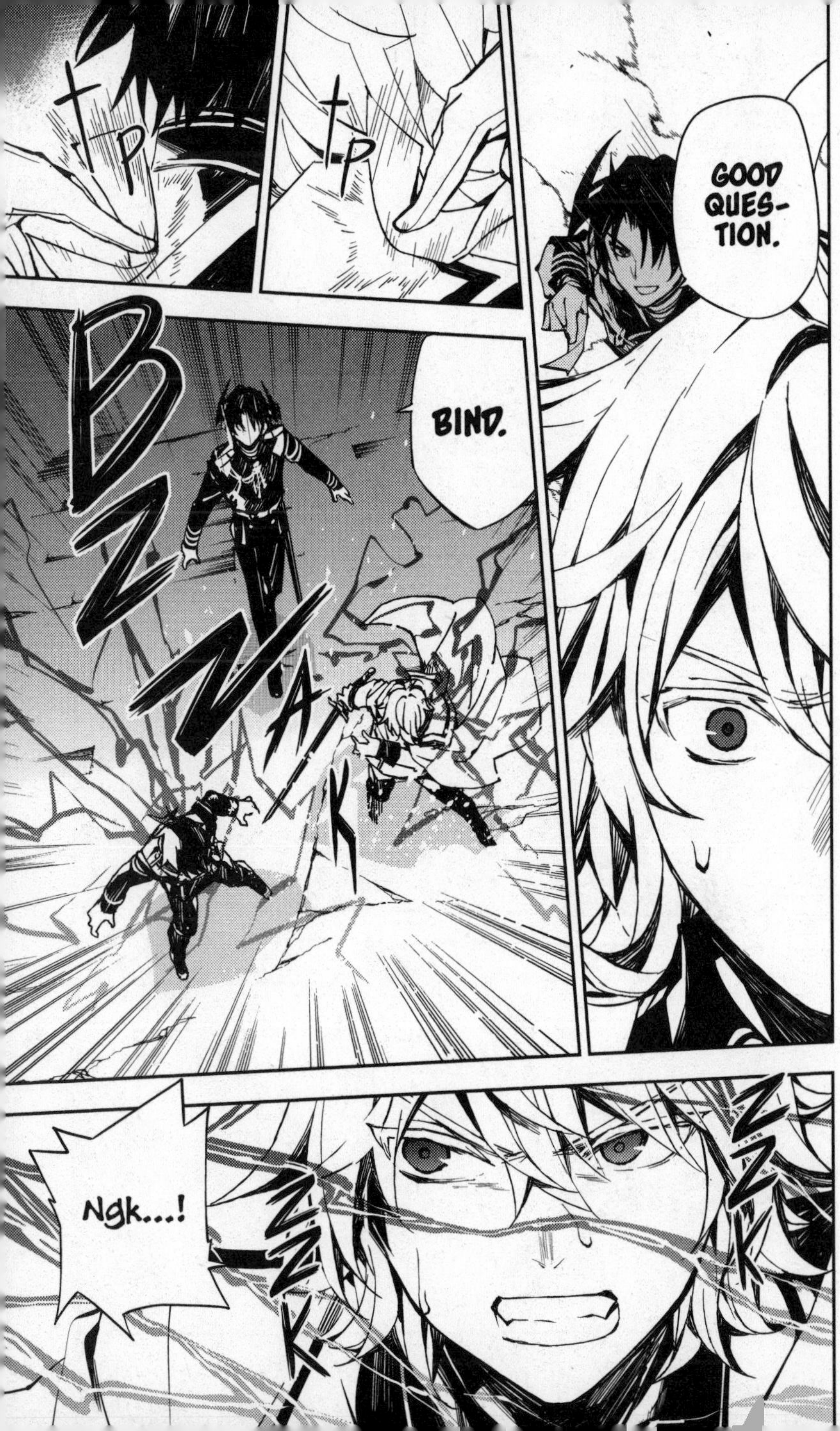
TP
TP
GOOD QUES-TION.
BIND.
BZZZZ
ZAK
ZZZZAK
ZZZK
Ngk...!

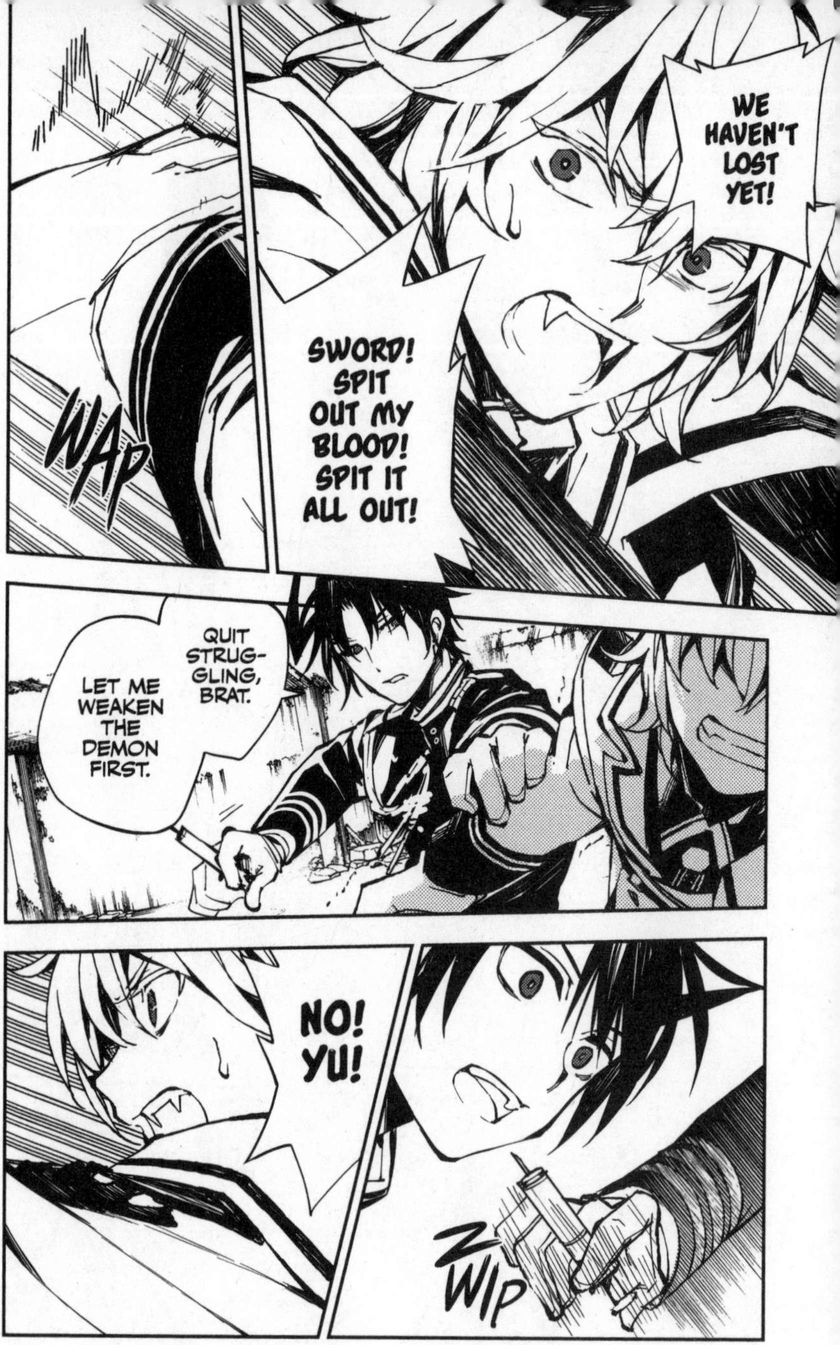
WE HAVEN'T LOST YET!
SWORD! SPIT OUT MY BLOOD! SPIT IT ALL OUT!
WAP
QUIT STRUG-GLING, BRAT.
LET ME WEAKEN THE DEMON FIRST.
ZWIP
NO! YU!

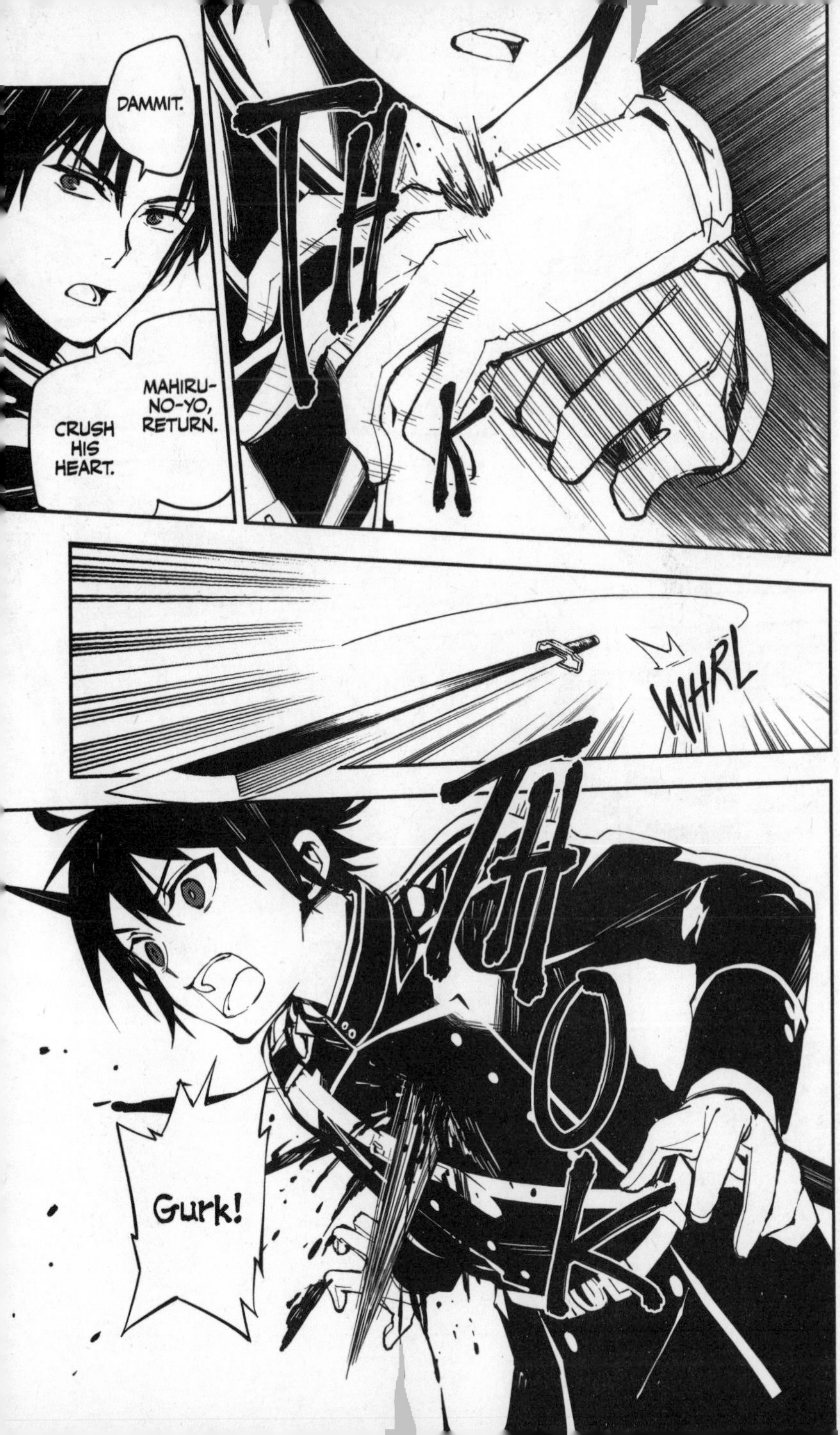
THK
DAMMIT.
MAHIRU-NO-YO, RETURN.
CRUSH HIS HEART.
WHRL
THOK
Gurk!

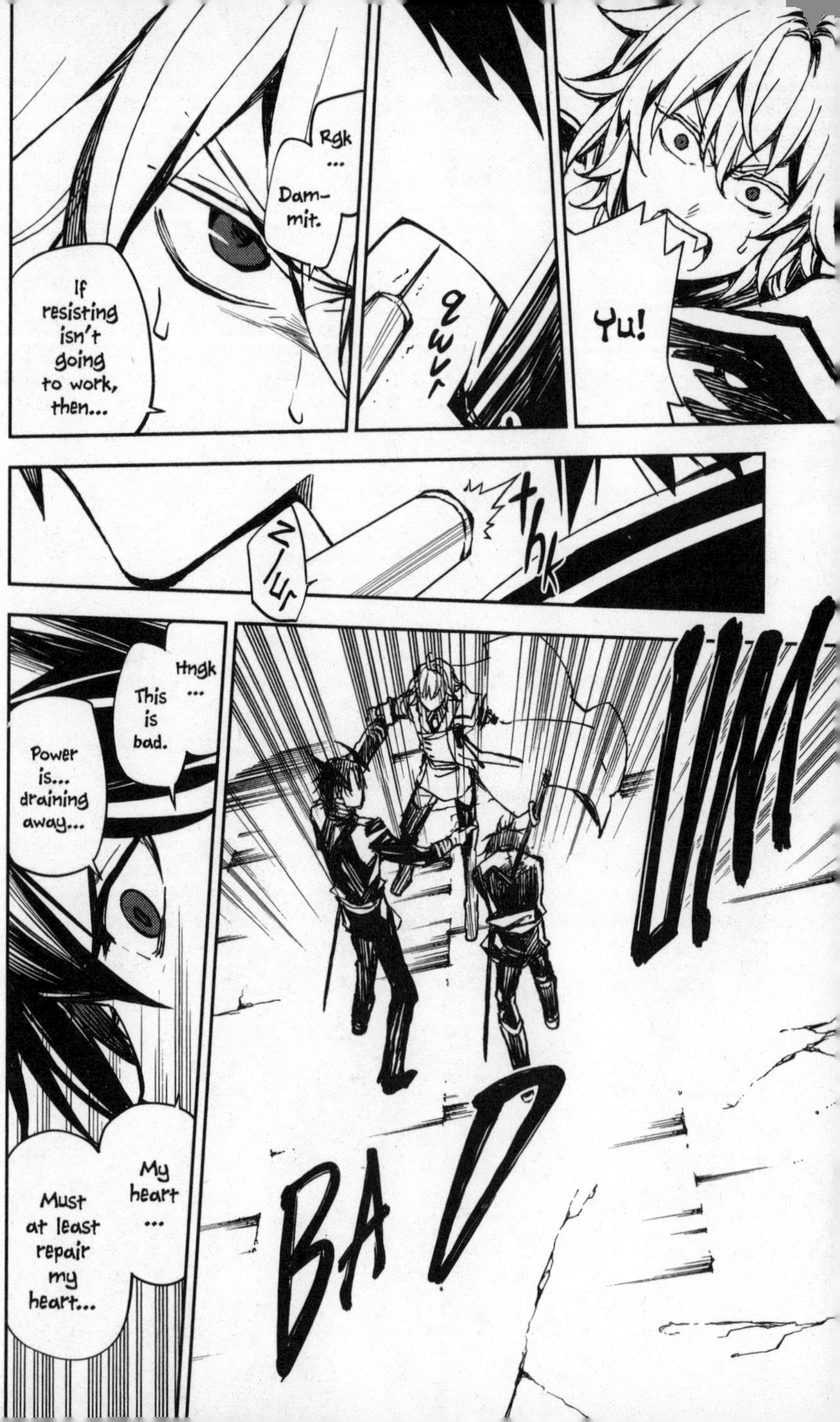

Yu!
Rgk ... Dam-mit.
qwvr
If resisting isn't going to work, then...
thk
zlur
UM
BA D
Hngk ... This is bad.
Power is... draining away...
My heart ...
Must at least repair my heart...

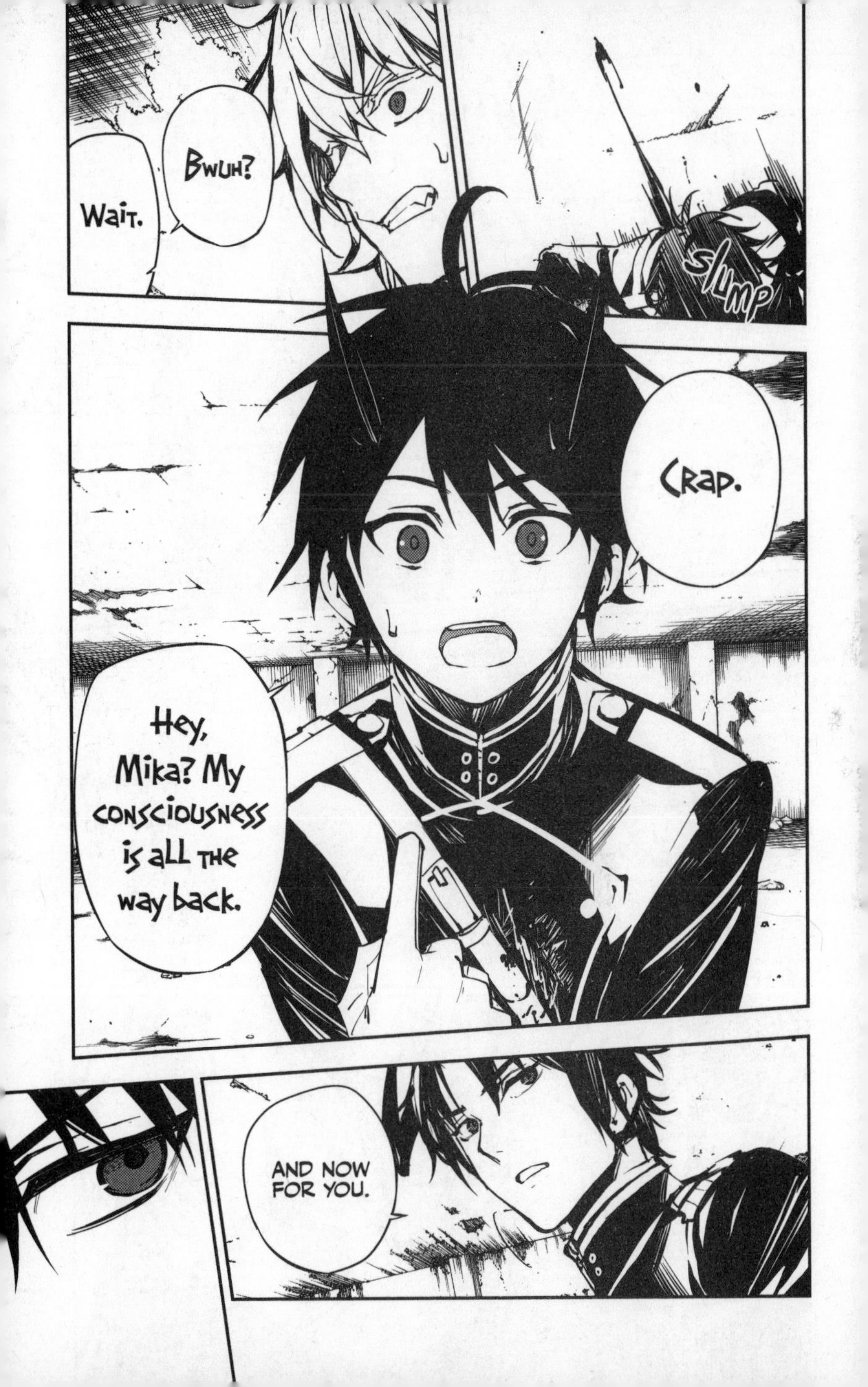
SLUMP
BWUH?
WAIT.
CRAP.
HEY, MIKA? MY CONSCIOUSNESS IS ALL THE WAY BACK.
AND NOW FOR YOU.

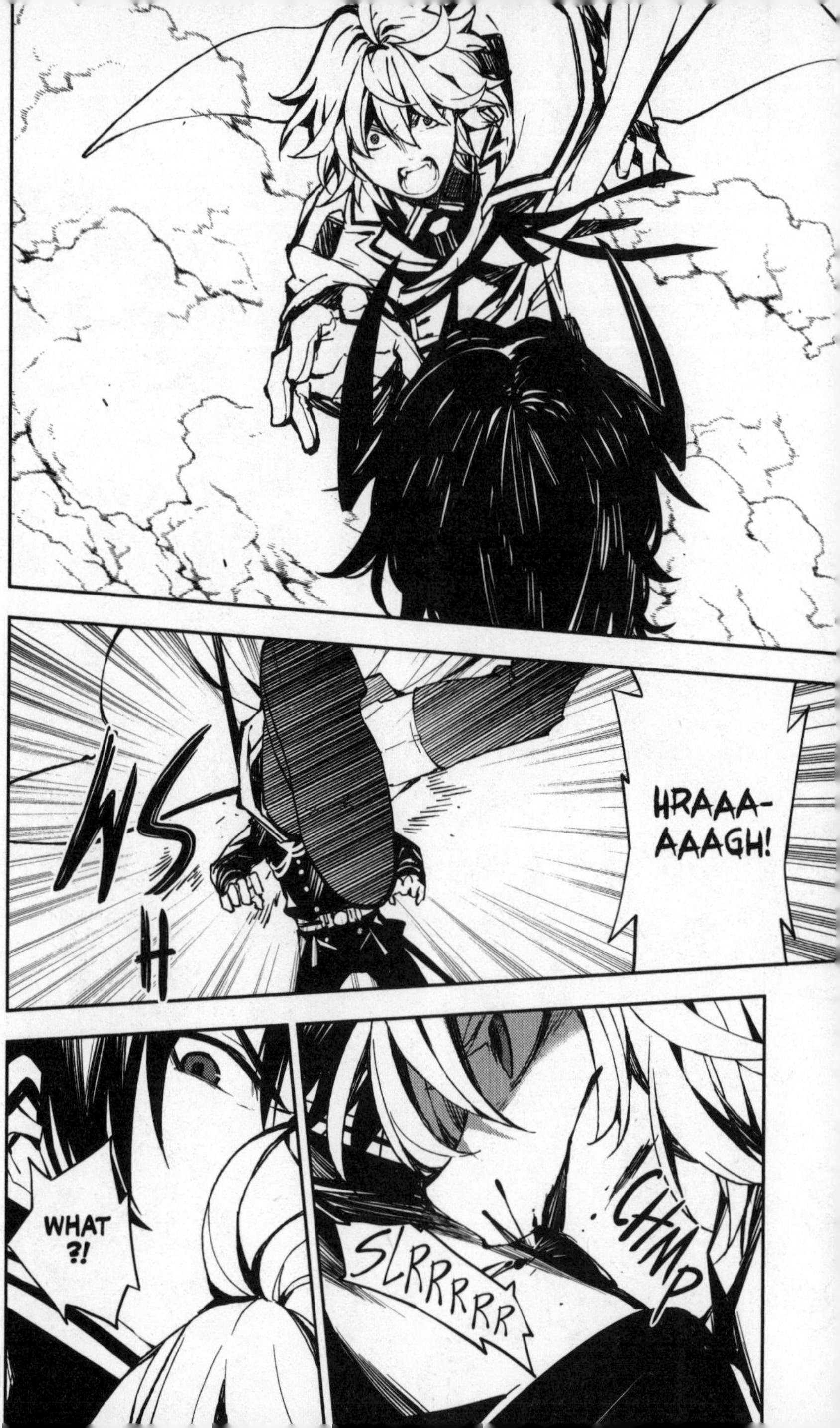
HRAAA-
AAAGH!
WSH
CHMP
SLRRRRRR
WHAT
?!

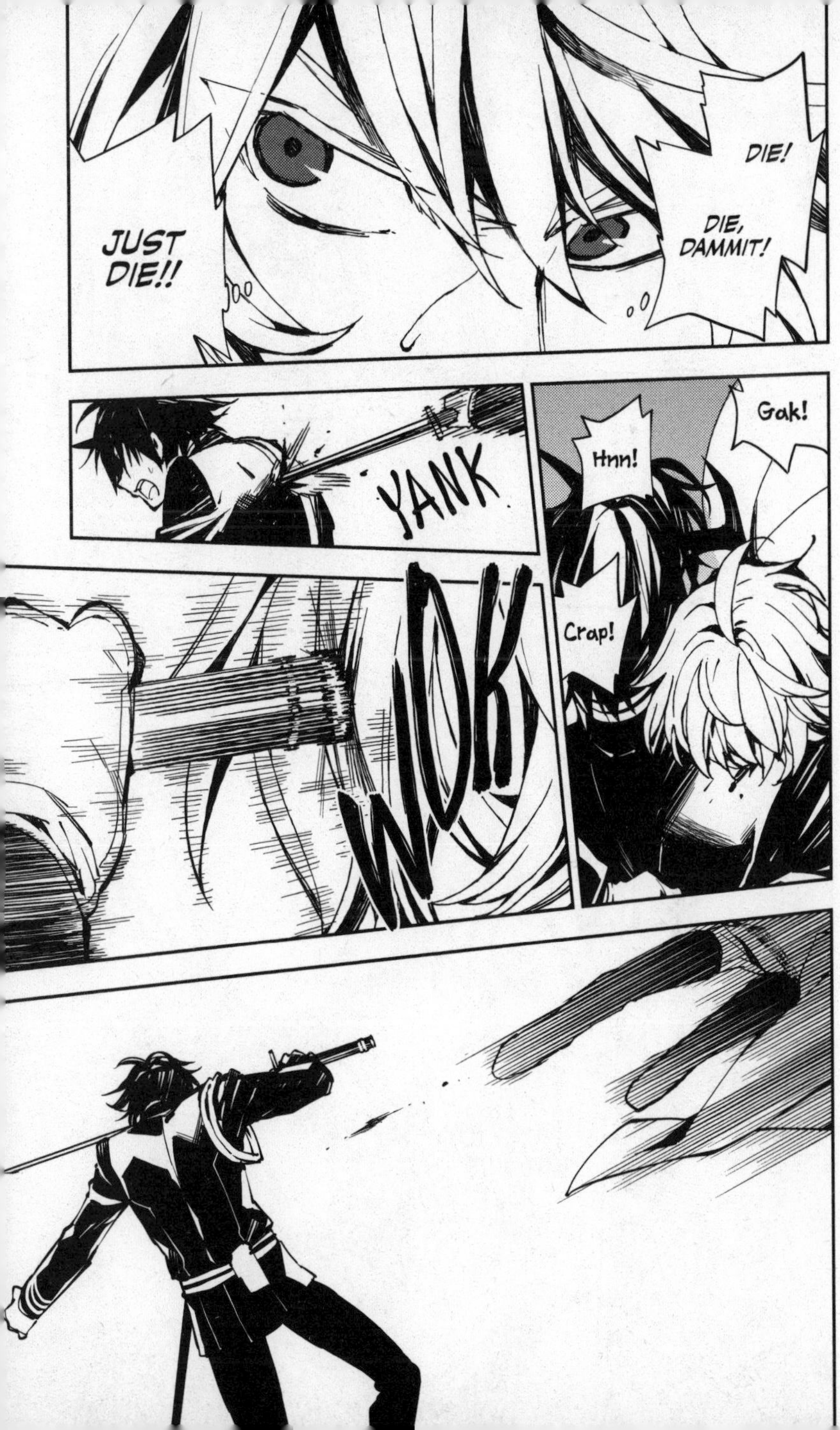
DIE!
DIE, DAMMIT!
JUST DIE!!
Gak!
Hnn!
Crap!
YANK
WOK

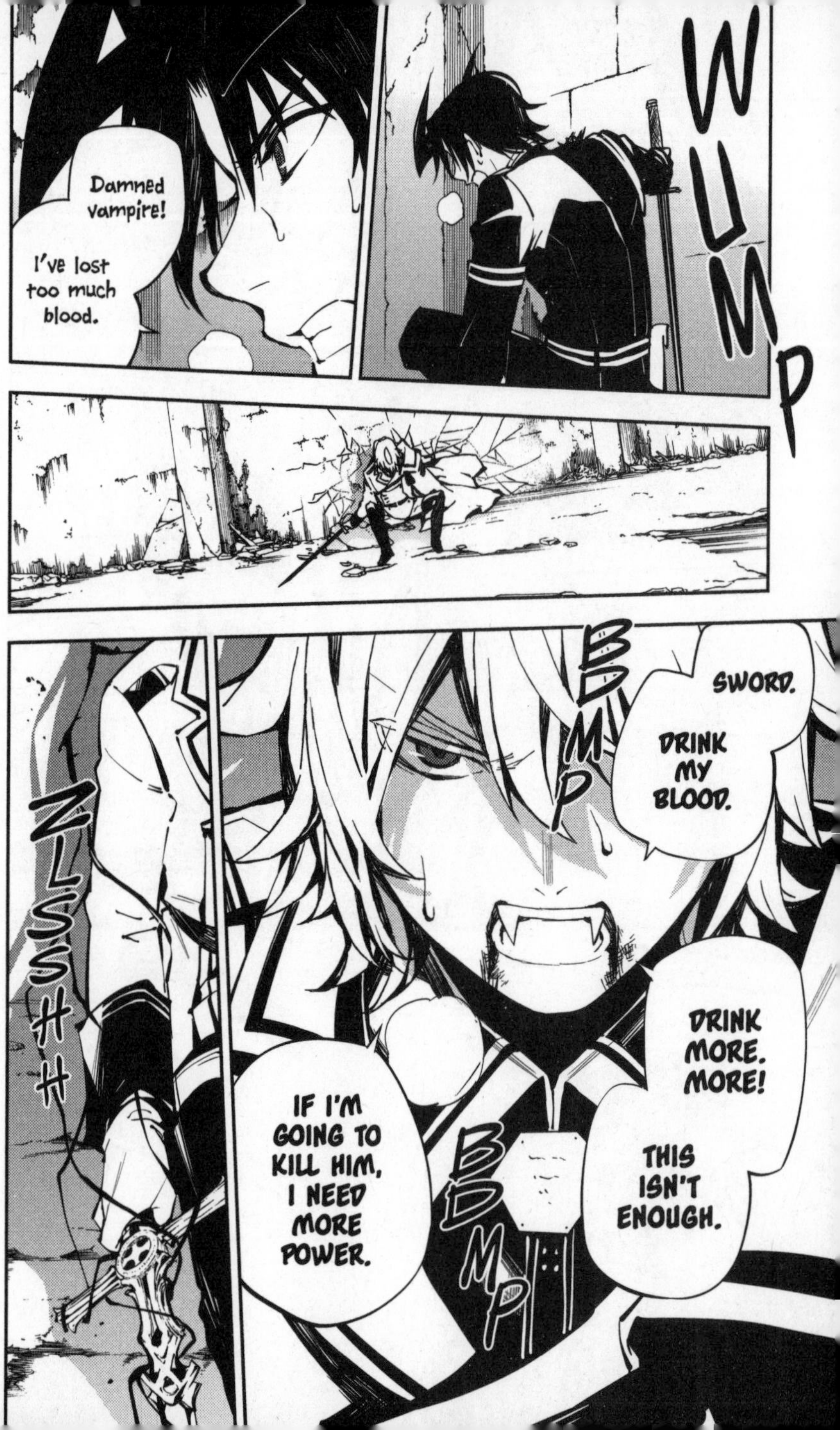
WUMP
Damned vampire!
I've lost too much blood.
BMP
SWORD.
DRINK MY BLOOD.
DRINK MORE. MORE!
THIS ISN'T ENOUGH.
BDMP
IF I'M GOING TO KILL HIM, I NEED MORE POWER.
ZLSSHH

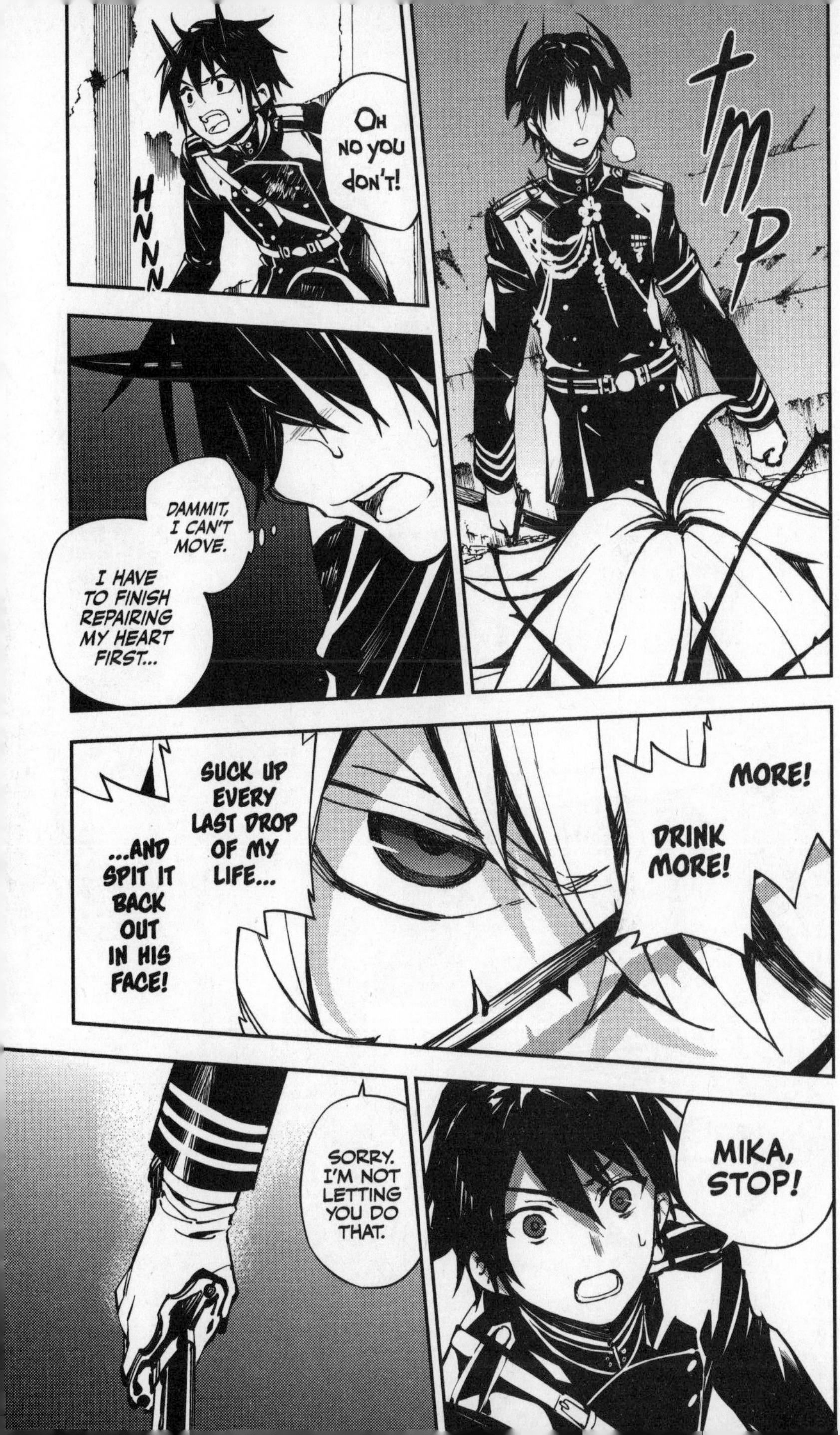
TMP
OH NO YOU DON'T!
HNNN
DAMMIT, I CAN'T MOVE.
I HAVE TO FINISH REPAIRING MY HEART FIRST...
MORE!
DRINK MORE!
SUCK UP EVERY LAST DROP OF MY LIFE...
...AND SPIT IT BACK OUT IN HIS FACE!
MIKA, STOP!
SORRY. I'M NOT LETTING YOU DO THAT.

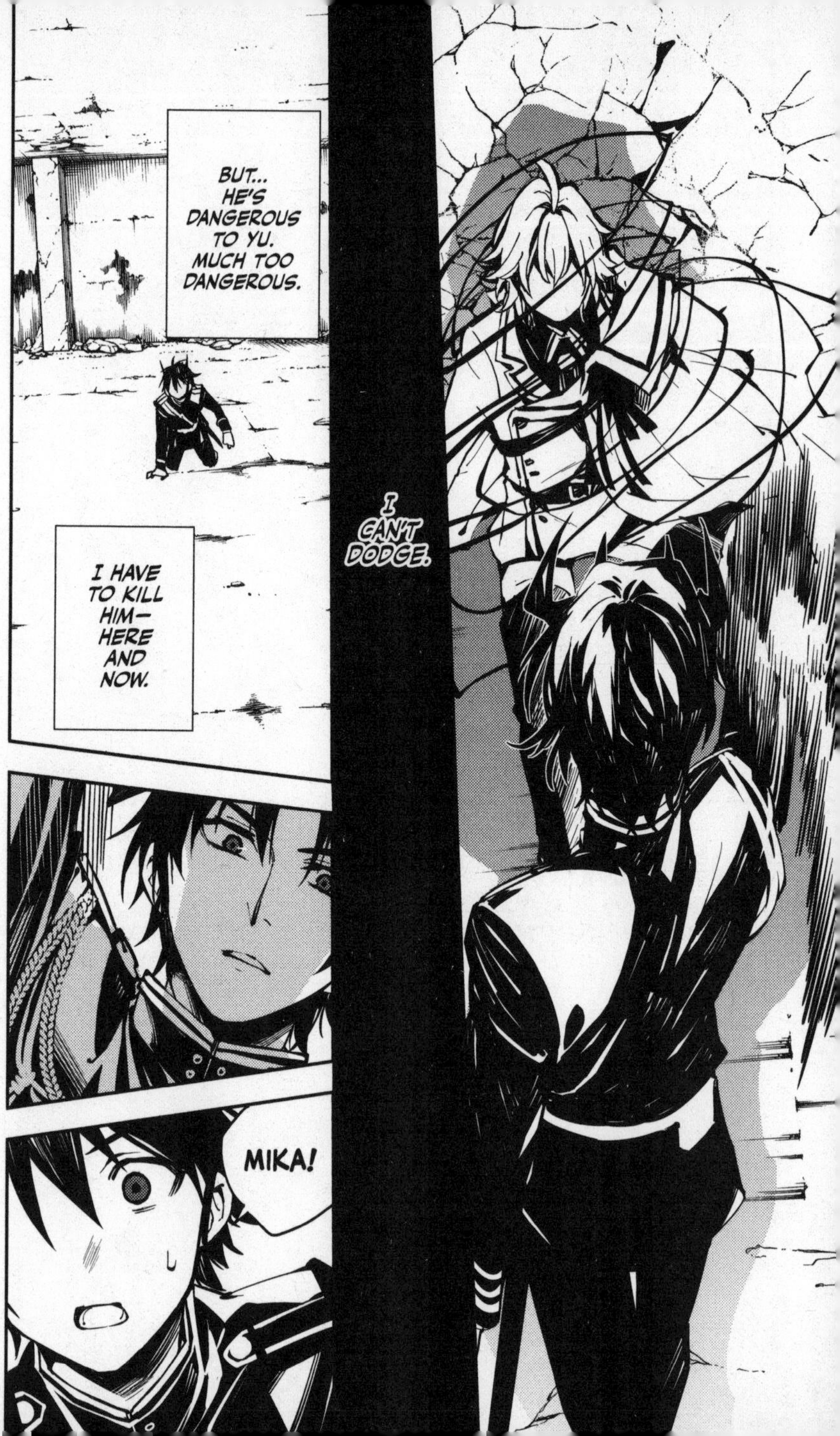
I CAN'T DODGE.
BUT... HE'S DANGEROUS TO YU. MUCH TOO DANGEROUS.
I HAVE TO KILL HIM—HERE AND NOW.
MIKA!

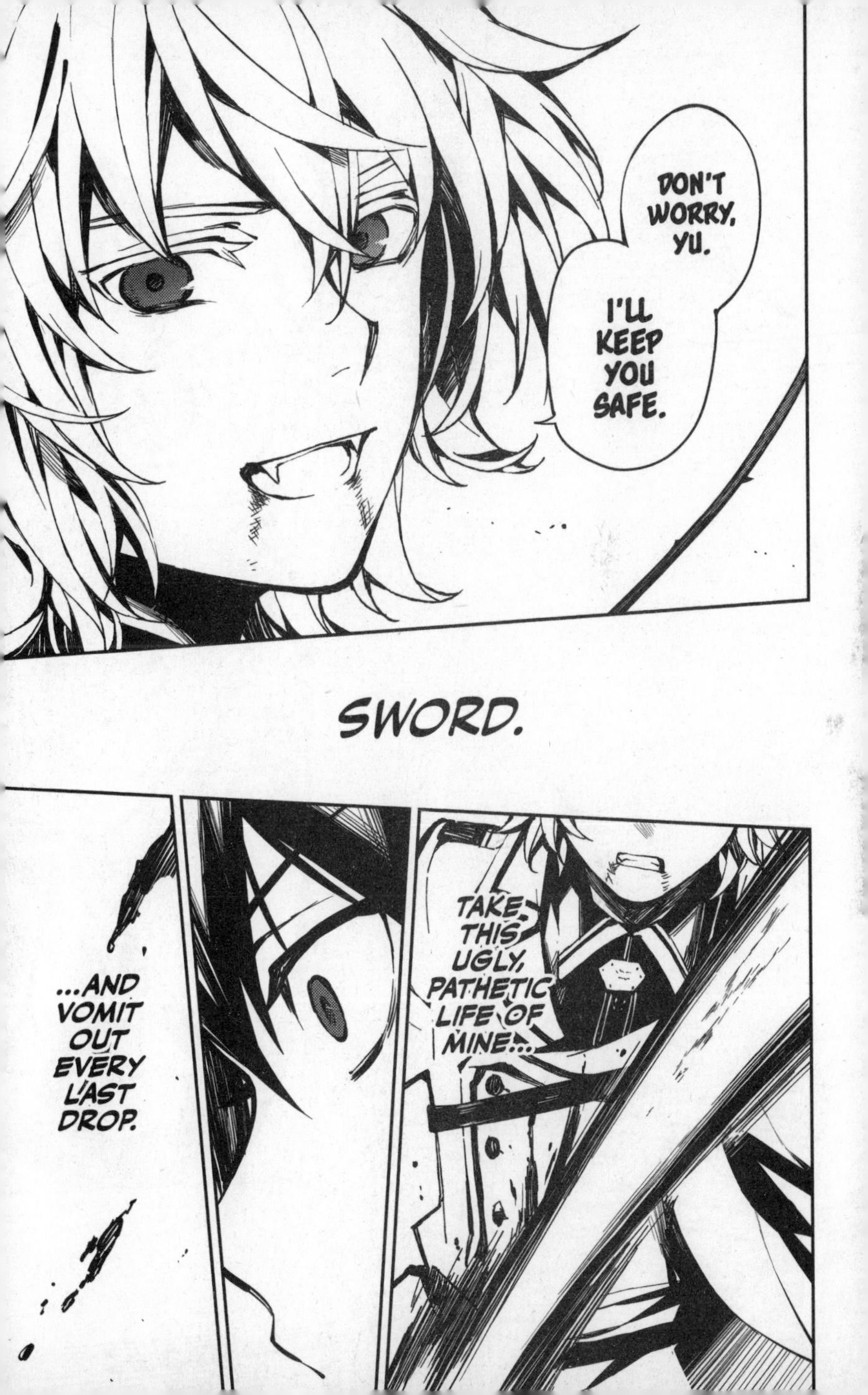
DON'T WORRY, YU.
I'LL KEEP YOU SAFE.
SWORD.
TAKE THIS UGLY, PATHETIC LIFE OF MINE...
...AND VOMIT OUT EVERY LAST DROP.

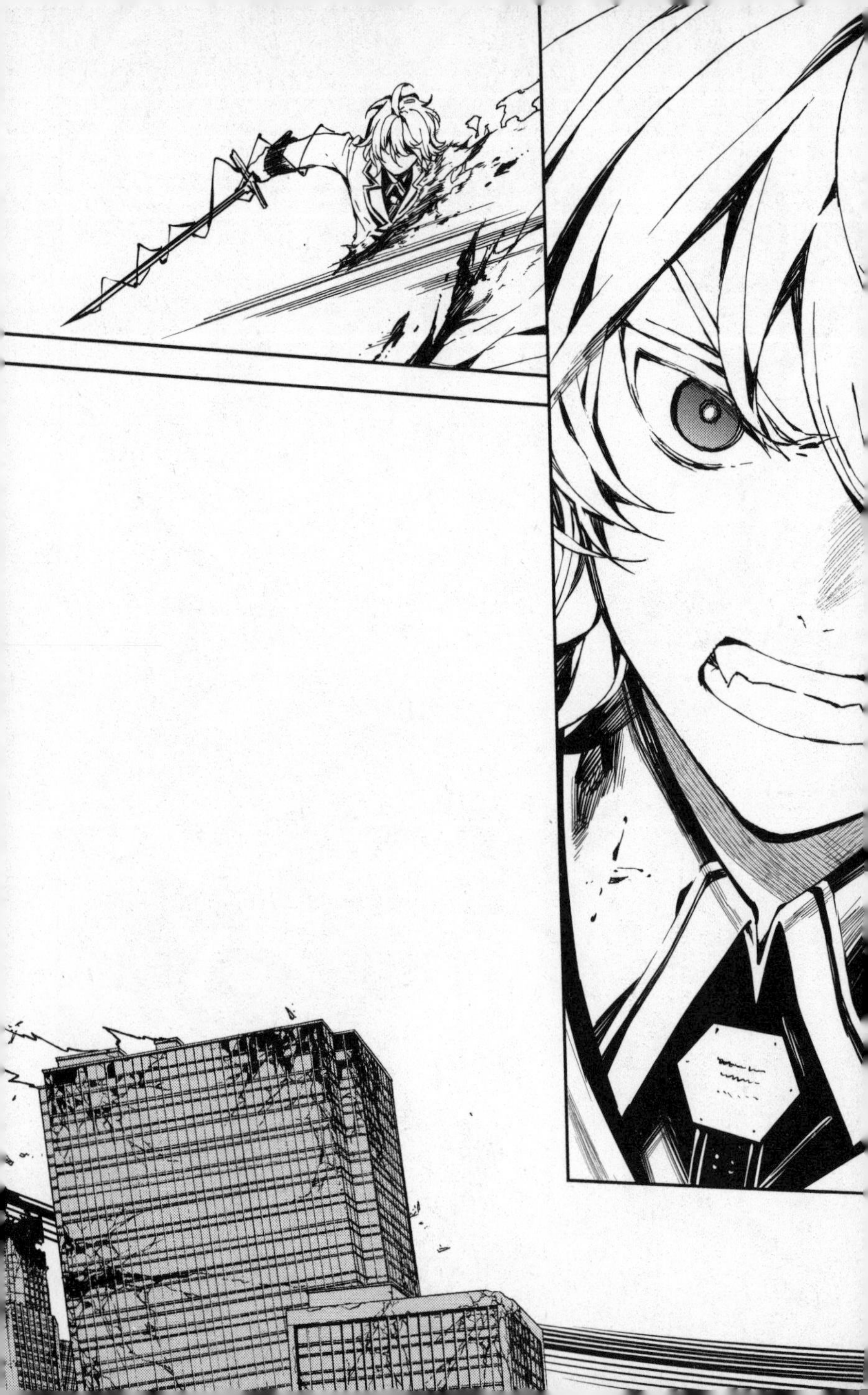

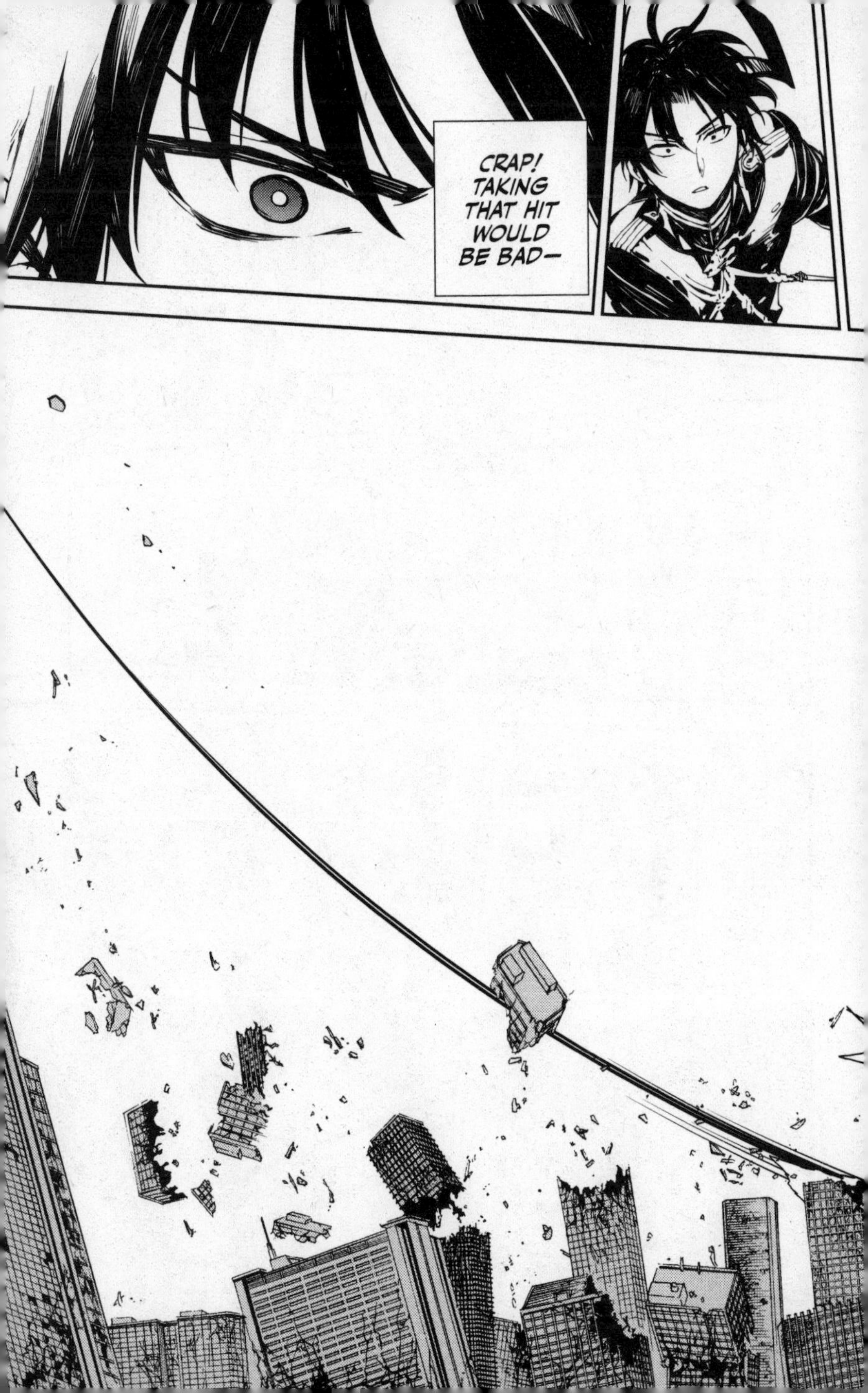
CRAP! TAKING THAT HIT WOULD BE BAD—

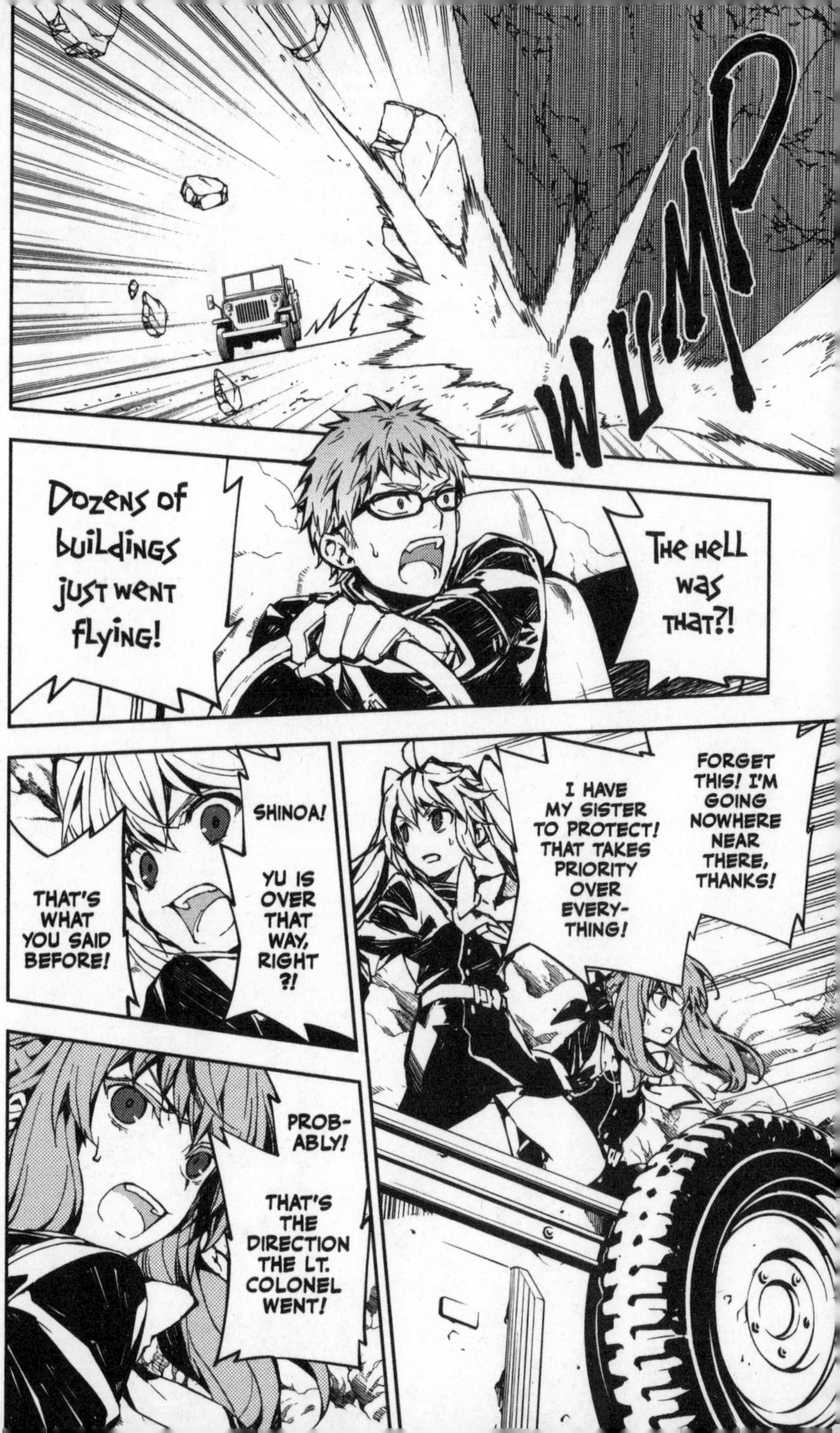
WUMP
The hell was that?!
Dozens of buildings just went flying!
FORGET THIS! I'M GOING NOWHERE NEAR THERE, THANKS!
I HAVE MY SISTER TO PROTECT! THAT TAKES PRIORITY OVER EVERY-THING!
SHINOA!
YU IS OVER THAT WAY, RIGHT?!
THAT'S WHAT YOU SAID BEFORE!
PROB-ABLY!
THAT'S THE DIRECTION THE LT. COLONEL WENT!

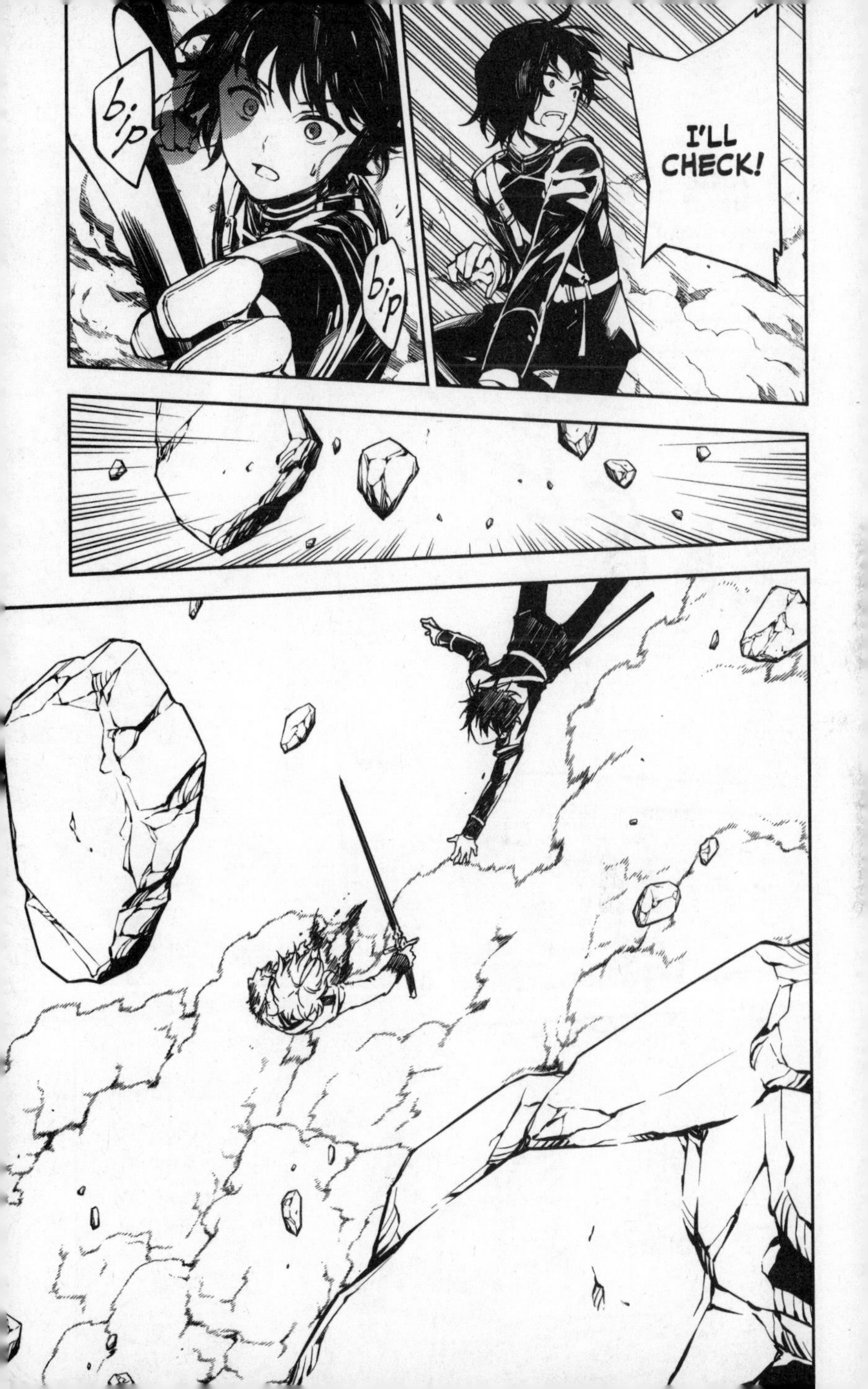
I'LL CHECK!
bip
bip

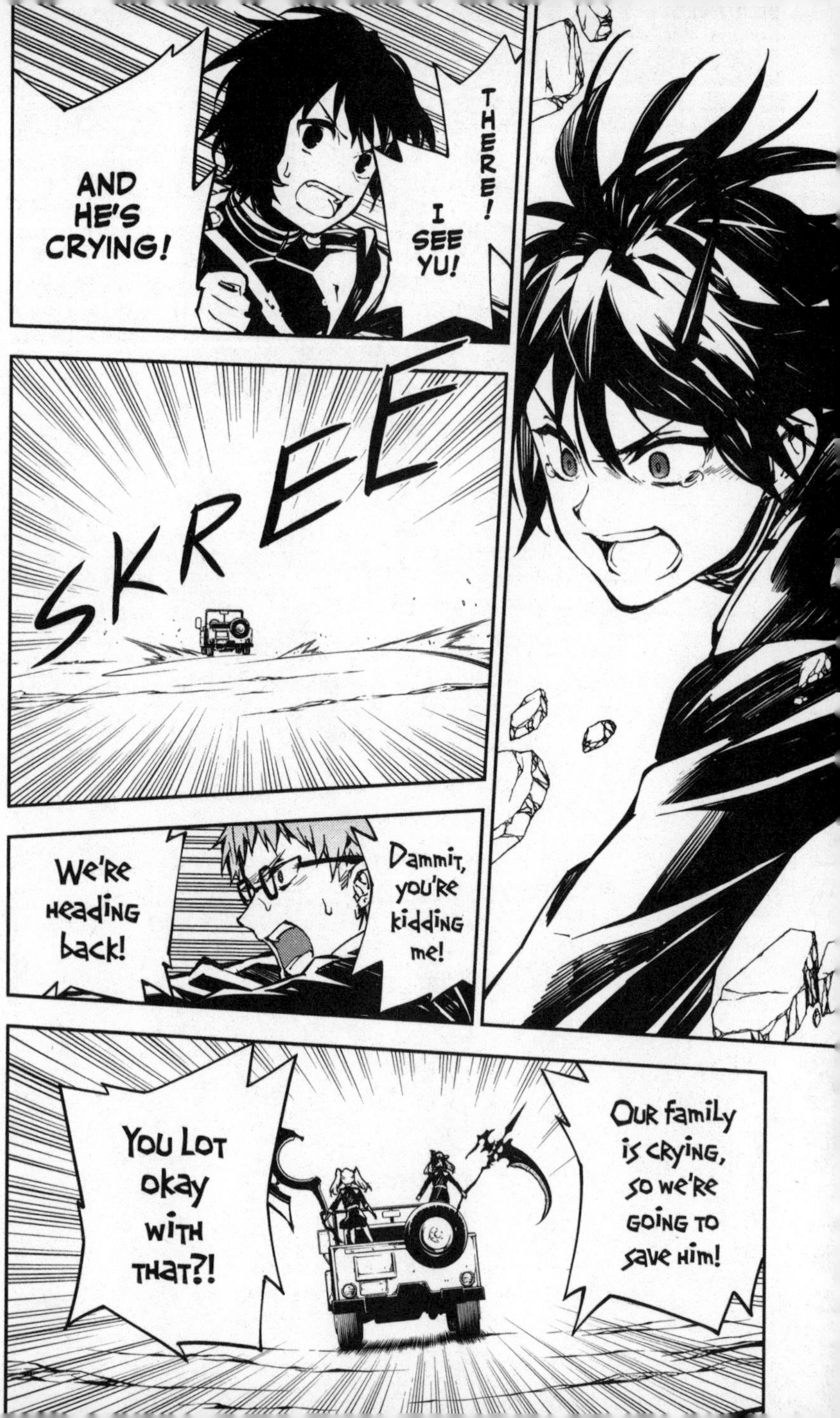
THERE! I SEE YU!
AND HE'S CRYING!
SKREE
Dammit, you're kidding me!
We're heading back!
Our family is crying, so we're going to save him!
You lot okay with that?!

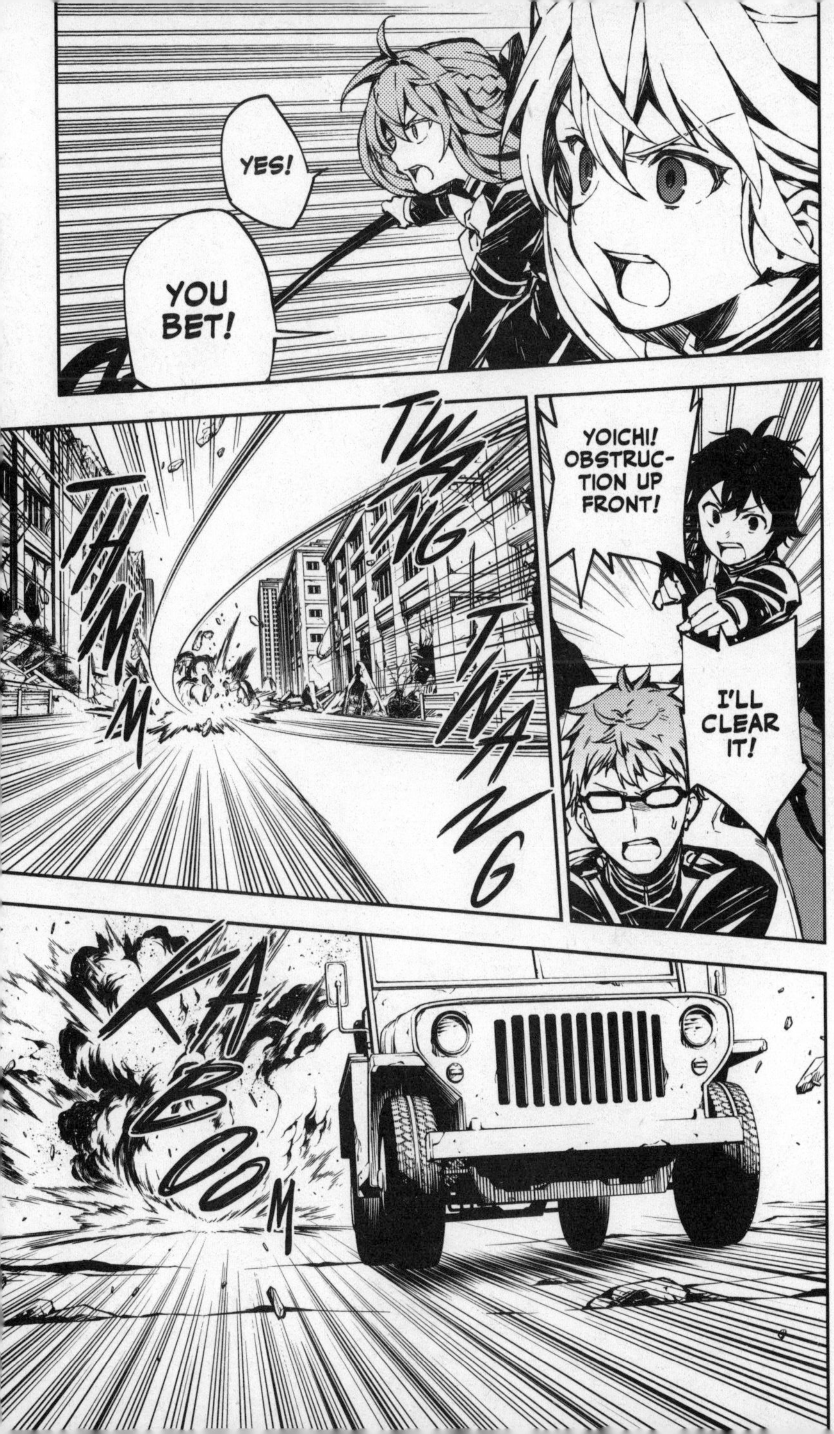
YES!
YOU BET!
YOICHI! OBSTRUCTION UP FRONT!
I'LL CLEAR IT!
TWANG TWANG
THMM
KABOOM

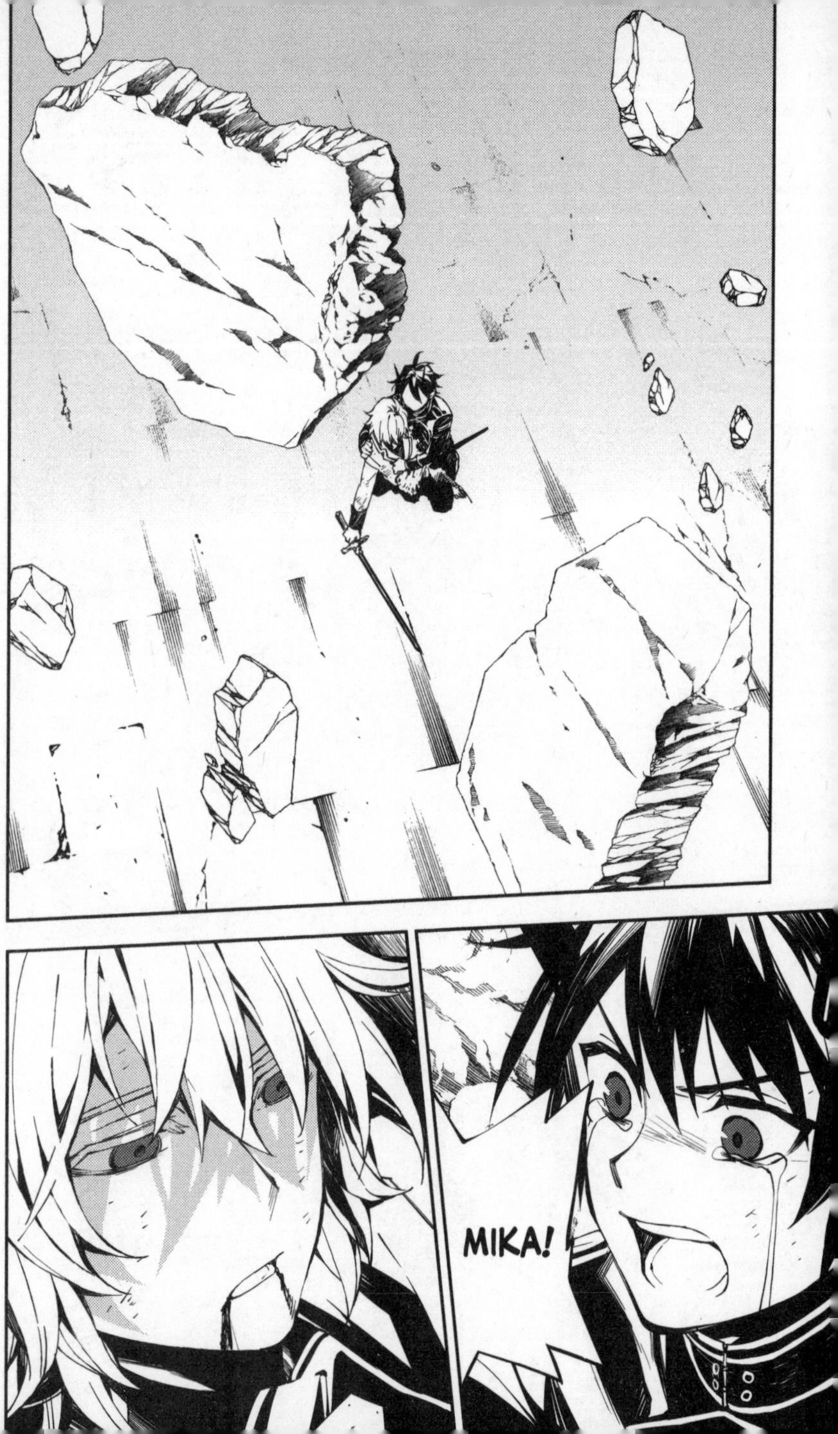
MIKA!

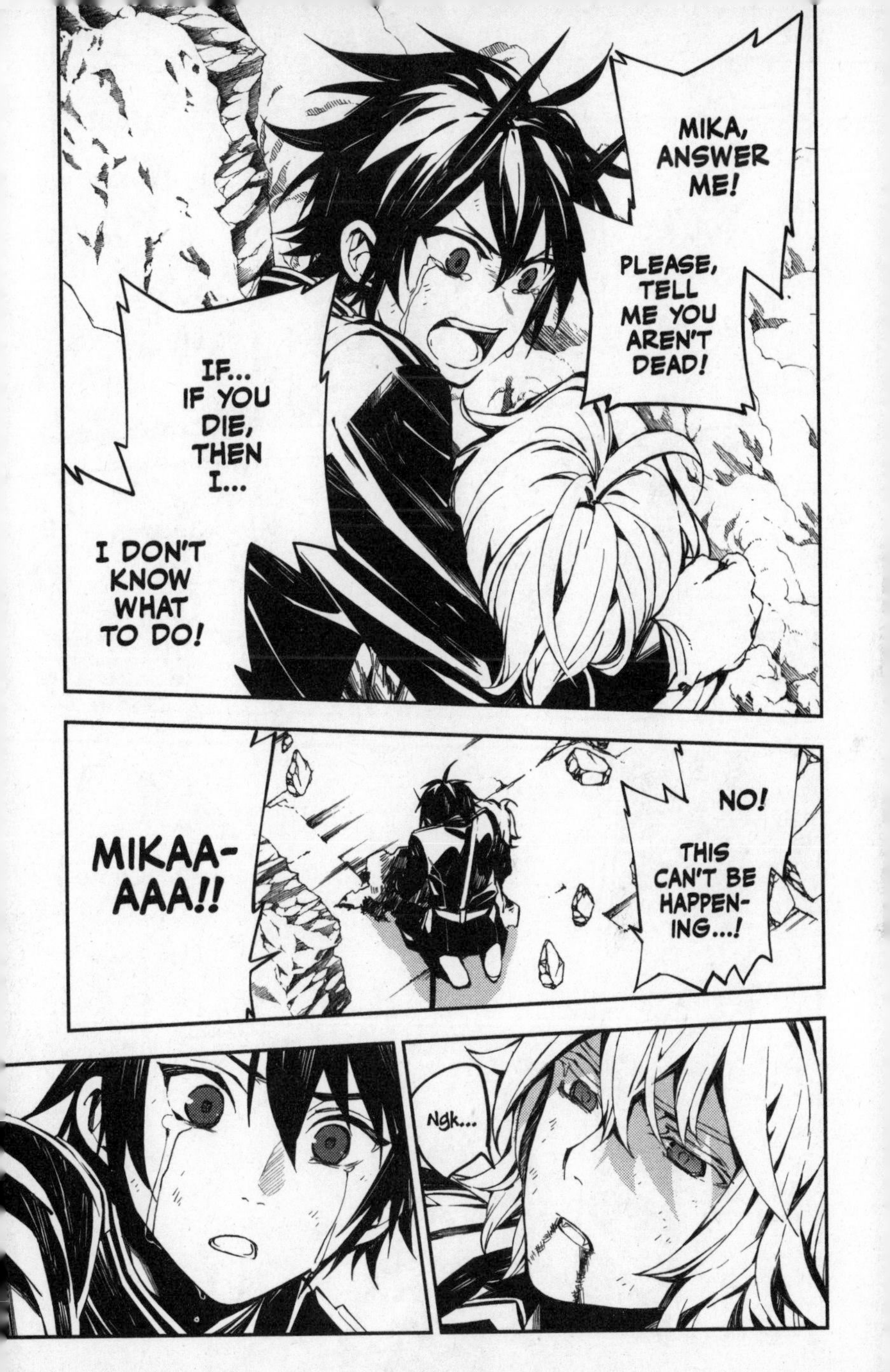
MIKA, ANSWER ME!
PLEASE, TELL ME YOU AREN'T DEAD!
IF... IF YOU DIE, THEN I...
I DON'T KNOW WHAT TO DO!
NO!
THIS CAN'T BE HAPPENING...!
MIKAA-AAA!!
Ngk...

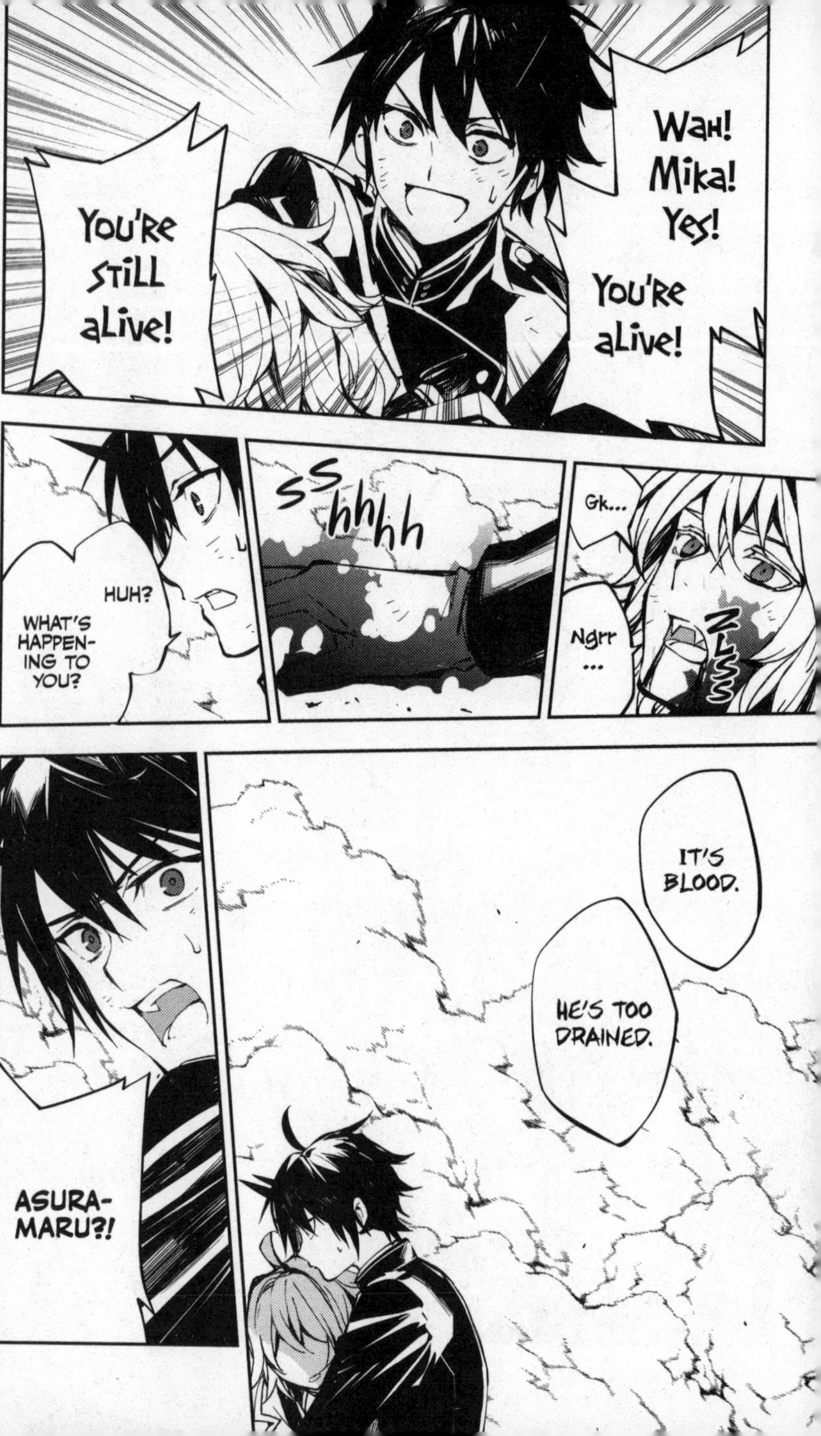
Wah! Mika! Yes!
You're alive!
You're still alive!
Gk...
Ngrr ...
ZLSS
sshhhh
HUH?
WHAT'S HAPPENING TO YOU?
IT'S BLOOD.
HE'S TOO DRAINED.
ASURA-MARU?!

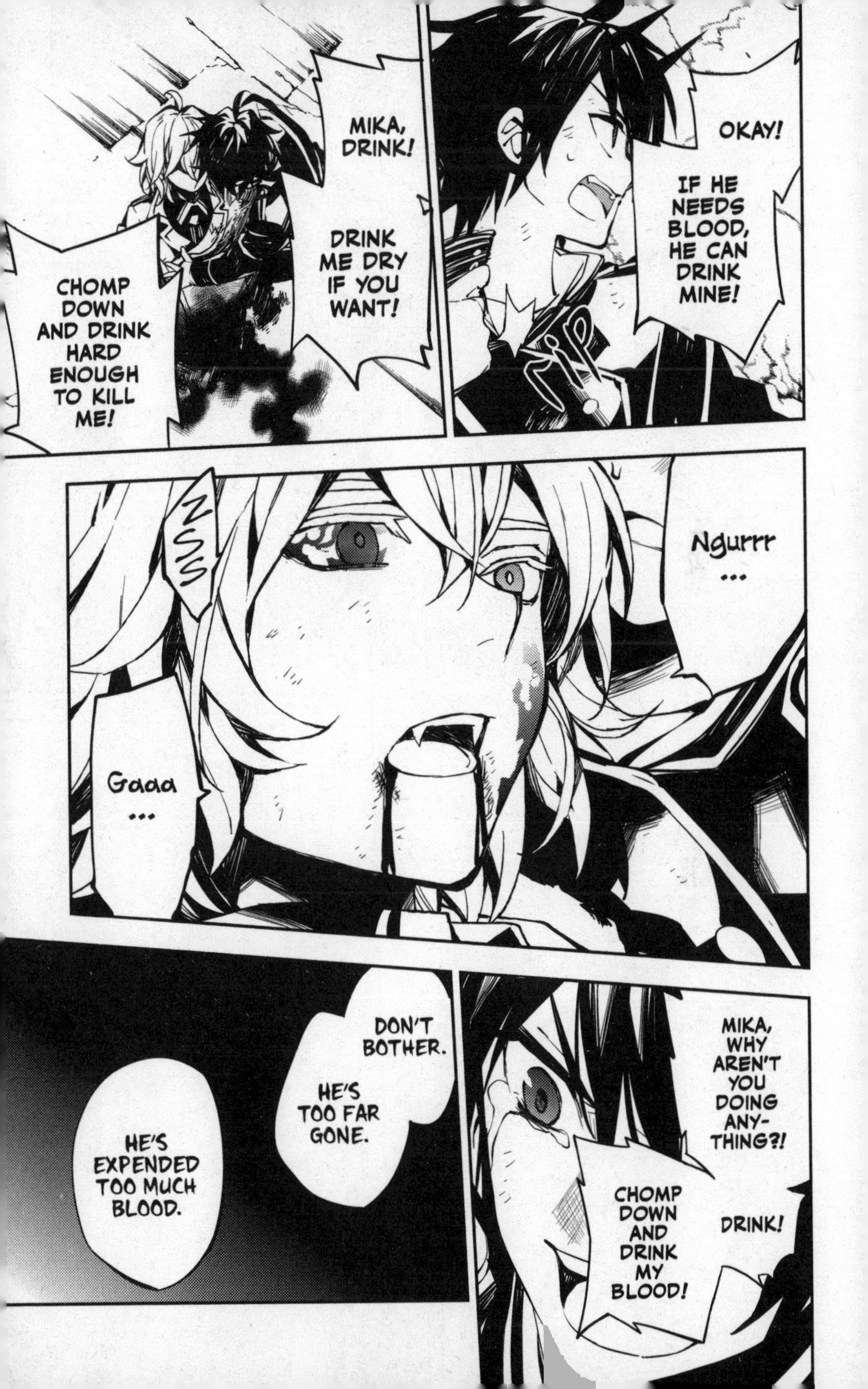
OKAY!
IF HE NEEDS BLOOD, HE CAN DRINK MINE!
rip
MIKA, DRINK!
DRINK ME DRY IF YOU WANT!
CHOMP DOWN AND DRINK HARD ENOUGH TO KILL ME!
Ngurrr ...
ZSS
Gaaa ...
MIKA, WHY AREN'T YOU DOING ANY-THING?!
DRINK!
CHOMP DOWN AND DRINK MY BLOOD!
DON'T BOTHER.
HE'S TOO FAR GONE.
HE'S EXPENDED TOO MUCH BLOOD.

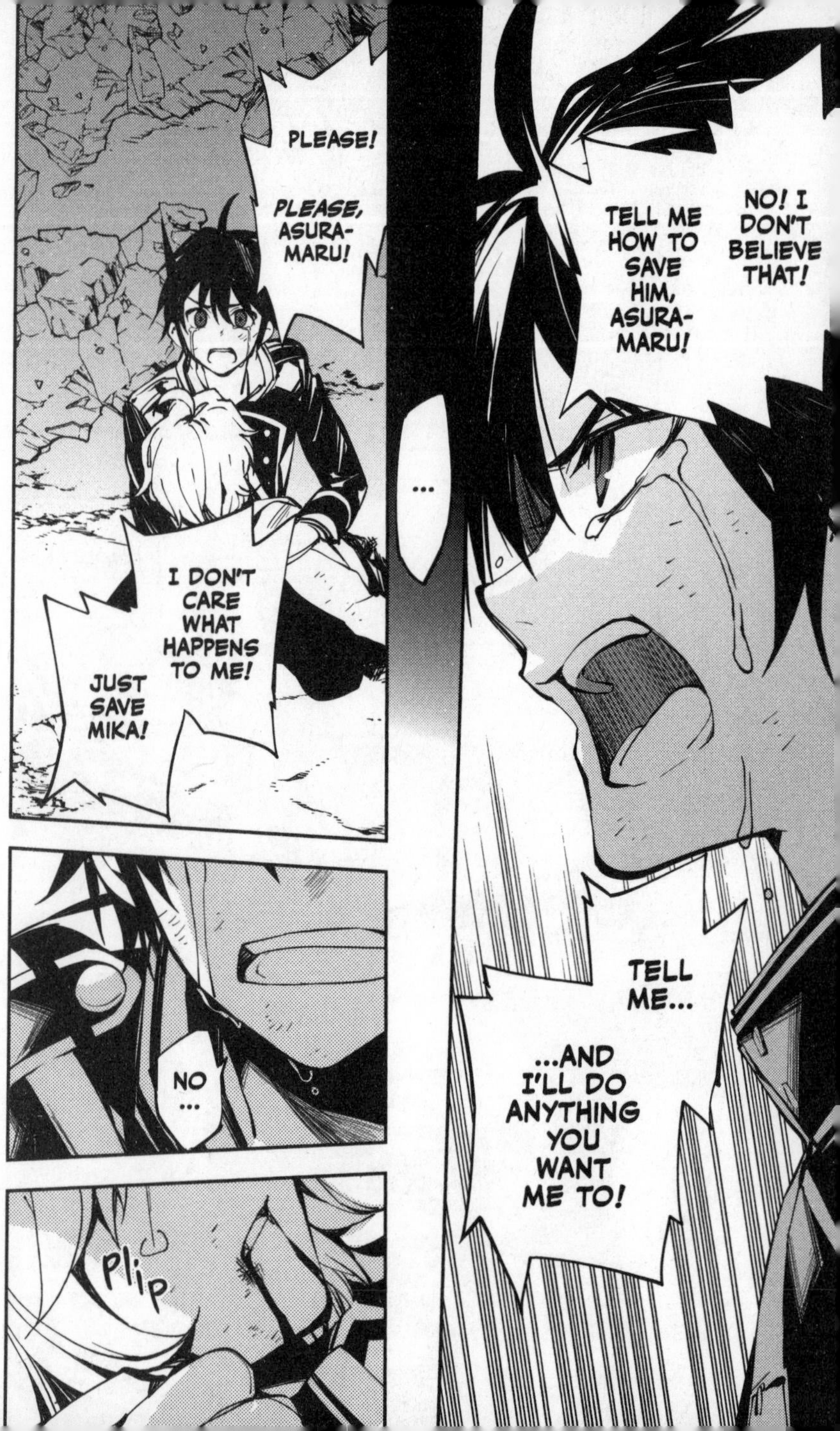
NO! I DON'T BELIEVE THAT!
TELL ME HOW TO SAVE HIM, ASURA-MARU!
...
TELL ME...
...AND I'LL DO ANYTHING YOU WANT ME TO!
PLEASE!
PLEASE, ASURA-MARU!
I DON'T CARE WHAT HAPPENS TO ME!
JUST SAVE MIKA!
NO ...
Plip

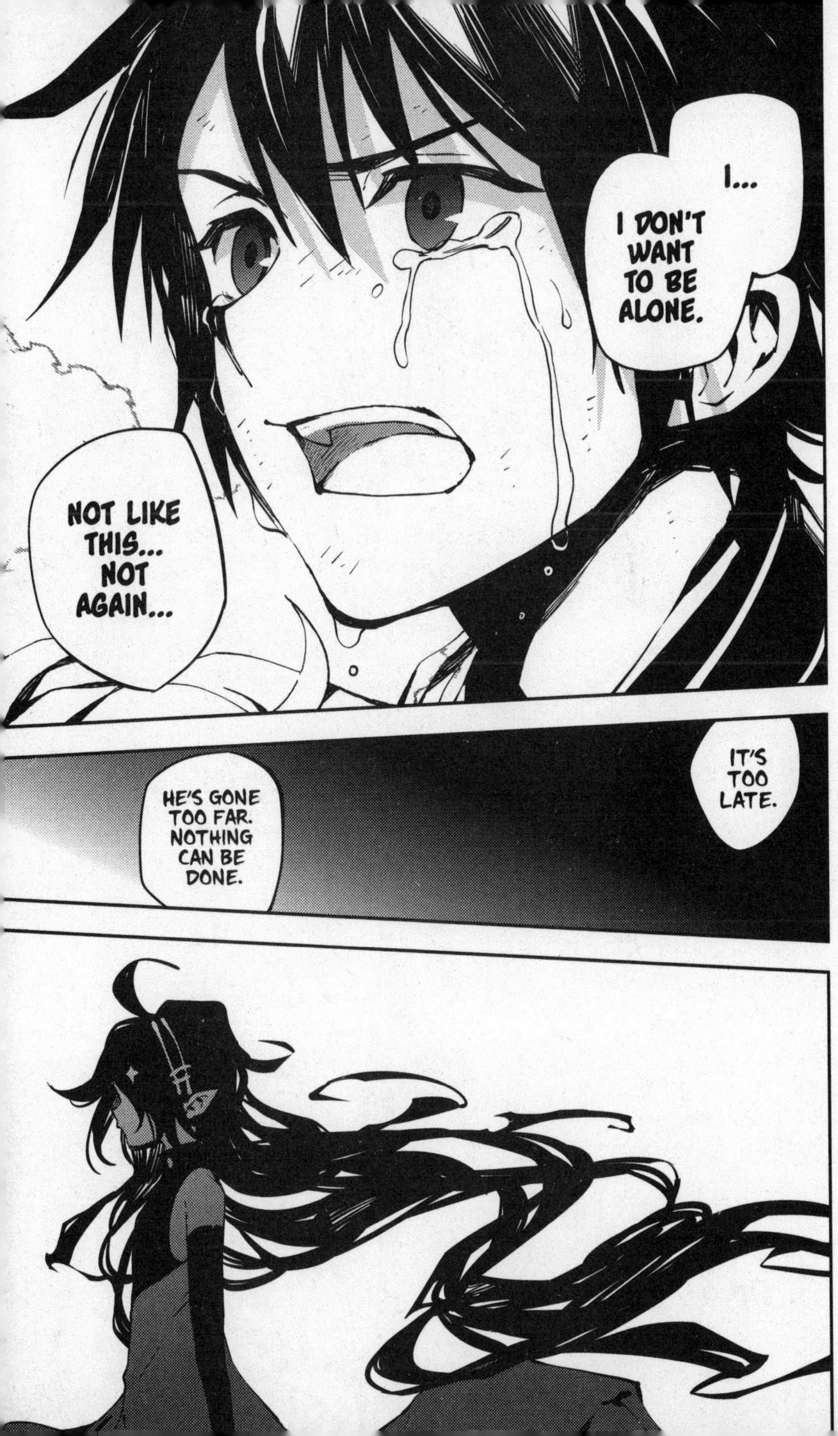
I...
I DON'T WANT TO BE ALONE.
NOT LIKE THIS... NOT AGAIN...
IT'S TOO LATE.
HE'S GONE TOO FAR. NOTHING CAN BE DONE.

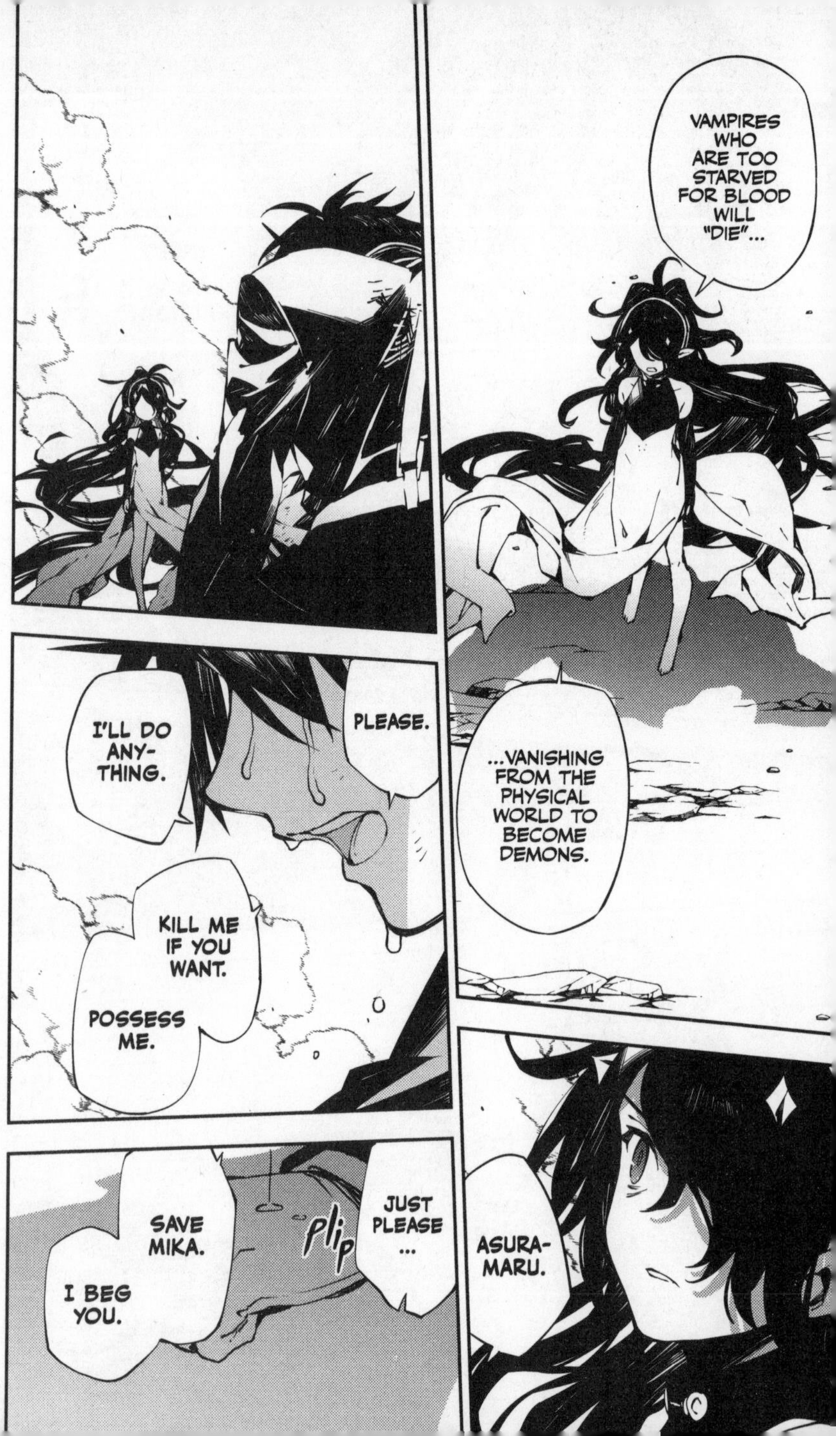
VAMPIRES WHO ARE TOO STARVED FOR BLOOD WILL "DIE"...
...VANISHING FROM THE PHYSICAL WORLD TO BECOME DEMONS.
PLEASE.
I'LL DO ANYTHING.
KILL ME IF YOU WANT.
POSSESS ME.
ASURA-MARU.
JUST PLEASE...
Plip
SAVE MIKA.
I BEG YOU.

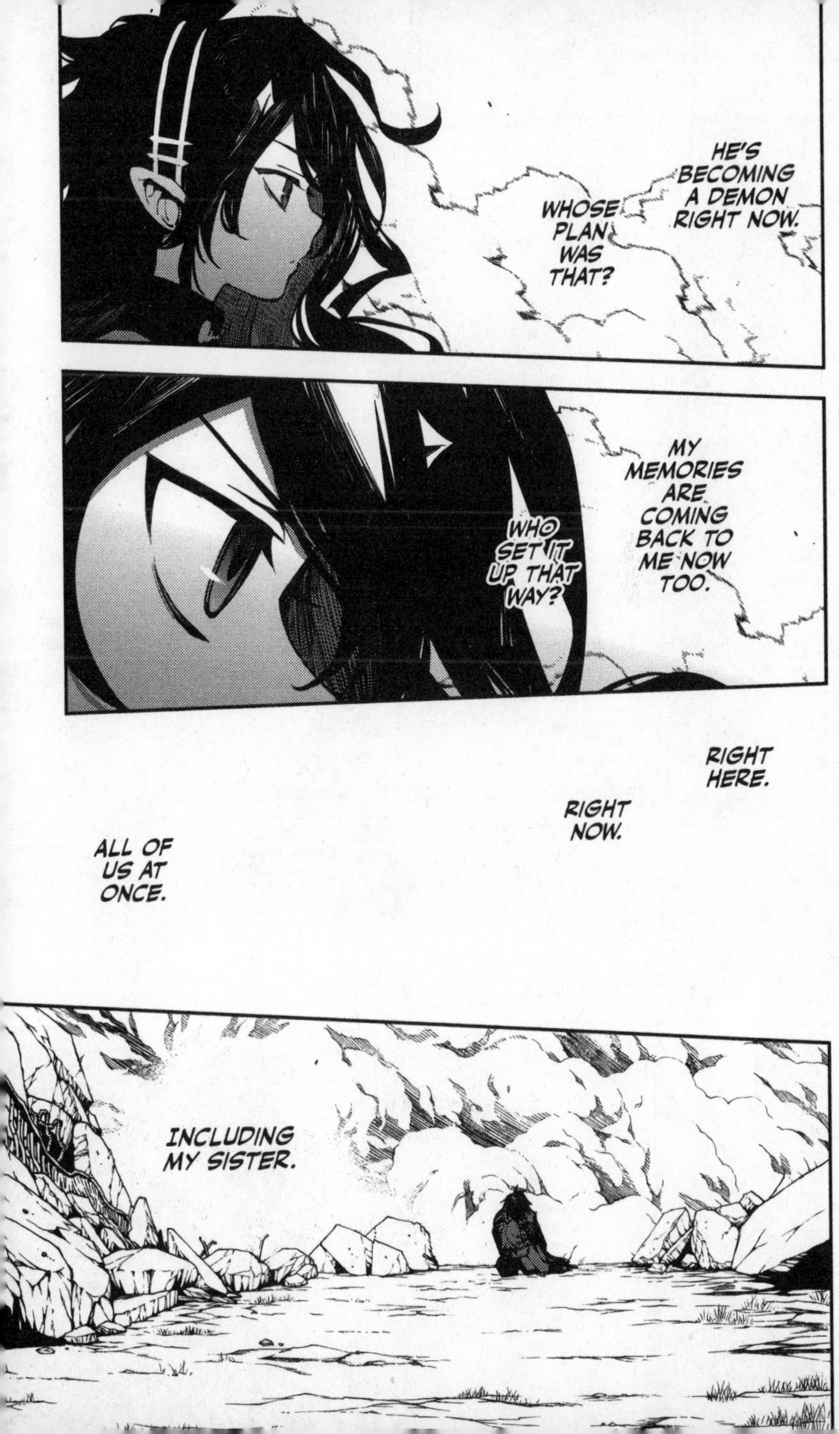
HE'S BECOMING A DEMON RIGHT NOW.
WHOSE PLAN WAS THAT?
MY MEMORIES ARE COMING BACK TO ME NOW TOO.
WHO SET IT UP THAT WAY?
RIGHT HERE.
RIGHT NOW.
ALL OF US AT ONCE.
INCLUDING MY SISTER.

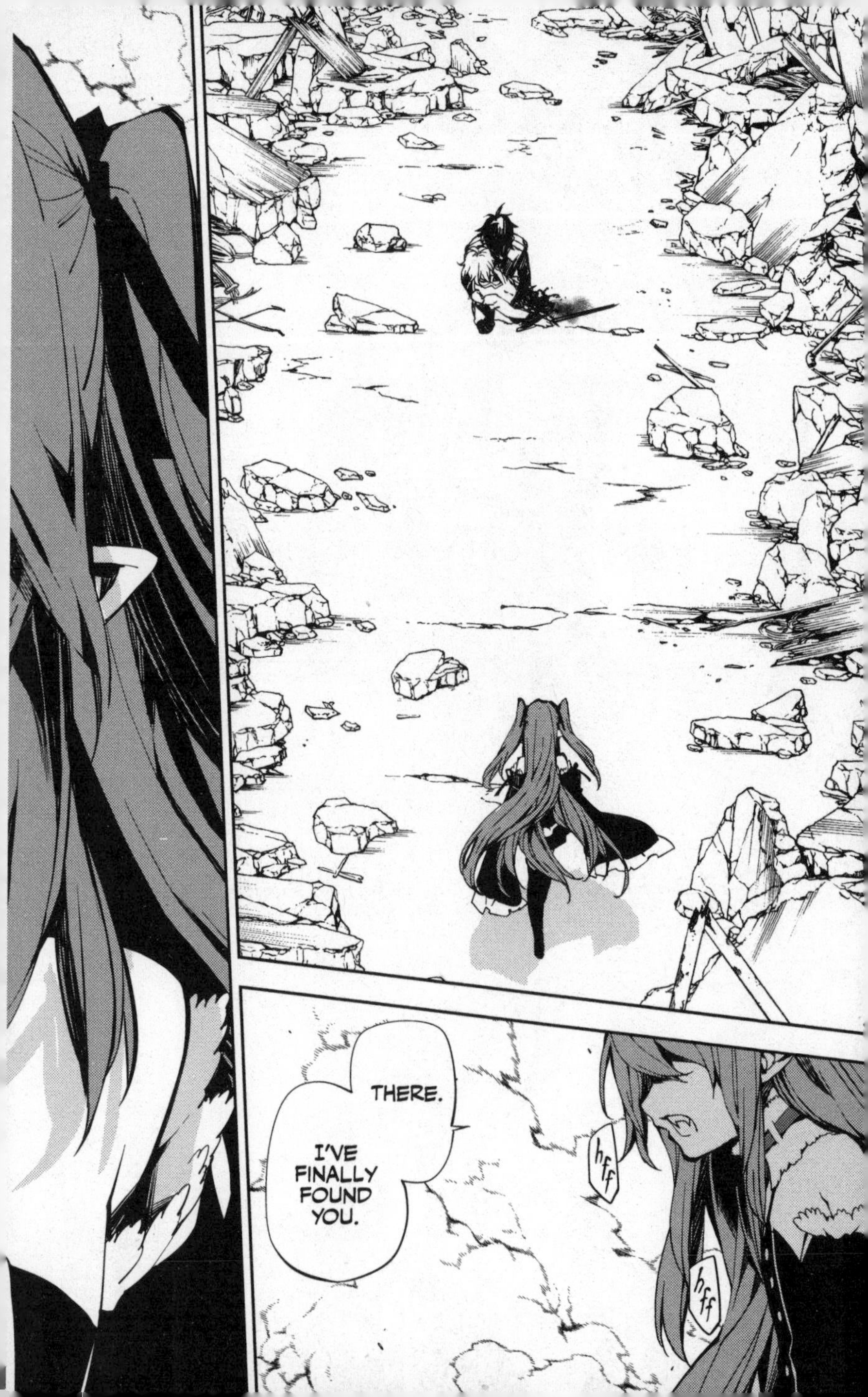
hff
hff
THERE.
I'VE FINALLY FOUND YOU.

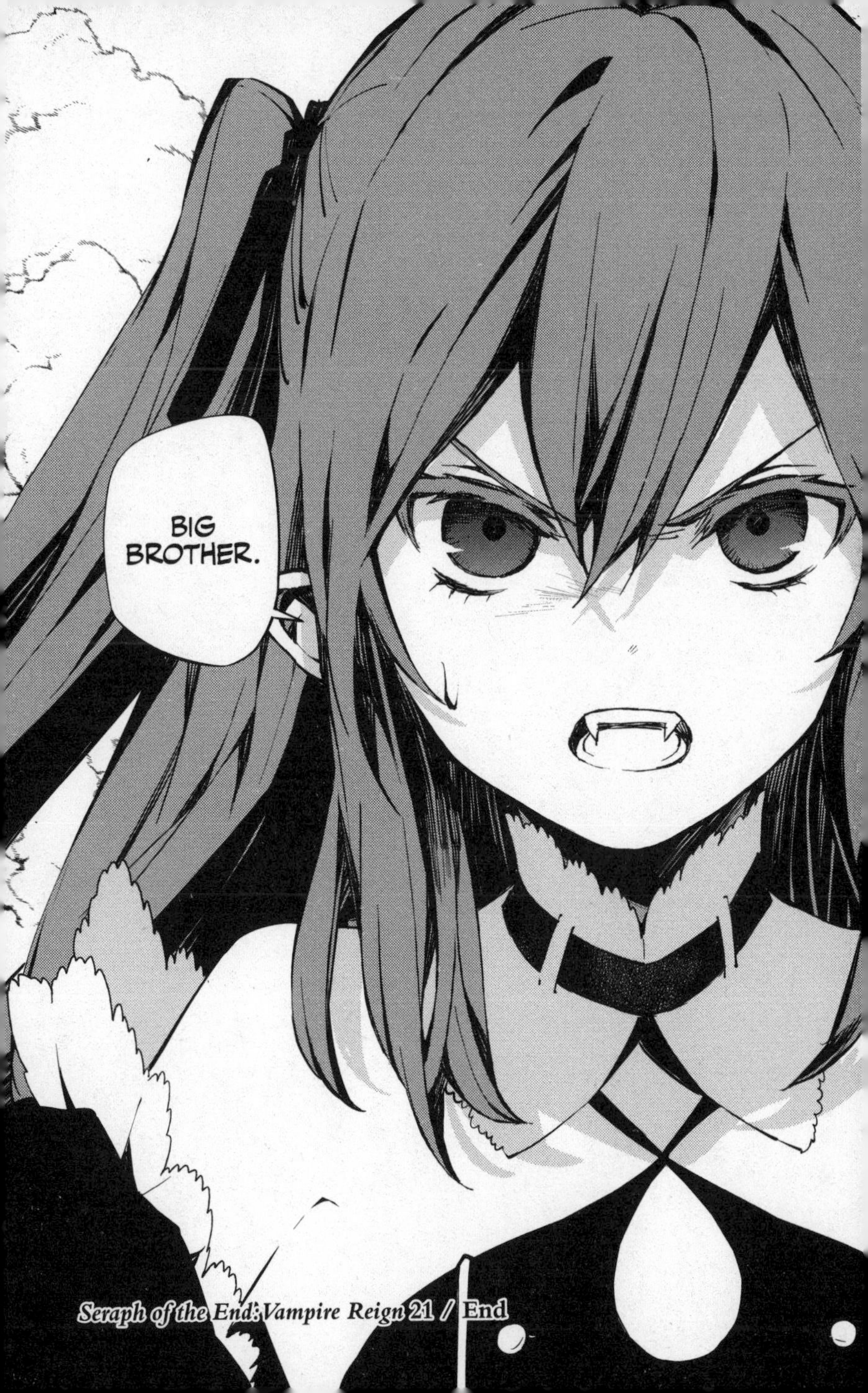
BIG BROTHER.
Seraph of the End: Vampire Reign 21 / End

of the **End**

REIGN——

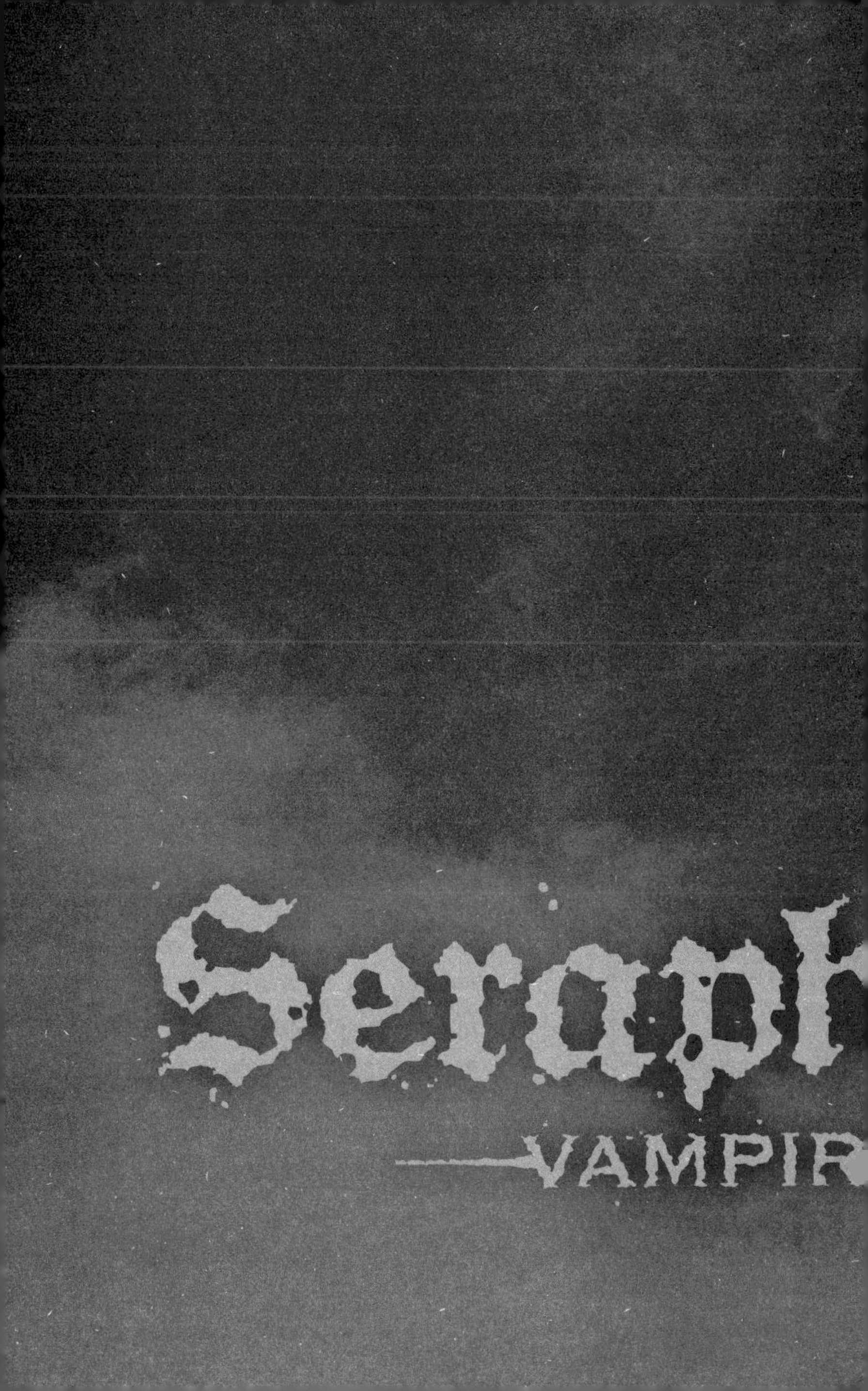
Seraph
VAMPIR

AFTERWORD

HELLO, EVERYONE! IT'S BEEN A WHILE!

THIS IS A NEW VOLUME *SERAPH OF THE END!*

SO I WRITE WITH HAPPY EXCITED LITTLE EXCLAMATION MARKS AT THE END OF EACH OF MY SENTENCES. BUT BY THE TIME YOU'RE READING THIS AFTERWORD, IT'S GOING TO BE AT LEAST JUNE OF 2020, IF NOT LATER. RIGHT NOW, AS I'M WRITING IT, IT'S APRIL 2020. I CANNOT EVEN IMAGINE WHAT THE WORLD WILL BE LIKE COME JUNE.

YOU SEE, RIGHT NOW THE WORLD IS SUFFERING FROM A VIRUS. SCHOOLS ARE CLOSED. PEOPLE CAN'T GO TO WORK. OR THEY'RE FORCED TO GO TO WORK EVEN THOUGH THEY WOULD REALLY RATHER NOT.

SERAPH OF THE END BEGAN WITH AN UNKNOWN VIRUS INFECTING THE WORLD, LEAVING ONLY THE CHILDREN BEHIND. FROM THERE, TWO CHILDREN, YUICHIRO AND MIKA, DID THEIR BEST TO SURVIVE. WHEN THE FIRST EVENTS OF THE STORY BEGAN, GUREN AND HIS FRIENDS—IN KODANSHA'S *SERAPH OF THE END: GUREN ICHINOSE: CATASTROPHE AT 16*—WERE ONLY 16 YEARS OLD. THEY WERE CHILDREN, BUT THEY WERE LEFT TO MAKE THEIR OWN WAY IN THE WORLD.

WE'RE MORE FORTUNATE THAN THEY, AS THIS VIRUS ISN'T NEARLY SO BAD (THOUGH WE CAN'T SAY ANYTHING FOR CERTAIN YET). BUT EVEN SO, THINGS ARE STILL PLENTY TERRIBLE ENOUGH.

NOW THAT SOMETHING LIKE THIS IS ACTUALLY AFFECTING OUR LIVES, IT BRINGS A LOT OF UNCERTAINTY AND ANXIETY. WHO KNEW IT WOULD BE SO DIFFICULT? WHO KNOWS WHAT WILL HAPPEN NEXT?

I'VE WRITTEN SO MANY STORIES ABOUT WHAT PEOPLE MIGHT TRULY DO AND NEED IN A CATASTROPHIC WORLD.

WHAT POINT IS THERE TO LIVING?

WHAT SHOULD WE CLING TO?

THAT AND OTHER CONCEPTS LIKE IT FORMED THE BASIS OF MANY OF MY WORKS. *SERAPH OF THE END* IS A WORK THAT I REALLY THINK EMBODIES THAT IDEA.

WHAT DOES IT MEAN TO HAVE FRIENDS?

WHAT DOES IT MEAN TO HAVE FAMILY?

WHAT DOES IT MEAN TO TAKE THE HANDS OF THOSE AROUND YOU AND LIVE, NO MATTER HOW HORRIBLE THE WORLD HAS BECOME?

AND WHAT IS THE TRUE, HUMAN STRENGTH THAT WILL SHINE THROUGH AT THE END?

CURRENT WORLD EVENTS ARE GIVING ME MORE INCENTIVE TO THINK EVEN MORE DEEPLY ON THAT.

IT MAKES ME FEEL THAT THERE'S SOMETHING WE CAN LEARN FROM HOW YU LIVES. FROM HOW MIKAELA, GUREN, SHINYA AND SHINOA LIVE. IT MAKES ME FEEL THAT MAYBE WE CAN FIND SOME ENCOURAGEMENT LOOKING AT THE *SERAPH OF THE END* WORLD, WHICH WAS STRUCK BY A DEVASTATING VIRUS FIRST. IT GIVES HOPE THAT, NO MATTER HOW BAD IT GETS, PEOPLE CAN STILL TAKE EACH OTHER'S HANDS AND PUSH FORWARD.

TODAY, I GO BACK TO WRITING ON THIS WORK HOPING THAT THIS MAY PROVIDE SOME SMALL ENCOURAGEMENT FOR OTHERS IN THE WORLD TODAY. I THINK THAT I CAN SAY THE SAME FOR YAMATO YAMAMOTO AND DAISUKE FURUYA, WHO WORK ON IT WITH ME. I WOULD BE HONORED IF THIS STORY COULD HELP BRING A LITTLE BIT OF FUN INTO YOUR LIVES.

IN OTHER NEWS, *SERAPH OF THE END*'S STORY IS DIVING EVER CLOSER TO THE CORE OF THE PLOT. I HOPE EVERYONE WILL KEEP READING! NOT ONLY THAT, IT'S GOING TO START TOUCHING ON ANOTHER, EVEN BIGGER STORYLINE THAT HAS BEEN AROUND SINCE EVEN BEFORE THE FIRST KERNELS OF THE *SERAPH OF THE END* PLOT FORMED IN MY MIND. I HATE TO END ON THAT TEASER, BUT STAY TUNED!

—TAKAYA KAGAMI

A brilliant sketch of Yuichiro by the author!

TAKAYA KAGAMI is a prolific light novelist whose works include the action and fantasy series *The Legend of the Legendary Heroes*, which has been adapted into manga, anime and a video game. His previous series, *A Dark Rabbit Has Seven Lives*, also spawned a manga and anime series.

❝ I've been an indoor person ever since I debuted as a creator. I never expected the day would come when it was recommended that everybody become indoor people. ❞

YAMATO YAMAMOTO, born 1983, is an artist and illustrator whose works include the *Kure-nai* manga and the light novels *Kure-nai*, *9S -Nine S-* and *Denpa Teki na Kanojo*. Both *Denpa Teki na Kanojo* and *Kure-nai* have been adapted into anime.

❝ Volume 21 sees unbelievable things happen to Yuichiro and Mika. What's going to come next?! Don't miss it! ❞

DAISUKE FURUYA previously assisted Yamato Yamamoto with storyboards for *Kure-nai*.

Seraph of the End

⟶VAMPIRE REIGN⟵

VOLUME 21
SHONEN JUMP MANGA EDITION

STORY BY **TAKAYA KAGAMI**

ART BY **YAMATO YAMAMOTO**

STORYBOARDS BY **DAISUKE FURUYA**

TRANSLATION **Adrienne Beck**
TOUCH-UP ART & LETTERING **Sabrina Heep**
DESIGN **Shawn Carrico**
EDITOR **Marlene First**

OWARI NO SERAPH © 2012 by Takaya Kagami,
Yamato Yamamoto, Daisuke Furuya
All rights reserved. First published in Japan in 2012 by SHUEISHA Inc., Tokyo.
English translation rights arranged by SHUEISHA Inc.

The stories, characters and incidents mentioned in this
publication are entirely fictional.

Printed in the U.S.A.

Published by VIZ Media, LLC
P.O. Box 77010
San Francisco, CA 94107

10 9 8 7 6 5 4 3 2 1
First printing, June 2021

 MEDIA
viz.com

Twin Star Exorcists

ＯＮＭＹＯＪＩ

STORY AND ART BY Yoshiaki Sukeno

**The action-packed romantic comedy
from the creator of *Good Luck Girl!***

Rokuro dreams of becoming *anything* but an exorcist!
Then mysterious Benio turns up. The pair are dubbed the
"Twin Star Exorcists" and learn they are fated to marry...

Can Rokuro escape both fates?

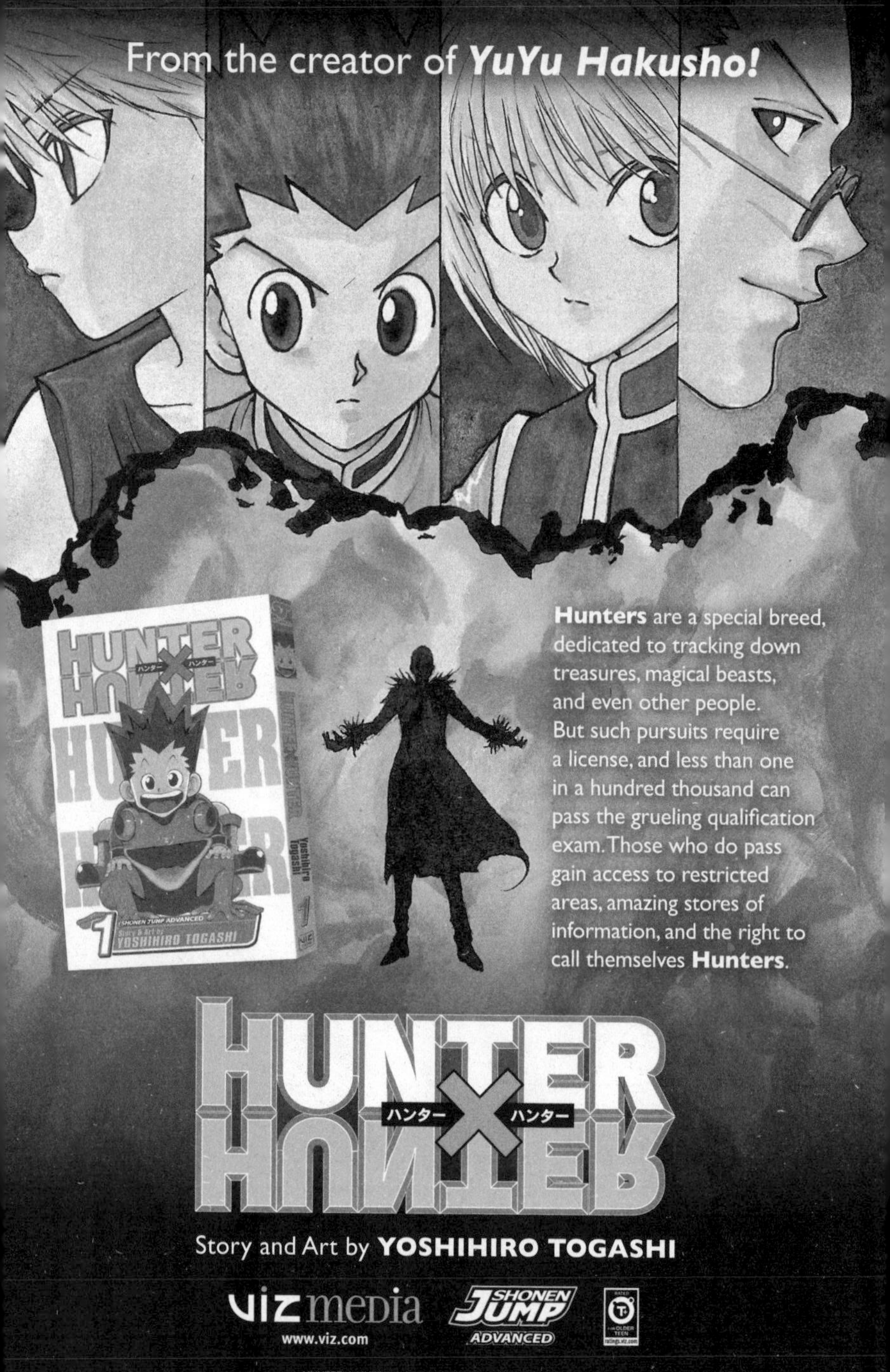
From the creator of YuYu Hakusho!
HUNTER × HUNTER ハンター ハンター
SHONEN JUMP ADVANCED
1
Story & Art by YOSHIHIRO TOGASHI
Hunters are a special breed, dedicated to tracking down treasures, magical beasts, and even other people. But such pursuits require a license, and less than one in a hundred thousand can pass the grueling qualification exam. Those who do pass gain access to restricted areas, amazing stores of information, and the right to call themselves Hunters.
HUNTER × HUNTER ハンター ハンター
Story and Art by YOSHIHIRO TOGASHI
viz media
www.viz.com
SHONEN JUMP ADVANCED
OLDER TEEN
ratings.viz.com

Black✳Clover

STORY & ART BY YŪKI TABATA

Asta is a young boy who dreams of becoming the greatest mage in the kingdom. Only one problem—he can't use any magic! Luckily for Asta, he receives the incredibly rare five-leaf clover grimoire that gives him the power of anti-magic. Can someone who can't use magic really become the Wizard King? One thing's for sure—Asta will never give up!

SHONEN JUMP

vizmedia
www.viz.com

YOU'RE READING THE

WRONG WAY!

SERAPH OF THE END reads from right to left, starting in the upper-right corner. Japanese is read from right to left, meaning that action, sound effects, and word-balloon order are completely reversed from English order.

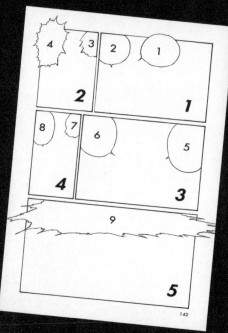